Foundations
for
a
Theory
of
Instruction
and
Educational
Psychology

Foundations for a Theory of Instruction and Educational Psychology

C. H. PATTERSON
University of Illinois
Urbana–Champaign

HARPER & ROW, PUBLISHERS
NEW YORK, HAGERSTOWN, SAN FRANCISCO, LONDON

Sponsoring Editor: George A. Middendorf
Project Editor: David Nickol
Designer: Michel Craig
Production Supervisor: Kewal K. Sharma
Compositor: American Book–Stratford Press, Inc.
Printer and binder: R. R. Donnelley & Company

**FOUNDATIONS FOR
A THEORY OF INSTRUCTION AND
EDUCATIONAL PSYCHOLOGY**

Library of Congress Cataloging in Publication Data
Patterson, Cecil Holden, Date–
    Foundations for a theory of instruction and educational
psychology.
    Includes indexes.
    1. Education–Philosophy–History. 2. Educational
psychology. I. Title.
LA21.P37   370.1   77–2707
ISBN 0–06–045057–6

How we teach is dependent, to some extent at least, on the theories we accept. Whatever the approach, the strategies employed, and the relationships generated, the choice is related to one or more theoretical constructs that may or may not be consciously identified. Nevertheless, many who teach are unaware of the role that various theories play in their work.

L. J. Stiles, Theories for Learning

Despite the books and articles that are beginning to appear on the subject, the process of education goes forward today without any clearly defined or widely accepted theory of instruction. We have had to make do and are still making do on clever maxims and moralistic resolutions about what instruction is and should be.

Jerome Bruner, The Relevance of Education

CONTENTS

PREFACE

Theories of learning have been the object of attention for several decades. Theories of instruction or teaching have received consideration only in the last decade. Thus they are in an early stage of development, so early that no full-fledged, systematic theories—or even approximations of systematic theories—exist. It is premature to title a book *Theories of Instruction*. Bruner titled one of his books *Toward a Theory of Instruction*, and if he had not preempted the title, it would be appropriate for the present book.

Yet there have been a number of writers who have attempted to consider instruction and teaching in a systematic way, usually developing their ideas from another major field of activity than education. (Montessori is the only writer represented in this book who can be considered an educator.) It seems desirable to bring together for the student the major approaches to a theory of instruction.

The term *theories of instruction* was perhaps first used in its present sense by Jerome Bruner in 1963. In 1965 it was used as the title for the Ninth Curriculum Research Institute of the Association for Supervision and Curriculum Development.[1] In that year the association appointed a Commission on Instructional Theory, which published a report on criteria for theories of instruction in 1968.[2]

In 1972, Atkinson, noting the widespread usage of the term *theory of instruction* (with, however, little agreement on the requirements of such a theory) and the growing literature, suggested that a significant contribution could be made by someone who would summarize the literature in the way Hilgard did in his *Theories of Learning*, first published in 1948.[3] Atkinson's concept of such a book appears to differ somewhat from that suggested by Hilgard's work, however. Hilgard's *Theories of Learning* contained chapters summarizing each of a number of recognized theories.[4] Atkinson seems to suggest a book which would summarize the diverse writing on instruction, from speculation to computer-assisted instruction, including a chapter on decision-theoretic analysis of instruction, of which he provides an overview in his article.

Actually it does not appear to be possible at this time to produce a book on theories of instruction similar to Hilgard's *Theories of Learning*. There are few if any candidates for inclusion in such a book; that is, there are no statements which warrant designation as a theory, even by liberal standards. There are no theoretical statements on instruction which have been developed to the level of the theories of learning summarized by Hilgard.

This lag in the development of theories of instruction is puzzling when one considers that the practice of education has been a concern of society for centuries. Counseling or psychotherapy, another applied field or practice, though more recent in origin, suffers from a surfeit of theories. Both education and counseling or psychotherapy deal with changing or influencing human behavior in ways which involve learning. Books summarizing theories of counseling or psychotherapy appeared over a decade ago.[5] There have, of course, been many thinkers and scholars who have been concerned with education and who have made theoretical contributions. But none could be said to have developed a theory of instruction.

A major factor, no doubt, is the extent and complexity of instruction and teaching. Although it is not necessary that there be some agreed-upon or generally accepted theories of learning, motivation, development, and personality before a theory of instruction can be developed, it is necessary that some progress have been made in these areas, since a theory of instruction must be based on knowledge in these areas.

The materials presented in this book do not, then, constitute theories. They are rather systems, and very loose systems at that. A more accurate term might be approaches. They are only the beginnings toward theories of instruction.

Three approaches selected are those which are currently the focus of attention in educational psychology. Almost everyone closely connected with education is familiar with the names Piaget, Bruner, and Skinner. Any consideration of instruction and teaching must include their writings and ideas.

The other two approaches included here may be less familiar to educators, but are currently the objects of increasing attention. Montessori was one of the first of the moderns to attempt to present a systematic approach to teaching based on more than speculation and limited personal experience. There has been a revival of interest in her work. Thus it is included here not simply for historical interest but for its current relevance. (No approach is included simply for historical interest.) Some earlier approaches might also have been included for their continuing relevance, but these are adequately treated in books dealing with the history and philosophy of education.

The second approach that may not be too familiar to educators represents perhaps the newest development in education: humanistic education. The person most closely associated with this approach—though he does not use the term—is Carl Rogers, whose work has revolutionized the field of counseling and psychotherapy, being the greatest influence since Freud. Rogers' writing in the field of education has not been systematic, though he has influenced the work of a number of other writers (most of whom, again, have not been systematic). The present author has elsewhere attempted a systematic development of an approach derived from Rogers (*Humanistic Education*, Prentice-Hall, 1973). He has drawn from his own work for this section, identifying his own contribution.

Almost every textbook in educational psychology devotes from a paragraph to a few pages to a consideration of each of these five writers. None, however, presents an adequate summary of their extensive work. In the case of Piaget and Skinner, there are now numerous paperback summaries available. The others are not available in extended summaries. And nowhere are all five brought together in summaries extensive enough to give even a basic understanding of them. This book does so and also includes critical evaluations of their contributions.

The sections of the book consist of extensive organized summaries of the relevant writings of the authors represented. By necessity, the material is condensed and concentrated. This may make for relatively slow, if not difficult, reading. This is especially so where the original writing, such as that of Piaget, is particularly difficult. Every effort has been made to keep the writing as simple and as clear as possible, and the material on Piaget, even in its highly condensed form, is probably not as difficult as the original. It is suggested that the reader first read the summary before reading each presentation, to get an overview of the main ideas, which should then provide some background for the presentation.

The student who is interested in a particular approach should read something of the original writer, selected from the references. The instructor who wants students to become more familiar with a particular approach can assign selections, such as one of the books of Bruner or Skinner, or Rogers' *Freedom to Learn*.

This book is designed to be used at the upper undergraduate and beginning graduate levels by education students in courses in foundations of education, methods of teaching, and educational psychology. An introductory psychology course and/or a basic course in educational psychology should be adequate preparation for students using it as a text or as supplementary reading.

The plan of the five major sections is as follows: First, there is a brief biography of the scholar whose work is being considered. Although students will be familiar with the names of these scholars, they will probably know very little about them as people or about their academic histories and achievements. These summaries should contribute to an interest in them as people.

Second, there is a presentation of the theoretical position of each theorist. An attempt is made at comprehensiveness and completeness, although by necessity in condensed form. The writer has aimed at presenting the theory in as unbiased a way as possible, following closely the writings of the theorist. In fact, in immersing himself in the writings, the present author has found himself identifying to some extent with each, and as a result has probably presented each position in a rather favorable light. Accuracy and clarity of presentation has been striven for in each case, however.

Third, the relevance of the theoretical position for the educational process has been considered. Here as in the presentation of the theoretical material, the original writings of the theorists have been drawn upon, though references to other sources are made, and the present writer has attempted to organize the material in some form. The applications are in most cases general rather than specific and do not take a how-to-do-it form.

Fourth, there is an evaluation by the writer, drawing upon other evaluations also, of the theoretical position. This is separated from the presentation to avoid the writer's involvement while summarizing the theory, thus keeping the presentation of the theory uncontaminated by criticism.

Because the material is condensed and frequently difficult and because of the length of the presentations, frequent summaries are provided within the sections, in addition to the final summary. These should be helpful to students in reviewing the materials.

While research relevant to the theories is frequently referred to, no attempt has been made to review or evaluate all the research related to the theories or their applications. This would extend each presentation to book length. The presentations are thus introductions to the theoretical positions, and the student interested in a particular approach can further explore it, beginning with the references included here.

As was the case with my book *Theories of Counseling and Psychotherapy*, now in its second edition, I am indebted to my editor at Harper & Row, George Middendorf, with whom I have worked for almost 20 years, for the suggestion that I write this book.

Jean K. Miller, Executive Director of the Montessori Development Foundation of Cleveland, read the material on Montessori and made a number of helpful suggestions, for which I wish to express my appreciation.

C. H. Patterson

REFERENCES

1. J. B. Macdonald and R. R. Leeper, eds., *Theories of Instruction*. Washington, D.C.: Association for Supervision and Curriculum Development, 1965.
2. I. J. Gordon, ed., *Criteria for Theories of Instruction*. Washington, D.C.: Association for Supervision and Curriculum Development, 1968.
3. R. C. Atkinson, "Ingredients for a Theory of Instruction." *American Psychologist*, 1972, 27, 921–931.
4. E. R. Hilgard, *Theories of Learning*. Englewood Cliffs, N.J.: Prentice-Hall, 1948.
5. D. H. Ford and H. B. Urban, *Systems of Psychotherapy*. New York: Wiley, 1963; B. Stefflre, ed., *Theories of Counseling*. New York: McGraw-Hill, 1965; C. H. Patterson, *Theories of Counseling and Psychotherapy*. New York: Harper & Row, 1966.

Foundations
for
a
Theory
of
Instruction
and
Educational
Psychology

Introduction:
theories of
instruction

1

CHAPTER
1

Teaching is perhaps as old as the human race. There is even some suggestion that animals intentionally teach their young. The prolonged infancy and childhood of the human species is related to the need for teaching to prepare the child to occupy a place in society.

In a simple or primitive society, education and teaching can be informal, and left to individuals or families, but in a complex society, teaching becomes organized and formalized. Since learning is inherent in the nature of a growing, developing organism, little direct teaching is necessary where the child is in direct contact with the world of adults, and can learn from real experiences and observation of and modeling upon adults. But as human society has become more complex, the child is not in direct contact with the world of adults. Obstacles are placed in the way of natural learning. It becomes necessary to prepare children for a future world that, because they are not now faced with it, has limited interest or relevance for them. Formal teaching has become necessary, and society has invented or developed extensive educational systems in which children are placed, apart from the "real" world, for instruction.

It is curious that, in spite of the fact that informal teaching of the young has gone on for thousands of years and that formal instruction has been provided for hundreds of years, there is today no generally accepted or agreed-upon method of education. There have of course been educators throughout history who have developed and promulgated methods or approaches to teaching. But their methods have not persisted or been built upon systematically by others. New methods have appeared to displace old methods. Discrete methods and techniques have proliferated, but no general system or theory of instruction has emerged. Considering the importance of education in society and the tremendous cost involved, it is indeed curious why we have not progressed farther in systematizing the process of education.

LEARNING THEORY AND EDUCATION

One apparent reason for the lack of progress in developing a theory of instruction has been the emphasis upon learning and a theory of learning as the basis for teaching or instruction. Education involves changes in a class of people called learners or students—a class which at one time or another and for varying periods of time includes the total population. (It is of course true that most people learn continuously, whether they are being educated, or taught, or not. Learning can, and most frequently does, occur without direct or intentional teaching.) Education as formalized teaching or instruction is conducted for the purpose of deliberately inducing certain changes considered desirable in all persons in a society. (But teaching can, and often does, occur without learning taking place.) Since these changes are called learning, then it seems obvious that education should be concerned with the psychology of learning. Thus, many scholars have assumed that theories of learning would be the foundation for teaching, or would lead to principles of instruction.

In spite of the fact that learning is a natural function of the organism and occurs without the necessity of formal teaching in natural environments, it is a highly complex process. In the complicated social environments in which people live, learning becomes very involved and elaborate. As a result, the conditions under which learning will occur are not well known. Tremendous amounts of time and money have been spent in this century on research on learning. Yet there is no agreement on what learning is, how learning occurs, or whether there is only one, or more than one, kind of learning. As a result, rather than there being one learning theory, there are a number of learning theories.[1]

The applicability of learning theory to classroom learning is limited by other factors. Learning theories have been derived mainly from research with animals, principally rats. The research which has been done upon human beings is in the main highly controlled laboratory research with limited learning objectives, such as the memorization of lists of nonsense syllables. Experiments in classrooms are extremely difficult to conduct, because of the influence of so many variables. When some of these variables are controlled, there is the problem of generalizing results to classrooms where there is no control of these variables. The social character of classrooms introduces conditions not present in research studies on individuals.

If, as has often been assumed, teaching or instruction is an application of theories and principles of learning, then the state of teaching depends directly upon the state of our knowledge of learning and learning theory. With different theories of learning in existence, there is the problem of which one to select as the basis for teaching. Teaching and instruction have been influenced by different theories, including Thorndike's connectionism, Watson's behaviorism, Gestalt psychology, and Skinner's behaviorism.

Hilgard has argued, however, that it is not necessary to wait until learning theorists are in agreement to develop a scientifically based method of instruction.[2] Disagreement among theorists may be more about the interpretation of the facts than about the facts themselves, and thus there may be no problem in applying factual knowledge. Hilgard also points out that even if there were an agreed-upon theory of learning, the principles of instruction would not be clearly evident, since technology does not flow directly and simply from theory. But he notes that learning theory can be useful even though it does not dictate instructional practices. There are some direct applications in the classroom of knowledge and principles from the laboratory. "A skilled teacher may understand better why some practices work and others do not because of acquaintance with basic learning principles. Such principles permit a better analysis by pointing out where to look and what to expect."[3] A theory of instruction, according to Hilgard, is a theory of application of theories of learning, differing in goals and content in relation to the school setting and its social contexts. It goes beyond the descriptive and explanatory to the prescription of practice.

NEED FOR A THEORY OF INSTRUCTION

Jackson has noted that the hopes of psychologists and teachers that a scientific theory of learning would speak to the problems of importance to classroom teachers have not been realized.[4] Teaching or instruction does not derive from or relate to learning theory in any simple way. Nor is it only an application of learning theory. While a theory of learning would appear to be necessary for instruction, it is not sufficient. Jerome Bruner is reported to have said (at the 1963 Conference of the Association for Supervision and Curriculum Development) that it is a mistake to look to learning theory for guidance in teaching. Teaching practice, he felt, cannot be directly derived from learning theories. Rather, they must be derived from a theory of instruction.[5]

Teaching or instruction needs a theory to organize and integrate what is known about teaching as a systematic foundation for teaching. A theory provides a framework for the organization of principles. It provides a rationale for specific practices. It changes teaching from simply a trade or an art into a profession.

In addition to organizing existing knowledge and methods of teaching, a theory provides a basis for evaluating and selecting proposed innovative methods or practices. Even more basically, a theory points to areas for research and investigation which may lead to the *development* of useful innovations. Without a theory, teaching or instruction becomes a bag of tricks, a succession of new fads and techniques.

A theoretical formulation facilitates the education of teachers, providing an organization for teacher education, so that each student teacher, or each practicing teacher, does not have either to develop his or her own system or, as is probably the case most frequently now, to operate with no integrative system. The need for a theory is evident in teacher education. Most teacher education programs include courses in the philosophy of education, usually emphasizing Dewey's philosophy. But no psychological theory of instruction is provided as a bridge between philosophy and practice. Methods courses are universally rated as of little value and are disliked by students. In part, at least, this is because of the lack of a theoretical base. Similarly, educational psychology courses often are of little help to prospective teachers. They consist almost entirely of isolated facts or summaries of empirical research (that is, research not directed by a theory). Although they may include summaries of theories of development, theories of motivation, theories of personality and adjustment, as well as theories of learning, there is little if anything on a theory of instruction. The student is left to acquire this by inference. But as Gage points out, "farmers need to know more than how plants grow. Mechanics need to know more than how a machine works. Physicians need to know more than how the body functions. Teachers need to know more than how a pupil learns."[6]

Theory also guides research, leading to more relevant and significant research. Not all research has to be theory-oriented. As Skinner emphasizes, in the early stages of knowledge in an area, research must be empirical in nature. But it would appear that good theory would lead to more efficient use of research time and money. Most current research in education is not based on theory, and as a result there is little relationship among research projects, and thus great difficulty in integrating the results into a system of practice. Research in education —as distinguished from personal observations and experience—is quite new, and the accumulation of empirical data serves a purpose. One of the purposes is to provide a basis for a theory. Perhaps we have now reached the point where theoretical formulations could lead to a significant advance in research in education.

In addition to the hope that learning theory would be sufficient as a basis for teaching, other factors have contributed to the neglect of instructional theory. Gage refers to one of these—the concept of teaching as an art, coupled with the fear that the development of a science of teaching would leave feelings and emotions out of teaching.[7] Yet teaching as a technology is being welcomed by many. Perhaps the way practitioners view the nature of theory—as abstract and impractical—has inhibited the development of both a theory of instruction and teachers' and administrators' interest in such a theory.

Interest in a theory or theories of instruction has been increasing over the last 10 or 15 years. Psychologists and educators have directed attention to the need for such a theory. A theory of instruction must incorporate or take into consideration all that we know about human beings, biologically and psychologically. In psychology, this would include theories of motivation, perception, personality, and development, as well as learning. In none of these areas do we have enough knowledge to lead to agreement on a single theory. In addition to psychology, other sciences must be considered in a theory of instruction: biology (maturation and development), anthropology (cultural factors), and sociology (social psychology of roles, relationships, and interactions). There is much that we do not yet know in these fields. But we should not, and cannot, postpone development of a theory of instruction until we have complete knowledge or agreement in all these fields. We know enough about the nature of man and about teaching and the educational process, to begin to develop a theory of instruction. The results of experience and research in teaching and learning are waiting to be put together in a systematic way so that principles can be derived, formulated, and integrated into a theoretical orientation which can guide application and suggest new principles or applications. Yet we must recognize that because of the multitude of disciplines involved in the teaching-learning situation, any theory at this stage of our knowledge can only be tentative and incomplete.

THE NATURE OF THEORY

A theory is more than an opinion, a speculation, a statement of position, or a point of view. It is more than a collection of principles or techniques. It is more than a summary of knowledge, principles, or methods derived from research. A theory is an attempt to organize and integrate knowledge to answer the question "Why?" A theory organizes, interprets, and states in the form of laws or principles the facts and knowledge in an area or field. Theory, from the Greek word *theōria,* is defined as "an act of viewing, contemplating, considering, and arranging what we know in some way that makes possible description, prescription, prediction, explanation, and the systematic testing of ideas."[8] Theories are invented or constructed for these purposes; they do not exist by themselves somewhere to be discovered. Although a theory of instruction may go beyond the explanatory to the prescriptive, prescriptions are based upon explanation. Practice may be based upon empirical knowledge. But an explanatory theory gives a sense of understanding, direction, and rationality to practice. It provides a guide to application, extension, extrapolation, and modification in new or different situations.

A formal scientific theory has certain characteristics. First there is a set of stated *postulates* or *assumptions*. (Assumptions are sometimes distinguished from postulates; the difference is in the degree of acceptance as being true, with postulates being more tentative.) These state the premises of the field with which the theory is concerned. They are the givens which are accepted and for which proof is not required. Second, there is a set of *definitions* of the terms or concepts in the theory. These definitions relate the concepts to observational data or to operations and thus make possible the study of the concepts in research and experimentation. Third, the terms or concepts bear certain stated *relationships* to each other; these relationships derive from a set of rules, usually rules of logic. They include cause-and-effect relationships. Fourth, from these assumptions, definitions, and relationships *hypotheses* are constructed or deduced. These are essentially predictions of what should be true if the assumptions, definitions, relationships, and the reasoning involved in the deductions are true, that is, if the theory is valid. Given certain assumptions, definitions, and relationships, certain things should follow or be true. Hypotheses state, in a form that can be tested, what these things are. The testing of hypotheses leads to new knowledge. If hypotheses are not supported by adequate observation and experiment, the theory must be revised and corrected, and new hypotheses deduced and tested. Theory thus directs research, providing hypotheses to be tested and directing observation and experiment.

Theory not only predicts new facts and relations; it organizes and integrates what is known in a meaningful framework. Whether this organization of existing knowledge comes with the formulation of the theory or follows its formulation is not always clear; some writers appear to think of organization as a late development or result of a theory. However, the assumptions and postulates of a theory do not arise out of thin air or apart from reality and experience. They are developed upon the basis of observation and experience, or empirical research. That is, existing facts and knowledge are the bases for the assumptions and definitions of a theory. The process of theory construction, testing, modification or reconstruction, and further testing is a continuing process.

Theories cannot be evaluated as to their correctness or validity until they are tested. A theory may be good without being totally correct; in fact, few if any theories, even after considerable testing, can be accepted as valid in any complete or absolute sense. A good theory, however, is one which is more likely to be true than a poor one. Certain formal criteria have been proposed for evaluating a theory.[9]

1. *Importance.* A theory should not be trivial, but should be significant. It should be applicable to more than a highly restricted, limited situation such as the behavior of rats in a T maze or the learning of nonsense syllables. It should have some relevance to life or real behavior. Importance is very difficult to evaluate, however, since the criteria are vague or subjective and dependent upon the times or the current state of knowledge in a field. Acceptance by competent professionals or recognition and persistence in the professional literature may be indicative of importance. Also, if a theory meets other formal criteria, it is probably important.

2. *Preciseness and clarity.* A theory should be understandable, internally consistent, free from ambiguities. Clarity may be tested by observing the ease of relating the theory or its data to practice and the ease of developing hypotheses or making predictions from it and specifying the methods of testing them.

3. *Parsimony or simplicity.* Parsimony has long been accepted as a characteristic of a good theory. This involves few assumptions and a minimum of complexity.

   Maddi questions this criterion, however, suggesting that one cannot determine which of two theories is more parsimonious until everything is known about the area to which the theory applies. He questions its value on the grounds that the most parsimonious theory based on current data may not be the best theory: "It is distinctly possible that a theory which looks parsimonious in explaining today's facts may be actually such an oversimplification in terms of explaining all human functioning as to be wholly inadequate to cope with tomorrow's facts without major overhaul."[10]

   Nevertheless, it might be maintained that the phenomena of the world and of nature are relatively simple in terms of basic principles. Weaver writes that "as man's control of his environment has proceeded . . . he has progressively uncovered more and more complication, but, at the same time he has succeeded in discovering more and more unifying principles which accept the ever increasing variety, but recognize an underlying unity. He has, in short, discovered the many and the one. . . . The diversity . . . is a surface phenomenon: When one looks underneath and within, the universal unity again becomes apparent."[11]

   The law of parsimony appears to be the most widely violated in theory construction. This may be because of the stage of knowledge we are at, where the diversity is more apparent than the underlying unifying principles. Hall and Lindzey propose that parsimony is important only after the criteria of comprehensiveness and verifiability (see below) have been met. They write: "This becomes an issue only under circumstances where two theories generate exactly the same consequences."[12]

4. *Comprehensiveness.* A theory should be complete, covering the area of interest and including all known data in the field. The area of interest, however, can be restricted.

5. *Operationality.* A theory should be capable of being reduced to procedures for testing its propositions or predictions. Its concepts must be precise enough to be measurable. A strict operationism can be restrictive, however, as Maddi points out, when a concept is defined by a restricted or limited measurement operation.[13] The concept should be defined first, and then a method of measurement chosen or developed. A current lack of measurement to operationalize a concept should not rule out the use of a concept which is essential for a theory. Not all concepts of a theory need to be operational. Concepts may be used to indicate relationships and organization among concepts.

6. *Fruitfulness.* The capacity of a theory to lead to predictions that can be tested, thus producing new knowledge—even where predictions are not verified—has often been referred to as its fruitfulness. But a theory can also be fruitful in the early stages of development of a field, even if it is not capable of leading to specific predictions. It may provoke thinking and the development of new ideas or theories, sometimes because it leads to disbelief or questioning by others.

7. *Empirical validity or verifiability.* The preceding criteria are rational in nature and do not directly relate to the correctness or validity of the theory. Eventually, however, a theory must be supported by experience or experiments which confirm it. Thus, in addition to its consistency with, or ability to account for, what is already known, it must generate new knowledge. However, a theory which is disconfirmed by experiment may indirectly lead to new knowledge by stimulating the development of a better theory.

8. *Practicality.* There is a final criterion of a good theory, from the standpoint of the practitioner rather than that of the researcher, which is seldom mentioned or recognized. A good theory helps the practitioner organize his thinking and practice by providing a conceptual framework. A theory allows the practitioner to move beyond the empirical level of trial-and-error application of techniques to the rational application of principles. Practitioners too often think of theory as something that is irrelevant to what they do, unrelated to practice or real life. But, as Kurt Lewin, the field or Gestalt psychologist, is reputed to have said, "There is nothing as practical as a good theory."[14] Operating on the basis of a theory is the difference between being a technician and being a professional.

INSTRUCTIONAL THEORY

Scientific theories developed in the physical sciences, where observations of data are easily quantifiable, specific predictions can be made, and the predictions can be tested by controlled experiments. In the social and behavioral sciences, theory building and testing are much more difficult. Yet the general established procedure is accepted as being the method most likely to yield knowledge and understanding.

Ideas, speculations, or "theories" about education have been proposed for centuries. The work of such educators as Rousseau, Pestalozzi, Herbart, and Froebel, as well as that of John Dewey, is of this nature. This work has not led to scientific theories, because of limitations in methods of observation, collection, and measurement of data. It is only relatively recently that it has been possible to build upon and incorporate some of these early ideas and personal observations in a system which can meet the requirements of a scientific theory. Although ideas and speculations unrelated to empirical observation can often be stimulating, a theory must derive from a data base and be related to experience and empirical observations.

In the mid-1960s the Association for Supervision and Curriculum Development of the National Education Association appointed a Commission on Instructional Theory, chaired by Ira Gordon. The commission did not attempt the task of developing a theory of instruction, believing that to be the task of the scholar-scientist, requiring ongoing investigation or research. It decided instead to develop a set of criteria for a theory of instruction, based upon the nature and requirements of scientific theory. These criteria were presented not only as a guide for theory builders, but also for educators, particularly curriculum builders, to use in the process of evaluating new programs, since such programs are implicitly related to theory and/or have theoretical implications.[15] The commission dealt with a number of issues in the development of the criteria.

Theories of Instruction and Values

A theory of instruction, according to Gordon, is not concerned with values, aside from the belief that the development of a theory is desirable. A theory does not specify the goals or objectives of instruction and thus "could be used by those who subscribed to fundamentally different educational philosophies. . . . [A theory of instruction would] represent a statement of empirically established ways of achieving a great range of different goals. The user of such a theory would have to decide what goals he wished to achieve, and he could then consult the theory to determine what had been established as the best ways of achieving his goals."[16]

There is, however, some question as to whether a theory in the behavioral as contrasted to the physical sciences can avoid or ignore the matter of goals or objectives, and thus be neutral or value free. It is in part a question of whether means can be independent of ends and whether an integrated, cohesive theory can include means of achieving a great range of different goals. The concept of a value-free science, even of the physical world, is now being questioned. If values are implicit in a theory, then they should be recognized and dealt with explicitly. Although the commission avoided the value question, theorists cannot do so, as is evident in the presentations included in this book.

Bruner represents this view when he writes:

> A pedagogical theory is perforce quite different from, and hardly as neutral as, the usual type of scientific theory in the explanatory sense. Nor is it a purely normative theory such as a grammatical theory, prescribing rules for reaching specific goals (such as "well formed sentences"). A theory of instruction is a political theory in the proper sense that it derives from consensus concerning the distribution of power within the society—who shall be educated and to fulfill what roles?[17]

A theory which is prescriptive involves goals and ends—what should be done—which are values. While values may be considered as preferences which lie outside the realm of science—what ought to be as compared to what is—science, as the study of the effects of various acts, may be concerned with the selection of actions which lead to results—or goals—which are demonstrated as being necessary for the survival of society and mankind. In other words, science may provide the criteria for survival, or even for a life which enhances the nature and development of the organism. Furthermore, science is itself a value, as is its objective, the advancement of knowledge.

Values are also involved in science in another way. Bronowski, in his essay on science and human values, says that the values of science derive from its methods, which require both independence, which leads to originality, and freedom, which allows for dissent. Thus, "the values of science turn out to be the recognizably human values"[18] of democracy, which provides tolerance and respect for the views of others. But these values do not actually derive from science; these values—and honesty, accuracy, and objectivity—existed before science developed, and are necessary for the existence of science.

Science, in its methods, objectivities, and results, is inextricably involved in values. Neither science nor scientific theories can be divorced from values. Thus the commission's poistion on values cannot be accepted.

Relationship of Theory to Data

Apart from postulates or assumptions, the statements or propositions in a theory from which hypotheses or predictions are derived must be based upon empirical data. They must be consistent with all that is known, not simply with a single observation or study, which may not be consistent with other studies. Each statement is a generalization and must be based upon data which are reliable and valid. In the current state of research, there are always some disagreements, often related to known inadequacies of particular studies. But until there is considerable agreement upon basic data, a theory cannot be developed.

Components of a Statement of Theory

Theories include three main classes of terms: (1) Primitive terms. These are terms which cannot be operationally defined. They are intuitive and accepted by agreement. Such terms should be kept to a minimum. Theories which consist mainly of such terms are not scientific and cannot be tested. (2) Key terms. These are the basic terms related to the area or content of the theory which are defined operationally. The key terms must be part of a system of concepts or ideas, so that they can be used in relational statements or propositions. Terms which can be operationally defined in laboratory experiments are often much more difficult to define in real life situations like the classroom. This makes the development of a theory applicable to classroom learning difficult. But theories relating to terms operationally defined in restricted laboratory procedures may be useless in the classroom. (3) Theoretical terms. Theoretical terms are not operationally defined but represent concepts based on or related to terms which are operationally defined. *Motivation* and *attitudes* are such terms.

These three kinds of terms enter into two main classes of statements which comprise a theory: definitional statements and relationship statements. The statements or propositions in a theory may also be divided into two classes on a different basis. There are statements which are generalizations of empirical data, and there are other statements going beyond empirical data which lead to or are hypotheses about empirical data.

Language Problems

Theories involve technical language, the technical language of empirical research and the technical language of theoretical terms. Definitions of terms are not always clear or generally accepted or agreed upon. Operational definitions are not always possible or are limited or may vary from researcher to researcher. Some terms are used in both an empirical or operational sense and in a theoretical or conceptual sense, as, for example, the term *reinforcement*, which may refer to a specific operation such as giving a child an M&M, or to any operation or event that changes the probability of a response.

Validation of Theories

A theory must be stated in such a form that it can be tested, that is, that its hypotheses or predictions can be empirically validated. Theories which possess certain formal properties are capable of being validated empirically. These formal properties provide criteria for evaluating a theory prior to its empirical validation.

CRITERIA FOR A FORMAL THEORY

The formal properties necessary if a theory can be validated empirically were stated by the Commission on Instructional Theory as criteria. They are presented as necessary but not sufficient conditions for a satisfactory theory:

1. A statement of instructional theory should include a set of postulates and definitions of terms involved in these postulates. The number of primitive terms should be minimal. Terms dealing with three elements of the theory should be operationally defined: (a) Pupil characteristics related to learning or to the particular area of learning or instruction covered by the theory, if it is a limited theory, must be specified. These characteristics include biosocial variables (age, sex, social class, level of physical maturity) and psychological variables (level of intellectual development, academic achievement, cognitive style, self-concept, achievement motivation). Their relationship to goals must be specified. (b) The characteristics of the instructional situations and their relationship to goals must be specified. Some of the dimensions to be specified include the following: organization variables (time, space, class size, class composition); content variables (tasks, media, sequence); teacher behavior variables (acts to be performed, management techniques); and teacher personality variables (warmth, openness, control, style). The relationships of instructional characteristics to pupil characteristics must be specified. (c) Goal characteristics should be dimensionalized; that is, objectives should be described in terms of change on a scale. Outcomes are defined as performances on tasks, or actions undertaken to reach a goal. Goals and tasks must be specified in terms of pupil characteristics. In addition, a theory must specify how, as pupils change and progress toward goals, the instructional situation must change.

   This criterion is similar to the criterion of operationality described earlier for theories in general.

2. The statement of an instructional theory or subtheory should make explicit the boundaries of its concern and the limitations under which it is proposed. These boundaries include such things as kind of learning (psychomotor, conceptual, and so forth), goals, classes of children, and the instructional situation (e.g., directed or open ended). This criterion relates to the criterion of importance described earlier.

3. A theoretical construction must have internal consistency—a logical set of interrelationships. This is similar to the criterion of preciseness and clarity noted earlier.

4. An instructional theory should be congruent with empirical data. The theory should incorporate all that is known in a way that can be examined and checked against the sources of the evidence. The nature of the inductive inferences leading to generalizations should be specified. This criterion also relates to clarity and preciseness, as well as to parsimony and simplicity.

5. An instructional theory must be capable of generating hypotheses. This requires clarity, specificity and adequate definitions. This criterion also involves preciseness and includes the criterion of being stimulating.

6. An instructional theory must contain generalizations which go beyond the data. This is necessary for developing hypotheses and making predictions. This criterion is similar to that of comprehensiveness in the earlier list.

7. An instructional theory must be verifiable. It must lead to hypotheses and predictions which can be tested, that is, for which relevant data are available or can be obtained. (It should be interjected here that this could be a hampering restriction, depending upon the current state of knowledge and instrumentation. The writer believes that scientific theories have made predictions which could not at the time have been verified, but which led to the development of methods by which they could be verified.) This is the criterion of empirical validity or verifiability mentioned earlier.

8. An instructional theory must be stated in such a way that it is possible to collect data to disprove it. Statements can be tautological and reasoning circular, so that it is impossible to disprove them. For instance, the statement that a reinforcer is anything which changes the probability of response is viewed by some as tautological and incapable of disproof. This criterion involves the importance criterion.

9. An instructional theory must not only explain past events but must also be capable of predicting future events. Explanation of the past is useful, but is insufficient. The crucial test of an explanation is its ability to predict future events, which can be in terms of probabilities in stated situations. This criterion would appear to be related to the criterion of being fruitful noted earlier.

10. At the present time, instructional theories may be expected to represent qualitative syntheses. Ultimately, or ideally, a theory should state quantitative relationships, specifying not only changes in pupil behaviors or understandings under certain conditions of instruction, but the amount of change occurring with given degrees of the presence of the conditions. For most practical uses, however, qualitative statements are sufficient. In the behavioral sciences, precise mathematical statements regarding nonlaboratory situations may not be possible and are unnecessary. This criterion is similar to that of comprehensiveness.

Applications of the Criteria

The commission suggests two main uses for the criteria it developed. One is to guide those who are involved in the development or construction of theories of instruction. The second, and the one of interest here, is to evaluate existing theories.

Since, as noted in the Preface, it can be questioned whether any real theories of instruction exist, there is no opportunity for the second use of the criteria. The materials presented in this book are not theories of instruction. They are considered to be foundations for a theory or theories of instruction and, perhaps in some cases, approaches to a theory. None of the authors of the materials covered represent their work as theories of instruction. In most instances, their concern with education or teaching is not their primary interest, which has usually been some area of psychology—and not necessarily the psychology of learning per se. It would therefore be inappropriate and unfair to evaluate their contributions in terms of the criteria listed above.

The criteria can be useful, however, as a general frame of reference from which to look at and consider the presentations. But even this is a difficult task: Since the authors of the materials were not attempting to develop formal theories, their writings are not organized or expressed in a manner which allows one to look at them from the frame of reference of a formal theory. The terms *postulate, assumption, propositions, operational definition,* and *hypothesis* seldom occur. In order to evaluate, or even to compare, the various approaches or systems, one would first have to cast each one in the form of a theoretical statement organized according to these terms. The present writer does not, and probably the student reader will not, want to spend the time and effort necessary to do this. It is not the purpose of this book to attempt a comparative evaluation of the systems in terms of criteria for a formal theory. At this stage of development of instructional theory it seems to be useful to present (summaries of) the systems as the original writers have expressed them, along with a discussion of the nature of a theory and the criteria for an instructional theory as a general framework for viewing the systems.

ONE THEORY OR MULTIPLE THEORIES?

Teaching and instruction are complex, highly varied areas. Instruction is broader than teaching, covering all the processes of influencing learners, including curriculum and instruction through printed materials. Teaching is instruction through personal interaction. Teaching is a complex activity, involving one or more actions such as explaining, demonstrating, guiding, maintenance of order or classroom management, record keeping, assignment making, curriculum planning, testing and evaluation, and affective or mental hygiene activities.

Then there are different areas of learning: motor or psychomotor, cognitive and affective. There are different learning theories, which may be grouped as conditioning, cognitive restructuring, and modeling or identification. Within each type there may be quite different subtypes, such as rote memory and conceptual or meaningful learning in the cognitive area. Different subject matters may involve different kinds of learning: reading as compared to arithmetic, for example.

In view of this complexity and variety, Gage has proposed that there are many different potential theories involved in teaching, since no single theory could be adequate.[19] Stiles and his colleagues agree that there is no single theory for teaching appropriate for all teachers in every situation, and they even doubt that a single theory is possible.[20] With the tremendous number of conditions or variables involved in the human behavior of learning, both personal and environmental, one might despair of ever developing a theory of learning or a theory of instruction that could include them all in their infinite number and relationships.

Thus there are those who are concerned with the development of subtheories of varying degrees of comprehensiveness, selecting limited pupil groups, instructional methods, and goals or objectives. Thus one could focus on a theory of reading instruction, or even on a theory of reading instruction for blind pupils using Braille. Certainly there is nothing wrong with doing this. But if, as most educators and psychologists seem to believe, there are common elements among differing groupings of pupils, different subject matters, different learning methods, and different instructional methods, then it would appear to follow that all subtheories would be related to all other subtheories in some ways and that together they would constitute a general theory. It would then seem to be more efficient to attempt to develop a general theory, which could then be modified for subgroups of various kinds, than to approach a general theory from the development and integration of a large number of subtheories. At present there seems to be more effort devoted to the development of subtheories than to a general theory. The work of Piaget, Skinner, and Bruner seems to be more of this nature; the work of Montessori and Rogers seems to be of a more holistic nature.

That there are common elements in all learning and instruction, or that subtheories or part theories are interrelated, seems to be the case when one examines the work of many apparently different writers. Much in the differing approaches—the behavioristic, the cognitive, the humanistic—is not necessarily inconsistent, in conflict, or irreconcilable. To some extent, differences are a matter of differing terminology. Some are a matter of differing levels of analysis. Much is supplementary and can be related or integrated into a more comprehensive theory.

We are certainly at an early stage in the development of a comprehensive theory of instruction. Yet many of the ingredients are now available, and many of them are included in the approaches presented in this book. We do not yet have a theory, or even a number of sub-theories or part theories. But we do seem to have some of the foundations of a theory, which can be built upon by theorists and researchers. Students should be familiar with those who may be considered, at this time, the major contributors to an eventual theory of instruction.

REFERENCES

1. E. R. Hilgard and G. H. Bower, *Theories of Learning*, 4th ed. (Englewood Cliffs, N.J.: Prentice-Hall, 1975).
2. Hilgard, "A Perspective on the Relationship Between Learning Theory and Educational Practices, in Hilgard, ed., *Theories of Learning and Instruction, The Sixty-third Yearbook of the National Society for the Study of Education*, part I. (Chicago: distributed by the University of Chicago Press, 1964), pp. 402–416.
3. Hilgard and Bower, op. cit., p. 607.
4. P. W. Jackson, *Life in Classrooms* (New York: Holt, Rinehart and Winston, 1968).
5. W. H. Beatty, "Theories of Instruction for What? A Projection," in J. B. McDonald & R. R. Leeper, eds., *Theories of Instruction* (Washington, D.C.: Association for Supervision and Curriculum Development, 1965), pp. 114–118.
6. N. L. Gage, "Theories of Teaching," in Hilgard, op. cit., pp. 268–285.
7. Ibid.
8. J. Park, S. Stone, and W. Barron, "Scientific Theory for Teaching: Its Nature and Role," in L. J. Stiles, et al, *Theories for Teaching* (New York: Dodd, Mead, 1974), pp. 9–29.
9. C. S. Hall and G. Lindzey, *Theories of Personality*, 2nd ed. (New York: Wiley, 1979); S. R. Maddi, *Personality Theories: A Comparative Analysis* (Homewood, Ill.: Dorsey), 1968.
10. Maddi, ibid., p. 468.
11. W. Weaver, "Confessions of a Scientist-Humanist," *Saturday Review*, May 28, 1966.
12. Hall and Lindzey, op. cit., p. 13.
13. Maddi, op. cit., p. 454.
14. K. Lewin, "Science, Power and Education," in G. W. Lewin, ed., *Studies in Topological and Vector Psychology*, 1944.
15. I. J. Gordon, ed., *Criteria for Theories of Instruction* (Washington, D.C.: Association for Supervision and Curriculum Development, 1968).
16. Ibid., pp. 6–7.
17. J. S. Bruner, *The Relevance of Education* (New York: Norton, 1971), p. 100.
18. J. Bronowski, *Science and Human Values* (New York: Julian Messmer, 1956). (Also Harper Torchbooks, New York: Harper & Row, 1959.)
19. Gage, op. cit.
20. Stiles et al, op. cit.

The
Montessori
method

2

CHAPTER

2

INTRODUCTION

Maria Montessori (1870–1952) was born in Chiaravalle, in the province of Ancona, Italy, on August 31, 1870. When she was 12, the family moved to Rome in order that she might have a better education, in preparation for becoming a teacher. Maria, however, was interested in mathematics and engineering, and attended a technical school for boys. Her interest then moved to biology, and she applied for admission to medical school. Her first application was denied, but she persisted, was finally accepted, and was awarded scholarships each year. Her father disapproved of her career choice, and she engaged in private tutoring to help pay her expenses. In 1896 she received the first MD awarded to a woman by the University of Rome Medical School.

She was then appointed to the staff of the psychiatric clinic of the university, and came into contact with mentally retarded children. She became convinced that education, rather than physical or medical treatment, was necessary to alleviate their condition. She learned of the work of Edward Séguin (1812–1880) with retarded children,[1] and of the work of Séguin's teacher, the French physician Jean Itard (1775–1838), who had spent five years attempting to educate and humanize a "wild" boy discovered in the forest.[2]

In 1899 she presented a paper entitled "Moral Education" at the Pedagogical Congress in Turin. In part as a result of this paper, she was invited by the minister of education to give a series of lectures to teachers in Rome on the education of mentally retarded children. The courses became the foundation for the State Orthophrenic School, which Montessori directed for two years (1899–1901). She taught in the school daily (from eight in the morning until seven at night) and pursued her interest in the work of Itard and Séguin. She went to London and Paris to study methods of teaching the retarded. In Paris she observed the classes at the Salpetrière which Séguin had founded, and also visited the Bicêtre to study their methods. She realized that Séguin's methods were not actually being followed.

Drawing from Séguin and Itard, she developed her own didactic materials. But she recognized that it was not simply the materials which were the source of her effectiveness, "but my voice which called to them, awakened the children, and encouraged them to use the didactic material, and through it, to educate themselves. I was guided in my work by the deep respect which I felt for their misfortune, and by the love which these unhappy children know how to awaken in those who are near them."[3]

Going beyond Séguin and Itard, Montessori developed her own system for teaching reading and writing. She reports that she "succeeded in teaching a number of the idiots from the asylums both to read and to write so well that I was able to present them at a public school for an examination together with the normal children. And they passed the examination successfully."[4]

Feeling the need for more preparation, Montessori enrolled as a student again in the University of Rome, studying philosophy, anthropology, and psychology. She made a more thorough study of Séguin and Itard, translating their writings into Italian. She also continued studying and publishing on the nervous diseases of children, practiced medicine in clinics and in private practice, and was a member of the staff of the Women's Training College in Rome, where she held the chair of hygiene from 1896 to 1906. In 1904 she was appointed professor of pedagogic anthropology at the University of Rome, a position she held for four years. Her first book was entitled *Pedagogical Anthropology*.

It was in 1906 that she began working with children in a tenement in a slum housing project in Rome. All children between the ages of 3 and 7 in the tenement comprised the school, which was called the Casa dei Bambini, or the Children's House. During the next two years two other Children's Houses were opened in Rome, and one in Milan. The third was in a new building in a middle class neighborhood. In these houses Montessori had the oportunity to apply her methods to normal children. She felt that if her methods could achieve so much with retarded children, they should lead to results with normal children much greater than those achieved by the standard methods of instruction. Though normal, the children in the first two Children's Houses, born of illiterate working parents, were apparently retarded through neglect and lack of stimulation, and were also fearful, shy, and bewildered. They were also, in general, younger than the retarded institutionalized children with whom Montessori had previously worked. But the materials and methods that enabled the retarded children to learn also enabled the "normal" children to learn—spontaneously and independently.

Montessori soon became the object of much attention, and her fame spread throughout the world. She resigned her lectureships and gave up her private practice, devoting all her time to her new work, including training teachers and writing. In 1909 her first publication dealing with the Montessori schools appeared: *The Method of Scientific Pedagogy as Applied to Infant Education and the Children's House.* A Montessori Society was organized in Rome, and branches of it and Montessori schools were established in Milan, Naples, and elsewhere. The movement spread to other countries in Europe and to Russia, China, Japan, Canada, Argentina, India, Ceylon, and America.

She traveled widely, lecturing and establishing schools and teacher-training centers and conducting training courses. In 1913 she made her first visit to the United States, where she was given a White House reception, lectured at Carnegie Hall, and met many famous Americans. A Montessori Association was formed. She rejected an offer by the publisher McClure to build her an institution in America. Nevertheless, Montessori schools were established, and numerous laudatory articles were published in magazines and journals about her work. She returned to America in 1915, led a training course in California, and was involved in setting up a Montessori class at the San Francisco World's Fair, conducted by Helen Parkhurst, one of her students and followers in America. It received the only two gold medal awards given at the exhibition.

Her popularity in America rapidly subsided, however, as criticism by professional educators mounted. Professor William Heard Kilpatrick of the Teachers College, Columbia University, was the most devastating critic. In a book published in 1914,[5] based on the reading of her book (*The Montessori Method*), a visit to Montessori classes in Rome, and an interview with Dr. Montessori, he rejected her methods as outdated and not based upon current theorists or research in learning. We shall consider his specific criticisms later, since some of them are still being made. The Montessori movement died out in America, though it continued in other countries. Dr. Montessori's last visit to the United States was in 1918.

In 1922, she was appointed government inspector of schools in Italy, but gradually, because of Fascist interference with her work, spent more of her time in Barcelona, Spain, where she had established a pedagogical seminary. Her effigy and books were burned in Nazi Germany. Her last visit to Italy until after the war was for the Fourth International Montessori Congress in Rome in 1934. With the 1936 revolution in Spain, she moved to Holland. In 1939 she went to India for a visit, where she was interned as an Italian national during World War II, although she was allowed to continue her work. Numerous schools were established in India, which is still a center of Montessori activity.

After the war she went England (1946) and returned to Italy in 1947. The next year she went to India again, and in 1949 began a course for teachers in Pakistan. She left before its completion to preside over the Eighth International Montessori Congress in San Remo. The previous congresses (1925, 1932, 1933, 1934, 1936, 1937, 1938) had also been held under her presidency. She attended her last congress in London in 1951.

During the years from 1949 to 1952 she traveled extensively in Europe, receiving the Medal of the Legion of Honor in France in 1949, touring Norway and Sweden, and directing a teacher-training course in Italy in 1950. She lectured at Innsbruck, Austria, and then returned to Holland, which had become her headquarters after she left India in 1946. She was given the rank of officer of the Order of Orange-Nassau by Queen Wilhelmina, and received an honorary doctor of philosophy degree from the University of Amsterdam. She died in Holland in May 1952, after having appointed her son, Mario Montessori, her successor in directing the Association Montessori Internationale.[6]

PHILOSOPHY AND THEORY

The Nature of Man

Montessori was familiar with the writings of Rousseau, Froebel, and Pestalozzi and was influenced by their ideas. Human beings, she recognized, are unlike the other animals; they are not born with fixed characteristics, or instincts, which determine their behavior in specific ways. On the contrary, they have the potential for developing many different behaviors, for learning to adapt to varied circumstances. Their behavior is less fixed by heredity, and is thus more adaptable than that of the lower animal species.

The human infant, lacking the instinctive behaviors of the animals is more helpless, and dependent for a longer period on the care of adults. Children must therefore go through a long period of learning. They do not begin to communicate, as other animals do (in a limited way, of course), almost immediately after birth, without learning, naturally and instinctively. They must learn to speak over a period of time, beginning some months after birth. They speak a language not by heredity, but by learning the language of their associates.

Yet children learn to speak without being taught specifically to do so. The capacity to learn is present, and when the opportunity is there—that is, where the child is in the presence of others who talk—it learns when it is ready developmentally. According to Montessori, this learning is preceded by "an *inner development* during the long period when the baby was unable to express himself. He was actually elaborating in the mysterious recesses of his unconscious mind a whole language with the grammatical order of words necessary to express thought. This children achieve in all possible languages. . . . In every race the child begins to speak at about two years of age and it was certainly so in the past also."[7]

She continues:

> It appears, therefore, that the ear does not merely hear as a sense
> organ, but is guided by special sensitivities to collect the sounds of
> human speech only from the environment. These sounds are not merely
> heard, they provide motor reactions in the delicate fibres of the vocal
> chords—the tongue, lips, etc. Thus among all these muscle-fibres runs a
> tendency to reproduce those sounds. Nevertheless, this is not immedi-
> ately revealed, but stored away until that time when language is to be
> born, just as the child during the intra-uterine life is being formed with-
> out functioning, and is then, at a given moment, stimulated to enter the
> world and starts functioning all of a sudden.
>
> These, of course, are suppositions, but the fact remains that there are
> inner developments, directed by creative energies and that these de-
> velopments can reach maturity before they become outwardly manifest.[8]

Development is spontaneous, but only in the appropriate environment. The learning of the mother tongue is not like the learning of a
foreign language by an adult. No conscious effort is involved.

Children learn to walk, as well as to talk, without specific instruction. From these natural learnings, involving the development of the
child's potentials, Montessori derived two related ideas.

Sensitive Periods

The first concept is that of sensitive periods of development. As the
child develops, there appear to be periods when he becomes ripe for
certain learnings. If the environment provides the opportunities, these
learnings occur naturally and easily. If, however, the environmental
opportunities are not present, these learnings do not occur. When this
is the case and the learnings are postponed, the process becomes a
difficult and often painful one. Thus, the wild boy of Aveyron, who
walked on all fours when he was discovered, learned to walk upright
under Itard's tutelage only after a long and laborious process. He never
learned to speak.

The optimum stages for learning to walk and talk are only two examples of the existence of sensitive developmental periods. Montessori
describes five major sensitive periods. (There is a large number of
more specific skills which have optimum periods for their acquisition.)

The first and earliest period, apearing in the first year and extending into the third year, is represented by a strong interest in, even a
need for, order in the environment. Things must be in their "right"
places, and follow the "right" order; children may become quite
ritualistic in these matters. They become upset amid disorder or by a
change in schedule. Order is necessary for the child's constructing of
(or ordering of) himself out of the elements of his environment,
which must be ordered for his use. The child whose need for order is

not met finds difficulty in adjusting to or accepting order later. The child whose need is met is able to tolerate some disorder later.

A second sensitive period, which overlaps the period of order in its beginning, sees the development of walking. The child spontaneously learns to walk when it is ready. Preventing the young child from walking when it is naturally ready makes the process a more difficult one later.

A third sensitive period is the period of the development of language, beginning in the second year. This process includes the exploration of the environment by the tongue and hands—through taste and touch. The acquisition of a new language by an adult is a difficult process, but the child acquires language naturally and easily. The adult may never learn to speak the new language like a native, but children learn their native language with no "unnatural" accent. This sensitive period lasts for several years, longer than any of the others.

A fourth period is characterized by interest in and attention to small or tiny objects. It accompanies the period for order, beginning in the second year. Children are attracted to small articles—beads, beans, pebbles. insects, and so on.

The fifth period is the period of development of social interest, first manifested by the child becoming aware of and observing others, then by its interacting with and relating to them, followed by its understanding and respecting the rights of others. This last stage is sometimes referred to as the period for learning good manners.

A period for the refinement of the senses is also often referred to, when the child is interested in colors, sounds, shapes, and textures, and their nuances and discriminable differences.

The failure of the environment to provide the conditions for the development of the activities represented in these sensitive periods leads to retardation or inhibition of their development, the failure to achieve their optimum or highest form, and even, in cases of severe and prolonged deprivation, lack of their development.

While there appears to be a sequence to the sensitive periods, they overlap considerably. The sensitive period for language, for example, while becoming clear or obvious in the latter part of the second year and the first part of the third year, may be considered to begin in the first weeks of the infant's life, with babbling sounds; it then continues after the third year for several more years before it becomes impossible for the child to learn speech. Likewise, the stages of social development also encompass a period of several years.

Language includes writing as well as speech, and the sensitive periods for these aspects of language development are, according to Montessori's experience, earlier than usually assumed. When Montessori was working with retarded children, 4-year-olds began to "write." They were not interested in writing, but in the shapes and feel of letters. They began writing by tracing cutout letters with their fingers. They then arranged the letters into words and sentences. This happened spontaneously, about three months after they were exposed to the letters of the alphabet. When they began to write on paper, Montessori observed that their penmanship was "well nigh perfect and all children write in the same way because all have touched the same letters."[9] This spontaneous writing was called by Montessori "the explosion into writing." Reading soon followed, at the age of 5. Montessori contrasted the spontaneity and ease with which these young children learned to read and write with the painful and disagreeable experiences of older children learning to read and write at a later age in the schools: "Written language can be acquired much more easily by children of four years than by those of six years of age—the time at which compulsory education usually starts. While children of six years of age need at least two years to learn how to write, and do so with much difficulty and against nature, children of four years learn this second language within a few months, and with enthusiasm."[10]

Because the experience of learning to read and to write was so difficult for older children, educators could not believe her discovery, and felt that young children should be spared the "painful labor of intellectual study."[11] If strain and resistance were present in older children, they reasoned, it would be undesirable to "force" younger children to engage in such learning.

Observation as the Basis for Practice

The second idea which Montessori developed from her experience was that *educational methods and practices should derive from observation of children rather than from preconceived notions about their development.* She felt that contemporary education was based upon such preconceived notions and that these biases were the source of the resistance to her ideas. She asked: "Who then can reveal the natural ways along which the psychic development of man proceeds but the child himself once he is placed in conditions permitting him to do so?"[12] Education, she insisted, must be based upon the laws of the child's natural development. She believed that "the subconscious impulse during the period of growth—that is, of the construction of the individual—urges it to realize its growth, and the child is supremely happy when it is simply given the opportunity of doing this and is urged on to make the greatest effort to achieve it. It can be said that the period of childhood is an age of 'inner life' which leads to the developing, maturing and perfecting of all the faculties. The outer world has value only insomuch as it offers the necessary means to reach the goal set by Nature."[13]

The child's mental state is creative in nature, open to learning. Montessori used the term *absorbent mind* to distinguish this natural, effortless, unconscious state of learning from the conscious, effortful learning of adults. Whereas the adult adapts with difficulty to new situations, children adapt easily to the environment in which they find themselves. They learn without being taught.

If the child's nature, or natural development, is to be observed, the child needs freedom in the classroom or environment. But "to let the pupils do what they like, to amuse them with light occupations, to lead them back to an almost wild state, does not solve the problem."[14] The environment must provide opportunities for development if potentialities are to develop. Appropriate materials must be present. For preschool children to exercise their natural capacity to learn to read and write, the materials—letters of the alphabet—must be provided. "The prepared environment" is the designation used by Montessori to refer to an environment of the child's potentialities.

In a prepared environment children learn spontaneously. They do not have to be forced; indeed, sometimes their eagerness must be restrained. "Indirect intervention" may be provided to facilitate natural development. "The child learns from his own activity, taking culture from the environment and not from the teacher."[15] Spontaneous interest leads the child to become absorbed in what he or she is doing for long periods of time. The child's absorption and persistence contrast with the wandering of attention of older children in classrooms. Montessori gives examples of this persistence. One child spent days consulting geographies and drawing, with instruments, the Rhine River, with all its tributaries. Another boy multiplied a 30-digit number by another of 25 digits, pasting sheets of paper together to continue the computations, spending over two days, with the help of two other boys, with no sign of fatigue or boredom. Children, unlike most adults, are oblivious of time; they have all the time in the world. They are absorbed in a process, while adults focus on the outcome of a project. Unlike those who believed that children should "play"—that is, engage in useless activity—Montessori believed that the child needs to engage in "work"—meaningful, constructive, creative activity utilizing and developing his or her capacities. The lack of this experience in early childhood becomes the basis for restlessness, inactivity, and lack of interest in and resistance to meaningful activity—that is, learning—later in childhood.

Montessori did not contend that man is born good (or evil), but only that nature follows an established order, that development is a lawful process. When this process is recognized, learning occurs without stress or strain. Moreover, disciplinary problems do not occur. Misbehavior or naughtiness in the child "represents a disorder regarding the natural laws of psychic life in the course of construction," that is, it is the result of obstructions to the natural, spontaneous, constructive activities of the child. Children who are "unstable, lazy, disorderly, violent, disobedient . . . are 'functionally' ill and can be cured by a hygienic form of psychic life. . . .   They start again to function normally," according to their nature.[16]

The quietness, order, and discipline of the children in Montessori's classroom attracted the attention of observers, who attributed it to her control. But it was not enforced by the teacher, and it continued when she left the room. The discipline was thus not achieved by force, by commands, or repression. It was the natural result of the children being engaged in activities in which they were absorbed.

There were of course rules establishing limits of acceptable behavior, and teaching of respect and consideration for the rights of others, as well as "silence exercises" or "lessons in silence." Montessori felt that there is a natural tendency toward obedience, an instinct related to the need for order, which leads, in the appropriate environment, to self-discipline.

Motivation

It is apparent from the foregoing that motivation was not a problem to Montessori. Children do not have to be motivated, either by the carrot or by the stick. Unless they are restricted or live in a bare or deprived environment, they engage in continuous spontaneous activity and interact with their environment. Their activities are purposeful, not necessarily in the sense that they have a conscious future goal or objective, but in the sense that they provide intrinsic pleasure or satisfaction. Children engage in activity that realizes their potential—they are innately motivated towards self-realization; or, in a favorite phrase of Montessori and her followers, children construct themselves, or engage in self-construction.

During the sensitive periods, the child naturally engages in activities relevant to the development of the potentials seeking expression. Where the environment—persons and materials—provides the opportunities for such expression, there is no problem of motivation. After the critical period has passed, artificial, extrinsic efforts to motivate the child may become necessary. But for children engaged in activities related to the exercise of their potentials during the sensitive periods, extrinsic reinforcement and encouragement—by competition for stars, grades, and such—have no place. Learning is its own reward.

Montessori's observations and experience not only confirmed her assumptions about the nature of children and their development, they also led her to develop a deep respect for children and a trust in their capacity to grow toward independence and to develop as persons.

Montessori was interested in the growth and development of the whole child, not simply his or her academic or intellectual growth. An important aspect of growth is the physical. Montessori recognized this aspect of development in her emphasis on movement. Her concern with sensorimotor activities derived from her study of Séguin. It is through sensorimotor exploration that the child learns abouts its physical environment. Sensorimotor development is a foundation for intellectual development. The materials which she developed had the purpose of fostering sensorimotor development. These materials were designed to facilitate fine motor activities which were deemed especially important, but gross motor activities were not neglected. They involved gymnastic equipment as well as other materials.

The Montessori approach is not simply a technique or the application of certain methods or the use of certain materials, however, as becomes clear in reading Montessori's writings. There is a basic attitude toward the child which influences the activities of the teacher and the conduct of the classroom. It consists of a basic respect for the child as an individual and for his or her potentialities and capacities. Implicit in this attitude of respect is an acceptance of children as they are, a trust in their ability to develop, and patience in allowing them to do so, with help and suggestions when they ask for it or clearly need it, but without tight control and direction of their learning experiences.

Stages of Development

The child is not a miniature adult, either physically or mentally. In fact, one cannot say what "the child" is or in what specific ways he or she differs from the adult, because a child is different from age to age. The child is in a continuous process of growth and change. It is in this basic respect that the child differs from the adult, who has reached the developmental norm or maturity. The child passes through a series of stages, separated by transition periods or metamorphoses, so that the stages are not simply quantitatively different but are also qualitatively different. There are stages of physical, mental, and social development, but Montessori is concerned mainly with mental development.

Infancy: The absorbent mind (0–6 years). The stage of infancy is a stage of creativity and transformation. It is divided into two periods:

1. *The Unconscious Mind (0–3 years).* During this period the mind is constantly absorbing impressions from its environment without awareness of the process. The absorption of language is perhaps the prime example. But there is also the absorption of the difference between the real and the unreal, of bodily activities and coordination, of habits of self-care and independence. The various senses permit the absorption of the environment.
2. *The Conscious Mind (3–6 years).* Consciousness develops with movement—the awareness of activity and its effect on the environment. The powers of concentration, will, and memory develop. There is a shift from control by the environment to control of the environment. The hand is a conscious instrument rather than a reac-

tor to stimuli. Learning is spontaneous and only requires the opportunities provided in an appropriate environment.

The period of childhood (6–12 years). The stage of childhood is a period of development without much transformation, a period of stability. Information acquired earlier and new information are used to reason, to answer the questions why, how, and when. Interest develops in broad areas: the development of the universe, the development of life, the history of eary man and civilization, and science and scientific classification. Social interests become strong, and concern about moral issues develops.

Adolescence (12–18 years). Adolescence is divided into two periods:

1. *Puberty (12–15 years).* Puberty is a period of transformation or creation. The rapid changes make the child susceptible to weaknesses and diseases—tuberculosis, in Montessori's time. Montessori compares this period of "new birth" to that of birth and neonate development. In addition to physical changes, there are psychological changes, characterized by doubts, uncertainties, emotional upheavals, discouragement, and a decline in intellectual functioning. Academic activity, Montessori felt, should be subordinated to the facilitation of social development.

2. *Adolescence (15–18 years).* The period following puberty is a period of consolidation and a development of interests, with concern about one's place in the adult world. This concern involves the place in one's life of work and economic independence, marriage, and social responsibility.

Maturity (18–24 years). The above stages of development culminate in maturity. The individual enters adult society, finds his life work, becomes established socially and emotionally, and settles into a stable period of development.

APPLICATION AND PRACTICE

The Preschool Age

For the 60 children in Montessori's first school, she provided equipment suited to their size. The furniture included lightweight rectangular tables which two 4-year-olds could carry, long enough for two children to sit at the long sides; as well as smaller tables at which a single child could work. Chairs were also lightweight: armchairs were also provided. Washstands low enough for use by a 3-year-old were provided, with basins, and shelves for soap dishes, towels, and so on. Long, low cupboards provided places for keeping materials, and plants, acquariums, and toys were placed on top. Numerous blackboards were hung on the walls, and pictures were placed on the walls above them; Raphael's Madonna was one of these.

Exercises of practical life. Practical activities of everyday living were an important part of the schedule of Montessori's schools. These were of three types: self-care, care of the environment, and the practice of grace and courtesy in interactions with others. Exercises and role playing enable the child to practice these activities. Thus, in addition to learning to put on and take off their outer clothes, children practiced buttoning and unbuttoning, using hooks and eyes, and lacing, on equipment which Montessori constructed. Self-care also included washing, blowing one's nose, and covering the mouth when coughing or sneezing.

Care of the environment included carrying chairs and tables quietly, opening and shutting doors, sweeping and dusting, carrying water in pitchers, assisting in preparations for lunch, and cleaning up afterward. Washing windows, cleaning and polishing silver and utensils, and other household activities have been included in the activities of Montessori schools. Table washing is an activity frequently mentioned as being liked by children. Many if not most of these activities are of real value or use, but often children engage in them for the activities themselves, enjoying them so much that they sometimes continue them repetitively without their being necessary.

Social activities practiced include watching another child at work without interfering, walking around another child's work rug and materials, learning how to interrupt a child engaged in an activity, how to ask for something, how to accept something, how to refuse politely, how to shake hands in greeting, how to introduce someone, how to verbalize feelings, and so on.

In the Montessori classroom, all materials have their assigned places and are always returned there when the child no longer wishes to use them, so they will be available to another child who wants to use them. Thus the development of order is encouraged.

These practical activities are among the first in the daily schedule of children of all ages. Their purpose is to aid children in development of skills and attitudes which will be useful to them in their social and academic lives, as well as enabling them to develop a positive self-image based on competence. In addition to social skills, the skills developed include the following:

> *Problem-solving techniques and attack skills.* Children learn to order materials and sequence activities in order to achieve solutions and success.
>
> *Coordination and refinement of movement.* Carrying and manipulating materials of varying sizes and shapes develops increasing control and precision of movement.

Concentration. Building from interesting activities of short duration to those of long duration increases attention span and the ability to concentrate. Freedom from interruption and interference by others also contributes.

Independence. Activities of self-care and care of the environment lead to the development of independence from adults.

Muscular education.   Although Montessori used the word *gymnastics,* she did not mean by it the usual exercises and physical activities. Rather she meant activities related to the child's normal physical development, like walking and balancing. Thus, a chalk line provided the opportunity for the child to walk a straight line. Small circular stairs with one railing for support allowed practice in going up and down stairs. Marching, not for rhythm but for poise, was recommended by Montessori. The usual children's games were encouraged.

Montessori also used respiratory or breathing exercises, and exercises for the lips, tongue, and teeth, involving the pronunciation of basic consonant sounds.

The planting and care of a garden and care of animals were also a part of Montessori's school and provided practice in a variety of large- and small-muscle activities.

Education of the senses.   The didactic materials developed by Montessori were designed for the education of the senses, which she considered to be of the greatest importance for the young child. Some of the materials which she had used with mentally deficient children were not used with those in the children's houses. Others which were used were modified. Some materials were taken from or adapted from psychometric tests. She felt she had "arrived at a *selection of objects* (which I do not here wish to speak of in the technical language of psychology as stimuli) representing the minimum *necessary* to a practical sense education, . . . [which constitutes] the didactic system."[17]

Materials and exercises were devised to develop all of the senses. The thermal and tactile senses were combined in washing, rinsing, and drying the hands, using soap, and water of differing temperatures. She also used a series of thin metal bowls holding water at different temperatures. Children were asked to touch materials with eyes closed. Sandpapers of varying degrees of coarseness and papers of different textures were used. The baric (pressure) sense was developed by having the children close their eyes and discriminate between wooden tablets of the same size but different weights (being made of different woods), held in the upturned palm and fingers of each hand.

The stereognostic sense exercises utilized cubes and rectangular solids to be sorted by touch, as well as common objects to be named with eyes closed. The education of smell included recognizing odors

of flowers and of foods at lunch. Taste exercises used various solutions that were sweet, bitter, salty, and so on.

Exercises for the discrimination of sounds were difficult to find. Bells of 13 different tones were developed by Anna Maria Macceroni, one of Montessori's associates; intensities varied with the force with which they were struck, however. The activities with bells in teaching discrimination, as well as other musical activities, were developed by Maccheroni in collaboration with Montessori and have been expanded in use. Series of whistles were also used. Montessori constructed small boxes containing sand and pebbles of different sizes which produced different sounds when the boxes were shaken. She reports that the children did not like the whistles or boxes.

It is in the visual and the visual-tactile-motor areas that the materials and exercises were most extensive. For the differential perception of dimensions, four sets of blocks of wood, each with ten holes varying in diameter and depth, were constructed. Ten wooden cylinders fitted into the holes. A small wooden or metal button on the tops served as a handle. In one set the cylinders were all of the same height, but varied in diameter (by half-centimeter increments) from 1 centimeter to 5½ centimeters. In the second set the cylinders were of equal diameter (27 millimeters), but varied in height from 1 centimeter to 5½ centimeters. The third set consisted of cylinders increasing both in diameter, like the first set, and in height, like the second set. In the fourth set, the cylinders increased in diameter and decreased in height. Children of 2½ to 3 years of age began with the first set, fitting the disarranged cylinders into the holes. The children learned to place the cylinders correctly without direction: "The didactic material *controls every error*. The child proceeds to correct himself, doing this in varying ways."[18]

The "Pink Tower" consisted of ten blocks or cubes from 10 centimeters to 1 centimeter in size. Three dimensions were represented. The child built them into a tower, starting with the largest and placing each block successively on the one next largest. This exercise could be used with the youngest children, under 3 years of age.

The "Big Stair," or the "Brown Stair," consisted of ten blocks of wood, each 20 centimeters long but increasing in width and height from 1 centimeter to 10 centimeters. These blocks were to be placed in order, forming stairs. The concept of thickness and thinness was thus represented.

Length was represented by ten rods, each 3 centimeters wide and 3 centimeters high but varying in length by decimeters, from 1 decimeter to a meter. Each 1-decimeter space was painted red or blue, the colors alternating along the rod. When placed side by side in order the rods formed a large triangular shape like half of a pipe organ, with the

red and blue sections matching transversely. These rods were used with the older childern in teaching arithmetic. (Currently, the rods are all red.)

Montessori also constructed various sets of wooden geometric forms of varying sizes, which could be arranged in order of size and placed in the appropriate places as insets on a cutout frame. Placement of these forms combines the visual and the muscular-tactile senses. For use with these forms, three sets of cards were prepared. In one set, geometric forms cut from blue paper were mounted on white cards. In the second set, blue-paper outlines of the same forms, 1 centimeter wide, were mounted on white cards. In the third set, the figures were outlined in black lines on the white cards. Exercises included placing the wooden insets on the appropriate cards (the wooden figures and the figures on the cards were of the same size). These exercises combine the tactile-muscular senses but move toward emphasizing the visual sense.

For the education of the chromatic sense, Montessori constructed tablets presenting eight colors, each in eight intensities. Silk or wool materials were used. Two sets allowed for matching exercises, beginning with three colors and proceeding through the eight colors, then adding tones, beginning with the eight tones of two colors. (Currently, painted tablets are used.)

In all of the materials and exercises, there is a progression from presenting the materials with the greatest differences for discrimination to those with the least differences, leading to the development of sensitivity to small differences.

Montessori wrote: "I do not claim to have brought to perfection the method of sense training as applied to young children."[19] But as noted earlier, she recognized the necessity of sense training as a foundation for intellectual activity. Rather than education beginning with ideas, it should begin with sensorimotor activities. It is through the senses that man is in contact with his environment and receives the stimuli for thought and action. It was Aristotle who said: "There is nothing in the intellect that was not first in the senses." The Montessori materials and exercises presented the elements of the environment to the child in an orderly way, related to the natural development of the child's capacities to use them.

Intellectual education. From the education of the senses, the teacher led the child to ideas, from the concrete to the abstract. The direction of the teacher was minimal, and the child was not urged or pushed. Experience with the materials or objects came first, with the child watching the teacher handle them. Then the association of an object with its name was begun. This was done simply by naming the object

or quality while touching it. Thus, touching a rough object, Montessori repeated, "Rough. This is rough." Or "This is cold" and "This is warm." Then the teacher tested, by asking after a waiting period, "Which is rough?" or "Which is smooth?" If the child could not point to the correct object, the teacher did not correct her or him; the child was not ready, and the teacher waited for another time. If the child was correct, the teacher then proceeded to have the child pronounce the word by asking, "What is this?" She might repeat the word correctly if the child's pronunciation was not distinct. The teacher did not go beyond this to teaching the child to generalize. This the child usually did spontaneously when ready, and thus the child experienced the joy of discovery. "The greatest triumph of our educational method should always be this: *to bring about the spontaneous progress of the child.*"[20] The materials were thus used by the teacher to enable the child to discover such concepts as dimension and form. Games were also used. For example, Montessori had the children play a game in which one child, blindfolded and sitting at a table, was asked to identify different objects or to name qualities by touch or to discriminate weight. The watching children showed intense interest.

Reading and writing. Earlier mention was made of what Montessori called "the explosion into writing," when retarded children of 4 to 5½ years began to write "spontaneously." They were, however, prepared for the actual writing. The first step was the tracing of the letters of the alphabet with their fingers. The letters were in script and were made of wood, the small letters being 8 centimeters high and half a centimeter thick. The consonants were painted in blue enamel and the vowels in red. Montessori also prepared cards on which the letters were painted. Pictures of objects beginning with each letter were used in conjunction with the letters. The children repeatedly traced the letters in the form of flowing writing. To prepare the child for holding a pen, a small wooden stick was held like a pen and used for tracing. Since the children had difficulty following the letters smoothly with the stick, Montessori planned to prepare indented letter forms, but notes that these were not constructed because of the expense.

The use of these materials led to the children learning to write. Montessori writes: "It was with great surprise that I noted the *facility* with which a deficient child, to whom I had one day given a piece of chalk, traced upon the blackboard, in a firm hand, the letters of the entire alphabet, writing for the first time. This had arrived much more quickly than I had supposed."[21]

When Montessori began working with the normal children in the Children's Houses, she did not plan to attempt to teach writing. The children and the mothers asked for such instruction, however, so she decided to do so beginning in October, when the elementary schools opened. But she could not find anyone to manufacture the materials she had used eight years earlier. Finally, she made large cutout paper letters which were colored. It was then that she cut letters out of sandpaper and glued them to smooth cards, for tracing with the fingers. She found these to be superior to the wooden letters, and they could be made easily in quantity. These and other materials were used in a series of exercises progressing to actual writing.

Montessori reports that, though starting later in the year than elementary school children, by Christmas two of her 4-year-olds wrote letters of thanks and good wishes while the elementary-school children were still struggling to write single letters. The writing was judged equal to that of third-grade children. Montessori comments on the joy of the children in one class when they first discovered they could write and thus communicate silently. Once they realized that they could write, it became apparent that they were not limited to the first word they happened to write. They were able to write many words, and they covered the blackboards, floors, and every available place with their writing, not only in the classroom but at home. In this group all of them apparently broke into writing at about the same time. Montessori suggests that in groups where the children are at different stages, the individual children may begin writing at different times, some perhaps earlier than in the group described, but to a more limited extent. The teacher can recognize when a child is ready to write, and if the child does not do so spontaneously, after a week of waiting she or he can invite the child to write.

The teaching of writing includes the beginning of the teaching of reading, since the images of the letters and their sounds are associated. Writing precedes reading by about two weeks, though it may be longer. The assembling of letters into words during the teaching of writing leads to their pronunciation, that is, the reading of the words. But this is not reading. Reading requires the comprehension of ideas.

Montessori's materials for teaching reading were cards or pieces of paper on which words and phrases were written in large script, and toys corresponding to words. The slow pronunciation of the sounds of the words is not reading, because there is no meaning. When the words are repeated rapidly, the meaning appears, since the child has already learned the spoken word.

One of the games used by Montessori in the teaching of reading was to write the names of toys on pieces of paper, fold them, and put them in a basket. The children then one by one pick one out of the basket, look at the word, take the paper to the teacher who is at the table containing the toys, pronounce the word and give the paper to the teacher, and receive the toy to play with. Montessori writes: "But what was my amazement when the children, having learned to understand the written cards, *refused* to take the toys! They explained that they did not wish to waste time playing, and with a species of insatiable desire, preferred to draw out and read the cards one after another!"[22] She therefore abandoned the game and simply wrote hundreds of slips with names of objects, cities, children, colors, and so on, and placed the slips in open boxes from which the children could freely draw them to read.

Finding no suitable books for the children to read, Montessori fostered reading by communicating to children through writing on the blackboard. "Little by little, they *discovered* the great quality of writing—that it communicates thought. Whenever I began to write, they fairly *trembled* in their eagerness to understand what was my meaning without hearing me speak a word."[23] She also wrote long sentences on cards ("command cards"), describing actions to be taken by the children, which the children read, afterward performing the required actions.

The perfection of reading proceeded more slowly than the perfection of writing, but Montessori states that "almost all of the normal children treated with our method begin to write at four years, and at five know how to read and write, at least as well as children who have finished the first elementary. They could enter the second elementary a year in advance of the time when they are admitted to first."[24] But no child was forced to learn to read or write: "We do not even *invite* him, or in any way attempt to coax him to do that which he does not wish to do. So it sometimes happens that certain children, *not having spontaneously presented themselves* for these lessons, are left in peace, and do not know how to read or write."[25]

Numeration and arithmetic. Counting with coins was used with the youngest children. It was next done with rods which, as noted above, varied from 1 to 10 decimeters, each rod being marked off in decimeters by alternating red and blue sections. When placed in order, they constituted "The Long Stair," a triangle with the hypotenuse constituting the ten stairs.

Numbers cut from sandpaper were used like the letters: Children were asked to give the teacher the number requested, and they traced the numbers with their fingers. Cards with numbers were sorted into compartments in a tray. Montessori also cut numbers from calendars and mounted them on slips of paper. For an exercise in memory, the slips were folded and placed in a box. The children drew numbers, went to their seats, and read the numbers; then, leaving the slips, the children went to a table to take the number of objects specified on their slips.

Addition and subtraction up to 20 and simple multiplication and division of numbers up to ten were taught by using the rods referred to above.

Conclusion. Montessori wrote that the Children's Houses eliminated "the old-time teacher, who wore herself out maintaining discipline of immobility, and who wasted her breath in loud and continued discourse. . . . For this teacher we have substituted the *didactic* material, which contains within itself the control of errors and which makes auto-education possible to each child. The teacher has thus become a *director* of the spontaneous work of the children."[26] When one reads Montessori's writings, however, it becomes clear that she was a successful teacher not simply because of her method and her materials, but because of the person she was, including her attitudes and feelings —interest, concern, caring, and respect—toward the children. She obviously loved the children. Montessori recognized the importance of the personal relationship, as indicated by her statement quoted earlier (p. 21), and by her statement that "education is fundamentally a 'contact of souls.' "[27]

A preschool class in a Montessori school includes children ranging in age from 2½ or 3 years to 6 years of age. Children thus become accustomed to being with both older and younger children. Older children help the younger children, both by serving as models and as actual teachers. The older children gain by clarifying their own knowledge as they teach the younger ones. This functioning of the older children as assistants or aides to the teacher, together with the correlation of materials and teaching with the sensitive periods, enables a Montessori class to function with a much higher student-teacher ratio than other classrooms. In the first group of 60 children in the Children's House, apparently only Montessori (who was absent much of the time) and one other young woman (the porter's daughter), who was not trained as a teacher, were present.

The description of the materials and exercises given here is based upon the early writings of Montessori. As the movement spread and developed, the materials changed, being modified and added to over time by teachers in different countries and cultures. The cylinders, for example, have varied in size. In one reference to Montessori schools in America, the cylinders are described as varying in height from 5 to 10 centimeters,[28] rather than from half a centimeter to 5 centimeters as described by Montessori. Illustrations, in this source, of the stairs and the tower of blocks clearly indicate that they are much larger than the original materials. Nowhere, however, is there as systematic, detailed, and complete a description of materials as in Montessori's original writing. (In 1914, Montessori published *Dr. Montessori's Own Handbook*, which describes in detail the materials and their use. This manual was reprinted in 1964 by Bentley in England and in paperback in 1965 by Schocken Books, Inc.) The basic nature of the materials and their uses have remained essentially the same. Standardized materials are now available from A Neemhuis BV, Zelhem, Holland.

Elementary and Secondary Education

Montessori's work was mainly with preschool children. However, she had experience with children up to 9 years of age, using the same method of approach as with younger children. She further states, "We found that the procedure adopted by us, with children under nine years of age, could be applied to those of more advanced age, and we can affirm that at all stages of school life it is essential that no obstruction be placed in the way of the individual activity of the children in the course of development. Only thus can they obey the 'natural process of psychic development.' "[29] The basic principle of adapting teaching and education to the natural developmental capacities and interests of the child applies at all ages. When Montessori was living in Holland, she obtained government endorsement for the application of her methods at all educational levels, and a system of Montessori schools through high school was established. In 1920, she began to apply her methods at the university level at the University of Amsterdam.

Montessori defined three levels of education: (1) the period from birth to 7 years, with three subdivisions (the first two years, the third to fifth years, and the sixth and seventh years); (2) the period from 7 to 12 years; and (3) the period from 12 to 18 years, or adolescence. It appears that Montessori viewed the third subdivision of the first period as an extension of the preschool years, in which the methods and materials used in the earlier years would continue to be used. As indicated above, these first two years of elementary school would differ from the traditional school, assuming the children had experienced three years of a Montessori preschool. Montessori does not specify the changes necessary, however.

Montessori writes that doubts were expressed to her about the extension of her methods to children over 7 years of age. Critics suggested that children at this age should begin to respect the will of others in contrast to their own, to carry out necessary rather than chosen tasks, and to learn self-sacrifice. Even before this age, they suggested, children must learn the arithmetic tables and grammar. These unpleasant necessities, it was assumed, must be forced upon the child, and this would certainly be inconsistent with the liberty which was the basis of Montessori's system.

Montessori's answer was that liberty is not neglect or abandonment of the child, but includes the provision of an environment that allows the child to grow and develop according to its nature. She pointed to the advances in physical hygiene which had led to the improved health of the child by allowing it to grow and develop according to its nature. As the young child develops spontaneously in an appropriate environment, so will the older child.

The child from age 7 to 12. The levels of education are related to the characteristics of the child at the different age levels. The child from 7 to 12 has certain characteristics and needs which education must recognize. An environment must be created and provided to meet the child's needs. This environment must allow for the enlarged field of action required by the child from 7 to 12. It must provide opportunities for the child's total development. The traditional school does not do this; it is a closed environment. Therefore, the child attempts to escape from it.

Besides this need for a widening of the environment, there are two other major developments in the child during this period. The first is the beginning and growth of a moral sense; the second is the movement from the sensorial, material level to the abstract. This age level is the sensitive period for the development of a moral conscience and abstract intelligence.

The development of a moral conscience takes place in a social setting. Montessori believed that there is an inborn, natural sense of justice in the child, which manifests itself in an appropriate environment. Instruction is not to be forced upon the child. "We have not made our children moral by any special means; we have not taught them to 'overcome their caprices' and to sit quietly at work; we have not inculcated calm and order by exhorting them to follow the examples of others, and explaining how necessary order is to man; we have not lectured them on mutual courtesy, to instill the respect due to the work of others, and the patience with which they should wait in order not to infringe on the rights of others. There has been none of this; we have merely set the child free, and helped him to 'live.' "[30] Although this statement apparently was written about younger children, the principle applies to older children. A moral sense is not learned by memorizing words, according to Montessori. It is an internal response based upon sympathy and love for others and is learned in interaction with others. "It is up to the teacher to arrange that the moral teachings of life are taught through social experience."[31]

When children become interested in questions of how and why, they are entering the stage of abstract thinking. Their many questions need answering if they are to progress. They must be allowed the freedom to pursue answers to their questions in their environment, through observation and exploration of nature. "Thus, when the child wants to understand everything, the world, which he has before him, can fill that need."[32]

Since everything cannot be physically presented to the child, instruction must appeal to the imagination. Through imagination, the child can reconstruct the whole from the details, if they are precise. Imagining is for the older child what touching is to the young child.

In this sensitive period for the imagination, one can begin the study of each of the sciences in some detail. Since everything is part of a whole, the details can be selected at random. Montessori illustrates this by choosing water; she shows how one can proceed to the study of marine life or zoology, physical geography, mineralogy, physics, and chemistry, and goes on to describe exercises or experiments that can be performed. She presents the four basic elements (hydrogen, oxygen, nitrogen, and carbon) and their simple combinations pictorially, and develops some simple ideas in inorganic and organic chemistry. All this is presented simply, with visual symbols, since children at this stage (9 years) are not ready for formulas and theories. But their interest is stimulated, and they acquire the foundation which allows them later to study and to understand the sciences in less time than otherwise. By the age of 12, according to Montessori, the child educated in her system had attained an academic level three years beyond that of children from regular schools, as well as being advanced in social relations.[33]

Instruction is given to children 7 to 12 in large groups (the total class), in small groups, and individually. The purpose of large group lessons is to give general introductions to the development of the universe, of life on earth, of the human race, and of various subject areas in order to awaken the interest and strike the imagination of the children. Topics for those lessons include such things as the development of the universe, of the alphabet, of writing, of systems of numeration, of fractions, and so on. These general lessons give background material, so the children will approach the study of any particular area with a feeling for its historical beginnings.

In small group lessons, the makeup of the group is determined largely by the level of functioning of the children. Other interested children are usually not turned away.

In the first type of small group lesson, the adult gives more details about the topics that were introduced in the large group lessons. For example, if the adult were going to help the children gain a deeper understanding of the development of the universe and life on earth, he would introduce appropriate experiments in physics, biology, botany, and zoology. For an expansion on the introduction to the degrees of a circle as calculated by the Babylonians, the children could be introduced to the protractor and its use.

The second type of small group lesson is given to prepare children for excursions into the external environment. For example, if children are going to look at leaves, then leaf classification is reviewed before the children go out to observe or collect specimens.

The third type of small group lesson involves giving exact techniques for such things as experiments, art work, and other such activities. Dr. Montessori felt that the development of perserverance grows through experience of success; therefore, the children are helped to gain the techniques which will enable them to reach their aims in the shortest possible time with the fewest possible failures.

The large and small group lessons are all meant as introductions to activities which children may pursue in their own ways, as their interests and abilities allow. The lessons for individuals involve the types of work whose sequential nature demands that one master certain aspects before one can proceed to a higher level of work in the sequence. These lessons are mainly for mathematics, geometry, and language. They are usually for individual children, although it is sometimes appropriate to form a small group when there are several children who are at the same level. Other children who are interested in the lesson may observe. If some of those children have already had the presentation, seeing it again becomes a review. They may, at times, take over the adult's role and continue to work with the child who has just had the lesson. As for children who are not yet ready for the material nor the activity involved, observation stimulates them to work with the prerequisite activities and/or materials. Then when they are ready for the lesson, it will not be totally new and strange to them.

Each child must have the possibility of making choices and of pursuing those choices. Large, uninterrupted time blocks are provided in order to allow each child to pursue work to an end and to achieve satisfaction. In this manner a natural work cycle and long concentration span develops which is refreshing—*not fatiguing*—to the child.

The task of the Montessori center during the grade-school period is to aid the child in developing naturally the basic physical, emotional, and cognitive skills necessary for functioning in society and the world; and to help the child gain an overview of the development of the universe, of the solar system, of the earth, of life on earth, of early humanity, of civilizations, and of scientific classification. This knowledge is an aid to the child's own natural inner development. Before making an intelligent choice about what to do with his life and how to fit into the culture, the child needs to know how the culture developed and what developed. Intelligent choice is based on knowledge. The infant has to make order out of the apparent chaos of the world. Education is simply an extension of the same thing, that is, ordering and classifying the world and life as we know it in order to understand it. It is the responsibility of the Montessori center to provide this kind of overview and the means by which children can pursue those aspects which are particularly of interest to them. This bare-bones curriculum provides organizing centers as starters; the child takes it from there.

Perhaps the most important aspect of the Montessori process is that abstractions are not taught directly; instead, the necessary "keys" or components are provided, so that the children can make their own abstractions. Teaching begins with the concrete or the specific and moves to the abstract or the general, from sensorimotor to visual to symbolic. This means that children arrive at abstraction through their own creative thought, developed during their struggle to understand. It is a joyful process. It is part of the children's inner development and creation of themselves rather than an intellectual veneer.

The child from age 12 to 18. Montessori called for a reform of secondary education.[34] Education of the adolescent, she insisted, must be related to the physical and psychological changes which result in the child becoming an adult, moving from living in the family to living in society. The primary focus of earlier education should be nature; after the age of 12 the focus should move to society and the development of greater understanding (and thus love) among men. The child should participate in social work of some kind.

Montessori criticized existing schools because they had no aim other than to prepare pupils for a career. But in a world of change, the future is characterized by uncertainty and insecurity. Preparation for such a world must focus upon the personality development of the pupils. Adolescence is the sensitive period for the development of feelings of justice and personal dignity.

Montessori proposed "an experimental school of social life," in which the adolescent would acquire economic independence through paid work. The work would not be specialized, but would be such as to allow talents to reveal themselves. The general principle would be that work itself is of greater importance than a specific kind of work, since all work is noble.

Montessori also advocated that the adolescent be educated away from the family, in a rural environment conducive to good physical health and to reflection and meditation. Work and study would be combined and related. She called the work-school organization *Erdkinder*, that is, "Children of the Soil" or "Rural Children."[35] The work would be varied, including the operation of the boarding school or hotel, a farm, and a store in a nearby city where farm and other products would be sold. The school would operate on a year-round basis, without vacations, which "are a loss of time and a break in the continuity of life. Rest comes from *a change of occupation*."[36] Study, if it meets a psychic need of the individual, does not cause "mental fatigue."

There would be liberty within the limits necessary for order. The children would be treated with the greatest respect. "It is of greater value to treat them as if their worth were superior to their real worth than to minimize their merits and risk injury to their sense of personal dignity. . . . One must not give the adolescents the impression that they are not conscientious, that they are unable to discipline themselves."[37] In this setting, social morality will develop.

Physical development would be fostered by physical education, taking into account the differential rates of development of the parts of the body during adolescence, and by attention to diet, which should not include meat during this period, according to Montessori.

The educational program would encourage personal expression, through the choice by the students of exercises in music, language, and the arts. The bases of personality would be developed through "creative" culture, consisting of moral education, mathematics, and languages. The program would put the adolescent into relation with current civilization through the study of the earth and living nature; of the physical, chemical, and other sciences, including laboratory experiments; and of the history of humanity. Each student would be expected also to engage in a detailed study of a specific subject, era, event, or person. The last two years, from age 16 to 18, would include preparation for university or diploma examinations.

Montessori felt that it was the methods, even more than the curriculum, which needed to be changed. Methods should arouse and sustain the interests of students, give them the opportunity to work alone and to experiment, and alternate study with the practical activities of life.

The Function of the University

Universities as they exist, Montessori wrote,[38] are a continuation of the lower schools, and students live as, and are treated as, children. The universities have lost the sense of dignity and grandeur which they had in the Middle Ages and have become professional schools. Students want to work as little as possible and want to pass examinations so they can obtain a position.

The function of the university is to teach one how to study, so that one can continue to learn. This should not require three to six years. Learning can continue while one works and is thus financially independent. The university is for adults.

Students, if they are adequately prepared, will be "ardent apostles, intelligent critics, and veritable collaborators" with the professors.[39] The university ought to be concerned not only with culture, but with other needs of man, which if not met, disturb his mental state. These include the need to feel of value, to be appreciated and loved. The perfection of a skill in a freely chosen field and a sense of accomplishment lead to the development of a feeling of one's worth. University education cannot be limited to the confines of classrooms, but includes associations with others and practical experiences. "A man who has never worked, who has never tried to earn his living, who has never approached the different age levels and the different social classes, will have great difficulty being worthy of a position of leadership."[40]

Conclusion

Montessori never developed her approach to secondary and higher education, or even to elementary education, to the extent that she did her approach to preschool education. However, she did develop in considerable detail a curriculum for grammar, reading, and arithmetic.[41] Advances since Montessori's time have included the development of curriculum in many subject areas for the elementary school.

Essentially, Montessori reiterated the application of the basic principles which she implemented at the preschool level. These include the importance of recognizing that there is a natural developmental process in human beings that continues beyond childhood and that education must be aware of and adapt to this process. This process involves "sensitive periods," and for learning to progress optimally and with the least pain and strain, education must be geared to these periods. Since learning depends upon the natural development of the child, then the child should be allowed the greatest liberty or freedom within the limits of the freedom of others who are in association with her or him. The appropriate materials and resources must, of course, be made available to the child in a "prepared environment." Respect for children, trust in their ability to grow and develop through use of and interaction with their environment, and patience in allowing them to progress at their own time and rate, are fundamental to the Montessori method.

The materials in a Montessori environment are not teaching devices whose purpose is to teach specific intellectual skills and concepts. Nor do they constitute, as some observers perceive them, a canned program through which children are led. They are rather developmental materials which aid children in the development, or construction, of themselves.

THE TEACHER IN THE MONTESSORI SCHOOL

The Montessori teacher is called a directress. As noted earlier (p. 38), the teacher directs the spontaneous activities of the child along constructive lines. *Guiding* might be a better term than *directing*. For the teacher is not the center of the class or of the children's activities. The children are not all engaged in the same activity at the same time. Each child is free to choose an activity and the materials with which to work, within the limits of his or her level of experience or achievement. The teacher must be a close observer of each child, ready to step in with help when the child asks for it or gives evidence of needing it, to guide the child to the next level of activity with given materials or to new materials when the child appears to be ready, and to lead the child to new activities when he or she gives evidence of not being able to continue with the current activity. If the child, when guided to the next step or level, does not become involved in it, however, the teacher does not press it on him or her, and moves to something else to avoid allowing the child to feel like a failure.

In short, the teacher facilitates children's interactions with and use of the prepared environment at the level for which they are capable of utilizing it with some anticipation of success. Montessori speaks of the teacher as an experimenter working with each child individually on the basis of observation. Individual contacts, or "lessons," are brief, simple, and objective, in the sense that the teacher puts the child in contact with the materials or objects from which to learn.

This objectivity does not mean, however, that the teacher is impersonal. As has been indicated earlier, the teacher has a personal interest in and concern for each child. The preparation of teachers involves more than intellectual study; it must prepare them to respect and understand the child. The teacher must be able to empathize with children, understand them, and be able to predict what they will or are ready to do.

While the children spend much of their time in individual activities, there are also times when the teacher works with groups of children. This is more common with elementary-school children than with preschool children. While preserving order, the teacher does not interfere with the interactions of individual children unless it is necessary to protect the rights of a child who is unable to do so itself. The development of order and structure, as well as the principles of respect for others and consideration in social relationships, are taught by the behavior of the teacher rather than didactically. The teacher is thus a model. The concept of modeling is involved also in instruction with the materials; the teacher shows the child how to use them rather than simply telling how. Education is not obtained by listening to words, but by activity on the environment.

The teacher's activities must contribute to the goals of Montessori education: the development of a sense of self, of competence, independence, self-confidence, responsibility. "Education should no longer be mostly imparting of knowledge, but must take a new path, seeking the release of human potentialities."[42] "To stimulate life—leaving it then free to develop, to unfold—herein lies the first task of the educator."[43]

Montessori teachers have special training, usually following the attainment of a bachelor's degree. Montessori designed an international training course which was six months in length and included 50 hours of observation in a Montessori school. It later became a one-year course for college graduates, combining didactic teaching with practice or an internship. Some courses in European teacher-training institutions are three years in length, at the undergraduate level. The American Montessori Society teaching certificate requires a nine-month, half-day internship under the supervision of a certified teacher, in addition to academic courses. If courses and internship are taken together, the total program can be completed in one year. Most of the courses of the American Montessori Society have an academic phase of six or seven weeks in the summer, with an internship during the school year. The courses conducted in this country by the Association Montessori Internationale have an academic phase of one or two school years combined with observation in Montessori classes, supervised practice with materials, and practice teaching.

The length and specific nature of the training vary among the different training institutions and centers, some of which are affiliated with colleges or universities. Xavier University in Cincinnati, Ohio, was the first university to offer a master of education degree with specialization in Montessori education. Here, the internship may be taken concurrently, or arranged for through the American Montessori Society after completion of the degree. Not all the instruction has been by persons trained in the Montessori method.

MONTESSORI IN AMERICA TODAY

The renaissance of Montessori in this country can be dated from the establishment of the Whitby School in Greenwich, Connecticut, in 1958, although this was not the first school in America. The directress of the school (and one of the founders) was Nancy McCormick Rambusch, who received her Montessori training in London in 1953. In the same year she published an article entitled "Learning Made Easy," in *Jubilee*. There had, of course, been a continuous stream—sometimes thin—of publications about Montessori and her approach in American journals. But for years no one attempted to implement the method. In 1959, E. M. Standing's book *Maria Montessori: Her Life and Work* (Fresno, California: The Academy Guild Press. Now available in paperback, New American Library of World Literature) was published in America. In 1962 Mrs. Rambusch published her book entitled *Learning How to Learn* (Baltimore: Helicon Press). Included in the book is a bibliography of publications by and about Montessori in the English language from 1909 to 1961, compiled by Gilbert E. Donahue. In the same year, E. M. Standing's book entitled *The Montessori Method: A Revolution in Education* (Fresno, California: The Academy Guild Press) was also published. The American Montessori Society was founded in 1960.

In the past 20 years the number of Montessori schools has grown to an estimated 2500, and numerous training centers or schools for teachers have been established. Montessori's books have been reprinted and other books on the Montessori approach have been published, including *Montessori Today* by R. C. Orem (New York: G. P. Putnam's Sons, 1971); *A Montessori Guide* by Paula P. Lillard (New York: American Montessori Society, 1970); and *Montessori—A Modern Approach*, also by Lillard (New York: Schocken, 1972).

The revival of Montessori coincided with the post-Sputnik concern about the quality of the American system of teaching academic subjects, especially science and mathematics. Some feel that the resultant emphasis upon cognitive learning was one of the reasons for the interest in Montessori, particularly among middle-class parents, who were ready to support a preschool program which seemed to be cognitively oriented. In this connection it is important to note that almost all Montessori schools are private schools and depend upon financial support from paying parents. (There *are* a number of Montessori classes in elementary schools, as well as Montessori Headstart classes.)

Another factor was perhaps the changes in psychology, which brought psychological theories in harmony with many of the ideas of Montessori. (See the next section for a consideration of these changes.) Whereas Montessori had earlier appeared to be in disagreement with what was accepted in psychology, her ideas were now consonant with the new ideas and theories. Among these were changes in concepts of child rearing, with a rejection of extreme permissiveness and concern for discipline and limits to aggressive, antisocial behavior. (It should be noted that extreme permissiveness, though attributed to Dewey and progressive education, was a misreading or misunderstanding of Dewey.) Montessori schools thus appeal to parents who value seriousness, order, freedom combined with discipline, and a learning curriculum rather than the emphasis on free play and socialization of the traditional American nursery school and kindergarten.

Montessori in America is not a homogeneous movement, free from internal disagreements. Schools range from those which follow Montessori closely, on the one hand, to those which would hardly be recognized as deriving from Montessori. The majority are probably in the middle. It is unlike America to accept anything from outside without alteration. It is argued that the American setting requires adaptation, and that Montessori could not have developed a method appropriate for all times and places. The adaptations went so far, however, that in 1963 the Association Montessori Internationale (AMI) removed its seal of approval from the American Montessori Society. The AMI was founded in 1929, with Maria Montessori as its president until her death in 1952, when she was succeeded by her adopted son Mario.

There are still teacher-training institutions in America which are approved by AMI, however.

It is difficult to determine just how closely American Montessori schools follow the Montessori method. There is no systematic textbook or manual. The publications of Standing, Rambusch, and Lillard referred to above are brief, descriptive, and not particularly systematic, and are popular summaries of Montessori aimed at the general public. The title of Rambusch's book (*Learning How to Learn*) is in contradiction to the basic principle of Montessori that learning is the natural activity of the child. It was probably selected for its popular appeal, whether with or without recognition of the contradiction. Rambusch emphasized the necessity of adapting Montessori to America: The subtitle of her book is *An American Approach to Montessori*. Some of her statements, such as the following, precipitated the break between the American Montessori Society and the Association Montessori Internationale: "There is good reason to believe that the American Montessori Movement will be destroyed as intellectually and pedagogically substantive if it is representative of the fossilized outlook of those Europeans whose fidelity to Dr. Montessori's memory is as unquestioned as is their innocence of the complexity of American culture."[44]

In her book, however, Rambusch hews very closely to the basic ideas and principles of Montessori, casting them in a form related to the American sociocultural environment. It is difficult to understand the vehemence of the preceding quotation, unless she was attempting to appeal to those Americans (including parents and educators) who might reject what would be perceived as a 50-year-old European import. It can also probably be understood in relation to the conflict and struggle for power within the movement.

It appears that Rambusch no longer subscribes to what was presented in her book. But no revision or new presentation has appeared. That the American adaptation of Montessori has continued to remain close to the basic ideas and principles is indicated by Orem's book referred to earlier. Orem gathered material for his book through a survey (by questionnaires, structured telephone interviews, and personal visits) of a majority of the then 700 Montessori schools in America, as well as a number of schools which utilized Montessori techniques along with other methods. In addition to the information obtained from his survey, he utilized data gathered from conferences, brochures, newsletters, and articles from schools, study groups and teacher-training programs.

While Orem notes that the original Montessori materials are being supplemented by contemporary technological innovations in education, the consistency of the programs with Montessori is made apparent by the repetitiousness that occurs in the reporting of the data, which includes numerous quotations from the survey data. The book is rather monotonous to read because of this repetitiousness of both Montessori's original words and paraphrases.

The major difference in the American Montessori schools as compared to the original schools described by Montessori, aside from the differences in customs and appearance of the surroundings attributable to the passage of 50 years, is that the American schools, while containing many—if not most—of the didactic materials, also include other materials and equipment. Often these have been developed along the ideas of the Montessori method; sometimes, however, they are of the kind found in the nursery school, included as an accommodation or concession, or to avoid the charge that the Montessori school is rigid and narrow in its method and approach.

The books by Standing, Rambusch, Lillard, and Orem are no substitute for Montessori's writings. Montessori has been criticized for her writing style, which has been called flowery, impassioned, zealous, and inspirational. It is, of course, influenced by its era, and also by the strong personality of Montessori. She did perhaps take literary liberty at times, as when she wrote that the children carried large tureens of hot soup without ever spilling a single drop. But the detailed descriptions of the method as developed and elaborated by its originator should be read by any serious student of Montessori.

EVALUATION AND DISCUSSION

It will be recalled that Montessori was widely acclaimed in America in the early part of the second decade of this century. The enthusiasm waned sharply, however, and Montessori was unrecognized and virtually unknown for close to 50 years. The demise of the movement occurred in part because it failed to find acceptance and support from the major schools of psychology (functionalism and behaviorism) and in part because it coincided with the rise of psychoanalysis in America.[45] Perhaps of even greater importance was the publication in 1914 of a critique by William Heard Kilpatrick, then an assistant professor of the philosophy of education at Teachers College, Columbia University.[46] Although an assistant professor, he was not a young neophyte, but was 44 years of age, had taught mathematics for many years before entering into graduate work at Columbia, and was a popular and influential lecturer and teacher.

The Kilpatrick Critique

Kilpatrick's critique was based on a visit to Rome in 1912 (with a committee of Columbia faculty), the details of which are not known (though it appears there were translation or interpreter problems), and on Montessori's book, *The Montessori Method*. His influence began to be felt before his book was published, since he was presenting his criticisms in his lectures at Columbia even before Montessori's visit to America. Kilpatrick's rejection was particularly important in light of the development of the progressive education movement at this time. One might expect that, since Montessori's ideas were similar in many respects to those of progressive education, Montessori might have continued to enjoy recognition and influence. But Kilpatrick's criticism, in which he placed Montessori in disagreement with John Dewey in some respects, denied her acceptance by those identified with the progressive education movement. Although she was in other respects in agreement with Dewey, and although Dewey appears to have accepted her (he introduced her Carnegie Hall lecture and allowed a book about her method to be dedicated to him), it is probable that the native, homegrown progressive education movement felt no need for outside support, nor was it ready to accept ideas from an outsider.

While Kilpatrick lauded Montessori's scientific attitude, he lamented her lack of knowledge of science, particularly of psychology. His specific criticisms of her method focused upon seven areas, and are summarized below:

1. *Education as Development.* The doctrine that education should be considered as a development from within was not new, said Kilpatrick—it was espoused by Rousseau, Pestalozzi, and Froebel. While it has some value, it is incomplete and presents a danger. It is incomplete in that while education is the most complete development of the individual possible, this involves mastering the complexity of civilization as well as "the living out of the impulsive life. More exactly, the two elements of mastering the environment and expressing one's self are but outer and inner aspects of one and the same process." Montessori, Kilpatrick said, took the position "that in the child's nature as given at birth there is contained—in some unique sense—all the child is to become."[47] The danger in this doctrine is that it leads to the rejection of society as bad, as in Rousseau, and the rejection of "the most useful of modern conceptions, that of intelligent, self-directing adaptation to a novel environment. . . . Still further, this erroneous notion of education gives to the doctrine of child liberty a wrong and misleading foundation. If the child already uniquely contains that which he is properly destined to manifest, then the duty of the educator is to allow the fullest expression of what is implicitly given. But such a doctrine of liberty is notoriously disastrous."[48] It leads many observers to the rejection of all liberty. Montessori, Kilpatrick said, did not reach these conclusions from her doctrine because she did not think logically enough.

2. *The Doctrine of Liberty.* Kilpatrick contrasted the centralization of control in the teacher in the American kindergarten with the freedom of the child in the Montessori classroom to engage in whatever activity he wanted to for as long as he wanted to, and approved of the

freedom in the Montessori classroom. He recognized that Montessori imposed limits on the freedom of the children. He agreed that freedom is necessary for genuine self-expression in the child. But he criticized Montessori because she did not create the socially conditioned environment which would lead to the development of group cooperation among the children; such social cooperation as there was, he said, was imposed from outside by the teacher.

Kilpatrick agreed that the freedom allowed by Montessori did not penalize the child in terms of his learning the things he should know on entrance to the primary school. The natural interests of the child could be depended on to lead to such learning. Here Montessori was in agreement with John Dewey, who was Kilpatrick's model.

Free expression could also be allowed without fear of the expression of undesirable behaviors, if the desirable behaviors were encouraged so that the undesirable impulses would have little opportunity for expression. There would be little need for punishment then. The child would also respond to the social approval and disapproval of his fellows. All this would occur in Montessori's system. This, Kilpatrick conceded, was a valuable, practical contribution of Montessori, but it was not a theoretical contribution.

3. *Adequacy of Self-Expression.* "Freedom without self-expression," Kilpatrick said, "is a contradiction in terms. But," he continued, "the didactic materials of Montessori were not varied enough to provide for self-expression. Without discussing here the grounds for this restriction, it suffices to say that this apparatus by its very theory presents a limited series of exactly distinct and very precise activities, formal in character and very remote from social interests and connections."[49] While the materials are interesting and the child enjoys the exercises with them, they provide, in Kilpatrick's phrase, a meager diet, especially since the children could not *play* with them, and there were no other play materials for the children. In contrast, the then-current American practice in kindergarten, of which Kilpatrick approved, made play, particularly social play, the major activity of the child. The activities of practical life in the Montessori school, Kilpatrick conceded, partially offset the deficiencies in the rest of the program. Nevertheless, he concluded that the Montessori curriculum was inadequate.

4. *Autoeducation.* Kilpatrick sympathized (his word) with the effort to have the child learn from experience, as with self-corrective exercises with the Montessori materials, but he contended that achieving this by limiting the child to a "relatively mechanical manipulation of very formal apparatus" was a severe limitation of the child's freedom or liberty. It was also a restriction in learning, since one could not depend upon the child to extend this learning beyond the specific materials. The principle of autoeducation would be effective if the school provided experiences close to the conditions of normal life.

5. *Exercises of Practical Life.* Kilpatrick noted that the attention of Montessori to the practical aspects of self-care and living, and the long school day, while the result of and particularly appropriate to

the children in the tenements of Rome, offer suggestions for American schools to meet the demand that the school function as a social institution related to its environment and the requirements of living. But he questioned the contention that the skills of the children in handling luncheon activities were related to the muscular control developed from the use of the didactic materials. Rather, he felt, they were the result of direct practice. Moreover, he questioned Montessori's claims of the perfection of the children—for example, that they never spilled a drop of soup—relating that he saw soup spilled and dishes dropped and broken during his visit.

6. *Sense Training by Means of the Didactic Apparatus.* Kilpatrick's most devastating criticism revolved about the use of the didactic materials in sense training. Here he placed Montessori among those who held the doctrine of formal discipline: that the training of the senses is possible and that the training transfers to objects and areas not specifically included in the training. This view, known as faculty psychology, had been rejected, Kilpatrick pointed out. Sense discrimination learned from the Montessori materials would not lead to the ability to discriminate in everyday life, since there is no sense, or faculty, of discrimination. Discrimination must be learned in the specific circumstances; and such learning as is necessary occurs in the course of normal experience. Kilpatrick admitted that experience with color, form, or weight helps to develop these concepts. Yet later he rejected Montessori's statement that the child can be led from sensations to ideas, on the basis that this is not in agreement with Dewey's insistence that the total experience is the unit from which the parts are learned by differentiation. He contended that opportunity for sense experience is desirable in education, but that it does not require and should not be limited to the Montessori materials and should not be depended on to lead to general transfer.

7. *Reading, Writing, and Arithmetic.* Kilpatrick dismissed Montessori's success in teaching reading at an early age as being possible because of the phonetic nature of the Italian language. It would not be, and had not been, successful in America. The appraisal of Montessori's contribution to writing, Kilpatrick wrote, was difficult, though he grudgingly admitted that there was one. But he qualified this admission by stating that the value in the case of the English language was uncertain. Montessori's contribution to arithmetic was dismissed with reference of the "Long Stair" as the only new element. Regarding the introduction of the three R's before the age of 6, Kilpatrick said that the question was open. He felt, however, that it was better to postpone book learning, and thus reading and writing, to a later period, when it would not divert time and attention from more relevant learnings.

Kilpatrick evaluated Montessori against Dewey. That in her approach which agreed with Dewey was acceptable, that which did not was not. More generally, what was acceptable was not new or original with Montessori; what was new or original was not acceptable, because it was not in agreement with the then-current educational theory, according to Kilpatrick. Dewey not only included all that was valid in the Montessori method, but also provided the criteria for correcting her errors and for going much farther in educational methods. Because Montessori based her work on Séguin (whose ideas were first published in 1846, he noted) and on other old but rejected doctrines, he wrote that "we feel impelled to say that in the content of her doctrine, she belongs essentially to the mid-nineteenth century, some fifty years behind the present development of educational theory."[50]

Kilpatrick's critique is an interesting document. He says many positive things about Montessori, but then he qualifies them, using a "yes-but" approach. He gives the appearance of impartiality, yet many of his statements are far from impartial. He appears to have misread or misunderstood Montessori, but this may be the result of the bias inherent in his period in time. The net result is a strong condemnation and rejection of the idea that Montessori contributed anything new or original. That the impact of his rejection of Montessori could be devastating appears clear.

Kilpatrick's criticisms require some comment, because they appear to be accepted by some people today; apparently, in some instances, because of lack of knowledge or understanding of Montessori. Brief comments on each of Kilpatrick's categories are thus provided here.

1. Kilpatrick gives the impression that Montessori accepted the position that development is simply the predetermined unfolding of what is present in the child, with no direction or assistance from outside. This is not the case, of course. Montessori attempted to provide an environment which would assist and facilitate the development of the child when the child was ready to utilize what was offered.

2. In his criticism that Montessori neglected the social development of the child because she did not directly teach social behaviors, Kilpatrick was not only inconsistent with his approval of liberty and freedom of the child, but failed to recognize that the child learned social behaviors in the Montessori classroom through experience in associating with other children. Socialization in the Montessori school was developed in the child through natural interaction with other children, rather than in the forced and organized manner of American schools, which imposed group activities upon the child. It is relevant here to note that social isolation was the only punishment Montessori imposed on her children. This is interesting in relation to the "time-out" practice of the behaviorists. Montessori's procedure was superior to that of the behaviorists, since the isolated child was able to observe the acceptable behavior of the other children and use them as models. There is some evidence that children in Montessori classes are better socializers than those in other preschool classes.

3. Contrary to Kilpatrick's contention that the child in Montessori's school almost never engaged in play, a reading of Montessori's writings indicates that there was considerable play involved. It is true that the child was not permitted to use the materials for purposes other than those for which they were intended. This would seem to be a reasonable restriction based on educational principles. That this restriction inhibited creative and imaginative activities was suggested, but not proven, by Kilpatrick. The emphasis on play by Kilpatrick (and in the American kindergarten) was not supported by evidence as to its desirability, or by evidence that children could not engage in serious learning. In fact, Montessori showed that children could learn and enjoy doing it, that is, that work (as defined by adults) was play, or pleasure for the child. In other words, the work of the child is learning, and learning can be enjoyable.

4. In his discussion of autoeducation, Kilpatrick overestimated or overemphasized the dependence of Montessori upon the didactic materials, giving an erroneous impression of the narrowness of the curriculum.

5. Kilpatrick's criticism that the children were not perfect in their practical activities is, of course, only a quibble with the literary liberty in Montessori's writing. It is also quite possible that the children were disturbed by the presence and observation of a committee. Wanton breakage of materials in Montessori classes is almost nonexistent, and accidental breakage rare.

6. The criticism of the emphasis upon sense training represents a lack of concern with such training that still exists in American education. Montessori recognized a stage of development in the child which had not previously been adequately recognized, and proceeded to provide the child with assistance in the development of sensory learning. Hunt notes that "perhaps Montessori's pedagogical emphasis on 'sensory learning,' based as it was on careful clinical observation of the learning of mentally retarded children was closer to reality than the theories of those who held such emphasis in contempt."[51]

7. Finally, Kilpatrick's evaluation of Montessori's methods of teaching reading and writing to preschool children and the desirability of doing so, represents an opinion, one which is still held but which has not been supported by adequate evidence or research. The method continues to be effective when used by trained Montessori teachers.

Kilpatrick's conclusion was that while Montessori might have made some practical contributions to education, she had made no contribution to educational theory. In the 1960s, the Association for Supervision and Curriculum Development of the National Education Association appointed a Commission on Instructional Theory. This commission developed a set of criteria for evaluating such theories. These criteria included the following (see pp. 13–15 for further detail):

1. A theory of instruction should state the characteristics of pupils that are implied in the teaching procedures. These characteristics must be well defined, relevant to the instructional procedures, and demonstrated to be related to learning.
2. The instructional procedures must be specified, together with the relationship they have to goals.
3. Tasks involved in the instructional procedures should have identifiable characteristics specified in terms of task variables.
4. An instructional theory should include the identification of variables that are involved in moving from one point to another in the instructional process (or from level to level, phase to phase, stage to stage).[52]

In a discussion following a paper given at a conference on guided learning, I. J. Gordon, a member of the commission, commented as follows: "We (the Commission) have also checked the Montessori method of education against our criteria, and although we approached the method with hostility, we were quite amazed. If you want what is probably the most complete theoretical statement about instruction—although it may not be correct—I refer you to Maria Montessori's writing."[53]

Hunt's Evaluation

J. McV. Hunt, a psychologist at the University of Illinois, became interested in Montessori because of his concern about early childhood education, particularly the preschool education of the culturally disadvantaged. In his introduction to the Schocken edition of *The Montessori Method* he discusses the early rise and fall of Montessori in America. In addition to her being hurt by the Kilpatrick criticisms, Hunt feels that Montessori suffered because her conceptions were at variance with those of American psychology at the time. Some of these conceptions were the following:

1. The idea that school experience for young children could be important for later development was unacceptable. Early experiences were not considered important because they could seldom be recalled. Preschool education was not looked on with favor because it would increase school taxes, and to some it was an intrusion on the responsibility of the family. Nonetheless, though Hunt does not note this, the kindergarten movement had begun in America by this time; it was, however, concerned with the social, not the cognitive, development of the child.
2. The belief in fixed intelligence as one of the characteristics of the individual determined by heredity (the concept of "the constant IQ") was inconsistent with Montessori's conception of mental retardation as a defect which could be remedied by pedagogical treatment.

3. The belief in predetermined development, that "ontogeny recapitulates phylogeny," was the focus of G. Stanley Hall's developmental psychology. Studies showing the evanescence of the effects of practice were appearing at this time. The futility of efforts to teach young children reading, writing, and arithmetic was accepted.

4. The belief in the motivation of behavior by instincts, by painful stimuli, or my homeostatic needs, and the belief in behavior as an attempt to reduce or eliminate such internal and external stimuli, so that in the absence of such stimuli the organism—or the child—is not active, was inconsistent with the claim of Montessori that children have a spontaneous interest in learning, and that the organism is actively curious, exploring and manipulating without specific stimuli.

5. The interest in stimulus-response psychology (the work of E. L. Thorndike and J. B. Watson), and particularly the interest in responses as evidence of learning, overshadowed concern with perception and central process in the brain. Thus, Montessori's emphasis on sensory training was dismissed.

6. The traditional concern of the teacher for control and an orderly classroom clashed with the freedom and focus on the individual of the Montessori classroom.

Hunt points out that all of these beliefs or conceptions are no longer supported. The importance of early experience has been clearly demonstrated. The belief in fixed intelligence has been seriously challenged; Hunt summarizes some of the evidence. The belief in predetermined development is no longer tenable. Practice is effective when it occurs at the age when a given ability is ready to be developed. Thus, there is evidence (Hunt does not state it this way) for "sensitive periods" in development: "During the earlier phases, the longer a developing organism is deprived of a given sort of experience, or, to put it another way, the longer an organism is deprived of a given kind of informational interaction with the environment, the more likely is the effect of that deprivation to become permanent."[54]

The belief that the organism is quiescent unless motivated by painful stimuli, homeostatic imbalance, sex or other drives, has not been supported. The facts seem to justify the idea that children have a spontaneous interest in learning. Finally, "the belief that it is the motor response that is all-important in learning is less tenable than it was half a century ago. Although this issue is still far from settled, recent evidence appears to indicate that the role of the eyes and the ears, and perhaps the tactile organs, may be more important in the organism's on-going informational interaction with the environment than are the motor outlets."[55] Thus, as noted earlier (p. 55), Hunt suggests that Montessori's emphasis on sense training is justified. It appears that rather than being 50 years behind the times, Montessori may have been 50 years ahead of her time.

Hunt felt that Montessori's approach offered "a promising ante-dote" to cultural deprivation. His recommendation that her approach be used in compensatory education (made in 1962) was not acted upon, however.[56] He does offer some words of caution: Montessori's theory is not adequate: There is danger of a cult focusing on the didactic materials as sufficient for all children, and on prescribed ways and se-quences of using them; and there might be danger of underemphasis on the social, affective, and aesthetic aspects of life.

Research Support

Many of the basic ideas and concepts of Montessori are supported by a wide variety of research studies. Hunt refers to many of these.[57] Elkind refers to some of the research support for the conceptions held in common by Montessori and Piaget.[58]

Research evidence for the effectiveness of the method or practice is sparse. There have been a few studies, however. Banta reports a com-parison of four groups of children in preschool programs. The Mon-tessori group demonstrated higher achievement in learning skills and evidenced ability to engage in sustained activity without supervision for longer periods of time. A nongraded group ranked second.[59]

In a study supported by the U.S. Office of Education, Montessori children showed more initiative, self-confidence, self-control, persis-tence, independence, acuity in sensory perception, concentration, pur-posefulness of activity, and positive attitudes toward learning as compared with another group of children with equal preschool ex-perience. The Montessori children were higher in verbal ability and social interaction. They were rated by their public school teachers as equal to or superior to the control group in their classroom behavior and performance. The results must be considered tentative because of difficulties in controlling for ability and in measuring relevant vari-ables.[60]

Certainly more and better studies of the effects of the Montessori approach are needed. With the large number of Montessori schools now in existence such research is possible and can be anticipated.

Discussion

It appears that Montessori was beyond her times in her understanding of children and in providing an educational environment to promote their development. The use of observation of children as the basis for her approach was a departure from the usual armchair reasoning about the nature of children and their needs. Montessori clearly was a gifted observer; although she writes about her method as scientific and ex-perimental, it was not the kind of controlled experimental research which is now engaged in. Yet she anticipated many of the results of later research.

She also anticipated practices which have developed since then, apparently independently. One of these, not commented on earlier, is the placing together of children of differing ages, now referred to as the ungraded classroom. A classroom of children with a range in ages of 2, 3, or 4 years makes it possible for younger children to learn from the older ones, and for the older children to supplement the teacher by helping the younger ones. It also provides a group in which a child whose intellectual, social, and emotional developmental levels are not equivalent can find children of differing chronological ages who have a similar intellectual, social, or emotional level.

The demonstration by Montessori that preschool children can engage in serious learning, intellectual or academic as well as practical, is a contribution which is even now not adequately recognized or accepted. Some, like Kilpatrick, while conceding that it is possible, question its desirability as a preschool activity. Childhood, they believe, should be reserved for play; serious learning is work, and therefore unpleasant. But Montessori showed that learning is not necessarily unpleasant. Her concept of sensitive periods (similar in some respects to the current concept of readiness) is relevant here also. Learning is pleasant when the child is ready for it; later it may be unpleasant, if the optimum time has passed. Here also, Montessori is relevant for the intrinsic-extrinsic motivation problem. When the child is ready to learn, the learning is pleasant and interesting, and the child persists in learning because it is intrinsically satisfying. The activity is rewarding in itself; extrinsic rewards—prizes, M&M's, or other reinforcements—are not necessary. As illustrated by anecdotes reported by Montessori, they may be ignored or considered insulting. Montessori opens the way to the solution of the problem of motivation which plagues education today.

The method also has relevance for the problem of boredom and lack of interest in school, which leads to "behavior problems." Presenting, and encouraging the use of materials that are interesting and challenging minimizes the development of boredom in the classroom.

Introducing serious learning in the preschool period provides a better preparation for school than limiting preschool experience to play. The latter fails to prepare the child for the reality of school and is the basis for the difficulty in adapting to the school experienced by many children.

Montessori anticipated Piaget in many of her ideas and beliefs. Elkind, referring to both as "giants of early childhood education," discusses "three original ideas about child thought and behavior which Piaget and Montessori arrived at independently but share in common."[61] (It may be noted that Piaget was aware of and interested in Montessori's work, attended international congresses of the Association Montessori Internationale, and served as president of the Swiss Montessori Society.) These three ideas are as follows:

1. *Nature and Nurture.* Montessori and Piaget take a similar view on the relation between nature and nurture. Mental development is an extension of physical growth, following a pattern which is determined by the genes. The environment provides, to a greater or lesser degree, the nourishment for mental development, and thus influences mental growth. The environment also determines the mental content —the particular language, concepts, percepts, and values which the child acquires.

2. *Capacity and Learning.* Whereas the experimental psychologist often views the capacity of the child for learning as no different from that of the adult, Piaget and Montessori take the view that the child's needs and capacities are different from those of the adult. Rather than learning determining capacity, learning is determined by capacity or development. Thus, contrary to some interpretations of Piaget and Montessori, growth cannot be indefinitely accelerated. The environment affects and can facilitate growth, but there is a limit imposed by the nature of the organism and its developmental level.

3. *Cognitive Needs and Repetitive Behavior.* While the popular view in psychology and education is that repetitive behavior ("rote learning" and "perseveration") is bad, Montessori and Piaget recognize the important role that repetitive behavior plays in mental growth. Such repetitive behavior is obvious and accepted as important in physical growth. Emerging mental abilities must also be practiced to become perfect.

There are other similarities which have been noted, some of which are corollaries of the nature-nurture and capacity-learning relationships. Both Montessori and Piaget recognize similar developmental stages or levels in the mental growth of the child. These stages or levels are related to "sensitive periods" (Montessori) or "optimal times" (Piaget) for particular aspects of mental development.

Related to the developmental stages or levels is the matter of social development and its relation to educational programs. Here Montessori and Piaget are in agreement. Piaget has noted the egocentrism of young children, which is related to their individual activities rather than group activities. Montessori observed this and adapted her methods to it, with no effort to socialize the child by forcing it into group activities. The sensitive period for socialization begins at about age seven. Piaget writes, "There is . . . no real social life among children of less than seven or eight."[62]

Piaget is also in agreement with Montessori's attention to sensorimotor activities in the education of the young child. Learning, according to Piaget, begins with, and is facilitated by, contact with materials. Thinking proceeds from the concrete to the abstract, from experience with things (perceptual and judgmental experience as well as motor) to concepts. He wrote: "Sensori-motor intelligence lies at the source of thought, and continues to affect it throughout life through perceptions and practical sets."[63]

Piaget has, however, criticized the Montessori materials and their use as being limited and restricted. Others have also contended that the restriction of their use discourages creativity. However, the materials were constructed for specific educational or developmental purposes. They focus the child's attention on one attribute (or a set of attributes) of the objects at a time, not only for a particular educational purpose, but to foster concentration and to avoid confusion. The materials are also used for different purposes over time as the child develops. Their self-correcting nature provides immediate relevant feedback, which facilitates the learning for which they are designed. They are not designed to foster creativity, which, however, is encouraged by other aspects of the Montessori school.

SUMMARY

Seventy-five years ago, Maria Montessori developed a method of education which was clearly beyond her time. Starting with no a priori ideas or theory, she observed the children in her classes and developed methods and materials which seemed to be suited to their developmental level and needs and thus to be intrinsically interesting. The materials emphasized sensorimotor activities, as did other activities of practical life which were included in her programs.

Following activities using the materials, which included large cutout letters, she found that children 4 to 5 years of age began to form words and to proceed to writing and reading without direct or specific instruction in reading and writing.

While Montessori's work was concentrated on preschool children, she became interested in elementary, secondary, and higher education and proposed changes in educational methods at these levels.

In her emphasis on freedom within limits, the provision of a prepared environment related to the developmental level of the child, her concern for the individual child's own rate of growth, and the grouping of children of differing ages, Montessori anticipated current developments in education.

Montessori was concerned with the whole child, his physical, social, emotional, and cognitive development. The attitudes of the teacher toward the child, and the relationship between the teacher and the child were recognized as important. Montessori knew and understood children. Elkind states that when one reads Montessori (and Piaget), "one often has the uncanny feeling that they are somehow able to get inside the child and know exactly what he is thinking and feeling and why he is doing what he is doing at any given moment. It is this genius for empathy with the child which, or so it seems to me, gives their observations and insights—even without the buttressing of systematic research—the solid ring of truth."[64] Montessori was an early representative of a humanistic approach to education.

\ Although her practice developed from observation and experience, rather than being derived from theory, the Montessori approach has a theoretical base. Montessori never developed her theory in a highly systematic fashion, but her observations led to the development of ideas and concepts which are of theoretical relevance. It is because her work was based upon sound observations that it has passed the test of time and is so relevant today.

REFERENCES

1. See E. Séguin, *Traitement moral, hygiène et éducation des idiots* (Paris: Bibliothèque d'éducation spéciale, 1960; originally published in 1846); E. Séguin, *Idiocy: and Its Treatment by the Physiological Method* (Albany: Columbia University Teachers College Educational Reprints, 1907; originally published in 1866).
2. J. M. G. Itard, *The Wild Boy of Aveyron,* trans. George and Murial Humphrey (New York: Appleton-Century-Crofts, 1932).
3. M. Montessori, *The Montessori Method,* trans. Anne E. George (New York: Schocken, 1964), p. 37. (First published in Italian in 1909, and in English in 1912).
4. Ibid., p. 38.
5. W. H. Kilpatrick, *The Montessori System Examined* (Boston: Houghton Mifflin, 1914).
6. For a biography of Maria Montessori, see E. M. Standing. *Maria Montessori: Her Life and Work* (Fresno, Calif.: Academy Guild Press, 1959).
7. Montessori, *The Formation of Man, trans,* A. M. Joosten (Madras, India: The Theosophical Publishing House, 1955), p. 79.
8. Ibid., p. 82.
9. Ibid., p. 126.
10. Ibid., p. 110.
11. Ibid., p. 30.
12. Ibid., p. 21.
13. Ibid., pp. 47–48.
14. Ibid., p. 19.
15. Ibid., p. 52.
16. Ibid., pp. 45–46.
17. Montessori, *The Montessori Method,* op. cit., p. 169.
18. Ibid., p. 171.
19. Ibid., p. 251.
20. Ibid., p. 228.
21. Ibid., p. 266.
22. Ibid., p. 300.
23. Ibid., p. 306.
24. Ibid., pp. 302–303.
25. Ibid., p. 302.
26. Ibid., p. 370.
27. Montessori, *The Discovery of the Child: Revised and Enlarged Edition of the Montessori Method,* trans. Mary A. Johnstone (Madras, India: Kalakshetra Publications, 1948), p. 33.

28. E. M. Standing, *The Montessori Method: A Revolution in Education* (Fresno, Calif.: The Academy Guild Press, 1962), p. 31.
29. Montessori, *The Formation of Man*, op. cit., p. 54.
30. Montessori, *Spontaneous Activity in Education* (New York: Frederich A. Stokes Co., 1917), p. 324.
31. Montessori, *From Childhood to Adolescence.* (New York: Schocken Books, 1973), p. 27. (First published in French in 1948.)
32. Ibid., p. 36.
33. Ibid., p. 76.
34. Montessori, *The Erdkinder: A Scheme for a Reform of Secondary Education,* published in Amsterdam in 1939. Included as Appendix A in *From Childhood to Adolescence,* ibid., pp. 95–109.
35. Ibid., pp. 106–107.
36. Montessori, *The Reform of Education During and After Adolescence,* published in Amsterdam in 1939. Included as Appendix B in *From Childhood to Adolescence,* ibid., pp. 113–126.
37. Ibid., p. 115.
38. Montessori, *The Function of the University,* published in Amsterdam in 1939. Included in *From Childhood to Adolescence,* ibid., pp. 129–140.
39. Ibid., p. 133.
40. Ibid., p. 138.
41. Montessori, *The Montessori Elementary Material,* translated, with additions and adaptations to English grammar, by Arthur Livingston (New York: Schocken, 1973). (First published in Italian in 1917.)
42. Montessori, *Education for a New World* (Wheaton, Ill.: Theosophical Press, 1963), p. 2.
43. Montessori, *The Montessori Method,* op. cit., p. 115.
44. Nancy McCormick Rambusch, *The American Montessori Bulletin,* 1963, 1 (1).
45. J. McV. Hunt, introduction to Montessori, *The Montessori Method,* op. cit., p. xiv.
46. W. H. Kilpatrick, *The Montessori System Examined* (New York: Arno Press, 1971). (Originally published in 1914 by Houghton Mifflin, Boston.)
47. Ibid., pp. 8–9.
48. Ibid., p. 10.
49. Ibid., p. 27.
50. Ibid., p. 63.
51. Hunt, intro. to *The Montessori Method,* op. cit., p. xxxi.
52. I. J. Gordon, "Guided Learning Experiences and New Curricula," in R. H. Ojemann and Karen Prickett, eds., *Giving Emphasis to Guided Learning* (Cleveland: Educational Research Council of Greater Cleveland, 1966), p. 73.
53. Ibid., p. 91.
54. Hunt, intro. to *The Montessori Method,* op. cit., pp. xxv–xxvi.
55. Ibid., p. xxix.
56. Hunt, referred to in D. N. Campbell, "A Critical Analysis of William Heard Kilpatrick's *The Montessori System Examined*" (Ph.D. diss., University of Illinois at Urbana-Champaign, 1970), p. 80.
57. Hunt, intro. to *The Montessori Method,* op. cit.
58. D. Elkind, "Piaget and Montessori," *Harvard Education Review* 37 (1967):535–545. [Also in D. Elkind, *Children and Adolescents: Interpretive Essays on Jean Piaget* (New York: Oxford, 1970), pp. 104–114].

59. T. J. Banta, "The Montessori Research Project," *The American Montessori Bulletin*, 1969, 7, (1).
60. O. Fleege, M. Black, and J. Rackaiskas, *Montessori Preschool Education* (Washington, D.C.: U.S. Department of Health, Education and Welfare, Office of Education, 1967).
61. Elkind, *Children and Adolescents*, op. cit.
62. J. Piaget, *The Language and Thought of the Child* (New York: Harcourt, Brace, Jovanovich, 1926), p. 57.
63. Piaget, *The Psychology of Intelligence* (Totawa, N.J.: Littlefield, Adams, 1963), p. 119. (First published in 1942.)
64. Elkind, *Children and Adolescents*, op. cit., pp. 104–105.

Piaget: the origins and development of intellect

3

CHAPTER

3

INTRODUCTION

Jean Piaget has spent over 50 years studying children—their thinking, language, reasoning, judgment, and their conceptions of time, space, numbers and morals. It has been estimated that he has written some 20,000 pages of material, or the equivalent of 40 500-page books. He is the author or coauthor of over 30 books. Yet it was not until the 1960s that he achieved recognition in America. In effect, however, Piaget was rediscovered since there was considerable interest in him in the late twenties and early thirties. But the increasing preoccupation of American psychology with quantitative and statistical analysis in its research—indeed the virtual equating of research with quantification and statistics—turned attention away from Piaget. His methods and approach have been observational and clinical rather than statistical; for many he is not "scientific.".In addition, his writing, apart from the description of his observations on individual children, is highly technical, involving original terminology and propositional and symbolic logic, and is thus very difficult to read, even for many highly educated people. Fortunately, there are now a number of books by American psychologists which present Piaget's ideas and work in a more readable form.

Piaget was born in Neuchâtel, Switzerland, on August 9, 1896. He was a serious and prococious child; he published a brief (one-page) paper at the age of 10, and several others between the ages of 15 and 18. His interest in nature led him to the study of biology. He received the bachelors degree in 1915 and the PhD in 1918, from the University of Neuchâtel, his research centering on mollusks. His interests had broadened during his university years, influenced by his introduction to Bergson, an idealist, and philosophy by his grandfather, and he studied philosophy, sociology, theology, and psychology.

After obtaining his PhD, Piaget went to Zurich, where in addition to spending time in psychological laboratories, he read Freud and worked in Bleuler's psychiatric clinic for a year. He then went to Paris, where he studied at the Sorbonne and worked with Théophile Simon in the Binet Laboratory (the Simon and Binet of the Binet-Simon intelligence test). He became involved in the standardization of Cyril Burt's English reasoning tests on Paris children, and published several articles on this research in 1921 and 1922. It was while he was involved in the testing of children that he became interested in the processes by which children arrived at answers to the test questions, particularly the wrong answers. Drawing upon his experience with psychiatric examining procedures, he developed the clinical method of studying children's thinking which he later used in his own research. In addition to his work in the Binet Laboratory, Piaget also studied abnormal and retarded children at the Salpetrière Hospital. Here he found it necessary to supplement the verbal question-and-answer method with the use of materials or objects to be manipulated, a method which he was to use later in his study of normal children.

In 1921, Edward Claparède, director of the Institut Jean Jacques Rousseau in Geneva and professor of psychology at Geneva University —who as editor of *Archives de Psychologie* had seen Piaget's research articles—offered Piaget the position of director of studies (or research) at the Institut. The Institut was engaged in the scientific study of children and the training of teachers. Piaget was given the freedom to pursue his own interests. He began to study the children in the Maison des Petits, the preschool operated by the Institut.

His work with children on the reasoning tests led him to pursue the study of the child's thought through observations of children's responses to questions and their own questions. His early writings during this period (1921–1925), published between 1924 and 1932, attracted considerable attention in Europe and the United States. This work, based upon children's language rather than their behavior, was, however, the source of much criticism of Piaget by American experimental psychologists, leading to the decline of interest in his work in America. Piaget had been somewhat surprised by the recognition he had received, since he considered this work only preliminary in nature, and recognized the validity of the criticism. He then moved from the direct study of the (verbalized) thought of children to the study of the children's behavior—their manipulation of and experience with objects. His work during this early period produced *The Language and Thought of the Child* (1923), *Judgment and Reasoning in the Child* (1924), *The Child's Conception of the World* (1926), *The Child's Conception of Physical Causality* (1927), and *The Moral Judgment of the Child* (1932). (Dates here and below are those of the original French editions.)

The next few years (1925–1929) were occupied by the study of the manipulative behavior of children, including his own children (Jacqueline, born in 1925; Lucienne, born in 1927; and Laurent, born in 1931). He recognized the related perceptual and conceptual elements involved in manipulative behavior. He went on in the next ten years to study the development of the child's concepts of objects, space, causality, and time. His publications from this period include *The Origins of Intelligence in Children* (1936), *The Construction of Reality in the Child* (1937), and *Play, Dreams and Imitation in Childhood* (not published until 1945).

During the years following this period (1940 to the present), Piaget engaged in research which provided the basis for his theory of cognitive development through adolescence. He was concerned about what leads to the child's and adolescent's ability to construct a world view which conforms to reality—or the world as seen by the adult—and their understanding of scientific concepts. Publications include *The Child's Conception of Number* (with A. Szeminska, 1941); *The Psychology of Intelligence* (1947); *Traité de Logique* (1949); and with Bärbel Inhelder, who has collaborated with him since the 1930s, *The Child's Conception of Space* (1948), *The Child's Conception of Geometry* (with A. Szeminska also, 1948), and *The Growth of Logical Thinking from Childhood to Adolescence* (1955), as well as other books, some of which have not yet been translated from the French.

In addition to his research and writing, Piaget has been involved in teaching and other professional activities. In 1923 he accepted a part-time appointment at the University of Neuchâtel. He taught courses in psychology, sociology, and scientific thought there and at Geneva University, where in 1929 he was appointed professor of the history of scientific thought. In 1929 he returned to full-time status at the J. J. Rousseau Institute, becoming assistant director, and in 1932, codirector, assisting in its reorganization and its affiliation with Geneva University in 1948 as the Institut des Sciences de l'Education. He served as director of the Psychology Laboratory at Geneva, and taught experimental psychology at Lausanne University, where he was professor of psychology and sociology from 1938 to 1951. In 1952 he was appointed professor at the Sorbonne.

He held the chairmanship or directorship of the International Bureau of Education, later to become part of UNESCO, and continued his work with the bureau in the 1940s, and was head of the Swiss delegation to UNESCO. He has been director of the International Center for Genetic Epistemology at Geneva University since its establishment in 1955–1956, with support from the Rockefeller Foundation. This culminated a dream of Piaget for an interdisciplinary attack on the study of cognition. Each year, scholars from several fields or disciplines gather to work together on a cognitive problem, culminating in a symposium which is published in a monograph.

Piaget has continued publishing at a high rate: *The Early Growth of Logic in the Child* (with Inhelder, 1959), *The Psychology of the Child* (a brief summary of his earlier work, with Inhelder, 1966), and books on mental imagery in the child (with Inhelder, 1967), biology and cognitive processes (1968), and memory and intelligence (with Inhelder, 1968). Translations of his books into English, as well as other languages, have increased, and the number of articles and books about Piaget has increased by leaps and bounds. Piaget has served on the editorial boards of a number of journals, and as coeditor of *Archives de Psychology,* which has published much of the work of his institute.

Piaget has received many honorary degrees: from Harvard in 1936, the Sorbonne in 1946, the University of Brussels in 1949, and the University of Rio de Janeiro in 1949, among others. The award of an honorary degree from the University of Chicago in 1953 was a precursor of the revival of interest in Piaget in America. His first visit to America was to the University of California, Berkeley, in 1964. In 1967 he gave the Heinz Werner memorial lectures at Clark University (where Freud first lectured in America, in 1909). During this visit to America he also lectured in Montreal, Minnesota, Michigan, and New York. In 1969 he addressed the annual meeting of the American Educational Research Association in Chicago. In the same year Piaget received a Distinguished Scientific Award from the American Psychological Association "for his revolutionary perspective on the nature of human knowledge and biological intelligence." He was the first European to receive this award. (From 1956, the first year of such awards, through 1969, 41 awards were made, including two others in that year.)

Piaget has now (1976) retired from the chair in experimental psychology at Geneva University and as director of the Institute des Sciences de l'Education, but still directs the Center for Genetic Epistemology.

The question arises as to why American psychology and education has become so interested in the work of Piaget. This interest developed at just about the time interest in Montessori began to manifest itself. The increasing concern about the academic quality of American education has been cited as one of the sources of interest in Montessori. Elkind relates the interest in Piaget to the same concern, referring to the criticisms of American education by Bestor, Woodring, and Hutchins in the early 1950s, and the public reaction to the launching of the first space vehicle by the Russians in 1957.[1] This crisis in education prompted a whole series of curriculum reforms and the development of new math and new science curriculums. Curriculum developers, according to Elkind, found little in psychology to help them understand how the child acquires mathematical and scientific concepts, since most psychologists interested in learning studied the process in animals, particularly rats, rather than in children. Piaget, whose book *The Child's Conception of Number* had been translated into English in 1952, became a source to which they increasingly turned.

Although Elkind may be correct in his assessment of the source of the renewed interest in Piaget, there was little written or published on the contribution of Piaget to education, at least for the teacher or general reader. Recently, however, a number of books have appeared which are concerned with the application of Piaget's work to education.[2] Piaget himself has been mainly interested in research and theory rather than application or practice. His study of children has been a means to the development of knowledge and theory. But Piaget has also been interested in children as persons, and as far back as 1935, he and his colleagues were writing on the application of theory to teaching. A 1935 paper, entitled "The New Methods: Their Psychological Foundations" has been reprinted in Piaget's *The Science of Education and The Psychology of the Child* (New York: Orion Press, 1970). Two other papers published in French in 1948 and in English in 1951, under the titles "The Right to Education in the Modern World" and "A Structured Foundation for Tomorrow's Education," have been reprinted in book form under the title *To Understand is to Invent* (New York: Grossman, 1973).

There are a number of relatively brief,[3] as well as lengthier,[4] summaries of Piaget's work. There have also been, as noted above, a number of publications relating Piaget's theory and research to education. It might be questioned why another summary and consideration of Piaget's relevance to education is needed. The plan and purpose of this book, of course, does require it. There is, moreover, no brief but comprehensive presentation of Piaget's theory and its relevance for education. Although such a presentation is exceedingly difficult and this presentation suffers from brevity, as well as the inadequacies accompanying such an attempt by a single writer who does not claim to be an expert on Piaget, it is felt that this summary serves the purpose of introducing students in education and educational psychology to the significant contributions of Piaget.

PHILOSOPHICAL FOUNDATIONS AND CONCEPTS

Philosophy

Piaget has had a strong and continuing interest in philosophy. His focus has been on epistemology, or the origin and nature of knowledge; and logic, or the knowing process. Epistemology deals with the problems of how we come to know the external world through the visual, auditory, and tactile senses. There are two theoretical views of how the infant perceives objects in space and in time. One is that there is an inborn predisposition to order things in space and time. The other is that it is through experience with objects in space and time that the infant learns that space and time provide the framework for ordering objects and experiences. Piaget accepted neither of these a priori theories. He set about studying the origin and process of knowing empirically, to determine how conceptions of space, time, logic, mathematics, and casuality develop in children. This approach, which Piaget calls genetic epistemology, was influenced by his training as a biologist. It is based upon the assumption that observation and investigation of a small number of individual organisms, children in this case, will provide data that are common to all members of the species. In this method of research, the usual problems of reliability and validity of data are in effect bypassed or ignored. Data are inherently reliable (obtained from interviews with children or observation of their behavior), and validity is measured by their consistency with theoretical propositions. Empirical data lead to the construction of hypotheses through reasoning and logic, and also substantiate or refute such hypotheses.

For Piaget, science—biological, psychological, and social—is unitary, representing the order of the universe or cosmos. Variation is simply an irrelevant deviation from the natural order or process of development. The concept of cosmic order requires that the parts which constitute a whole must bear certain relationships to each other and to the whole. The whole may act upon itself (resulting in the law of preservation and survival); the parts may all act (resulting in the law of alteration and preservation); the parts may act upon themselves (resulting in the law of preservation and survival); and the parts may act upon the whole (resulting in the law of alteration and preservation). These actions of an organism lead to evolutionary development, with increased mobility, complexity, versatility, and unity. This increase in unity moves the whole towards equilibrium, of which there are three possible forms: (1) predominance of the whole, with alteration (or deformation) of the parts; (2) predominance of the parts, with alteration (or deformation) of the whole; and (3) reciprocal preservation of the parts and the whole. The third is the only good and stable equilibrium, and is the level toward which the evolutionary process moves, this end level being reached by the intellectually mature human being.

Piaget, as noted above, accepts neither the genetic nor the environmental theories regarding the child's development of his view of the world. His assumptions, however, incorporate both. The human infant is a biological organism with a system of reflexes and phylogenetically inherited drives. These drives are: (1) the hunger drive, which involves the capacity to seek and utilize food; (2) a drive toward balance, with emotion being a reflex reaction to sudden disturbance of this balance; and (3) a drive for independence from the environment, with the capacity to achieve a degree of independence through adaptation. The infant is not a passive subject acted upon by the environment;

it is active, seeking contact with the environment, seeking stimulation, showing a curiosity in exploring his environment. Its behavior is not simply an automatic reaction to its environment (except in the case of its few simple reflexes), but a reaction influenced or mediated by its interpretation of environmental stimuli.

Thus the organism functions in and interacts with an environment. Human beings are, then, a product of their genetic makeup and of environmental elements—they are neither predetermined by their heredity nor completely shaped by their environment. Growth and development are in part the result of inborn characteristics which set in motion certain processes, but growth and development are also in part the result of experience. Cognitive (or intellectual) organization and development, upon which Piaget focuses, evolve from an a priori pattern of intellectual development. It is this mode of intellectual functioning which is inherited. This mode generates cognitive structures which arise through functioning. But the intellect organizes its structure on the basis of experience with objects in space and time and the experience of causality. Thus, experiences, though influenced by the nature of the organism and its innate capacity to organize experience, shape the interests of the organism, which then influence the nature of later experiences.

Development involves both maturation and experience (learning). Piaget considers mental growth to consist of two processes: *development* (which results in real learning) and *learning* in a narrow sense. Development is spontaneous and includes four factors: (1) *maturation*, or the change and growth in physical structures; (2) *experience*, the opportunity to function and grow by acting on objects; (3) *social transmission*, or input from the social environment; and (4) *equilibration*, or the self-regulatory processes which integrate the other factors, and which allow the child to move from one state of equilibrium through a period of disequilibrium to the next state of equilibrium.

For Piaget there are two kinds of learning: (1) Learning includes the acquisition by the organism of new responses to specific situations, but without the organism necessarily understanding the reasoning behind the learning or being able to generalize the learning to other situations. (2) The second kind of learning consists of the acquisition of a new structure of mental operations from the equilibration process. This learning is stable and lasting as compared to the transitory first kind and leads to generalization based on understanding. It requires a certain level of cognitive structures dependent on the development of the organism.

Piaget's use of the term *genetic* (as in *genetic epistemology*) does not involve the usual etiological or causal connotations. *Genetic* for him is essentially equivalent to *developmental*. He is thus fundamentally a developmental psychologist, concerned with the description and theoretical analysis of successive ontogenetic states (stages or phases of development) in terms of preceding and succeeding states, progressing from simpler to more advanced levels of functioning.

Concepts

Piaget has been concerned with the structure of developing intelligence, rather than its content (specific behaviors) or its function, which is essentially the same at all ages. Structures stand between content and function, being organizational properties resulting from or required by functioning and imposed upon behavioral contents. Structures are explanatory concepts inferred from contents; and as contents, or behaviors, change as the organism attempts to function in a changing environment, the structures change. The changes in structures as the organism develops are the focus of Piaget's work. They include numerous concepts associated with Piaget's early work (for instance, egocentrism, syncretism, juxtaposition, reversibility, animism). Piaget did not ignore function and content, however; some of the concepts mentioned below (adaptation, for one) are functional concepts.

Cognition is characterized by *organization*. Although the specific characteristics of organization change with development, intellectual organizations are always wholes, composed of elements which are systematically related. Any specific act of intelligence is thus related to a system or totality of which it is a part. Organization applies also to wholes which consist of acts related in terms of means to ends, or of values to ideals.

Intellectual functioning which is organized is also an intellectual *adaptation*, a term taken from biology, along with the terms for its component processes (below), which retain their biological connotations. The function of intelligence at all levels of development is to structure the world or the environment. Organization and adaptation are both *invariant* functions; that is, they are constant, or continuous, processes present throughout the development of the individual.

Adaptation is the (inherited) cognitive striving of the organism to organize itself to achieve an equilibrium with its environment. There are two complementary processes in adaptation. One is the process of *assimilation*. In assimilation the organism adapts the environment to itself; it uses the environment, as in the ingestion and digestion of food. In assimilation, the organism can handle the environment without changing itself. The second process is *accommodation*. In accommodation the organism *adapts to* the environment. Here the organism changes to meet the demands of the environment. The processes are interrelated in that the organism must accommodate to an environmental situation before it can assimilate it. Both processes thus occur together, though they represent opposing or conflicting forces. The organism experiences a drive to act toward the environment as it has in the past, that is, to assimilate it, but also experiences the need to act differently in terms of the new situation, that is, to accommodate or adapt to it. Thus development is continuous with the past, using old structures to achieve new functions, but development also involves the changing of structures to achieve old functions under new conditions. The development of adaptations occurs in a total pattern, so that the whole organism is adapted to its environment. In other words, a dynamic *equilibrium* is achieved. Such a state, however, exists only momentarily, at best, and may be only a theoretical state. Nevertheless, the organism always strives toward equilibrium, and it is this striving and the resulting processes of change that constitute, for Piaget, the problem and subject matter of psychology.

Underlying the process of adaptation is the *schema*. (Some writers use the term *scheme*, since Piaget has adopted this in his more recent writing. *Schemata* is sometimes used as the plural of *schema*.) This is a difficult concept to define, because schemas are of varying degrees of complexity and refer to both sensorimotor and cognitive behaviors. Essentially, a schema is more than a simple response to a stimulus—it is almost a response seeking a stimulus. It is a pattern of behavior through which the organism contacts, or seeks contact with, its environment. Thus it includes such a simple reflex as the sucking reflex or grasping behavior in the infant, and also includes listening and looking, as well as such acts of conceptual thinking as visual imagery, drawing implications, and judging distances. Schemas are mobile, that is, they are not limited to single objects, and the schematic behaviors can be modified in instrumental acts, that is, when they are directed toward the attainment of a goal. Schemas relate to adaptation in that they place the organism in interaction with its environment and provide the basis for organizing and assimilating the environment. As an example, the child's grasping behavior derives from a grasping schema which, at the appropriate age, enables the child to pick up, or *functionally assimilate,* large objects. But the child is unable to pick up a small object until the grasping schema modifies itself to do so, or accommodates to its environment. Schemas are thus underlying and relatively enduring cognitive structures or organizations (wholes) to which new acts are assimilated. Thus, the grasping schema is the basis for the infant's accommodating to objects of different sizes and shapes by developing appropriate, specific grasping behaviors. Schemas recur or repeat themselves, leading to the generalizing of assimilation to new objects but also *differentiating* among objects in terms of appropriateness, thus leading to recognition of objects (*recognitory assimilation*) as appropriate for specific grasping behaviors. In the repeated process of accommodating and assimilating, schemas are modified or changed.

The relationship between assimilation and accommodation changes over the course of cognitive development, sometimes repeating itself. In early infancy, assimilation and accommodation are undifferentiated. The neonate is unable to distinguish its acts from the objects upon which it acts; they constitute a single experience. Assimilation is confused, or fused, with accommodation—the self is indistinguishable from the object. This is the initial state of *egocentrism:* "The external world therefore begins by being confused with the sensations of a self unaware of itself, before the two factors become detached from one another and are organized correlatively."[5] In his initial state of egocentrism, the subject, seeing the world from its own point of view, is unaware that there is any other viewpoint.

As the infant grows older and becomes able to separate itself from its surroundings, assimilation and accommodation become differentiated. Objects are perceived as separate from the self, and the self is perceived as an object among objects. Cognition moves from or beyond the boundary separating the self and the object, with developing knowledge of self and of objects in their relationships. "Intelligence thus begins neither with knowledge of the self nor of things as such, but with knowledge of their interaction, and it is by orienting itself simultaneously toward the two poles of that interaction that intelligence organizes the world by organizing itself."[6] Thus the assimilation-accommodation relationship changes from undifferentiation and opposition to one of differentiation and equilibrium.

But while 2-year-olds have achieved an equilibrium or balance in the sensorimotor area, they are at the undifferentiated and disequilibrium level in the symbolic or representations area. Children at the preschool and early school age are again egocentric, and unaware that their view is distorted because of their failure to see things from another point of view. It was at this age level that Piaget first recognized egocentrism. Later, he recognized another (third) period of egocentrism in middle childhood and early adolescence, with antagonism between assimilation and accommodation, and resulting disequilibrium related to abstract symbolic activities. These periods are interspersed with periods of differentiation and equilibrium, with objective perception of reality and awareness of the self. Cognition develops by conceptualizing the self as an object which perceives the world from a particular viewpoint, with increasing knowledge of the self and the world, or reality.

Whether the child wants to grasp the small object and thus wants to learn to do so, in the example above, involves *motivation.* Piaget recognizes the motivating nature of bodily needs or drives, but these are not the fundamental motives for intellectual activity. He posits an intrinsic need to cognize, which is an aspect of or indigenous to assimi-

latory activity. Using a biological analogy, Piaget says that the organism must continually "nourish" its cognitive schemas by repeatedly
assimilating the environmental "aliments" or "nutriments" for sustenance
of its schemas. Functioning inherently involves the need to function.
Learning (cognitive development) is thus a natural, innate process or
characteristic of an active (functioning) organism. When faced with
a new situation, that is, a situation which cannot be completely assimilated by an existing relevant schema, accommodation is required.
When it is achieved, an equilibrium is reached. Learning (a modification of the schema) has occurred. The organism is no longer motivated
in regard to that situation. New situations are challenges, and the
activities which they elicit are intrinsically appealing. In this respect,
Piaget's concept of motivation is similar to, or related to, what others
have called the curiosity and exploratory drives and the drive for
mastery.

Piaget's concept of *groups* and *groupings* is an extremely difficult
one to grasp, partly because it is a mathematical. Elements constitute
a group when certain conditions governing their relationships are met.
These conditions essentially are that the elements must be capable of
all logically or mathematically possible relationships or operations.
Groups or groupings (the latter being sets of elements which don't
quite meet all the criteria for a group) are thus adaptable. Schemas
which form groups or groupings are thus superior in achieving equilibrium, since they can react to and counteract disturbances in equilibrium—they are able, because they are complete systems, to change as
necessary to restore equilibrium. Groups and groupings are basic to an
advanced stage of thinking and will be considered in more detail later.

Piaget uses the term *primary processes* to refer to the original, immediate activities of the organism, particularly the early, undifferentiated processes of the child up to the age of logical thinking (age 7).
Intellectual organization develops out of the primary processes. But
affect (emotion) also arises from the same source. "When behavior is
studied in its cognitive aspect, we are concerned with structures; when
behavior is considered in its affective aspect, we are concerned with
its energetic (or 'economics,' as Pierre Janet used to say). While these
two aspects cannot be reduced to a single aspect, they are nevertheless inseparable and complementary."[7] And again: "Both are always
together as one. Both serve the adaptation to the environment."[8] They
are the two sides of the same coin. Feelings provide the interest and
value aspect of actions or behavior.

Personality thus appears to be a combination of intellectual and
affective functions and their interrelationships, the intellectual functions providing organization and integration, and the affective functions energy, drive, or desire.

Identification is a cognitive process, the recognition or conception of another as like onself. *Imitation* is also an intellectual function, recognizing another as a model. *Play* is an essential aspect of intellectual growth, involving assimilation and also, secondarily, adaptation. In play and imitation, assimilation and cognition are not in equilibrium. Play emphasizes assimilation—molding reality to the needs of the child. In imitation accommodation is emphasized, with the child adapting himself or his schemas to the reality which is being imitated. Neither represents a stable equilibrium, or intelligent adaptation. Play and imitation, since they do not achieve equilibrium, are in that sense not developmental. They are moment-to-moment or temporary, nondevelopmental shifts in the assimilation-accommodation balance superimposed on the developmental changes.[9] *Language* which is a product of mental activities, emerges along with intellectual development and is thus not a requirement of or a prerequisite of mental development.

Affective life, like the intellectual life, is adaptation, and its development thus involves the same processes. There are parallel structures, which in the case of affective development focus on persons rather than things. However, Piaget has not proposed stages of affective development as he has for intellectual development. This is not only because affect is not a main concern for Piaget, but because all behaviors (and all schemas) are both intellectual and affective. Affect and cognition cannot be separated except for purposes of discussions. But it appears that for Piaget the cognitive aspects of behavior are more important. This is reflected by Flavell's discussion:

> In Piaget's view, it is no accident that the child of, say, ten years is beginning to develop a hierarchy of values and well-ordered systems of beliefs about rules and laws, mutual obligations among peers, and the like [here Flavell refers to *The Moral Judgment of the Child*]; he has developed cognitive structures which make these things possible—possible at ten and not possible at four. What can happen in what might be loosely called "extracognitive adaptation" is at any age very much dependent upon the nature of the cognitive organization so far developed, and therefore the study of the latter is of prime importance for students of personality and social psychology: this seems to be the really important message of Piaget's writings in this area.[10]

There is a final aspect of Piaget's theory which must be given at least brief mention because of its significance for, among other things, education. Piaget bases his whole theory of cognition upon *actions* performed by the individual. In infancy the actions are overt sensorimotor behaviors. As the child grows older, the actions become progressively internalized, first at a simple, concrete level, and then at more and more complex levels as abstract, systematized thought—systems of internal *operations*. These are, however, *actions;* and conversely, the early actions are the substance of intellectual adaptation.

This concept of intelligence-as-action is the basis for viewing intelligence as a single, continuous process beginning at birth, if not before. Early motor behavior is not something different in kind from later symbolic or abstract thinking. Action constitutes the common element in a continuous developmental process. Sensorimotor behaviors are as much cognitive and intellectual as symbolic thinking; they are simply at an earlier developmental level. In fact, they, and later actions, are basic and fundamental—necessary—for all abstract and symbolic thinking.

Theory of Qualitative Stages

Piaget's system consists of a series of developmental stages, each of which is considered in terms of its similarities with and differences from preceding and succeeding stages. The nature of these stages will be considered in the next section. Here we are concerned with the general characteristics of stages.

The basic question which can be raised about the concept of stages or phases of development regards their reality. If development is continuous, can it be broken up into discrete units? For Piaget, intellectual development does manifest patterns which emerge sequentially and are sufficiently different from one another qualitatively to warrant analysis in terms of stages.

A requirement of stages is that they must follow each other in constant order, that is, their sequence is invariant, so that the second stage always follows the first stage in every child, and no stage can be skipped. The age at which a given stage occurs may vary with different children, depending on intelligence, experience, and culture. Development may be arrested so that some individuals (for example, the mentally retarded) do not reach the final stages of development. Individuals may also be at different stages with regard to different tasks or content areas.

A second requirement of the stage concept is that later stages incorporate the structures of earlier stages, which are necessary for the later stages. A third requirement is that each stage constitute a whole or total system, with the structures of earlier stages and present structures being interdependent. The whole may consist of many diverse and apparently unrelated behaviors, but they hold together as a grouping and are in equilibrium.

Stages do not, of course, emerge full-blown. There is an early period when structures of the preceding stage are tried along with the unperfected new structures. This preparatory phase gives way to a later period when the structures characterizing the stage become an integrated whole. Thus the process from a stage of disequilibrium to one of equilibrium is present within each stage.

Recurrent patterns in development are called *décalages,* or repetitions—or temporal displacements, to use the term of one translator. These are termed horizontal décalages when they occur within one stage, and vertical décalages when they occur at different stages of development. Recurrences within levels involve the application of the same cognitive structure to different tasks. J. H. Flavell, in his book on Piaget, gives as an example the recognition by the child that the *mass* or *quantity* of matter of an object remains the same (invariant) when the shape of the object changes. Later, the recognition that the *weight* also remains unchanged involves the application of the same cognitive structure. Although these applications are separated by a year, they are in the same stage. An example of a vertical décalage is the application of the same formal structure in a child's actual (motor) navigation of a room and, several years later, in his symbolic representation of a room and its contents.[11] Horizontal décalages indicate that stages are not homogeneous, but include different phases. Vertical décalages, on the other hand, suggest that there are some structural similarities or uniformities among stages.

The identification of stages is not an end in itself, but a means to understanding development. Underlying the stages there is a continuity, and transitional behavior or steps can be recognized. But "cognitive structures, i.e., the equilibrium stages which development yields, are essentially discontinuous and qualitatively distinct, one from another. However, each one arises from a developmental *equilibration process* which is continuous, more or less all of a piece, throughout ontogenesis."[12] This is in effect a statement of the major hypothesis involved in Piaget's theory, which his experiments are designed to demonstrate or prove.

Stage theories tend to underemphasize individual differences within stages and overemphasize differences between stages. Piaget emphasizes that the child is not a small adult—that the child's cognitive processes differ from those of the adult is one of his major contributions. Yet he recognizes that there are similarities and continuities. His theory of stages is one of the most complete and complex, avoiding the oversimplification which characterizes most such theories.

Summary

Piaget's concern has been with understanding the cognitive development of the child and adolescent. He recognizes the importance of affect or emotion in the total personality, but he focuses upon cognitive development. His empirical studies have been conducted in the context of a developing theory. Piaget's background in biology and philosophy has given his theory a biological and philosophical cast lacking in most other theories. Philosophically he has developed a theory of knowledge. Psychologically his theory may be considered a theory of intelligence, which may be compared, as indeed Piaget himself does compare his theory, with other theories of intelligence, such as associationism and Gestalt theory.[13]

The human organism is endowed with certain hereditary characteristics which influence the pattern of intellectual development. These characteristics affect each individual's perception of the world. The environment does not impose itself on the individual, shaping his or her behavior willy-nilly. Rather, the individual as an active organism organizes the environment in terms of his or her innate characteristics, the expression or manifestations of which vary over the course of development. The organism thus is not simply a reactor to external stimuli. Experience is an important element in cognitive development, but experience is an interaction between an active organism and its environment.

The use of the word *reality* by Piaget must be clearly understood. It will be remembered that earlier (p. 68), in noting that Piaget is concerned with how the child comes to know the world, the phrase "or the world as seen by adults" was used. Piaget recognizes that the world is ultimately unknowable, so that we can only approach a knowledge of it, and this knowledge is inherently shaped by, as well as limited by, our biological characteristics. The use by Piaget of the terms "conception of" and "construction of" in the titles of his books clearly recognizes this fact.

The child's interaction with the world is through the process of adaptation, which includes an accommodation of the individual to the object or stimulus—the "real" world—and also the assimilation of (a modification of or construction of) the object. The child can only come to know the world in distinction from, and in relation to, himself. The world exists only in relation to the individual; it has meaning only as it can be assimilated by the individual into a schema (or schematic whole).

Intellectual development can be divided into levels or chronological stages. The order of these stages is invariant (fixed), although the specific age ranges vary with the individual. The process of adaptation is common to all stages, but it manifests itself differently at different levels and with different contents. At each stage (and to some extent within stages), the process proceeds from phases where assimilation and accommodation are out of balance—disequilibrated—to phases where they are in balance—in equilibrium. While the function of cognition or intelligence remains the same throughout the developmental process—broadly, the apprehension of or adaptation to the world—its structure varies or changes, and it is these changes which are a major subject of Piaget's studies.

THE DEVELOPMENTAL PERIODS[14]

Piaget has divided the process of intellectual development into three major periods or levels: (1) the sensorimotor period (0–2 years); (2) the preoperational period, or the period of preparation for and organization of concrete operations (2–11 years); and (3) the period of formal operations or conceptual thought (11–15 years). Each period is divided into stages, and in some cases subperiods and substages, which are not always the same or consistent in Piaget's various publications. Since our concern is with Piaget's relevance for the formal education process, we shall give very brief attention to the first period and the first subperiod of the second period, and somewhat more attention to the second subperiod of the second period and the third period. Ages indicated for the periods as well as for the subperiods and stages are, it must be remembered, approximations, and will vary for individual children.

The Sensorimotor Period

During the sensorimotor period, the infant progresses from a reflex level in which the self and the world are indistinguishable, to the stage where it interacts in an organized manner with its environment. The interaction is on a perceptual-motor level; the infant does not have the ability to engage in symbolic manipulations of things or objects. There are six major stages in this period. It is important to reiterate here that behaviors characteristic of one stage do not necessarily disappear in the next stage; they may persist intact, or enter into the new behaviors by addition, combination, or modification. This is true not only of the sensorimotor period, but of the other periods as well. Detailed data and conclusions regarding this period are presented in *The Origins of Intelligence in Children, The Construction of Reality in the Child,* and *Play, Dreams and Imitation in Childhood.* They are based almost entirely on Piaget's observations of his own three children.

Stage 1: Reflexive or stimulus-response behavior (0–1 month). The behavior of the infant in the first month consists almost entirely of uncoordinated, spontaneous movements, and reflexes or reflexlike activities. While such behaviors do not warrant the designation intelligent, they are important because they are quickly modified and developed into learned adaptive behaviors, and are thus the sensorimotor basis of intelligence. They contain the beginnings of assimilation and accommodation and organization, which characterize all later intelligent behavior. But in its interaction with the environment the infant is purely egocentric; this egocentricity continues in the second stage.

Stage 2: Acquisition of the first adaptations and the primary circular reaction (1–4 months). Undifferentiated spontaneous and reflexive behaviors are rapidly modified as a result of experience. Simple habits develop: The sucking reflex becomes the habit of thumb sucking, an acquired accommodation involving learned coordination between the hand and the mouth. Such acquisitions are not intentional—they result from fortuitous connections of searching or grasping behaviors with elements of the environment. But they represent the beginnings of differentiation between assimilation and accommodation.

The connection of searching behaviors with environmental elements constitutes a *circular reaction* which tends to be repeated; primary circular reactions usually involve the infant's body rather than surrounding objects, as in the thumb-sucking behavior. Late in this stage, the grasping reflex is coordinated with vision; the infant looks at what he is grasping and tries to grasp everything he sees. Behavior becomes more organized.

Stage 3: The secondary circular reaction and procedures for making interesting sights last (4–8 months). The secondary circular reaction goes beyond the primary circular reaction in that the environmental consequences of the act are recognized: That is, the beginnings of the concept of causality appear, and also of intentionality, when the infant attempts to maintain or repeat effects of his actions. Piaget suggests that this reflects "a sort of magical belief in causality," but states that it "indicates that he is on the threshold of intelligence."[15]

Stage 4: The coordination and application of schemas to new situations (8–12 months). In this stage true intentionality emerges: That is, two (or more) schemas are coordinated, one being the goal and the other the means, in an intentional means-end sequence. The goal is first recognized, and the means then develops or is found from among previously learned behaviors to overcome obstacles and achieve it. Actions are performed in order to achieve something. Behavior is intentional, and thus intelligent.

Stage 5: The tertiary circular reaction and the search for new means through active experimentation (12–18 months). At the third level, circular reactions move from mechanical repetition to variations which constitute exploration of the potentialities of environmental objects. This represents a further differentiation of assimilation and accommodation beyond earlier stages, and of differentiation of the action from the object. At this stage, also, the means-ends process is advanced by experimentation leading to the discovery of new means, in addition to the means already in the child's behavior repertoire. For example, sticks, and strings attached to objects, are discovered as means to obtain the objects.

Stage 6: Invention of new means through mental comprehension or insights (18 months on). Here, rather than utilizing existing or obvious methods of reaching a goal, or even discovering new means by active experimentation, the child begins to solve problems by means of thought. Exploration is not by overt trial-and-error exploration, but by covert or internal exploration. This signifies the beginning of the ability to represent events not presently observable by symbolic images, prior to the development of language as a means of symbolic representation. This ending of the sensorimotor period marks the transition to the next period.

But before proceeding to the next period, it is necessary to note, without elaborating, that other developments are taking place during the sensorimotor period. These include the development of imitation; play; the object concept; the concepts of space, causality, and time; and the affective aspect of behavior. Each of these, as studied and presented by Piaget, is divided into six stages, corresponding to the six stages of sensorimotor development summarized above. These developments are interrelated with and interdependent with sensorimotor development, as well as with each other. It should also be noted that these aspects of development extend beyond the sensorimotor period. In the sensorimotor period, all aspects of development are tied to overt behaviors. In later periods development is freed from sensorimotor performance, moving into thinking and verbalizations about objects or reality, that is, into symbolic manipulations.

The Period of Preparation for and
Organization of Concrete Operations

The subperiod of preoperational thought (2–7 years). While the early years of this subperiod (2–4 years) represent the years least studied by Piaget, the later years are covered extensively in his studies of language, reasoning, space, time, and number. These studies are reported in his books with these terms in the title, and also in *The Psychology of Intelligence,* and *Logic and Psychology.*

In the preoperational subperiod the child develops the ability to manipulate reality by means of symbols. This is achieved by the development of *representational thought,* or the acquisition of the *symbolic function.* This requires the ability to differentiate what Piaget calls *signifiers* and *significates,* or the representation of an (absent) object or an event (the significate) by a word or symbol (the signifier). Representational thought or intelligence is superior to sensorimotor intelligence for the following reasons: (a) It is capable of grasping simultaneously a panorama of events, involving the past, present, and future. (b) In addition, it is not restricted to concrete or overt actions, but is capable of reflecting upon the nature and consequences of possible actions without the actions being performed. (c) It is free from the restriction of operating upon actual or concrete objects, being able to manipulate symbols, as in mathematical thinking. (d) Finally, conceptual intelligence, unlike sensorimotor intelligence, is not limited to the experiencing individual but can be shared with others who also possess the symbols.

Signifiers or symbols are first acquired by accommodation, in the form of an internalized imitation, which is an image of the action, object, or event, or (at the end of the sensorimotor period) of actions (often abbreviated) which symbolize the actions of people or objects. Images thus derive from an internalized imitation of activities or actions involved in perception and are acquired by the process of accommodation. The actual objects, events, or actions are the significates, and are provided of course by assimilation. In other words, the symbols refer to the meaning of the objects, that is, the objects as assimilated to the child's mental schemas. The process, involving absent (past) significates, becomes extremely complex. Thus it is difficult and time-consuming for the child to learn to cognize the world symbolically, and he vacillates between play, imitation, and adapted intelligence. The process is complicated also in that there are two kinds of signifiers—signs, which are socially or commonly shared, and *symbols*, which are private and idiosyncratic. The child's first signifiers are not signs—words appropriated from the social environment—but private, nonverbal symbols. The child's first words are "semisigns," having characteristics of private symbols, referring to specific objects rather than to a class of objects. The symbolic function is acquired between the ages of 2 and 4 years.

Preoperational thought is marked by a number of characteristics:

1. *Egocentrism.* The preoperational child, according to Piaget, is halfway between the autistic, purely egocentric thought of the Freudian unconscious and socialized adult thought. The child is unable to assume the role of another and to recognize its own view as one of a number of different views. The egocentric child recognizes no need to justify its reasonings nor to check its own thinking for logical contradictions. It cannot reconstruct a chain of reasoning after having gone through it. Such a child is unable to "think about his own thinking".[16] All these achievements require numerous interpersonal interactions, especially arguments, in which the child is required to become aware of the role of the other.

2. *Centration.* One of Piaget's well-known experiments, involving the concept of conservation, presents the preoperational child with two identical glass cylinders filled to the same level with liquid. Then, while the child observes, the contents of one cylinder are poured

into another, shorter and wider container. When asked whether the remaining taller and thinner container or the shorter and wider container holds the most liquid, the child will either choose the first because it is tall, or the second because it is wide, thus showing an inability to take into consideration both height and width simultaneously. This, Piaget states, indicates the tendency of the child to *center* on one aspect while reasoning, with an inability to *decenter*, or take into account balancing or compensating aspects, such as height and width.

3. *State Fixation.* The experiment described above illustrates another characteristic of preoperational thought. The child fixates upon what he is shown at the beginning and at the end of the experiment, but not upon the intervening process. That is, the child observes *states*, but not the *transformation* of states. His thought focuses upon static conditions rather than upon changes in the conditions. This is no doubt why the child at this age is so fascinated and mystified by the performances of magicians.

4. *Unstable Equilibrium.* There is a third characteristic which is manifested in the water-levels problem. The child is susceptible to the influence of apparent difference in states, leading to contradiction in its cognitions. The *balance or equilibrium between assimilation and accommodation is unstable*—the child cannot accommodate the new (the final state) with the old (the beginning state).

5. *Realism.* Although able to engage in mental operations on reality, the child in the preoperational stage does so primarily by use of concrete images or the replication of concrete actions (mental experiments) rather than by the use of abstract signs or symbols. Piaget refers to the child's *realism*, meaning that things are taken to be what they appear to be; for instance, nonobjective phenomena, such as dreams, are objectified.

6. *Irreversibility.* The water-level experiment reveals what is perhaps the most important characteristic of preoperational thought: The child is not only unable to recognize the transformation by which the amount of water remains the same (invariant) when poured from the narrow container into the wider container, but is also unable to recognize the possibility of the inverse transformation back to the original state. The child's thought is characterized by *irreversibility*.

7. *Transductive Reasoning.* The child in the preoperational stage is *unable to recognize identity in individuals over time.* An individual in a different costume or context is not the same. Conversely, similar members of a class or group are perceived as identical rather than as different individual members of the class. Piaget refers to the child's use of *preconcepts* which are related by transductive reasoning (from particular to particular) rather than by inductive or deductive reasoning. An example of transductive reasoning, taken from Piaget, is given by Ginsburg and Opper: Lucienne, who habitually had an afternoon nap, said on an afternoon when she didn't have a nap, "I haven't had my nap, so it isn't afternoon."[17] In addition, causal

relations are not recognized, but are seen as "and" relations, or simple juxtaposition. Thus, the child's reasoning is symmetric, with everything related to (or "caused by") everything else.

There are many other characteristics of preoperative thought identified by Piaget in his many experiments with children in this age period. Young children are animistic in their thinking, that is, they attribute life, consciousness, and will to physical objects and events. Their concepts of morality and justice, as well as of time, causality, space, and number are primitive. Their concept of reality is not clearly distinguished from play—indeed, play is reality to them. All of these characteristics are interrelated to form a single cognitive orientation, which may be designated by a number of terms—*concrete, static, acausal, illogical,* or, a term Piaget seems to favor, *egocentric.*

This period is a long one—about 5 years—during which many changes take place. There is movement from static, rigid, centered, irreversible thinking toward more flexible, decentered, and reversible thinking; and toward the concrete thinking which is the mark of the next period.

The subperiod of concrete operations (7–11 years). Because this period coincides with the early formal education of the child, it should be highly relevant to the teaching-learning process in schools. Therefore, the presentation will be more detailed than that of the earlier periods, although it still can be only a highly condensed summary.

In the period of concrete operations, children continue to develop in representational thinking; that is, they are not completely bound to the *actual,* but can deal to some extent, with the *potential.* They possess an organized, integrated cognitive system on the basis of which to organize, and operate in, their world. In contrast to the imbalance of assimilation and accommodation of the preoperational period, there is an equilibrium between a comprehensive, integrated assimilatory organization and a sensitive, discriminative accommodory apparatus.

The logicomathematical model. Piaget's writings on number, quantity, space, geometry, and moral judgment all deal with concrete-operational thought, and his general books, *The Psychology of Intelligence, Logic and Psychology,* and *The Early Growth of Logic in the Child* (with Inhelder), summarize the developments of the period. The concept of stages within the period is abandoned for another kind of organization of the material, deriving from Piaget's attempt to describe cognition in logicomathematical terms. Ordinary language, Piaget believes, is lacking in precision and therefore is inadequate for scientific theorizing and communication, so he has developed the logicomathematical model. This model includes a set of nine *groupings* applying to logical classes and relations (as well as to infralogical collections, to be mentioned later). These groupings describe the processes underlying the child's ability to understand classes and relations, and involve cognitive *operations*. Operations are cognitive actions or thought processes, integrated or organized into wholes with clear, strong structures. Operations may, but not necessarily, involve overt actions; they are usually internalized actions. They are characterized by their interrelatedness and by reversibility. They include logical and numerical operations (adding, subtracting, and so on), correspondences within systems of classes and relations, and the infralogical operations involving position and distance relationships and part-whole relationships. Infralogical operations deal with concrete, spatiotemporal objects or configurations, whereas logical operations are abstractions, independent of space and time. Two groups, in addition to the above groupings, are characteristic of the subperiod of concrete operations. (The distinction between groupings and groups will be considered below.) Cognitive operations are also involved in interpersonal relationships and the development of values and value systems.

In his study of the cognitive development of middle and late childhood, Piaget has departed from psychology; logic and mathematics constitute his major constructs. His mathematics is nonquantitative, involving operations which define relationships and thus processes and structures. (Piaget, however, uses the term *intensive quantification* to refer to the condition or relation where one knows that each of a number of subclasses is less than the whole, but where the relative sizes of the subclasses are not known. *Extensive quantification*, where the sizes of the classes are known, is characteristic of groups.) His use of logic is not the common use in psychology of deriving hypotheses from theorems and postulates and stating their relationships. The logical operations themselves are the content of the theory. The logicomathematical system constitutes a *model* of cognitive structure, representing the organization and process of cognition. It is the ideal, which actual cognition approximates.

The complex operations described in the groupings are not performed with complete conscious awareness. But they are implicit in the way the child deals with concrete problems. They explain the child's performance—he or she could not perform given experiments or answer given questions correctly without being able to perform the operations.

The logicomathematical model is not entirely an a priori conception of cognitive functioning imposed upon psychology. It appears to have been derived in part at least from Piaget's observations and to have developed further through his experiments. As will be noted, however, empirical or experimental evidence does not exist for some of the operations or groupings. They are logically necessary for his system, however. Thus, the fit of the model to actual cognition has not been completely tested or demonstrated. Piaget has tried, in various experiments, to detect the presence or absence of components of the groupings in the thinking of children.

Piaget's groupings are quasi-mathematical structures combining aspects of mathematical *groups* and *lattices*. A group has been referred to earlier (p. 76), as consisting of a set of elements and the relation governing them. Both this relation and the elements have the properties of composition, associativity, identity, and reversibility. A lattice consists of a set of elements and a relation between two or more of the elements such that any two elements have one *greatest lower bound* (g.l.b.) and one *least upper bound* (l.u.b.). As a simple example, given a set of positive integers (elements), two of which are 10 and 13, and the relation $\leqq$, the greatest lower bound is 10 (the largest number included in 10 and 13 simultaneously) and the least upper bound is 13 (the smallest number in which both 10 and 13 are included).

LOGICAL GROUPINGS

Eight of Piaget's major groupings are designated by Roman numerals. Four of them deal with the logic of classes, and an equivalent four deal with the logic of relations. The ninth (or first, in terms of simplicity) occurs as a special case in all the other groupings and is here considered first.

PRELIMINARY GROUPING OF EQUALITIES. This grouping is of the form (or *composition*) that if $A = B$ and $B = C$, then $A = C$. The composition is associative: $(A = B) + (B = C)$; *reversible:* $(A = B)$, $(B = A)$; includes the *general identity* $(A = A)$, and the *special identity* that each equality possesses identity with itself and with every other equality.

The preoperational child has difficulty with equalities; he may recognize that $A = B$ and that $B = C$, but fail to realize that $A = C$.

GROUPING I: PRIMARY ADDITION OF CLASSES. Grouping I describes the operations involved in simple hierarchies of classes, and the relationships among these operations. The figure on page 89 depicts a classification hierarchy of a zoological nature (suggested by Flavell)[18] using Piaget's class symbols.

Unprimed letters represent *primary classes,* and primed letters *secondary classes* (which may consist of an undetermined number). A particular primed and unprimed class have no elements in common; an unprimed class includes all the unprimed and primed classes below it in the hierarchy. Each class is an *element* of the system which can be subject to the binary operation (a binary operation is one that in-

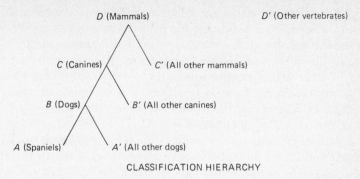

CLASSIFICATION HIERARCHY

volves only two elements at a time) of *combining*. There are five binary operations (according to five rules). These five ways constitute the properties of grouping:

1. *Composition*. The combination of any two elements yields another element or, in a hierarchy, the next higher class: $A + A' = B$; $B + B' = C$, and so on; or $(A + A' = B) + (B + B' = C) = (A + A' + B' = C)$, and so on, following the rule that only two elements can be combined at a time, but two elements once combined constitute an element which can then be combined with another element. (See 5 below for clarification if this is not clear.)

2. *Associativity*. Elements, or classes, can be combined in different orders with the same results. Thus $(A + B) + C = C$ and $A + (B + C) = C$. Or $[(B - A' = A) + (C - B' = B)] + (D - C' = C)$ and $(B - A' = A) + [(C - B' = B) + (D - C' = C)]$ are equal, and both are equal to $(D - C' - B' - A' = A)$.

3. *General Identity*. The identity element is a special element (set by Piaget as 0) which when added to any other element leaves the element unchanged $(0 + 0 = 0)$. Thus $(C - B' = B) + (0 + 0 = 0) = (C - B' = B)$; and so on.

4. *Reversibility*. For every element, there is another element, its *inverse*, which when combined with the first yields the identity element, or 0. Thus, $A - A = 0$; and $(A + A' = B) + (-A - A' - B) = 0$.

5. *Special Identities*. In addition to the general identity element, there are special identities in Grouping I. Every class is an identity element with respect to itself; that is, an element combined with itself remain the same: $A + A = A$. (The adding of a class to itself yields only the class itself.) Piaget calls this property *tautology*. In addition, a subclass combined with the class results in the class: $A + B = B$. This property is called *resorption*. The difference between a grouping and a mathematical group is apparent here. In a group, $A + A = 2A$. Classes and relations require a different structuring of operations. Grouping I has been more thoroughly studied by Piaget than any of the others.

The concrete-operational child, as compared to the preoperational child, grasps the direct and inverse operations of Grouping I, being able to combine classes in ascending a hierarchy and to decombine them in descending a hierarchy. He seems to look for or expect class hierarchies and can discard one classification system and apply another to the same data. He understands the *inclusion relation,* which consists of the ability to view subclasses as individual classes while at the same time seeing them as members of a superordinate class. He can think of wholes and their parts simultaneously: $A + A' = B$ and $B = A + A'; A = B - A'$ and $A' = B - A.$

Additive groupings were studied by the sorting task, in which Inhelder and Piaget presented various groups of children with various sets of objects with the instruction "Put together the things that are alike" or "Put them so that they are all the same." One set consisted of objects of various shapes: squares, triangles, rings or circles, and half-rings; some of wood and others of plastic; some of one color and some another. Thus the child could classify by shape, material, or color, or a combination of two or all three.

The young child forms *graphic collections,* or arrangements in rows or other geometric forms. The older preoperational child may group some objects in classes but not include all the objects in the sorting, or may include all the objects but with no homogeneity of classes and with multiple criteria for grouping. Later a single criterion may be used, but without an hierarchical classification.

The concrete-operational child classifies in a *hierarchical arrangement,* with various criteria separating the subclasses. Thus, for example, all the wooden objects are separated from all the plastic objects. Then each is subdivided into sharp-edged and round-edged objects, and these in turn are further grouped into squares and rectangles, and circles and half-circles. Inhelder and Piaget established a number of criteria for or properties of adequate classification: (1) Classes are *mutually exclusive;* that is, no object can be a member of more than one class at the same time. (2) Each class has a defining property, or *intension;* that is, all members share some similarity. (3) The *extension* of a class is simply a list of the objects in the class. (4) *Intension defines extension;* that is, the defining property determines the membership of the class. (5) There is an *inclusion relationship;* that is, the higher classes in a hierarchy include all subclasses and are larger than any subclass; and, conversely, each subclass is not inclusive of the major class. Nevertheless, it may be difficult to determine whether a child has arrived at an adequate system of classification on the basis of a conceptual plan involving cognitive organization or by some other method or process.

To test the understanding of *all* and *some* in a classification system, Inhelder and Piaget presented children with four boxes containing red circles, blue circles, red squares, and blue squares, and asked which boxes were needed to construct a row that included red squares, blue squares, and blue circles, but no red circles. Children were then asked: "Are all the circles blue?" and "Are all the squares red?" To answer correctly the child must be able to understand the nature of a logical class and to recognize that every member has a particular characteristic. The child of 9 or 10 can answer the first question correctly, but 9-year-olds may not be able to answer the second correctly.

To determine whether the child recognizes that there are more members in a class of higher rank than in one of its subclasses, Inhelder and Piaget used several similar experiments. In one, the child was shown a number of flowers: primulas, violets, tulips, and so on. Check questions were asked to determine that the child understood that all the primulas were flowers, and that there were other flowers that are not primulas. He or she was then asked if there were more primulas or flowers. An 8-year-old child answered that there was the same number of each. A child of 11 years 6 months, though recognizing that all ducks are birds and that there are other birds which are not ducks $(C + C' = B)$ and that there are other animals than birds (B'), did not recognize that the class of animals (A) minus ducks (C) is larger than the class of animals (A) minus birds (B), or $(A - C > A - B)$.

Children find it much more difficult to develop a hierarchy when given a set of objects if one class has only one object, and even more difficult to conceive of a class with no objects in it. Even up to the age of 10 or 11, children presented with blank cards along with cards with pictures may not construct a class of blank cards.

GROUPING II: THE SECONDARY ADDITION OF CLASSES. In Grouping I, the secondary classes $(A', B', C',$ and so on) denote an unspecified number of classes at the same level. Alternate divisions of the superordinate class are possible. For example, one can classify dogs as beagles and nonbeagles $(A_2 + A'_2)$, as well as classifying them as spaniels and nonspaniels, or terriers and nonterriers $(A_3 + A'_3)$, and so forth. In each case, the two secondary classes combined constitute the primary class: $A + A' = B, A_2 + A_2' = B, A_3 + A'_3 = B$, and so on; and $A + A' = A_2 + A'_2 = A_3 + A'_3$, and so on $= B$. Thus there are parallel series, each joining the others at the next higher class level. These equations, according to Piaget, are *complementary substitutions*, or vicariances. The grouping structures formed by vicariance equations have the properties of composition, associativity, general identity, reversibility, and special identities.

The concrete-operational child, whose thinking includes the operations of Grouping II, recognizes that beagles are included in the class of nonspaniels and that spaniels are included in the class of nonbeagles; that there are more nonspaniels than there are beagles (since all beagles are nonspaniels and in addition there are other dogs, terriers, for example, that are nonspaniels); and that there are more nonbeagles than there are spaniels. He is able to classify a given group of objects in different ways, which represent vicariance equations.

GROUPING III: BI-UNIVOCAL MULTIPLICATION OF CLASSES. Classes can be multiplied and divided as well as added and subtracted. Multiplication involves the distribution of all the elements in a set on the basis of two different properties. Thus, a set of objects may be red and nonred $(A + A')$ and square and nonsquare $(B + B')$, each dichotomy including all the objects; A and B are thus not mutually exclusive. The multiplication of the dichotomy yields four subclasses, or $(A + A')$ $(B + B') = AB + A'B + AB' + A'B'$, that is, red square objects, nonred square objects, red nonsquare objects, and nonred nonsquare objects. Each is the largest class containing the defining attributes of both classes. Class multiplication of this type is called bi-univocal by Piaget, and is not limited to two series or characteristics. The properties of composition and association hold for class multiplication. The special identity or tautology also holds, but resorption is replaced by *absorption* of the superordinate class into its subordinate class, and the inverse operation is division instead of subtraction. Multiplication of two classes generates a smaller class; dividing a class produces a larger class. That is, a class characterized by two qualities (red and square) is smaller than either red or square classes; and conversely, a class from which a quality (red or square) is disassociated, becomes a larger class, red or square, but not both. The general identity element in Grouping III is Z, representing the largest, most general class. If the defining limit is removed from a class, say "animalness," then the most general possible class left is "animalness-nonanimalness."

To study the logical multiplication of classes, Piaget has used the following problem: "There are only three knives in a store. Two of these knives have two blades: they cost 8 francs and 10 francs. Two of these knives have a corkscrew: they cost 10 francs and 12 francs. I choose the one which has two blades and a corkscrew: how much does it cost?"[19] Younger children had great difficulty in solving this. Other tasks involving the capacity to find the classification (intersect) involving two attributes were solved only by children at the level of concrete operations.

GROUPING IV: CO-UNIVOCAL MULTIPLICATION OF CLASSES. In Grouping III, there is a one-to-one correspondence between each of the component members of two or more series of classes, resulting in a square or rectangular matrix with numbers in all cells. In Grouping IV, one member of a series is set in correspondence with (or multiplied with) several members of each of one or more other series. The resulting matrix is triangular, since there are cells with no members. The grouping properties are the same as those in Grouping III. Piaget uses as an example a geneological tree. The details of the example will not be given, since the grouping, while a logically necessary member of the set involving groupings of classes, has not been studied by Piaget, so there are no data on its existence or importance in cognitive development.

GROUPING V: ADDITION OF ASYMMETRICAL RELATIONS. Groupings V through VIII involve operations on relations between individuals or classes, rather than upon classes (Groupings I through IV).

Asymmetrical relations are ordered differences of the type "less than" and "greater than" (seriation). Order is represented by the fact that the differences are directional; if $A < B$, then $B > A$, and $A < B \neq A > B$. The relations are *transitive*, that is, $A < B + B < C$ implies $A < C$.

Grouping V consists of the logical addition, and substraction, of ordered differences in a series of asymmetrical relations. The formal properties are similar to those of classes. For example, for class A and subclasses A and A' we know that $A < B$ and $A' < B$ (the *intensive quantification* property referred to earlier) without knowing or measuring the actual magnitudes of the classes; that is, classes and subclasses are in an ordered relationship. The inverse property in Grouping V differs from that in Grouping I: The *inverse* is not the *negative* or *annulling* of the relation but the *reciprocal;* that is, $A < B$ is the reciprocal of the relation $B > A$.

Preoperational children (ages 4 through 5) have difficulty in composing a series such as $A < B < C < D < E$ (seriation). At the age of 5 or 6 the child can do this, though with some difficulty, and usually by trial and error rather than by logic or by a rule or principle. Also, given two sets of ordered objects—the sets differing in absolute size, length, or difference between adjacent objects—children of this age can place the sets in correspondence, that is, match the objects of each set in order by relative size and length; but only on a trial-and-error basis. However, when the orders are presented out of spatial alignment, the child is unable to match the corresponding pairs. In the concrete-operational period, all these tasks can be perfromed easily and without trial and error, according to a plan or order. The child is still limited to doing this at a concrete level, with actual objects.

In another experiment a child is given three or more objects clearly differing in weight, but without volume being related to weight, and is asked to order them by weight, comparing only two objects at a time. The younger child bases the order on only two objects and is unsure that $A < C$ when $A < B$ and $B < C$. Piaget thinks that the failure to see the reversibility in asymmetrical relations causes both this difficulty and the willingness to conclude that $B < C$ from $A < C$ and $A < B$. Children as old as 13 have difficulty with problems of the type "If $B < C$ and $B > A$, which is the largest?"

GROUPING VI: ADDITION OF SYMMETRICAL RELATIONS. Grouping VI involves additive compositions of several distinct and different kinds of symmetrical relations, involving transitive and intransitive and reflexive and irreflexive relations. Piaget again uses the genealogical tree as an example. Stated in common terms, examples would be the relationships among X, Y, and Z, male members of a family. If X and Y are brothers and Y and Z are brothers, then X and Z must be brothers; if X and Y are brothers and Y and Z have the same grandfather, then X and Z have the same grandfather (they could be either brothers or first cousins; if Z is first cousin to one of two brothers, X and Y, he is also first cousin to the other).

As with Grouping IV, Piaget has developed little evidence of the functioning of this grouping in children. He has shown that the pre-operational child may recognize that X is his brother, but deny that X in turn has a brother.

GROUPING VII: BI-UNIVOCAL MULTIPLICATION OF RELATIONS. As in Grouping III, the multiplication of elements (objects) in Grouping VII yields products (cells in a matrix) having a given combination of attributes. Thus, multiplying a weight relation by a volume relation yields a matrix in which all the objects in the same column have the same weight, though differing in volume; and all the objects in the same row have the same volume, though differing in weight; and all the objects in a given cell are the same weight and volume; and the cells bear systematic relationships to each other.

Many of Piaget's experiments involve Grouping VII. In one experiment, the child is given a series of ten dolls varying in height and a series of walking sticks or canes varying in height, and is asked to arrange the dolls and the canes so the right cane goes with the right doll. This problem represents the diagonal cells in the matrix. Piaget assumes that the pairing of one asymmetrical series with another in one-to-one correspondence requires an understanding of the possibility of multiplying the two series. It is solved by the concrete-operational child. In another experiment, the child is given 49 cutouts of leaves of 7 different sizes and 7 different colors and is asked to arrange them. The concrete-operational child puts them in a 7-by-7 matrix.

The conservation studies described earlier involve this grouping. In these problems, and equality between two objects is kept unchanged ("conserved") across a transformation—for instance, the amount of water across a series of containers of differing widths and heights; this corresponds to a row or column in the Grouping VII matrix. Piaget believes the solution is facilitated by the ability to multiply relations such as "shorter than" and "wider than," leading to statements such as "The column of liquid in B is shorter than in A, but it is wider, and thus the amounts are equal." The concrete-operational child conserves on the basis of *negation* (if the water were returned to the original container, it would be the same); *identity* (the water is the same); *compensation* or *reciprocity* (the third jar is shorter, but wider). But there is an irregularity in the achievement of conservation in different areas (the *horizontal décalage* phenomenon). The child achieves the conservation of number and discontinuous quantity (rows with the same number of objects but differently spaced) at about 6 or 7; of continuous quantity and substance somewhat later, at 7 or 8 to 10; of weight, at 9 or 10 to 12; and of volume at 11 or 12 or later.

GROUPING VIII: CO-UNIVOCAL MULTIPLICATION OF RELATIONS. Grouping VIII is similar for relations to Grouping IV for classes. Here again, Piaget uses genealogical hierarchies to illustrate the operations. The grouping involves the multiplication of symmetrical and asymmetrical relations. The rules are very complex. Since there are no experiments related to this grouping, no further descriptions will be given. It completes the logically possible cognitive structures in Piaget's system.

INFRALOGICAL GROUPING

Logical operations apply to classes and relations, and involve classifying, seriating (ordering of classes), and multiplication operations. They deal with sets of discrete, dicontinuous objects, are independent of space and time, and do not involve any changes in their objects, either in their structure or in their spatial or temporal position.

Infralogical operations, though formally similar to logical operations, involve part-whole relationships and spatiotemporal relationships. The manipulation of part-whole relations differs from the manipulation of class relations, because (1) the whole is a single, continuous entity, whose parts are not separate or distinct when combined into the whole, and (2) its existence as a whole depends on the spatial proximity of its parts. A class is an abstraction, a whole exists in space and time.

Piaget's groupings apply, with adaptations, to infralogical collections. The adaptations relate to space-time proximities and relations. Thus, instead of stating that if $A = B$, then $B = A$, we state that if A is next to B, then B is next to A $(A \leftrightarrow B)$. $A \rightarrow B$ means that A is to the left of B, or A precedes B in time.

Infralogical groupings may appear to be less complex than logical groupings, but both develop together and characterize the concrete-operational child when she or he is dealing with part-whole relationships in the physical world of time and space.

ARITHMETIC GROUPS AND MEASUREMENT

There are two arithmetic groups: (1) The additive groups of whole numbers and (2) the multiplication group of positive numbers. The operations are the usual arithmetical computations. There are logical relationships between the arithmetic groups and the logical groupings.

These relationships account for the fact that the understanding of the properties of number develops contemporaneously with the understanding of the properties of the logical groupings.

The operations of logical and infralogical groupings are *intensive*, that is, the magnitudes are not exact. Arithmetic systems allow for exact comparisons, since their compositions are numerical and the elements *iterate*—they are equal units which lead to exact comparisons. The conversion of intensive logical units into iterable units makes possible *arithmetic operations;* the conversion of infralogical elements into iterable units yields *measurement operations.* As $1 + 1 + 1 = 3$, so unit measures enable one to measure the length of a rod or a time interval.

Piaget reports most of his studies on the development of number operations in *The Child's Conception of Number.* The experiments on measurement appear in several sources, including *The Child's Conception of Geometry* (Piaget, Inhelder, and Szeminska).

Much of Piaget's experimentation in this area has focused upon two basic ideas: (1) one-to-one correspondence and (2) the conservation of the equivalence of two numbers.

One-to-one correspondence is simple, but not obvious to young children. Piaget's test of this concept consists of asking the child to construct a set of objects which will have the property of being equal in number to a given set. Counting the number in the given set and then counting out the same number for the new set is the solution most adults would use, but this solution requires the ability to count. The problem can be solved, however, without the ability to count, if the child places with each object in the given set another object, until all are paired with another object. The pairing can be done mentally as well as physically.

The concept of conservation of number also appears to be simple to adults. If two sets of objects are presented in a one-to-one correspondence, so that it can be seen that they are equal in number, and then the arrangement is changed so that the objects of one set are either closer together or farther apart (so that one-to-one correspondence is no longer present), does the child recognize that the two sets are equal in number?

Piaget tested these concepts in experiments with children ranging in age from 4 through 11. The youngest children (4 through 5) do not have the concept of one-to-one correspondence. When asked to construct a set equal in number to one given by the experimenter, children of this age level produce a set which is not equal in number (or density) but equal in length, though placed closer together or farther apart than the given set. They *center* on one dimension only, and that is not the number dimension. When a child is helped to construct two sets in one-to-one correspondence and then one set is bunched up by the experimenter, the child fails to recognize that the two sets are equal in number, continuing to fail to do so even after the one-to-one correspondence is reestablished and broken again. Even when the child is able to count each set, he or she does not comprehend that they are equal in number and thus fails to conserve the equivalence.

The child a little older (5 through 7) easily constructs sets equivalent in number, but fails to conserve the equivalence. In addition to length, the child sometimes centers on density as representing the greater, or lesser, number.

At the concrete-operational level, the child has both the concepts of equivalency and conservation. Some children achieve this by counting, but others do so by a matching process that does not depend upon direct spatial relations. The process involves ordering, but of a different nature then ordering objects differing in size, length, and so on. Piaget uses the term *vicariant ordering* to indicate that the exact order doesn't matter as long as there is an order and every object is matched with another in the given set. There is also *classification,* in that all the members of each set are the same. *Relations* are also involved in some of the operations in constructing equivalent sets. The skills are *operations* since they are mental actions; the operations are also reversible. They are *concrete,* since they are performed on objects actually present.

Concrete-operational children are capable of *decentering;* that is, they can coordinate two related dimensions. Thus, they can understand that length and density are related in terms of *reciprocity,* or *compensation,* which is one form of *reversibility:* An increase in length can be balanced by a decrease in density. *Negation* is also comprehended by concrete-operational children: Contraction (increase of density) can be negated by expansion (decrease of density). They can also use *identity,* reasoning that the number of objects in a set must be the same since nothing has been added or taken away in rearrangement. In all of these cases, equality, or equivalence, is recognized. As children become experienced, they function quickly and automatically, and take conservation for granted as self-evident.

Conclusion. As noted at the beginning of the discussion of the subperiod of concrete operations, the major development in the child during this age span (7 to 11) is the acquisition of an organized and integrated cognitive system with which to structure and manipulate the world. Piaget's logicomathematical model attempts to provide a system which represents the cognitive structure and functioning of the child during this period. The model consists of a set of groupings which represent the logical operations involved in cognition, parallel infralogical groupings, and two groups of arithmetical operations. Piaget has conducted many studies of these operations in children, though there are gaps in some areas.

There are five major operations involved in the system: (1) composition, (2) associativity, (3) general identity, (4) reversibility, and (5) special identities. The reversibility operation is not simply one of the five operations, but the core of cognition-in-a-system in one or another of its expressions, including negation and reciprocity, so crucial in the concept of conservation.

In addition to the concrete-operational structures discussed here, Piaget has also dealt with cognitions involving the personal-social-affective spheres, including mental imagery, moral judgment and behavior, affective development, values, and interpersonal relations. The grouping structure is applied to these areas also. Interpersonal interactions are considered to be of special significance, since it is through such reciprocal interactions with peers that the logical grouping structures develop. The child meets viewpoints and ideas different from its own, which lead to the reduction of egocentricity and the acquisition of the capacity to see things differently, which includes reversibility. The makings of the grouping structures must, however, be present, laid down in the child's nature and earlier experiences.

Concrete operations have some limitations: (1) They are concrete, dealing with things and events in the present. (2) This concreteness limits generalization, so that, for example, the child has to learn conservation of mass, volume, and weight separately. (3) Similarly, the various concrete-operational systems do not yet form a single integrated system, so that the child cannot coordinate various operations or groupings to solve multivariable problems.

The Period of Formal Operations (12–15)

In the concrete-operational subperiod, the child begins to extend its thought from the *actual* towards the *potential*. However, this is limited to the concrete extension of the actual; the child can project the extension of a series of seriated elements $A < B < C$ to additional elements D, E, and so on, but is still tied to the concrete, the here and now. The adolescent, however, can transcend the present and the actual, can conceptualize possibilities which do not actually exist. This ability to conceptualize all possible relationships involves, in an intuitive way, formal logic. The adolescent can engage in abstract or hypothetical thinking. The ability to hypothesize possible relationships is the basis for designing situations to confirm or disconfirm the hypothesis, or to apply the scientific method. Not all possible relationships exist, or are real, and experiment and logical analysis attempt to determine which are real. Reality is a subset of possibilities. But it is only by being able to conceptualize the possible that one can determine the real.

Formal thought (or formal operations) has three essential characteristics. One is its *hypotheticodeductive* nature, just described. The second is that it is *propositional*. That is, it consists not of the manipulation of actual objects and events, but of statements, assertions, or propositions about data or the results of concrete operations. Formal operations, in Piaget's terminology, are second-degree or second-order operations, or *interpropositional* (involving logical relations among propositions) rather than *intrapropositional* (involving concrete operations on individual propositions). Third, formal operations involve *combinatorial* thinking, or analysis, which is the systematic or logical determination (or exhaustion) of all possible relations or combinations.

Such thought represents an advanced state of equilibrium, able to assimilate a variety of novel situations without extensive accommodation. Cognitive structures have reached a high stage of development, resulting in a mature state of cognition. Formal thought is scientific thinking.

Piaget has developed two logical models to describe the period of formal operations. The first is the model of 16 binary operations (a special case of a larger and more comprehensive combinatorial system); the second is the INRC Group, or the 4-group (identity, negation, reciprocity, and correlativity).

The 16 binary operations. The 16 binary operations comprise a lattice, in mathematical terminology. For two elements, statements, or propositions, they exhaust the possible combinations with one term (these being identified with the four subclasses resulting from the bi-univocal multiplication of two classes in Grouping III), two terms (six combinations), three terms (four combinations), four terms (one combination), and no terms (one combination). Piaget uses the notation of symbolic logic. For the symbols A, A', B, and B', the two elements or terms are p, $\bar{p}$, q, and $\bar{q}$: p is a positive statement or proposition (for instance, "This animal is a swan"), and $\bar{p}$ is the negative (for instance, "This animal is not a swan," or p is false); similarly, q is a positive statement ("This animal is white"), and $\bar{q}$ is the negative ("This animal is not white," or q is false). The class multiplication sign ($\times$) is replaced by · the conjunction sign; thus $p \cdot q$, equivalent to $A \times B$, means that propositions p and q hold true jointly. The disjunction sign $\vee$ (either-or, or both), replaces $+$; thus $p \vee q$ means that *either* p is true and q is false, *or* q is true and p is false, *or* both are true, the equivalent of $(p \cdot \bar{q}) \vee (\bar{p} \cdot q) \vee (p \cdot q)$. The 16 classes are then as follows:

1. The first class is the association $p \cdot q$, which, as $A \times B$, states that p is true and q is true; for instance, This animal is a swan, and this animal is white.
2. This class is represented by $p \cdot \bar{q}$ ($A \times B'$), which states that p is true and q is false; for instance, "This animal is a swan, and this animal is not white." Here is apparent the possibility that the asser-

tion that there are no swans which are not white is false. Piaget notes that the discovery of black swans in Australia confirms this statement, however.[20] This illustrates the fact that each proposition is a hypothesis to be tested.

3. This combination is stated by $\bar{p} \cdot q$ $(A' \times B)$; that is, "This animal is not a swan, and this animal is white." An animal may be white without being a swan.

4. The combination $\bar{p} \cdot \bar{q}$ $(A' \times B')$ states that this animal is not a swan and this animal is not white.

5. Here we go beyond Grouping III, with the first two-by-two combination: $(p \cdot q) \vee (p \cdot \bar{q})$, or the equivalent of $(A \times B) + (A \times B')$. This combination states that p is always true, whether q is or not; that is "This animal is a swan and this animal is white, *or* this animal is a swan and is not white."

6. Similarly, $(p \cdot q) \vee (\bar{p} \cdot q)$, or $(A \times B) + (A' \times B)$, states that q is always true: "This animal is a swan *or* this animal is not a swan, but this animal is, in either case, white."

7. This combination, $(p \cdot q) \vee (\bar{p} \cdot \bar{q})$, or $(A \times B) + (A' \times B')$, states that the two statements, p and q, are true or false in the same instances, that is, when p is true q is true, and when p is false q is false. "When an animal is a swan it is white, and when an animal is not a swan it is not white."

8. The combination $(p \cdot \bar{q}) \vee (\bar{p} \cdot q)$, or $(A \times B') + (A' \times B)$, states that p is incompatible with q: When p is true, q is false; when p is false, q is true. "When an animal is a swan, it is not white; when an animal is not a swan, it is white."

9. The combination $(p \cdot \bar{q}) \vee (\bar{p} \cdot \bar{q})$, or $(A \times B') + (A' \times B')$, states that q is never true, whether or not p is true. "If an animal is a swan, it is not white, and if an animal is not a swan, it is not white; that is, whether or not an animal is a swan, it is not white."

10. Similarly, the combination $(\bar{p} \cdot q) \vee (\bar{p} \cdot \bar{q})$, or $(A' \times B) + (A' \times B')$, states that p is false whether or not q is true. "If an animal is not a swan, it is white, and if an animal is not a swan it is not white; that is, whether or not the animal is white, it is not a swan."

11. This combination is the first of the four associations with three terms: $(p \cdot q) \vee (p \cdot \bar{q}) \vee (\bar{p} \cdot q)$, or $(A \times B) + (A \times B') + (A' \times B)$. Here either p or q is true, or both are true. "Either this animal is a swan, whether white or not white; this animal is white, whether or not a swan; or this animal is a swan and this animal is white."

12. This combination consists of $(p \cdot q) \vee (p \cdot \bar{q}) \vee (\bar{p} \cdot \bar{q})$, or $(A \times B) + (A \times B') + (A' \times B')$. It states that if q is true then p is true, but if q is false, p may be either true or false. "If this animal is white, it is also a swan; if this animal is not white, it may or may not be a swan."

13. The combination $(p \cdot q) \vee (\bar{p} \cdot q) \vee (\bar{p} \cdot \bar{q})$, or $(A \times B) + (A' \times B) + (A' \times B')$, is the converse of 12: If p is true than q is true, but if p is false, q may be either true or false. "If this animal is a

swan, it is also white; but if it is not a swan, it may be either white or not white."

14. Here the combination is $(p \cdot \bar{q}) \vee (\bar{p} \cdot q) \vee (\bar{p} \cdot \bar{q})$, or $(A \times B') + (A' \times B) + (A' \times B')$. It states that either p or q is false, or both are false. "This animal is a swan and not white, or it is not a swan and is white, or it is neither a swan nor white."

15. This is a combination of all four propositions: $(p \cdot q) \vee (p \cdot \bar{q}) \vee (\bar{p} \cdot q) \vee (\bar{p} \cdot \bar{q})$, or $(A \times B) + (A \times B') + (A' \times B) + (A' \times B')$. Here, the statement is that p and q are not related, so all four possibilities occur. "This animal is a swan and is white; or it is a swan and is not white; or it is not a swan and is white; or it is not a swan and is not white.

16. The final combination (sometimes listed as the first), is $(p \cdot \bar{q}) \vee (p \cdot \bar{q}) \vee (\bar{p} \cdot q) \vee (\bar{p} \cdot \bar{q})$. In this case, none of the possibilities occur. "There are no animals which are swans or which are white, nor any combination of these."

Now it is unlikely that the preadolescent or the adolescent consciously applies this system, nor does he "write down the formula for the number of all possible combinations."[21] Rather, he intuitively engages in use of the operations of implication (if-then), disjunction (either-or, or both), exclusion (either-or, or neither-neither), reciprocal implication, and so on.

The major experiment involving the combinatorial system consists of placing before the child four bottles of colorless liquids, plus a smaller bottle with a dropper. The first four bottles contain, respectively, (1) dilute sulfuric acid, (2) water, (3) oxygenated water, and (4) thiosulphate. The fifth, smaller bottle, labeled g, contains potassium iodide. Oxygenated water oxidizes potassium chloride in an acid medium: $(1 + 3 + g)$ will yield a yellow liguid. The addition of (4) will neutralize the color, while the adition of (2) does not change it.

The experimenter then presents the child with two glasses, one containing dilute sulphuric acid and oxygenated water $(1 + 3)$ and the other water (2). With the child watching, he adds a few drops from bottle g to the contents of each glass, so that the combined liquid from 1 and 3 turns yellow. He then asks the child to reproduce the yellow color, using liquids from the four larger bottles and bottle g.

The concrete-operational child does not respond unsystematically, as does the preoperational child. But he does not proceed as systematically as does the child at the level of formal operations. Compare the two following approaches:

REN (7 years, 1 month) tries $4 \times g$ then $2 \times g$ then $1 \times g$. "*I think I did everything; I tried them all.*"—"What else could you have done?"— "*I don't know.*" We give him the glasses again; he repeats $1 \times g$ and so forth. "You took each bottle separately; what else could you have done?"—*"Take two bottles at the same time."* (He tries $1 \times 4 \times g$, then $2 \times 3 \times g$, thus failing to cross over between the two sets of bottles, for example 1×2, 1×3, 2×4, and 3×4.—When we suggest that he add others, he puts $1 \times g$ in the glass already containing 2×3 which results in the appearance of the color: "Try to make the color again."—*"Do I put in two or three?"* (He tries with $2 \times 4 \times g$, then adds 3, then tries it with $1 \times 4 \times 2 \times g$.) "No, I don't remember any more."[22]

SAR (12 years, 3 months) "Make me some yellow." *Do you make the liquid from the yellow glass with all four?"*—"I won't tell you." (He tries first $4 \times 2 \times g$, then $2 \times g \times 4 \times g$.) "Not yet." (He tries to smell the odor of liquids, then tries $4 \times 1 \times g$.)—*"No yellow yet, quite a big mystery!"* (He tries the four, then each one independently with g; then he spontaneously proceeds to various two by two combinations but has the feeling he forgot some of them.) *"I better write it down to remind myself: 1×4 is done; 4×3 is done; and 2×3; several more that I haven't done."* (He finds all six, then adds the drops, then finds the yellow from 1 and 3 and g.) *"Ah, it's turning yellow. You need one and three and the drops."*—"Where is the yellow?" No answer. "In there?" Pointing to g.—*"No, they go together."* "And two?" *"I don't think it has any effect, it's water."*—"And 4?"—*"It doesn't do anything either; it's water too. But I want to try again, you can't ever be too sure."* (He tries $2 \times 4 \times g$.) *"Give me a glass of water."* (He takes it from the faucet and mixes $3 \times 1 \times$ water $\times g$, that is, the combination which gave him the color, plus water from the faucet, knowing that $1 \times 2 \times 3 \times 4 \times g$ produces nothing.) *"No, it isn't water. Maybe it's a substance that keeps it from coloring.* (He puts together $1 \times 3 \times 2 \times g$, then $1 \times 4 \times g$.) *"Ah, there it is, that one (4) keeps it from coloring."* "And that?" (2)— "It's water."[23]

These protocols illustrate, in part, the process of formal thinking involving the 16 binary operations. The essential characteristics consist of (1) determining all the possibilities inherent in the problem, (2) determining all those that actually exist, and (3) determining the causal structure implied by these actualities.

The determination of causation is facilitated when the child can not only use *negation* or *inversion*—that is, the removal of one variable to determine its influence or lack of influence—but can also use *reciprocity*, which is the neutralization of a variable by holding it constant. This ability is shown by the actions of the adolescent in the pendulum problem. The child is presented with a weight hanging from a string. The problem requires the child to discover whether it is length, height, or force, alone or in combination which determines the frequency of oscillation when the weight is given a push. To test the effect of weight, the adolescent will vary weight while holding the length of the string constant, and to test the effect of length, will vary the length of the string while holding the weight constant. (The other factors, of course, must also be held constant while the effect of length of string and weight are tested.)

The INRC group. The INRC group, or four-group, is a mathematical group whose elements consist of four transformations. Its properties can be exemplified in different systems; one involves the propositional operations summarized above.

The *identity* transformation is a *null* transformation and does nothing to change a proposition: For instance, the transformation $I(p \cdot \bar{q}) = p \cdot \bar{q}$.

Negation reverses everything in the proposition to which it is applied: Assertions become negations, conjunctions become disjunctions, and vice versa: For example, $N(p \vee q) = \bar{p} \cdot \bar{q}$, and $N(p \cdot q) = \bar{p} \vee \bar{q}$. The study of the development of the concept of inertia illustrates the transformation. A subject is presented with a situation in which balls of various sizes, weights, and volumes are released to run down a track or alley, and is asked to predict where they will stop. He or she succeeds in identifying factors which cause the ball to stop—air resistance, friction, or irregularities on the surface of the balls or track. If the subject wonders what would happen if all these factors were removed, he or she may conclude that the ball would not stop—which is the concept of inertia. The conclusion is reached by negation, that is, by reversing the statement that friction, air resistance, and so forth, lead to or imply stopping. This reasoning is not dependent on manipulation or observation, since inertia is a theoretical concept; it is a statement about the possible, the ideal, not the real.

Reciprocity transforms assertions and negations, leaving conjunctions and disjunctions unchanged. Thus $R(p \vee q) = \bar{p} \vee \bar{q}$, and $R(\bar{p} \vee \bar{q}) = p \vee q$. Reciprocity has already been illustrated in the situation where the child recognizes that length can be compensated for by density in the case of conservation. In the pendulum problem, also, the length of the string compensates for weight, and vice versa; the two variables reciprocate each other.

The *correlative* transformation changes conjunction to disjunction, and vice versa, but leaves assertions and negations unchanged. Thus $C(p \vee q)$ becomes $p \cdot q$, and $C(\bar{p} \cdot \bar{q}) = \bar{p} \vee \bar{q}$.

It is negation and reciprocity, which are two kinds of reversibility, that are the most significant transformations. At the period of formal operations, they are utilized at a higher level than earlier. Rather than operating at a concrete level in the manipulation of actual objects, as exhibited by children at the concrete-operational level, these transformations operate on an abstract level of logical thought. Adolescents functioning at the level of formal operations do of course engage in behaviors which involve the manipulation of objects, but they also become increasingly capable of transformation of propositions.

The INRC group combines with the lattice of binary operations to provide a model of adolescent cognition. It seems to represent one other important component of cognitive organization; not, however, independent of the binary system, though the interrelationships are not entirely clear. Both bring into equilibrium elements of the concrete-operational period; the binary model integrates concrete-operational groupings, and the INRC model integrates negation-reciprocal operations.

Conclusion. Adolescents are capable of functioning at a higher cognitive level than younger children, though they may not (indeed probably do not or could not) continually function at the highest level of which they are capable. There are of course individual differences, and the age at which a particular level of functioning is achieved varies. At this highest stage, also, some individuals, because of genetic or other limitations, may never reach the level which others, the more gifted, achieve.

There are several major characteristics of adolescent thought, which are advancements over concrete-operational thought. Adolescents are able to transcend actuality or reality and to think about the possible, that is, to entertain hypotheses. They are able to conceptualize the various possibilities inherent in a problem situation. They are then able to develop ways of testing the hypothesis or to determine which of several possibilities are actualities, doing this either by actual manipulation of objects or data, or by logical analysis. They proceed to test hypotheses in a logical manner, following the general process of holding all variables but one constant, to test the influence of that variable and to test whether one or another variable alone and/or in combination with others produces a given result, and other causal hypotheses.

In addition to these major characteristics, adolescents are flexible in their thinking, being able to look at a problem from different points of view. This is manifested in lack of egocentrism. The important characteristic of reversibility is a reflection of this flexibility. The social idealism of adolescents is an aspect of their ability to transcend reality. They may even appear at times to lose touch with reality. Piaget speaks of this as a form of cognitive egocentrism, related to the adolescent's belief in the unlimited power of her or his own thoughts.

The adolescent, like the child, lives in the present, but also, unlike the child, lives in the future, harboring ideas, theories, hypotheses, and plans relating to the future. This future involves occupational and marital choices, which become areas of concern. The adolescent recognizes that the future will take him or her beyond immediate family and friends, and bring involvement in occupational or professional groups and other organizations, including city, state, national and international institutions. Thus, formal operations can be applied to everyday problems of life: "Logic is not isolated from life; it is no more than the expression of operational coordinations essential to action."[24]

It is not too clear how the child moves from the concrete-operational period to the equilibrium of the period of formal operations. It appears that the same four factors underlying all development, listed earlier (p. 72), are involved. These include neurological development or maturation, individual experience, the social environment, and the activities of the child. While concrete operations are being perfected, their shortcomings become apparent, and the child searches for new methods of dealing with the world and the problems which it presents.

This suggests a possible weakness, or incompleteness, in Piaget's system. For if the results of development are homogeneous among all human beings, there must be not only a common genetic or neurological base, but also a common experiential base. Certain regularities in development, particularly the relation of formal operations to the scientific method, may be limited to a particular culture, such as Western civilization. Piaget recognizes the direct influence of the social environment in transmitting knowledge to the child; what is transmitted may be quite different in different cultures. Yet it may be questioned if, and to what extent, the basic concepts and operations of concrete and formal thought are transmitted or taught in our society. It is possible that these cognitive concepts and structures have some (universal) genetic basis that results in their development as a maturational process. However, Piaget places major emphasis upon the process of equilibration; and this process, involving recurring periods of experiences of conflict and contradiction leading to higher levels of equilibrium, is closely dependent upon social factors and social interaction.

A second possible incompleteness of Piaget's system, noted by Ginsburg and Opper,[25] is the limitation of the binary logical model. This model has the advantage of dealing with nonnumerical statements, that is, dichotomies such as short or long, heavy or light, white or black, presence or absence. But there are many situations involving more than two elements, and more than two values. It would appear, however, that theoretically the system could be extended to accommodate such data.

Summary: The Nature of Intellectual Development

Piaget has devoted his life to studying the origins and nature of intellect. His approach, however, has been quite different from that of American and English psychologists, who have focused upon statistical analyses of responses to standardized objective tests.

Trained in biology, Piaget views intelligence as an aspect of biological adaptation, which enables the individual to interact with his environment. This interaction tends toward a state of equilibrium: The individual attempts to achieve a balance between the complementary aspects of the process of adaptation (assimilation and accommodation). During his development, temporary states of equilibrium are achieved, only to be followed by disequilibrium and succeeded by a higher level of equilibrium, until adolescence, when the highest level is reached.

In the process of development the individual is an active participant, not a passive organism acted upon by the environment. Intelligence consists of a system of actions, mainly overt in the infant and young child and becoming covert, in the form of mental operations, as the child grows older.

Although recognizing the existence of individual differences, Piaget has concentrated upon the general aspects of the development of cognition. Piaget does not describe an average level of cognitive functioning, but represents optimal capability at different periods of development. He thus does not measure the performances of large samples of children at different ages. Rather, he focuses upon the intensive study, through observation and the clinical method, of a few subjects.

Piaget's research has led him to delineate three major periods in intellectual development. The first is the sensorimotor period, from birth to 2 years, which is further divided into six stages. This period is characterized by the development of the sensorimotor foundation of cognitive functioning and the beginnings of thought. The second period, that of preparation for and organization of concrete operations, consists of two subperiods, the preoperational subperiod (age 2 through 7) and the subperiod of concrete operations (age 7 through 11). The first subperiod is characterized by the development of the symbolic function, which enables the child to represent objects and events by means of symbols—words and images. The concrete-operational subperiod is characterized by development of an integrated and cohesive cognitive system with which the child is able to deal with the world. The system is limited, however, to dealing with concrete objects in the present, the here and now. Toward the end of this subperiod, the child begins to extend his thought from the actual to the potential. The period of formal operations sees the child—now becoming the adolescent—achieving the ability to free himself from the concrete and the actual and to deal with the abstract and the possible, following the model of the hypotheticodeductive method of science.

These periods and subperiods and their stages are not discrete, of course, but constitute a continuum. The ages are approximate and vary, of course, with individuals and cultures. Although Piaget's major focus is on cognitive development, he recognizes other aspects of human development—the affective, the interpersonal, and the area of values and morals. These are all interrelated and are also related to cognition, however, and their development can be viewed in the same framework or structure as cognitive development, including the delineation of periods and stages. Piaget's theoretical system is capable of being extended to encompass the whole of human development.

IMPLICATIONS FOR EDUCATION AND TEACHING

We have now completed the summary of Piaget's theory of cognitive development. Clearly, it is impossible to represent 50 years of research and writing, comprising some 30 volumes, in a few pages. This poses a very difficult problem in considering the implications and applications of the theory for education and teaching. There have been a number of books about Piaget directed to teachers. Most of them, however, have consisted almost entirely of a summary of aspects of Piaget's work, with only a few general comments on its relation to education and teaching.

An adequate summary of Piaget's work would require several volumes, and only such an extensive summary could serve as a basis for its detailed and specific application to education. Without such a summary and an extensive consideration of applications to education, the individual teacher would need to immerse himself or herself in Piaget's major writings to attain the necessary understanding for applying the theory or system. An alternative to such individual study would be the development of a whole curriculum by curriculum experts who were also experts on Piaget. This approach is particularly appropriate and necessary in regard to Piaget, as compared to the other scholars presented in this book, because Piaget's work is relevant not only to methods but also to the structure and organization of the actual content of education. In particular, a thorough familiarity with Piaget would be necessary in determining the grade placement of instructional content.

Ginsburg and Opper facetiously describe what might happen if a curriculum incorporating content from Piaget were developed at the preschool level. They write: "Consider the absurd situation that would result if traditional schools were entrusted with teaching the infant what he spontaneously learns during the first few years. The schools would develop organized curricula in secondary circular reactions; they would develop lesson plans for object permanence; they would construct audio-visual aids on causality; they would reinforce 'correct' speech; and they would set 'goals' for each child each week. One can speculate as to the outcome of such a program for early training!"[26]

While it might be possible to incorporate the content of Piaget's work into such a curriculum, it would of course be inconsistent with the implications of his work for teaching methods. It illustrates a danger in attempting to develop curriculums based on or derived from Piaget. This is the tendency of curriculums to become rigid and prescriptive, limiting teachers rather than freeing them to respond to children and situations. A ready-made curriculum is inconsistent with Piaget's open system of investigation. The introduction of kits of materials for teachers interested in the Piagetian approach could also lead to a restrictive technique, which is again inconsistent with Piaget's theory and philosophy.

The task of developing the implications for curriculums of Piaget's work is one which should be undertaken, but it is not possible to do this here—even if the writer were competent to do so—because of lack of space. It is also more appropriate in terms of the nature of this book to limit our concern to the implications for teaching methods and practice.[27]

The Purpose of and Need for Education
According to Piaget,

> "the principle goal of education is to create men who are capable of doing new things, not simply repeating what other generations have done—men who are creative, inventive, and discoverers. The second goal of education is to form minds which can be critical, can verify, and not accept everything they are offered. The great danger today is of slogans, collective opinions, ready-made trends of thought. We have to be able to resist individually, to criticize, to distinguish what is proven and what is not. So we need pupils who are active, who learn early to find out by themselves, partly by their own spontaneous activity and partly through material set up for them; who learn early to tell what is verified and what is simply the first idea to come to them."[28]

This process is essentially the acquisition of the basic tools of logic or the methods of logical thinking.[29]

Education is necessary because logical thinking is not innate. Education cannot, therefore, be limited to the transmission of information or knowledge; it must be concerned with the development of logical thinking. Education is "a necessary formative condition toward natural development itself. . . . The individual would not know how to acquire his most basic mental structures without some external influences. . . . On all levels the social or educational factor constitutes a condition for development."[30]

Intellectual development is not the same as learning. Learning is the acquisition of information and knowledge; intelligence provides, or is, the structure which is the basis of learning. The process of intellectual growth results in changes in the structure which make possible increasingly mature and abstract thinking. Intelligence develops naturally, or spontaneously, in a good general environment—functioning leads to or assures development. Intellectual development consists of the development of general concepts—of objects, of classes, of relations, of logic, and so on. Learning involves specifics, providing the information and knowledge upon which intelligence operates. Learning thus depends upon special experiences. Thus, while in a natural environment the structure of the intellect develops from within, utilizing the environment as raw material, in our society education is important to provide adequate opportunity and relevant specifics or content. There are some things and experiences in our complex modern world to which children are not normally exposed, and which they cannot spontaneously assimilate. Opportunities and experiences must be available for developing cognitive structures. But the school must be concerned with more than providing facts and information. Geographical, historical, and sociological facts have no meaning unless the child has a comprehension of spatial, temporal, and social relations. The development of these concepts, as well as others, such as number and causality, must be the concern of education also.

The idea that education should be concerned with the development of the ability to think is perhaps not new with Piaget, but it has not generally been implemented in curriculums, though it is at least implicit in attempts to apply Piaget to instruction in science and mathematics. Furth and Wachs, however, have made it the explicit goal.[31] They have developed a series of games, exercises, and activities for children aged 5 through 7, in kindergarten through the third grade, designed to help them learn to think. The activities begin with general movement thinking and continue with discriminative movement thinking, visual thinking games, auditory thinking games, hand-thinking games, and graphic thinking games, until finally logical-thinking games and social-thinking games are introduced. They are not subject-matter- or content-oriented; they provide the foundation for dealing successfully with academic subjects.

Education is not limited to cognitive or intellectual development. Quoting Article 26 of the Universal Declaration of Human Rights adopted by the General Assembly of the United Nations on December 10, 1948, that "education shall be directed to the full development of the human personality and to the strengthening of respect for human rights and fundamental freedoms," Piaget recognizes the need for education to encompass morals and ethics.[32] Such education enables the child to move from an egocentric centering upon self to a decentering of activity and the formation of reciprocal relationships with others, a process which involves being able to see the point of view of others. The most important indirect goal of education is to prepare individuals to take an active, intelligent part in improving life in society.

The Child is Not a Miniature Adult

Piaget's work clearly shows the differences in the thinking of the child at different age levels, and the differences between this thinking and the mature (formal) level of the adult. These differences are not simply quantitative—they are qualitative. While the *function* of mental activity (the achievement of adaptation and equilibrium) is the same at all ages, the *structure* (the methods and operations) is different. The child literally lives in a different world. This is epitomized in the titles of several of Piaget's books: *The Child's Conception of . . .* Children's concepts are different from those of adults, and while they learn to use the same words that adults use, these words may have different meanings for each of them. Thus, material presented by the teacher in verbal, or even visual, form may not be apprehended as desired by the teacher. It is changed or reduced by the child to a form which he or she can assimilate, since the child is unable to accommodate to it as given. To the adult this change is distortion, and the child is considered to be deficient in some respect. But the child really believes what he hears or sees—he cannot do otherwise.

The child of 7 or 8 and older recognizes, as do adults, that if two glasses of different shapes, A and B, contain the same quantity of water, and if another glass C also contains the same amount as B, then the amounts in A and C are equal, even though C is much different in shape than A or B. "On the other hand, according to children from four to five years old, there is no reason to admit that amounts A and C are equal when it has been said that A equals B and B equals C, and there is no decisive reason that the water remains the same although it changes containers."[33] But the child who recognizes the equality of water (quantity) may not accept equality of weight when the shape of one of two balls of clay of identical size and weight is altered. And the older child who does recognize the equivalence of weight may not accept the equivalence of volume in similar experiments.

Piaget discusses the difficulties arising in teaching mathematics when "the development of the spontaneous mathematical intelligence of the young child and the adolescent" is not recognized. He points out that when problems are posed not as mathematical problems, but as concrete problems involving rules, proportions, and other concrete operations, they are solved on the basis of general intelligence. He notes that "students are frequently found who, though mediocre in lessons of arithmetic, prove to have a comprehensive or even inventive spirit when the problems are posed in relation to any activity that interests them. . . . [But] they often remain passive and often even blocked in the school situation that consists of resolving problems in the abstract (that is, without relation to an actual need). Above all, they remain convinced of their inadequacy and give up beforehand, inwardly considering themselves defeated. . . . Every normal student is capable of mathematical reasoning if attention is directed to activities of his interest, and if by this method the emotional inhibitions that too often give him a feeling of inferiority in lessons in this area are removed. In most mathematical lessons the whole difference lies in the fact that the student is asked to accept from outside an already organized intellectual discipline which he may or may not understand. . . ."[34]

Piaget suggests that "if mathematics teachers would only take the trouble to learn about the 'natural' psychogenetic development of the logico-mathematical operations, they would see that there exists a much greater similarity than one would expect between the principal operations spontaneously employed by the child and the notions they attempt to instill into him abstractly."[35] It is necessary to recognize the nature of the development of thinking, from sensorimotor activity through concrete operations to abstract thinking. In each subject-matter area, the educational process should begin at the motor action level and proceed to the abstract level. The failure of teachers to do this in teaching mathematics is the source of much of the difficulty older children have in this area.

It is not easy for the adult, functioning at the stage of formal operations, to understand the child's world or his method of thinking. The adult must be capable of reciprocity with the child, that is, of placing himself in the position of the child—of being empathic, to use a term from another system of psychology. The basis for this should be present in the adult, since, as Piaget has emphasized, each new stage of intellectual development incorporates, and thus retains, the earlier stages. It is probably necessary for the adult to refresh his memory of his earlier cognitive functioning, however. The teacher who is dealing with subject matter related to any of the areas studied by Piaget could benefit by reading his work. The protocols recording the performances and responses of children at various stages of development would be very helpful to anyone interested in developing an understanding of the way the child functions at these stages.

An understanding of the stages of cognitive development must be combined with knowledge of the stage at which a particular student is functioning, if teaching is to be related to the students' level. Since the age levels assigned to the stages and periods or subperiods are only approximate, it cannot be assumed that a child of a particular chronological age is operating at a particular level. As a result of the wide range of individual differences, each child is functioning at a slightly different level than any other child. The teacher needs some way to determine at what level each child is functioning. School psy-

chologists, if properly trained, could ascertain this. Teachers could also
be trained to make such evaluations. The process of doing this would
be extremely time consuming; it would involve testing each child repeatedly across numerous physical and logical concepts such as relations, classifications, objects, number, space, time, causality, and so on,
since a child can be at somewhat different levels in each area. Perhaps
an alternative, suggested by Montessori's work, is the use of Piaget's
problems and experiments as a means of assessment and, at the same
time, for teaching or instructional purposes. The child would interact
with the materials at the level of which he or she was capable, and
would not be pushed to function at a higher level. The problems or
situations would be presented again later—or be available for use—
when the child might be ready to interact with them at a higher level.
In any attempt at evaluation, a thorough understanding of Piaget's
work and of the difference between the methods of evaluation appropriate to his system and the standard intelligence test is necessary.

There have been some attempts to develop ways to measure cognitive development in terms of Piaget's theory and research. Pinard
and Laurendeau, and Tuddenham, have been experimenting with the
development of scales of mental development based upon Piaget;
and Tanaka, Campbell, and Helmick have prepared some written exercises designed to give first-grade teachers an estimate of the child's
cognitive ability upon entrance to the first grade.[36]

This approach, however, may be inappropriate. The child cannot
be placed at a general level of functioning similar to that suggested by
an IQ score. And not only does the child's performance, or stage, vary
from area to area, but it fluctuates within the same area from time to
time as development progresses and ebbs in the early stage of a change
in cognitive structure. Stages and substages refer to the developmental
process in its various aspects or strands, not to the child himself. Thus,
Furth and Wachs state that "Piaget's theory is not consistent with a
diagnostic prescriptive approach to education where the weaknesses
of the child are systematically explored, nor does it encourage a premature emphasis upon achievement; rather it allows the teacher to accept and nourish at appropriate times what is positive and best in every
child, namely his capacity for further intellectual development."[37] In
their School for Thinking, Furth and Wachs provide series of tasks,
each progressing through Piaget's stages. The children are free to
perform each of them at their own level or stage of functioning on that
task. The child is not labeled as "preoperational" or "operational."

The recognition of the uniqueness of each individual child implies
that each child ideally should receive individualized instruction. But
this clearly is impossible in any system of universal education. Grouping is commonly used in every current educational system, although
there are arguments regarding homogeneous versus heterogeneous

grouping within grade levels. Involved in the problem of grouping is the relevance of the criteria on which grouping is based. Piaget's work provides a criterion which may be more appropriate than existing criteria.

However, it is a fact, as will be noted later, that interaction with others who are at slightly different cognitive levels stimulates learning. This suggests that some heterogeneity is desirable, as Montessori also found.

The development of tests incorporating Piaget's concepts and experiments could provide a basis for evaluating a child's level of cognitive development in order to determine readiness for particular levels of instruction, for grade placement or assignment, and for remedial programs.

Learning Is Activity

It will be remembered that Piaget equates cognition with action. During infancy the child operates upon or manipulates objects in his environment. This overt motor activity is the child's method of adapting to his environment, and it thus qualifies as intelligence. Later, the child's activity becomes increasingly covert, involving the mental manipulation of symbols. But in both instances, actions are involved, and overt actions precede and are necessary foundations for covert mental actions.

The individual is not a passive receptacle into which knowledge is poured. Nor is he or she simply a reactive system, responding to the environment or specific stimuli. Neither is learning simply maturation, or the unfolding of innate capacities. It is rather an interaction of the individual with the environment. The learner must therefore be an active participant. Assimilation and accommodation and equilibration are active processes which are inherent in the individual and lead to learning or cognitive development. Thinking is the natural, normal activity of the organism.

Piaget advocates what he calls an active method of education, which places stress on the spontaneous aspects of the child's activities. These methods "give broad scope to the spontaneous research of the child or adolescent and require that every new truth to be learned be rediscovered or at least reconstructed by the student, and not simply imparted to him. . . . To understand is to discover, or reconstruct by rediscovery, and such conditions must be complied with if in future individuals are to be formed who are capable of production and creativity and not simply repetition."[38] The teacher is not a lecturer, but a mentor, stimulating research and reflection. Information or knowledge acquired passively is not retained. "A student who achieves a certain knowledge through free investigation and spontaneous effort will later be able to retain it; he will have acquired a methodology that can serve him for the rest of his life, which will stimulate his curiosity without the risk of exhausting it."[39] Piaget states that research supports active methods of learning.

The difficulties students encounter in learning mathematics are related to nonactive methods of teaching. The use of an abstract, special language consisting of symbols removes mathematics from its relation to concrete objects. But while abstraction is a goal, it is the end result of a continuous series of concrete actions. "Mathematics is, first of all, and most importantly, actions exercised on things, and the operations themselves are more actions, but well coordinated among themselves and only imagined instead of being materially executed."[40] Instruction in mathematics should begin at the preschool level, with exercises related to concrete activities, and should progress to physical and mechanical experiments in secondary school, before mathematical abstractions are presented. All mathematical ideas, says Piaget, "begin by a qualitative construction before acquiring a metrical character."[41]

Active learning involves interaction with other students as well as with the teacher. "No real intellectual activity could be carried out in the form of experimental actions and spontaneous investigations without free collaboration among individuals—that is to say, among the students themselves, and not only between the teacher and the student."[42] Active learning thus involves cooperation and collaboration and working in groups as well as individually, rather than isolated, competitive study to prepare for an examination.

Interaction with others leads to the recognition or creation of conflicts, ambiguities, and questions, resulting from the different levels at which children are functioning and the different ways they see or perceive. The realization of the existence of such differences arises in part from the ability to see things from another's point of view, and this realization also facilitates the development of this ability, an important aspect of cognitive development, as well as of social development.

The active learning of Piaget is similar to what has been called inquiry learning and discovery learning by others. It is not applicable to all areas; Piaget notes that neither Latin nor history can be reinvented, and the teaching of these subjects consists of transmission. Other subjects, such as mathematics and physics, consist of truths that do not depend on society or opinion but on research and experimentation. The discovery method is particularly appropriate in the sciences, though not by the usual method of having students "do experiments" following detailed instructions, but by students making spontaneous explorations as they become interested and ready to experiment. Even the method of transmission, however, requires some activity on the part of the student—rather than passive reception and repetition—if learning is to take place; even assimilation involves a reconstruction or a reinvention, according to Piaget. As to the possibility that such learning is slow and inefficient, Piaget states that "learning to master the truth by oneself is a goal of education worth the risk of losing a lot of time and of going through all the roundabout ways that are inherent in real activity."[43] Piaget asks whether a truth is really assimilated or learned unless it is reconstructed or rediscovered through appropriate activity. Much if not most of the early learning of the child is probably discovery learning, a trait which may be related to its stability and persistence. In the case of the school-age child, much of the important learning occurring outside the school is also discovery learning.

The active learning which Piaget writes about is not activity stimulated by the teacher. The interest of the child is not the stimulated interest which the "good" teacher is supposed to arouse. Activity and interest are not the result of motivation induced somehow by the teacher. They are inherent in the child and are spontaneously expressed when instruction is appropriate for a child's level of development.

Providing appropriate instruction, involving the child in activities related to his or her level of development, is a difficult problem for the teacher. Certainly lecturing would appear to be inappropriate for students in the concrete-operational period. The use of audiovisual aids is criticized by Piaget. Although they may depict people involved in activities, the viewer is still passive and, at best, can engage only vicariously in activity. Demonstrations by the teacher similarly do not involve actual actions by the student. Materials and equipment must be provided for the student to act upon. The activities should include transformations: associativity, reversibility, reciprocity, as appropriate. And overt actions should be internalized, or transformed into mental operations.

Adaptation, Equilibrium, and Motivation

The function of intellect is to achieve equilibrium by adaptation, or a balance between assimilation and accommodation. Equilibrium is not static, however, but dynamic; it is constantly being disturbed by environmental stimuli and demands. These stimuli and demands can range from those which can be assimilated to the individual's present structure with no changes in the structure (that is, without accommodation being necessary) to those which overwhelm the individual and which are beyond his ability to accommodate to. In neither of these extreme cases does learning occur. In one case the discrepancy between the new situation and the cognitive structure is too small. The situation does not present inconsistencies or incongruities requiring resolution. It is not novel enough to stimulate interest or motivation leading to action. It is not necessary for the individual to do anything about the situation—it is assimilated without requiring any accommodation. In the other case, the discrepancy is too great. The situation presents too much novelty; it is beyond the power of the individual to deal with, or to relate to his cognitive structure. Learning thus requires a situation presenting an optimal discrepancy or novelty.

When, according to Piaget, an optimal discrepancy between the individual's present cognitive structure and a new situation exists, interest is aroused, and the individual is motivated to act to reduce the discrepancy, to accommodate to the situation, and to reestablish equilibrium at a higher level of thinking. Such motivation is intrinsic, leading to learning which occurs without external reinforcement.

The concept of optimal discrepancy is similar to what Hunt calls the "problem of the match,"[44] and the distinction of Combs and Snygg between a situation which is challenging and one which is threatening.[45] The difficulty of determining the level of discrepancy, the degree of the match, or the balance between challenge and threat is obvious. This discrepancy is more specific than the stage of development of the child, being different for every situation. It is here that individualized instruction would appear to be necessary if optimum learning is to occur.

The question of accelerating cognitive development by utilizing Piaget's work has been raised, particularly in America, where speed and efficiency are so highly valued. Piaget asks and answers this question: "Should passage from one stage of development be accelerated or not? To be sure all education, in one way or another, is just such an acceleration, but it remains to be decided to what extent it is beneficial. It is not without significance that it takes man much longer to reach maturity than other animals. Consequently, it is highly probable that there is an optimum rate of development, to exceed or fall behind which would be equally harmful. But we do not know its laws, and on this point as well it will be up to future research to enlighten us."[46]

Thus, there would appear to be limits to acceleration. Piaget stresses that every child must pass through all the stages, and cannot skip or omit any. Each stage builds upon and incorporates all the preceding stages. The level or stage at which the child is functioning limits what he is capable of learning. Thus, certain things cannot be taught or learned at a particular level regardless of the effort expended or the method used. For example, the principle of inertia cannot be comprehended by a child who has not reached the necessary level of development. This would seem to contradict Bruner's dictum that "any idea or problem or body of knowledge can be presented in a form simple enough so that any particular learner can understand it in recognizable form."[47]

The recognition of stages in intellectual development is relevant to the concept of readiness in learning. Learning of information by children when they are not ready is rote learning, that is, meaningless learning. Such learning is not retained. Meaningful learning is learning for which the intellectual structure is ready. Such learning is retained, as long as it is used, and the concept of memory is not necessary or relevant in explaining why it is retained, in the same way that the concept of motivation is unnecessary in explaining the learning in the first place. Attempting to force learning when the structure of intellectual development is not adequate may lead to rote learning, but it may also result in a child's lack of interest in meaningful learning at a later time, when the intellect has developed to the stage where meaningful learning can occur.

The sequential nature of cognitive development, progressing from sensorimotor activities to concrete-operational manipulation of objects to abstract manipulation of ideas or concepts, makes clear the importance of an adequate educational environment at every stage of development. It is true that the general intellectual or cognitive concepts studied by Piaget—concepts of space, time, number, causality, and so on—develop without formal education in a good, or ideal, environment. But the normal, everyday environment of most children is not an ideal or even a good, environment. It is becoming more and more restricted in an urban technological society moving away from nature. Therefore, the importance of the formal educational environment of the school is of great importance, particularly at the earlier ages. Inadequate educational or learning experiences in the earlier stages affect learning and development in later stages, as is particularly apparent, according to Piaget, in mathematics.

Language and Intellectual Development

Language or speech—verbalization or verbal ability— is not the essence or core of intelligence. This conclusion, derived from Piaget's work, may be surprising to many American teachers and educators. Intelligence is usually considered to be verbal intelligence. As a result of this, early education focuses upon language—the teaching of reading and writing. But, as Piaget has shown, the intellect begins to develop before language or speech is possible; thus the development of intellect does not depend upon language. Language is one of the means (mathematics is another) of expressing the operations of thinking. Earlier, language is tied to personal or concrete experiences or objects, and the child is not capable of manipulating words as abstract symbols in thinking. Language is essentially a means of communication and socialization, conveying information and feelings.

If thinking does not depend upon language, then it is not necessary for the child to be able to read or write or to be proficient in language in order to think. Early education should emphasize thinking rather than reading and writing, since early cognitive development is based upon figurative (imitative, pictorial, reproductive) and concrete knowing. Listening to children learning to read in the classroom clearly illustrates the figurative nature of the activity; words are read mechanically with no real understanding of their meaning. Language can be learned without comprehension. Furth points out that emphasis upon reading and writing in the first years of school interferes with the development of thinking.[48] Furth provides materials for teaching logical thinking to children in grades three to five, "sufficient for a symbol-logic course, two periods a week, throughout the school years."[49] The materials are nonverbal (using symbol-picture logic). He also describes other thinking games appropriate for children in the concrete-operational period. Reading instruction becomes appropriate when the child shows spontaneous interest in books and in using their contents in concrete-operative or early operative thinking.

Examinations

Piaget raises a number of questions about examinations. A basic question is the relevance of what is being tested. If education is concerned with learning how to think rather than with the acquisition of information or knowledge, then examinations which measure the latter are irrelevant.

Secondly, he questions the persistence of the information or knowledge demonstrated in examinations. We don't know, he says, what remains of the knowledge after several years, or if, when the specific knowledge is forgotten, anything else remains. The evidence seems to indicate clearly that facts and information acquired by rote learning are not retained for very long. If this is all that is learned, then nothing remains.

Thirdly, he points to the vicious circle created when teaching is influenced by the nature of the examinations. Examinations which emphasize information and knowledge are harmful "simply because they polarize around the pursuit of ephemeral and largely artificial results the majority of activities that ought to be concentrated upon the formation of the intelligence and good working methods. . . ." Furthermore, they emphasize memory, "a kind of memory that has no relation, generally speaking, to that which is employed consciously in life, since it is, in fact, no more than a deliberate and ephemeral accumulation, in other words, a mental artifact."[50] Memorization in the child is like the learning of nonsense syllables by college students in psychology experiments as far as meaningful learning is concerned.

Fourthly, he notes the undesirable emotional effects which examinations have on children.

Piaget suggests two other methods of evaluation of students. The first is the long-term observation of the students' work by the teacher.

He recognizes that such evaluations are influenced by the teacher's subjectivity and partiality, but still considers them superior to examinations. He favors the avoidance of grades or numerical evaluations which are "pseudo-mathematical." In addition, he feels that such evaluation over a period of time is only meaningful where active methods of education are used, so that the full abilities of students are manifested.

The second method, which Piaget feels would be acceptable if emotional elements of pressure and stress could be eliminated, is the use of open-book examinations. This method allows the student to demonstrate his ability to engage in thinking. Since this kind of examination is essentially a continuation of classroom activity and learning, it is essentially the same as the first method, though obviously the evaluation is based upon a briefer sample of behavior.

The Role of the Teacher

The role of the teacher is determined by the aims of education and the methods of instruction, which are related to the nature of the learner and the conditions necessary for his cognitive development. We have already made some statements about the role of the teacher in connection with earlier topics.

If the aim of education is not the acquisition of information, then the role of the teacher is not the imparting of information, through lecturing or other means, including films or other audiovisual aids. If the child learns spontaneously through his activities, then it is not the role of the teacher to motivate him, either by prodding, stimulation, rewards, or other means. By *active methods of instruction* Piaget does not mean active direction and control by the teacher. It is the child who is active. This does not mean, however, that the teacher merely stands by as a passive observer. Actually, according to Piaget, "active methods are much more difficult to employ than receptive methods. In the first place they require a much more varied and much more concentrated kind of work from the teacher, whereas giving lessons is much less tiring and corresponds to a much more natural tendency in the adult, generally, and in the adult pedagogue, in particular. Secondly, and above all, an active pedagogy presupposes a much more advanced kind of training, and without an advanced knowledge of child psychology . . . the teacher cannot properly understand the student's spontaneous procedures, and therefore fails to take advantage of reactions that appear to him quite insignificant and a mere waste of time."[51] The teacher is the facilitator of the natural development of the child, and as such must be able to provide the materials, resources, problems, and questioning and guidance which are appropriate for the level at which the child is operating, in order that the

child exercise its capabilities and move toward a higher level of thinking. The emphasis is always upon the development of the intellect, the
ability to think and to reason. Kamii suggests that when a child makes
a statement or a prediction about a situation or an experiment, the
teacher does not say "You are right" or "You are wrong," but "Let's
see." "She lets the child discover the truth by letting the object give
the answer."[52]

The Preparation of Teachers

The teacher who is to utilize Piaget's theory and research in teaching
obviously must, as indicated earlier, have a thorough grasp and understanding of Piaget's work. This is a formidable task, both for teacher-
educators and for the student teacher. This chapter can serve only as
an introductory survey. Piaget emphasizes the importance of the study
of developmental psychology in the preparation of teachers. He states
the recommendation of the International Conference of Public Education that teachers be trained in psychological development up to the
same level that they are to teach. This would mean that those who
teach adolescents would not only have training in the psychology of
adolescents, but in child psychology as well.

Training in developmental psychology should include, but not be
limited to, theory. Piaget deplores the limitations of teacher education
programs in teacher-training institutions divorced from universities,
where training in psychology is limited to lectures and examinations,
with no practical work except the administration of a few tests. In
addition to the study of theory, students should engage in research,
which involves participation in an ongoing research program or direct
study of children. Kamii says that "One cannot truly learn child psychology except by collaborating in new research projects and taking
part in experiments, and it is useless to limit courses to exercises or
practical work directed toward already known results. . . . It is even
truer in the case of psychology than in other fields that the only way to
understand the facts involved and their interpretation is to undertake
some research of one's own."[53] Piaget refers to a program for the
preparation of elementary-school teachers in Geneva, in which the
student, after receiving a baccalaureate degree, spends a year taking
practical courses; a year at the University taking courses in psychology,
pedogogy, and other courses at the Institut des Sciences de l'Education;
followed by a third year of practical work. The practical work is not
described, but at some period in their training, the students, in groups
of two or three, accompany assistants in research programs every
afternoon to schools, where the assistants question the children involved in the research of the Institute. The students "learn how to
record facts and how to question the children, and above all [how to]

make periodic reports, thus involving them with the progress of the research both in periods of failure and success."[54]

Conclusion

The implications for education and teaching which we have discussed are general rather than specific. Some specific applications have been suggested,[55] but the possible applications of Piaget to education are far from having been exhausted. No one has tackled the tremendous task of devising a system of education based on Piaget's theory and research. Such a system would involve more than a modification or revision of our current system, more than an innovation, or a series of innovations; it would be, as Furth has put it, a Copernican revolution "which should turn our theories, and consequently our practice, upside down."[56]

A good teacher who becomes thoroughly familiar with Piaget's work (admittedly a difficult and time-consuming process) will certainly be able to make many specific applications to facilitate the learning of individual children. However, the full-scale application of Piaget to education would require the support of the school administration to make the necessary changes in curriculum and the organization of the classroom instruction.

Certainly also it would be necessary to demonstrate through research that the new methods were effective. Flavell notes that Piaget "has so far shed little empirical hard-fact light on precisely how these [cognitive] forms work their way into the child's cognitive life. That is, he has not provided concrete evidence as to the conditions, within the child himself and in his circumambient reality which are necessary and sufficient to induce their acquisition."[57] Although Piaget's equilibrium model attempts to provide a systematic conception of the process of ontogenetic change, it has not been subjected to experimental test. There has been some research by others (summarized up to the early sixties by Flavell) but the results are not clear-cut and provide no tested methods or techniques for teaching.

EVALUATION

As was indicated earlier, Piaget's work has been criticized because it has not followed the procedures or methodology generally accepted by American experimental psychologists. This methodology requires the use of relatively large numbers of subjects, selected so as to be representative samples of a specified population (such as 8-year-old boys or girls from middle-class homes in an urban environment, and so on), who are subjected to a standard treatment (for example, the administration of a series of predetermined questions), the results of which can be reported in an objective or quantified manner, so that statistical analyses can be performed, resulting in means and standard deviations presented in tables. Instruments, such as tests, must be of known reliability. The reporting of the results of the research provides information on all these factors, as well as summary statistics, if not the raw data obtained.

In contrast to researchers who use these scientific methods, Piaget studied small numbers of children, often a single child of a given age, as in the case of his own children. Where more than one child was studied, the exact number is seldom mentioned. There is no indication of how they were selected for study nor descriptions of their intellectual or socioeconomic levels. His early method of study consisted of observation. This method was followed by the clinical method of inquiry or questioning and then by the presentation of problems or problem situations. The questions and problems were not rigidly standardized, so that each child was not necesarily subjected to the same objective stimulus. Rather, the procedure was adapted to the responses of the child. Questions and stimuli were thus modified as data were being obtained, a procedure which led to new questions or variations of the task. Thus, it can be argued that no two children were subjected to the same situation or experiment.

This method is thus subject to a number of criticisms. Its unstandardized nature can be questioned. It can also be questioned whether the experimenter could not unwittingly lead the child to produce certain responses, under the influence of the desire to find preconceived results. Preconceptions might also lead to the experimenter's failure to recognize or attend to other responses, or to record selectively or distort responses in the recording. There are also problems of evaluating and interpreting data. It must be noted that Piaget has recognized these difficulties. He has felt that there is no other way of approaching what he has wanted to study. His method makes it possible to study the process of thinking rather than simply the results of the process. His training as a biologist prepared him for acute observation of behavior. His co-workers and assistants have been thoroughly trained in the method before engaging in actual research studies. They learn to avoid suggesting answers and to test the meaning of children's responses and their justification of and certainty about them.

In regard to his methods of research, it should be noted that they are appropriate and acceptable for what is called exploratory research, as contrasted to experimental research. The former searches out a new field to define it, to locate the significant variables involved, and to develop ideas, or hypotheses, for experimental testing. Piaget does, however, also develop hypotheses which he attempts to test, and the two kinds of research are not clearly separated. But it could be maintained that much of the research in child development has been a premature study of variables and a testing of hypotheses which are not particularly significant. Piaget, in effect, entered the field with a fresh, unbiased approach which has resulted in a new outlook and the identification of different variables for study.

In addition to his methods of obtaining data being questioned, Piaget's methods of analysis and presentation of data have been criticized. He presents his data in the form of protocols recording the observations of individual children. There are no tables of averages of numerical scores for groups of children of differing ages. The number of children in a given study, and their ages, may be given, but there is little if any statistical analysis. He has not been interested in developing age norms or developmental scales and thus sees no need for statistical analyses. In addition he recognizes the indefensibility of statistical treatment of data obtained by somewhat different stimulus situations. It should be mentioned that some of the more recent research done in Geneva has utilized standard research designs and analyses.

The data which Piaget and his associates and assistants have collected have been explained or interpreted in terms of his theoretical system. His procedure of observing, testing, formulating new questions or hypotheses, testing again, revising his hypotheses and then checking them again, and so on, has involved a tremendous amount of work and has led to the formulation of a constantly developing theory. The question has been raised whether others could obtain the same results as he has. In recent years other investigators have obtained similar or consistent results. Thus there is independent support for his work. In other words, his research meets one of the major requirements of science, that is, that it can be replicated. However, the criticism has been made by Flavell (indeed, it is his major one) that the inadequacies of methodology, analysis, and reporting of Piaget's studies have made replication and validation necessary before others could build on or extend his work. "The reader is often left in considerable doubt as to what actual test and inquiry procedures were administered by whom under what testing conditions to how many children of what ages, backgrounds, previous testing experiences, and so on."[58]

A further question involves the inferences, conclusions, and theoretical implications which can be derived from his work. Here it appears that there is increasing acceptance of Piaget's theory. However, his theorizing is not always clearly related to the empirical data presented in his writings. This is in part because he has not published all the data on which he bases his theory and in part because his theoretical discussions extend beyond existing empirical data. While it is permissible to theorize beyond one's research, the difficulty with Piaget arises when the theory is apparently derived from empirical evidence which is inadequate or not clearly supportive of the theoretical elaboration. It also appears that data are sometimes converted into forced interpretations to fit the theory.

While it can be argued that Piaget's methods produce information and data which could not be obtained by the more limited methods commonly used in research, it must be conceded that his methods have not led to the production of data which are easily organized to lead to generalizations or conclusions. Nor has he presented his data in a complete, organized form as is customary in the reporting of research. This is no doubt in part because of the mass of data involved and in part because Piaget has not engaged in specific, delimited studies with beginnings and ends, but has moved continuously from one study to another, without completing exhaustive analysis of any of the data he has collected.

In addition to criticisms of data collection, analysis, and interpretation, there are others of various sorts. One focuses on the matter of the difficulty of Piaget's writing. According to Flavell, who read the French editions of his books, this is more than a matter of translation, or of complexity of the concepts and ideas. It is also due to lack of clarity and inconsistencies in definitions, meanings, or usage of terms. This is true, for example, of the concept of reversibility, which includes the confusing differentiation between negation and reciprocal operations.[59] Flavell also finds gaps between the empirical data and the theory, and feels that Piaget makes theoretical statements, or poses theoretical problems, which do not appear to be susceptible of testing by empirical research, as well as engaging in theorizing of a tenuous nature.

The criticism has been made that rather than revealing the development of cognition, Piaget's studies are simply studies of vocabulary development. An examination of the protocols reporting the performance of children in the experiments makes it difficult to accept this criticism. The method of inquiry, testing the child's understanding, goes beyond vocabulary. Moreover, the phenomenon of horizontal décalage, where, for example, the child demonstrates conservation in one area (mass) but not in another (volume), would appear to negate this criticism. Thinking appears to be more than verbalization. Some research by Inhelder, Bovet, Sinclair, and Smock, stimulated by Bruner's belief that language training would be effective in stimulating the acquisition of conservation, also refutes this criticism.[60] Vocabulary is related to cognitive development, but it is possible, and appears likely, that it follows rather than precedes the cognitive understandings studied by Piaget.

Flavell feels that Piaget has exaggerated the system and structure of the child's thought and questions whether it actually conforms to or follows the logicomathematical model of groupings and the four-group. He proposes a modification resulting in a simpler model, yet one which he believes could accommodate a greater variety of cognitive-developmental facts.[61] In this regard, it should be noted that for Piaget the highest or most mature level of cognition is thinking which follows the model of the scientific method. It can be argued that this is not necessarily the best or only method of thinking. The scientific method is considered by some to be appropriate for the testing or checking of hypotheses, or for verification, but not for the development of hypotheses, or for creative thinking. It is interesting to look at Piaget's work itself in this light. It is questionable whether his exploration of cognitive development and the formulation of his theory strictly followed the scientific method of reasoning. The adoption of this model as the highest level of cognition also must deal with the fact that many, if not most, adults do not function at this level. To be sure, it might be argued that most adults are not mature in their thinking and that their education in this respect has been inadequate. But it could also be argued that many of these adults are mature, but think in a different manner—the manner of creative thinking manifested in works of art, literature, music, and human relations. Flavell also thinks that Piaget's system does not adequately deal with or adequately allow for individual differences or variability, or for the development of semi-cognitive operations, in which affective factors influence perception and logic.

Finally, Flavell raises the problems with the concept of "stage," "level," or "period," including its multideterminateness, complexity, and heterogeneous elements.

In spite of these and other criticisms, there is no doubt about the tremendous contribution Piaget has made to developmental psychology. His theoretical system is one of the most extensive ever developed by one person—or a small group. Perhaps the only other system which rivals it is that of Freud. In comparison with psychoanalysis, Piaget's system is more solidly based on empirical observation and research—research which, as noted above, is not entirely acceptable to scientists in England and the United States, but which is more acceptable than psychoanalytic research, which is almost entirely clinical in nature. It is probably the most complete, detailed, empirically supported, and compelling theory of cognitive development. And it is capable of being expanded to include the affective and social aspects of development, thus becoming a theory of human development. As scientists are wont to say, it may eventually not be supported by further research, or it may be significantly modified by such research, but it is useful in that it stimulates thinking and research which can only advance scientific understanding. Its cognitive emphasis is significant and is no doubt a source of the increasing attention it is receiving, because of the increasing interest in cognitive development and in cognition in education. As Baldwin puts it, "In area after area he [Piaget] has broken new ground and performed new ingenious experiments; psychologists have been feeding upon his ingenuity since the 1950's and will undoubtedly continue to depend upon many of his innovations for years to come."[62] His approach of beginning with observation and clinical studies in an effort to develop insight and understanding, rather than applying standard methods which limit the data to be studied, has resulted in a contribution which appears to be capable of redirecting research to problems and issues which may be more productive than those which have been the focus of much if not most research in child development.

As to educational applications, while Piaget's research and theory are incomplete and not fully validated, there is much in his work that raises questions about current practices and which is sound enough to warrant changes in these practices. Certainly the effects of any applications should be studied, and compared with other practices. But there are a number of ideas discussed in the preceding section which are supported by other research and experience.

As Piaget notes, the concept of active learning has been recognized by almost all the great theoreticians in the history of pedagogy— Socrates, Rabelais, Montaigne, and Locke, culminating in Rousseau— and has been applied by Pestilozzi and Froebel.[63] They operated on the basis of intuition, however, since a "science of mental development" did not exist. Dewey, Decroly, and Montessori had the work of James, Baldwin, Bergson, Binet, Janet, Flournoy, and Claparadé to draw from, but they derived their practices mainly from their own experience with children. The concept of active education was thus well developed before Piaget began his research. But he has provided a strong research base for the concept.

The importance of sensorimotor activity as the beginning of and the basis for later cognition was recognized by Montessori. Here again, Piaget has provided research support, not only for the necessity of early sensorimotor activity but of experience with concrete objects in the later, preoperational period of cognitive development. It could be said that while it might appear that Piaget supports Dewey's concept of learning by doing and realizing the consequences of the act, there may be a subtle distinction, expressed in the statement that doing *is* learning.

It is true that many if not most of Piaget's suggestions regarding teaching methods are not new and have been developed and used by many teachers on an intuitive basis. Piaget provides theoretical understanding of why they are effective, and a research basis for their acceptance.

In the area of the content and organization of the curriculum, it appears that Piaget's work is an original or unique contribution. Here the application of his work will require considerable effort, and it is here also that research on the effects of the applications is necessary. It may well be that resistance to curriculum changes, perhaps in part based on the contention that Piaget's research must be replicated and validated before it can be applied, will delay its application. But beginnings are being made. If it should turn out that the applications are effective in the improvement of learning—and it appears that they may be—or even in the development of people capable of higher levels of thinking, this could lead to a revolution in the curriculum of education.

SUMMARY

Piaget's theory and research represent the individual as an active organism interacting with, rather than simply reacting to, his environment. Intelligence is an instance of biological adaptation, in which the individual organizes and structures first the immediate environment and then the universe so that he can deal with them.

The process of intellectual or cognitive development is influenced by the genetic makeup or nature of the organism. This genetic aspect is the "functional nucleus" which imposes "certain necessary and irreducible conditions"[64] on developing structures. The maturational process, through the development of physical readiness, also contributes to development, by making possible new actions or behaviors as the organism grows. The experiences of the organism—specific learnings—are also important, as are social influences.

Adaptation includes two processes: assimilation and accommodation. In assimilation the organism incorporates objects or experiences without itself changing. In accommodation, the organism changes in order to respond adequately to the environment. The two processes are complementary. One allows for continuity, the other for change. In the process of interacting with its environment the organism uses or attempts to use existing patterns of behavior, or schemas, but in accommodating to new demands these patterns become modified, and new schemas are developed.

While the function of intellect (adaptation) is the same at all levels of development, the structure of intellect changes as development proceeds, making possible successively higher levels of organization and functioning. Development is a process of organization and reorganization of structure, each reorganization incorporating the previous organization.

The process by which structures change is equilibration, a process which moves from equilibrium to disequilibrium to a new equilibrium. In equilibrium, structure is sharper or clearer. But this clarity directs attention to inconsistencies, conflicts, self-contradictions—and lack of adaptation, or inability to assimilate. Disequilibrium results, and the process of equilibration is set in motion, leading to the development of new structures and the restoration (temporarily) of a new equilibrium.

The process of intellectual development is orderly, progressing through stages. Although it is continuous, qualitative differences result. The same or similar problems are attacked differently at different stages of functioning. The thinking of the adolescent and the adult differs from that of the child qualitatively, not simply quantitatively. At the level of formal operations, thinking has moved from the concrete to the abstract, that is, it is capable of dealing with the possible, the hypothetical, as well as the real or actual. Its model is formal logic and scientific reasoning. It involves the negation, inversion, or removal of a variable to determine its influence, and reciprocity, or the neutralization of a variable by holding it constant in order to test the effects of other variables. These two methods of thinking constitute what Piaget calls reversibility. Formal thinking is also flexible, being able to view a problem from different points of view, and is thus not egocentric.

Piaget identifies three major periods of cognitive development: the sensorimotor period (0–2 years); the period of preparation and organization of concrete operations (2–11), including a subperiod of preoperational representations (2–7) and a subperiod of concrete operations 7–11); and the period of formal operations (12–15). The earlier periods are divided into stages. Although the age levels will vary among individual children, depending on intelligence and cultural factors, the sequence is invariant.

It is important to recognize that for Piaget intelligence or cognition is an active process. Its origins are in the early motor activities of the organism. "Intellectual adaptation is the progressive differentiation and integration of inborn reflex mechanisms under the impact of experience. The differentiations of inborn reflex structures and their functions give rise to the mental operations by which man conceives of objects, space, time, and causality, and of the logical relationships which constitute the basis of scientific thought."[65] From the simple reflexes of the infant to the scientific method is a long way, but they are the ends of the same continuum. Sensorimotor activities are not to be dismissed as simply "early motor behavior" but are the foundation of intelligence. As Flavell notes, "according to Piaget, the logical character of adult thought does not come about simply as a consequence of learning experiences vis-à-vis the physical, social, or linguistic milieu. Rather, the logical forms of thought—and here lies the importance of the action concept—constitute the end product of the internalization and coordination of cognitive actions. This coordination begins prior to language acquisition; one actually sees a kind of 'logic-of-action' in sensory behavior."[66]

The placing of the beginnings of intellect in the sensorimotor period distinguishes Piaget from most other cognitive theorists, who consider language as the essence or core of intelligence. For Piaget, language is a means of thinking, a tool—and not the only one—and not thought itself. It is only in the operational period that the structure of formal operations makes it possible for the older child to use language in developing thinking, as in reasoning by logical propositions. Earlier language is tied to personal or concrete experiences and objects; the child is not capable of manipulating words as abstract symbols.

The contention, or perhaps better, the recognition, that thinking precedes the acquisition of language constitutes a challenge to education, which almost universally places emphasis upon language as the foundation for all education. Piaget emphasizes that thinking begins with, is built upon, and grows out of sensorimotor activities. Thinking must begin with concrete objects and experiences before abstract or representational thinking can develop. The concept of cognition-as-action would radically change much of the instruction in schools.

> In trying to teach a child some general principle or rule, one should so far as feasible parallel the developmental process of internalization of actions. That is, the child should first work with the principle in the most concrete and action-oriented context possible, he should be allowed to manipulate objects himself and 'see' the principle operate in his own actions. Then, it should become progressively more internalized and schematic by reducing perceptual and motor supports, e.g., moving away from objects to symbols of objects, from motor action to speech, etc. Piaget's theoretical emphasis on the action (and active) character of intelligence thus provides the rationale for certain specific recommendations about the teaching process.[67]

Many of the specific implications of Piaget for education are not unique or new. They have been suggested, as indicated above, by educators and theorists. Piaget's work provides support for the ideas of Dewey and progressive education, for Montessori, and for the open classrooms of the English infant and primary schools. It also is consistent with the concept of discovery learning. Many of the methods and practices arrived at intuitively through experience by good teachers are also consistent with or supported by Piaget's work. Thus Piaget provides support for many of the changes in education which have been or are being proposed by others.

One of the most important of Piaget's ideas for education is his conception that the purpose of education is to facilitate the development of the thinking process. This is perhaps not original with Piaget; but heretofore there has been little basis for implementing it. Piaget provides a basis. With the information and knowledge explosion, it is becoming increasingly apparent that education cannot cram children with all they need to know; even if it could, much would be obsolete and useless by the time formal education was completed. The development of the ability to think, not only in cognitive areas but in areas such as social and interpersonal relations, values, and morality and ethics, is certainly a priority in our current world.

With all its difficulties and deficiencies, the work of Piaget, in quantity and in quality, provides one of the best existing foundations for a theory of instruction.

REFERENCES

1. D. Elkind, *Children and Adolescents: Interpretive Essays on Jean Piaget* (New York: Oxford, 1970), pp. viii–x.
2. I. J. Althey and D. O. Rubadeau, eds., *Educational Implications of Piaget's Theory* (Waltham, Mass.: Ginn-Blaisdell, 1970); M. Brearley, ed., *The Teaching of Young Children* (New York: Schocken, 1970); H. G. Furth, *Piaget for Teachers* (Englewood Cliffs, N.J.: Prentice-Hall, 1970); H. G. Furth and H. Wachs, *Thinking Goes to School: Piaget's Theory in Practice* (New York: Oxford, 1974) (paperback, 1975); M. Schwebel and J. Raph, eds., *Piaget in the Classroom* (New York: Basic Books, 1973).
3. H. W. Maier, *Three Theories of Child Development,* rev. ed. (New York: Harper & Row, 1969), chapter 3; A. L. Baldwin, *Theories of Child Development* (New York: Wiley, 1967), chapters 5–9; J. L. Phillips, *The Origins of Intellect: Piaget's Theory* (San Francisco: Freeman, 1969); N. Isaacs, *A Brief Introduction to Piaget* (New York: Agathon Press, 1972).
4. J. H. Flavell, *The Developmental Psychology of Jean Piaget* (New York: Van Nostrand Reinhold, 1963); H. G. Furth, *Piaget and Knowledge: Theoretical Foundations* (Englewood Cliffs, N.J.: Prentice-Hall, 1969); H. Ginsburg and S. Opper, *Piaget's Theory of Intellectual Development: An Introduction* (Englewood Cliffs, N.J.: Prentice-Hall, 1969); M. A. S. Pulaski, *Understanding Piaget: An Introduction to Children's Cognitive Development* (New York: Harper & Row, 1971); P. G. Richmond, *An Introduction to Piaget* (New York: Basic Books, 1971); B. J. Wadsworth, *Piaget's Theory of Cognitive Development* (New York: McKay, 1971).
5. J. Piaget, *The Construction of Reality in the Child* (New York: Basic Books, 1954), p. 351.
6. Ibid., p. 355.
7. J. Piaget and B. Inhelder, *The Psychology of the Child* (New York: Basic Books, 1969), p. 21.
8. Piaget "Psychologie der Fruehen Kindheit," in D. Katz, ed., *Handbuch de Psychologie,* 2nd ed. (Basle, Switzerland: Benno Schwahe), p. 275. Quoted in H. W. Maier, op. cit. p. 98.
9. Flavell, op. cit., pp. 66–67.
10. Ibid., pp. 81–82.
11. Ibid., pp. 22–23.
12. Ibid., p. 24 (emphasis added).
13. Flavell (ibid., pp. 67–77) summarizes these comparisons.
14. Flavell's excellent description and analysis is the main source drawn upon for a summary of Piaget's developmental periods.

15. Piaget and Inhelder, *The Psychology of the Child,* op. cit., p. 10.
16. Flavell, op. cit., p. 156.
17. Ginsburg and Opper, op. cit., p. 84.
18. Flavell, op. cit., p. 173.
19. Quoted in Flavell, ibid., p. 192.
20. Piaget and Inhelder, *The Psychology of the Child,* op. cit., p. 135, footnote.
21. Ibid., p. 135.
22. Inhelder and Piaget, *The Growth of Logical Thinking from Childhood to Adolescence.* (New York: Basic Books, 1958), p. 111.
23. Ibid., p. 117.
24. Ibid., p. 342.
25. Ginsburg and Opper, op. cit., pp. 201–202.
26. Ibid., p. 225.
27. The following represent some attempts to apply Piaget to curriculum: A. A. Carrin and R. B. Sund, *Teaching Science Through Discovery,* 3rd ed. (Columbus, Ohio: Merrill, 1975); R. W. Copeland, *How Children Learn Mathematics: Teaching Implications of Piaget's Research* (New York: Macmillan, 1970); K. D. George, M. A. Dietz, E. C. Abraham, and M. A. Nelson, *Elementary School Science: Why and How?* (Lexington, Mass.: Heath, 1974); W. Jacobson, *The New Elementary School Science* (New York: Van Nostrand Reinhold, 1970); C. Stendler-Lavatelli, *Piaget's Theory Applied to Early Childhood Education* (Boston: American Science and Engineering, 1970); H. D. Thier, *Teaching Elementary School Science: A Laboratory Approach* (Lexington, Mass.: Heath, 1970); B. J. Wadsworth, *Piaget for the Classroom Teacher* (New York: McKay, 1977).
28. Quoted in R. E. Ripple and V. N. Rockcastle, eds., *Piaget Rediscovered* (Ithaca, N.Y.: Cornell University Press, 1964), p. 5.
29. Piaget, *To Understand Is to Invent* (New York: Grossman, 1973), p. 50.
30. Ibid., p. 52.
31. Furth and Wachs, *Thinking Goes to School,* op. cit.
32. Piaget, *To Understand Is to Invent,* op. cit., pp. 87, 109–126.
33. Piaget, *To Understand Is to Invent,* op. cit., pp. 48–49.
34. Ibid., pp. 97–99.
35. Ibid., p. 17.
36. A. Pinard and M. Laurendeau, "A Scale of Mental Development Based on the Theory of Piaget: Description of a Project," in Althey and Rubadeau, op. cit., pp. 307–317; R. D. Tuddenham, "Psychometrizing Piaget's Méthode Clinique," ibid., pp. 317–324; M. Tanaka, J. T. Campbell, and J. S. Helmick, "Piaget for First-Grade Teachers: Written Exercises for Assessing Intellectual Development," ibid., pp. 324–328.
37. Furth and Wachs, op. cit. (1975 ed.), p. x.
38. Piaget, *To Understand Is to Invent,* op. cit., pp. 15–16, p. 20.
39. Ibid., p. 93.
40. Ibid., p. 103.
41. Ibid., p. 102.
42. Ibid., pp. 107–108.
43. Ibid., p. 106.
44. J. McV. Hunt, *Intelligence and Experience* (New York: Ronald, 1961), pp. 267ff.
45. A. W. Combs and D. Snygg, *Individual Behavior,* rev. ed. (New York: Harper & Row, 1959), pp. 178–179.
46. Piaget, *To Understand Is to Invent,* op. cit., pp. 22–23.

47. J. S. Bruner, *Toward a Theory of Instruction* (New York: Norton, 1968), p. 44.
48. Furth, *Piaget for Teachers,* op. cit., chapter 6.
49. Ibid., p. 96.
50. Piaget, *Science of Education and the Psychology of the Child,* op. cit., p. 108.
51. Ibid., p. 69.
52. C. Kamii, "Pedagogical Principles Derived from Piaget's Theory: Relevance for Educational Practice," In M. Schwebal and J. Raph, eds., *Piaget in the Classroom* (New York: Basic Books, 1973), p. 213.
53. Ibid., pp. 125, 129.
54. Ibid., p. 130.
55. See references listed in 2 above.
56. Furth, *Piaget for Teachers,* op. cit., p. 53.
57. Flavell, op. cit., p. 370.
58. Ibid., pp. 430–431.
59. Ibid., p. 427.
60. B. Inhelder, M. Bovet, H. Sinclair, and C. D. Smock, "On Cognitive Development," *American Psychologist* 21 (1966):160–164.
61. Flavell, op. cit., pp. 438–440.
62. Baldwin, op. cit., p. 278.
63. Piaget, *Science of Education and the Psychology of the Child,* op. cit., p. 139ff.
64. Piaget, *The Origins of Intelligence in Children* (New York: International Universities Press, 1952), p. 3.
65. P. H. Wolff, "The Developmental Psychology of Jean Piaget and Psychoanalysis," *Psychological Issues,* 1960, 2 (1), Whole No. 5.
66. Flavell, op. cit., pp. 83–84, footnote.
67. Ibid., p. 84.

Bruner: toward a theory of instruction

4

CHAPTER

4

INTRODUCTION

Jerome Seymour Bruner (1915–   ) was born in New York City. In 1937 he received the BA degree from Duke University, and in 1941, the PhD degree from Harvard University. During World War II he served with the Office of War Information, the Department of State, and Supreme Headquarters of the Allied Expeditionary Force, both in the United States and overseas, analyzing public opinion and propaganda.

In 1944 he was appointed a lecturer at Harvard University. In 1948 he became an associate professor, and in 1952 professor. During 1951–1952, Bruner was a visiting member of the Institute for Advanced Study at Princeton University and in 1952 lectured at the Salzberg Seminar. During 1955–1956 he was a Guggenheim fellow at Cambridge University, England, and in 1956 he was a guest lecturer at the Fédération Suisse de Psychologie. In 1962 he was Harper Lecturer at the University of Chicago. In 1965 he was Harvard's Bacon Professor at the University of Aix-en-Provence. Since 1972 he has been a fellow of Wolfson College and Watts Professor of Experimental Psychology at Oxford University, England.

Bruner has been an adviser or consultant to the United Nations, the White House, the National Institutes of Health, the United States Office of Education, the State Department, and Time-Life-Fortune, among other organizations. He is a fellow of the American Association for Advancement of Science and of the American Academy of Arts and Sciences, and a founding member of the Academy of Education. He is a fellow of the American Psychological Association (APA), in which he has been active, serving as president of the Division of Personality and Social Psychology (1959–1960), president of the Society for the Psychological Study of Social Issues (a division of APA) (1962–1963), and as president of the entire association (1965–1966). In 1975 he received the G. Stanley Hall Award of the Division of Developmental Psychology of the American Psychological Association for his contributions to human development and its applications. He has received honorary degrees from Lesley College, Duke University, Northwestern

University, Temple University, and the University of Cincinnati.

Although his interests as a graduate student were in the psychology of perception and learning, his experiences during the war years led him into social psychology and the study of public opinion. In 1956 he coauthored (with M. B. Smith and R. W. White) a book entitled *Opinions and Personality*. He also developed an interest in thinking, particularly the inferential processes involved in reasoning, and— also in 1956—published, with J. Goodnow and C. A. Austin, *A Study of Thinking*.

In 1959, following the concern with American education generated by the launching of Sputnik by the Russians, Bruner chaired the Woods Hole Conference on Education. Some 35 scientists spent ten days discussing how education in the sciences in elementary and secondary schools could be improved. This conference stimulated his interest in education. The book *The Process of Education* (first published in 1960) was an outcome of this conference. His earlier work represented interest in developmental psychology and curriculum; now he moved to an interest in the problem of representation in childhood.

It was also in part at least as a result of this conference that Bruner became involved in the development of a course in social studies for fifth and sixth graders which went beyond cognitive learning to deal with values and cultural differences. This course, known as "Man: A Course of Study" (MACOS) was supported by the National Science Foundation. For his work in developing MACOS, Bruner was given an award by the American Educational Research Association and the American Educational Publishers Institute, which cited the course as "one of the most important efforts of our time to relate research findings and theory in educational psychology to the development of new and better instructional material." The course arouses considerable affect in some students, and as a result is currently (1975) under attack in Congress by Representative John Conlon (R) of Arizona, who has charged that it deliberately manipulates the minds of children to lead them to reject the values, beliefs, and the religious and national loyalties of their parents.[1]

While he was a Guggenheim fellow at Cambridge he studied cognition and cognitive development and visited Piaget in Geneva. On his return to Harvard he spent two years studying learning efficiency in a group of normal 10-year-old children, focusing on patterns of individual differences. He moved from these studies, which were mainly observational, to more experimental studies of how children develop different strategies of problem solving, principally in mathematics. This work is represented in *The Process of Education* and *Toward a Theory of Instruction* (1966). During the next few years, beginning in 1960, he and a group of faculty and students at the Center for Cognitive Studies (founded by Bruner and George Miller) engaged in the study of cognitive or intellectual development. During 1961–1962 Barbel Inhelder was at the center, and studies relating to some of the work of Piaget, such as conservation and invariance, were begun, with subsequent exchanges of data and visits with Piaget at Geneva. Bruner also visited the Soviet Union, and researchers from Russia visited Harvard. He also studied children in Senegal, Africa, and two staff members were involved in studies of Eskimo children and children in Mexico. These studies resulted in the publication in 1966, in collaboration with others, of *Studies in Cognitive Growth*. The book is dedicated to Jean Piaget, "friend and mentor, whose brilliant insights have given new and powerful form to the study of cognitive growth," in honor of his seventieth birthday.

Between 1964 and 1970, Bruner became involved in educational questions and issues; this was the period of criticism of education by Paul Goodman, Ivan Illich, Jonathan Kozol, John Holt, Herbert Kohl, and James Herndon. The essays Bruner wrote during this period were published under the title *The Relevance of Education*, in 1971.

Bruner's work with older children led him to recognize that by the age of 3 the child has already achieved a level of intellectual competence. He then began to study the growth of skill in infancy, the early results of which are reported in *Progress of Cognitive Growth: Infancy* (1968).

In 1973, Jeremy Anglin edited a collection of Bruner's papers under the title *Beyond the Information Given: Studies in the Psychology of Knowing*. This collection includes most of Bruner's writings on cognition. However, neither this nor Bruner's other books, which are collections of essays and papers, present an organized, systematic statement of Bruner's theory and research and its conclusions and implications. The presentation here is derived from Bruner's writings, but for the reason just stated, it risks a greater danger of inadequacy, or even inaccuracy, than is the case with the other presentations included in this book.

PHILOSOPHICAL ASPECTS

Bruner does not present his philosophical foundation or assumptions in a systematic form. Philosophical statements, theoretical statements, and inferences and conclusions from research are often intermeshed. For this reason the word *aspects* is used here to refer to philosophically related or oriented statements which are extricated from Bruner's various reports and essays.

Psychological events must be explained, according to Bruner, in terms of psychological processes. It is not sufficient to reduce such events to, or to translate them into evolutionary, physiological, linguistic, or sociological concepts or terms. Evolutionary, physiological, cultural, linguistic, or logical reasons or causes must operate on the basis of or through psychological principles.

Bruner's view of people is that they are active beings engaged in the construction of their world. The human being is thus not simply a reactor to an environment, being shaped by that environment, as the behaviorists picture them. Bruner writes, for example: "It is apparent to many of us that the so-called associative connecting of physical stimuli and muscular responses cannot provide the major part of the explanation for how men learn to generate sentences never before spoken."[2] His research in reasoning that involves sequences of events supports the view that subjects do not mechanically associate specific responses with specific stimuli, but that they tend to infer principles or rules underlying the patterns, which makes it possible for them to generalize or transfer their learning to other problems.

Rather than being a simple reactor to stimuli, the individual engages actively, through perception, concept attainment, and reasoning in creating or constructing knowledge. Perception is not a passive process, the mirroring of the world, but a selective process by which, influenced by the organism's needs, beliefs, and values, the individual constructs a perceptual world on the basis of information given by his or her senses. Bruner thus appears to be essentially a phenomenological psychologist, recognizing that reality for the individual does not exist apart from the individual's perception, or creation, of it. "Man does not respond to a world that exists for direct touching. Nor is he locked in a prison of his own subjectivity. Rather, he represents the world to himself and acts in behalf of or in reaction to his representations."[3]

Conceptual behavior or activity, whether perception of events, attainment of a concept, solution of a problem, discovery of a scientific theory, or mastery of a skill, can be viewed as a problem whose solution is actively constructed. Implicit in this view of human beings and explicitly stated by Bruner is the concept of *intention*. Human behavior is purposive, in that it is intended to achieve certain objectives or results. "Intention viewed abstractly may be at issue philosophically, but it is a necessity for the biology of complex behavior, by whatever label we wish to call it."[4] Actions, and the search for meaning, are guided by intention. Bruner feels that the role of intention is a central concern in biology and psychology.

Bruner gives little attention to motivation as a concept. Behavior is ongoing, and—apart from activity being a characteristic of a living organism—is motivated by the drive toward competence and the drive of curiosity. Activities deriving from these drives are self-rewarding.

Cognitive development or growth is the process by which human beings increase their mastery in achieving and using knowledge. Cognition includes strategies for the reduction of the complexity of the world (which must be selective and directed toward the relevant or important aspects of the world) and for the organization of the environment. Cognition involves the means by which human beings represent their experience of the world and organize these experiences and their effects for future use. There are three modes of representation of the world:

1. *The enactive mode.* "At first the child's world is known to him by the habitual actions he uses for coping with it."[5]
2. *The ikonic mode.* "In time there is added a technique of representation through imagery that is relatively free of actions."[6]
3. *The symbolic mode.* "Gradually there is added a new and powerful method of translating action and imagery into language."[7]

Each of these modes has a powerful effect on mental life at different ages, and each continues to function and interact with the others throughout later intellectual life. The nature of these modes will be considered in more detail later.

Individual development proceeds by steps, discontinuously rather than smoothly. There are periods of rapid growth, or spurts, followed by periods of consolidation. The curve of growth is like a staircase rather than a straight line. The steps are not, however, discrete or sharply separated. Characteristics of earlier stages continue in later stages; enactment continues when the ikonic mode develops, and the ikonic mode is not abandoned when the symbolic mode develops.

Growth involves and requires "inside" and "outside" factors. The inside factors are not independent of outside factors. The "push" propelling growth is not adequately represented or explained by such concepts as "maturation," "unfolding," "will to learn," "competence motive," or "actualization." "Internal 'push' seems to be dependent on an external supply of stimulation,"[8] or "pull." There is no internal push without a corresponding external pull. The process is an interactive one.

Man's growth is related to his evolutionary history. The increased emphasis in primate evolution on distance receptors, the prolonged dependency of infancy, and the decreasing neurological specialization (reduction of instinctive behaviors) affects human development. Dependency requires continued intensive care and thus susceptibility to outside influences.

Early experiences are thus important in human development. Early isolation and early deprivation, particularly of caring or love, may result in irreversible damage. Separation from a parent or parent substitute leads to later psychopathy which may be extremely difficult to modify: Bruner has stated that "we may have exaggerated the effects of childrearing practices on the adult personality, but it has never crossed my mind that we have exaggerated the importance of identification in the childrearing process."[9] Further, "there seems to be a critical period during which isolation from the world of rich stimulation has its maximum deleterious effects—during the first year principally."[10] And elsewhere in the same source, he states, "Conceptions of reality early established tend to become the first editions of reality upon which later editions are fashioned." Changes which occur are from this reference point. "Early emotionally organized beliefs and guides to action often may be stubbornly incorrigible, partly because they are isolated from the language-bound literal structure of reality that develops later."[11]

Culture is an important factor in nurturing and shaping growth. "Cognitive growth in all its manifestations occurs as much from the outside in as from the inside out."[12]

The recent evolution of the human race (in the last 500,000 years) has not been marked by any major change in morphology, but by humans teaming up with implementation systems. These systems have included (1) amplifiers of motor capacities (tools and mechanical devices); (2) amplifiers of sensory capacities; and (3) amplifiers of ratiocinative capacities, which include language. Internal skills for organizing sensorimotor acts, percepts, and reasoning have been selected by evolution. Humans as a species have become specialized not in morphology but by the use of technological instruments. Our actions, perceptions, and reasoning depend on techniques rather than on the characteristics of our nervous system.

In effect, humans depend for survival on the inheritance of culture rather than on the inheritance of a set of genes. They are dependent on the cultural heritage because their morphological evolution has resulted in a long early period of helplessness. Bruner notes that the upright stature and bipedalism of the human, which frees the hands for tool using, resulted in a stronger but smaller pelvis, producing a smaller birth canal even though brain size in the adult was increasing. The necessary accommodation was a small and immature brain at birth.

Language is an aspect of culture which influences thinking; it "predisposes a mind to certain modes of thought and certain ways of arranging the shared subjective reality of a linguistic community."[13] Language is also important in "the conservation of cognitive capacity,"[14] by organizing, ordering, and simplifying the environment and experience. The myths of a culture also serve these purposes.

Language influences the content of equivalence groupings (categories or classes); a language with no word for a concept does not allow, or inhibits, grouping by that concept. (It should be noted, however, that if the language does not include a concept, but the concept becomes important in the activities of living, the concept may become incorporated in actions. For instance, the language of an African tribe studied by Bruner is restricted in color terms, but the children nevertheless were able to group objects by color, by pointing to objects to be included in the groups since they did not have words for colors.) The absence of higher-order words to integrate different domains of objects or words precludes the formation of hierarchical structures and their use in thought. Different value orientations influence the views of the world held by members of the different cultures. Young children in cultures which have a collective rather than an individualistic orientation (as in African cultures) do not appear to manifest the egocentrism which Piaget has found to characterize children of the same age in Geneva (and Western industrial cultures).

Cultural differences lead to differences in cognitive development; but cultural factors are involved even in developmental characteristics which are common across cultures. "Many of the universals of growth are also attributable to uniformities in human culture."[15] Languages have certain similarities across cultures. Inherent in what is learned from the culture, including language, are certain rules or principles, of which the learner is not aware even though he uses them. The contents of cultures are different, but there are universal aspects, one of which is the existence of linguistic rules or principles. Some linguists (for instance, Noam Chomsky) believe that there are genetic elements involved. The common biological heritage of humanity appears to provide a constraint which results in the absence of completely different and unrelated modes of thought in even the most divergent cultures.

Culture thus provides the technologies or nonnatural materials or artifacts which influence the development of cognitive capacities. Bruner has said that intelligence is, to a great extent, the internalization of the tools provided by a culture. The limits of growth, therefore, depend on the assistance which an individual obtains from culture, within the bounds of his or her potential. Culture also, through educational systems, influences the course of cognitive growth.

For Bruner, then, cognitive development, including the acquisition of knowledge, is an interactive process in which the individual constructs knowledge and reality from the materials provided by the environment. Knowledge, or the structure of knowledge, tells us something about the nature of mind, since mind constructs knowledge. But the structure of knowledge also respresents the influence of culture, through language and myth. "Nature is a symbolic construct, a creature of man's powers to represent experience through powerful abstractions. . . . Man lives in a symbolic world of his own collective creation, a symbolic world that has as one of its principal functions the ordering and explication of experience."[16]

A person's self-concept or image is related to her or his image of the world; the world view places limits on the self-view. "For it is characteristic of man not only that he creates a symbolic world but also that he then becomes its servant by conceiving of his own powers as limited by the powers he sees outside himself."[17]

Bruner's concern has not been with the development of the concept of the self, but with the development of a concept of the world, of "reality," by the process of knowing. Further, he has been concerned with the uses of knowledge, with how one's conception of reality influences action and commitment. The uses of knowledge or information include insight, understanding, and inferences, as well as competence in action. In this respect, the individual goes "beyond the information given," and is influenced by ways of knowing which go beyond scientific, objective methods to the use of intuition and hunches—metaphorically, to the use of the left hand as well as the right, or the influence of the right (nonverbal) hemisphere of the brain as well as the left (verbal) hemisphere. (See below, pp. 177–178).

Bruner has persistently been concerned with the relevance of research and theory to practice. For him, a theory of cognitive development goes hand in hand with a theory of pedagogy or of instruction. Thus he has been concerned with "how we impart knowledge, how we teach, how we lead the learner to construct a reality on his own terms."[18]

THE COURSE OF COGNITIVE GROWTH

Bruner began his studies of cognition with adults, and then moved downward, first to school-age children, then to children in their third year, and finally to infants. His studies of 3-year-olds showed that children at this age had already developed strategies for processing information. His studies of infants were for the purpose of understanding the origins of these strategies and seeking clues to the development of higher-order functions.

The objects of study of the development of new behaviors in infants were, first, of course simple skills—sucking, feeding, looking, reaching, and grasping. Three aspects or key features of these task behaviors which Bruner observed and formulated are *intention, feedback,* and *structure,* or *pattern.* Manual skill development involves an intended objective to be reached and a set of subactions (component acts) which can be performed in varying ways in line with feedback, so that the results can be compared with the objective until the objective is attained. The whole pattern of performance implies an organizing program, that is, a plan with a set of rules. These are also the characteristics of language production and problem solving. Thus, the development of manual skills "can tell us much about the nature of human problem solving and thought. I believe that the programmatic nature of human problem solving reflects the basic fact of primate evolution: that primates, increasingly, were able to use their hands as instruments of intelligence, that selection favored those that could, and that evolution favored in a variety of ways those organisms with a close link between hand an eye."[19]

Second, in addition to these task-directed behaviors, the infant engages in an early form of play behavior (Bruner calls it "mastery play"), which is crucial for the development of new behaviors during the first year or year and a half. It consists of pleasure-giving variations of the task-oriented behavior routines. Infants engage in such variations of an activity for relatively long periods of time. Such play "has the effect of maturing some modular routines for later incorporation in more encompassing programs of action. It also seems to trial run a range of possible routines for employing already established subroutines."[20]

A third way in which the infant develops new behaviors is through modeling, or imitation. To engage in such learning by observation and imitation of a model, the child must be able to construct complex behaviors to match the sample.

All three of these kinds of behaviors are directed toward dealing with or coping with the environment. In order to deal successfully with a complex environment individuals must reduce it to elements or situations which are manageable, or to which they can respond in ways which will achieve their intentions or objectives. In other words, the individual must *represent* the world in a form which he or she can handle.

Representation

Representation is a basic concept in Bruner's approach. Representation consists of a system of rules by which the individual conserves or represents for future use his or her encounters and experiences with events. It is a construction of the world—a model which represents the world to him or her. Representation occurs in three major media, which develop in order with age: (1) the action mode (enactive representation), (2) the imagery mode (ikonic representation), and (3) the symbolic mode (symbolic representation). Each mode, or medium has several subvarieties.

Each of the modes of representation, then, is directed to dealing with or coping with the environment, in order to reduce it to a manageable form. To deal successfully with a complex environment, individuals must select the most relevant elements or events to which they can respond in ways which will achieve their intentions or objectives. In other words the individual must represent it in a form which he or she can handle or work with.

Enactive representation.   The earliest form of representation, the enactive, develops in the second half of the first year of life. For the infant in this period, the actions in response to stimuli define, in major part, the stimuli. To be sure, visual perception precedes and is involved in enactive representation, but the meaning, or the "construction," given to objects, requires action on the objects. "Action . . . is the necessary condition for the infant's achievement of the ecologically valid 'correlations' that constitute the segmented and segregated objects of experience."[21] The enactive mode of representation is characteristic of the sensorimotor stage of development described by Piaget. Enactive representation is focused on the individual; it could be said to be self-centered or egocentric (Bruner does not specifically state this), lacking an "autonomous, external frame of reference."[22]

Ikonic representation.   As enactive representation fuses the percept with action, ikonic representation separates the percept from action. It appears that the repetition or "overlearning" of actions may lead to the development, or potential for development, of an image of the action—the placing of behavior in a spatial context. The spatial context frees perception from temporality. It then also frees representation from action, so that action-free imagery can develop. This transition is well under way by the end of the first year of life.

Yet it is many years before ikonic representation reaches its highest level. Young children's perceptual world, their "image of the world," is limited and unstable. They may focus on the whole and ignore parts, or focus on a detail and ignore the whole (either failing to see the trees because of the forest, or the forest because of the trees). Their images lack flexibility and are simple rather than complex in organization. Their world is self-centered and easily subject to distortions by need and affect. And, in the earliest years, it is still dependent on action checks. "It is as if the young child, having achieved a perceptual world that is no longer directly linked to action, now deals with the surface of things rather than with the deeper structures based on invariant features."[23]

Ikonic representation, while an advance over enactive representation, is inadequate for solving many problems which require attention to "invisible" features such as relations, hierarchies, and shared attributes as a basis for grouping. In the first two grades of school, good imagery appears to assist achievement, apparently because it is useful in associating arbitrary verbal labels to things or objects which are visualized. Children up to 8 or 9 years of age prefer perceptual bases for sorting objects, or for classification. Imagery thus characterizes early intellectual functioning, being a precursor of later "logical" operations. But its persistence may hinder later progress, which requires conceptual ability freed from objects or images. "It may be true that a picture is worth a thousand words, but if the object is to locate its functional equivalent in another context then perhaps one word is worth a thousand pictures if it contains the conceptual key."[24]

Symbolic representation. Symbolic representation derives from an (unknown) early, innate form of symbolic activity which becomes specialized into different systems. Action and imagery may show some of the properties of symbolic functioning. But language is the most highly specialized form of symbolic activity.

The child first uses words as signs rather than as symbols; they represent an object, or an aspect of the object, which is present. But the essence of a symbol is that the name attached to a thing is arbitrary. The symbol is not the thing; it is its *referent*. Thus the learning of reference is a slow process, not dependent on imagery, but on the ability to conceptualize, in that the extent and limits of the referent of the word, or symbol, must be learned.

Language, therefore, including early language, is *categorical*. Words refer to classes of things, and the classes are determined by rules. Categories can form hierarchies, so that language also has a *hierarchical* property.

All human language (other than the holophrase, or single-word utterance) is characterized by *grammar*. Although linguists do not entirely agree on the nature of grammar, all human languages exhibit three fundamental grammatical properties: causation (verb-object), predication (subject-predicate), and modification (the intersection of classes; that is, a member of a class—for example, a hat as a kind of clothing—modified by a member of another class—for example, green as a color). All languages also have rules for expressing or transforming an active sentence into three other forms: passive, interrogative, or negative.

The child's language from about the beginning of the third year of life is governed by a grammar (or set of rules) which can be inferred from his utterances. The first real language of a child is more than gestural vocalization; it involves a rule for combining even two words.

Grammar makes possible the production of an endless number of syntactically legitimate utterances. These utterances may or may not be semantically legitimate, that is, related to the "real world." But the fact that they need not be so related leads to "a form of *effective productivity* that makes symbolic representation such a powerful tool for thinking or problem solving: the range it permits for experimental alteration of the environment without having, so to speak, to raise a finger by way of trial and error or to picture anything in the mind's eye by imagery. 'What if there were never any apples?' a four-year-old asked upon finishing one with gusto."[25]

Language is not a direct copy of the perceptual world and thus does not represent its natural unity; language imposes a structure on the world. In this respect, language is a means not only for representing the world, but for transforming it. The hierarchy of linguistic categories is not present in the "real world" and is thus not experienced by the child. Nor is the child's experience organized by the other linguistic properties or principles. Moreover, the child's language is syntactically (grammatically) more advanced than it is semantically (in terms of meaning); that is, the child of 5 or 6 uses sentences involving highly abstract rules without being able to organize the things the words and sentences stand for. The words are "markers" for the ikonic or picturable aspects of the world, rather than representing the semantic properties of categories, hierarchies, prediction, causation, and modification. The child's "knowledge of the senses of words and the empirical implications of his sentence remain childish for many years, even after syntax has become fully developed. . . . Without special training in the symbolic *representation of experience,* the child grows to adulthood still depending in large measure on the enactive or ikonic modes of representing and organizing the world, no matter what language he speaks."[26]

Because of this partial independence of the syntactic sphere from the semantic sphere and from the experience of the child, Bruner believes that "in the linguistic domain the capacities for categorization and hierarchical organization are innate and so, too, are predication, causation, and modification. . . . One is strongly tempted to give credence to the insistence of various writers on linguistics that language is an innate pattern, based on innate 'ideas' that are gradually differentiated into the rules of grammar."[27] Thus it appears that children's ability to use language is ahead of their capacity to be aware of and to utilize its potential for representing or organizing the world, and of their ability to use it as an instrument of thought.

The process of transition from ikonic to symbolic representation continues over a period of years. Bruner presents some experiments illustrating the transition.[28] In one experiment, children between the ages of 5 and 7 are presented a double classification problem similar to an experiment of Piaget's. Nine glasses varying in three degrees in diameter and height are arranged in rows and columns on a 30-by-30-inch cardboard square divided into nine 10-inch squares. From left to right they increase in diameter, and from top to bottom they decrease in height. The smallest in both height and diameter is in the lower left square. The child is first asked to replace a glass after it is removed by the experimenter, then asked how the glasses in the columns and rows are alike and how they are different. Then the glasses are all removed and mixed up, and the child is asked to replace them as they were. Finally, the glasses are removed and mixed. The shortest, thinnest one is placed in the lower right square, rather than the lower left square, and the child is asked to make something like what was there before, leaving the one glass where it has been placed.

Children of 5, 6, or 7 years of age can all replace the glasses as they were originally (the older children doing it more rapidly), doing so as if they were copying from memory. But while most of the 7-year-olds can succeed in the transposed task, few of the younger children can do so. "The youngest children seem to be dominated by an image of the original matrix. They try to put the transposed glass 'back where it belongs,' to rotate the cardboard so that 'it will be like before,' and sometimes they will start placing a few glasses neighboring the transposed glass correctly only to revert to the original arrangement."[29] For the 7-year-old children the problem is one of reasoning, not copying, and this reasoning seems to be related to the language they use in the earlier part of the experiment. Children who say that the glasses in each row are alike because they are higher, and that the glasses in each column are different because some are shorter, and children who simply state that one is bigger and one is little, are likely to be successful on the transposed task. Those who confound a dimensional term (tall or short) with a global term (bigger or smaller) are twice as likely to fail. Bruner notes that "there is a suspicion that the language they bring to bear on the task is insufficient as a tool for ordering. . . . Improvement in language should aid this type of problem solving."[30] Activation by the experimenter of already acquired language (symbolic) habits before the experiment—saying before seeing—should also result in improved performance, by making it less likely that the perceptual-ikonic representation will dominate.

Bruner presents support for this reasoning in experiments performed by others involving the water-level or conservation problem of Piaget. Children who could see the water level change when it was poured from a thin glass into a wider glass were more likely to declare that the amount of water was not the same than children who saw only the tops of the thin and wide glasses. The latter were less influenced by perceptual-ikonic representation. In another experiment, the explanations of children who lacked conservation indicated that they were strongly influenced by the visual appearance of the problem situation.

Another experiment of Bruner's dealt with judging the emptiness or fullness of pairs of glasses of different sizes containing different amounts of water. It was found that children of 5, 6, and 7 years of age judged fullness and emptiness on observable sensory indexes rather than on proportion. And while the number of plain or simple errors decreased with age, it was found that contradictory errors increased with age. (Contradictory errors, for example, included the child's calling the same glass of a pair fuller when asked which was fuller, and emptier when asked which was emptier.) If such children were asked whether something could be fuller and emptier at the same time, they smiled, thinking they were being given a riddle, and said "That's silly."

Bruner suggests that these findings indicate a translation difficulty in moving from the ikonic to the symbolic realm. The younger child attends to one attribute—the volume of the water. The child of 7 or so attends to two—the volume of filled space and the volume of empty space—but is unable to relate them to a third attribute—the relative volume of the containers, which is not a perceptual variable. When this variable is introduced in the experiment, then the symbolic concept of proportion, which is not present perceptually, can be recognized. But although the older children are farther advanced than the younger children, they make more contradictory errors precisely because of their higher level.

The Relation and Interaction of Systems

A representation of an event is selective. In constructing a model of something, we do not include everything about it. The principle of selectivity is usually determined by the ends to which a representation is put—what we are going to do with what has been retained in this ordered way. Representations, by virtue of their summary nature, are rulebound in the sense that each representation is not an arbitrary or random sampling of what it stands for. . . . Much of spontaneous learning consists of inducing more general rules for more economical or more effective ways of representing similar events. And much of this learning consists of a kind of translation of one representational system into another, as when we became capable not only of following a given path habitually, but of representing it by an image in our mind's eye.[31]

Since representations are for a purpose, it follows that one may represent the same event differently for different purposes or *objectives*.

Symbolic representation, through language, can be used to describe states, images, and things, and their relations. It can also be used to prescribe actions. Language can also describe abstract relations among states and processes. Pictures or images can represent states, relationships (in a graphic way, through charts, diagrams, blueprints), and actions (flow charts). Enactive representation is more limited, but actions can be flexibly goal-directed; they are capable of adapting, being modified, or being extended through the use of tools, to achieve different goals and to overcome detours or obstacles.

While the three representational systems are unique and independent, paralleling each other, they can also be translated into each other and can interact with each other. Moreover, when two systems of representation are in conflict, as when what one sees does not correspond with how one must act, disequilibrium occurs, and there is a stimulus to cognitive growth. "It is usually when systems of representation come into conflict or contradiction that the child makes sharp revisions in his way of solving problems."[32]

There are three ways in which the three systems of representation can relate to each other: by *matching*, by *mismatching*, or by *independence* of each other. If the two systems match, there is no problem to solve, and the organism continues its ordinary operations. When there is a mismatch, one or the other is suppressed or a correction is made to coordinate the two. Preadolescents deal with mismatches between the action (enactive) and visual (ikonic) systems by choosing one or the other, either visual representation or the kinesthetic-labyrinthine (action derived), suggesting that preferences have developed through repeated problem solving.

Independence of these two modes (the action and the ikonic) of representation is not possible. But the symbolic mode can be independent of the other two, as suggested by the discrepancy between syntax and experience of actions in the young child. In this situation, where language (symbolization) as a mode of representation is independent of (ahead of) experience and thus of imagery and thought, language can be used as an abstract instrument to reach higher levels of mental operations when applied to experiences and thinking. When a child, in comparing objects, such as lumps of clay, which are the same in mass though different in shape, says "This one *looks* bigger," and then, recognizing that it actually is not bigger, says "But they are really alike," the child is restructuring her or his experience with the help of language. Experience and thought thus come to conform to language and their independence disappears. The contents of experience are prepared or modified to fit the requirements of being handled by (or represented by) language.

The independence of symbolic representation and action is evident in the impossibility of instructing someone how to skate or ride a bicycle by the use of language alone. However, if the action is broken up into parts or segments which correspond to words, instruction can be effective.

Equivalence, Information Seeking, and Invariance

Studies by Bruner and his associates have related to three issues in cognitive growth: equivalence, information seeking, and invariance. These issues are related to, or are aspects of, the development of the symbolic mode of representation, and thus this discussion overlaps somewhat with the above treatment of symbolic representation. These issues are worthy, however, of separate consideration.

Equivalence. Intellectual or cognitive growth involves the acquisition of ways of representing the recurrent regularities (equivalences) in the environment. This involves grouping, classifying, or categorizing objects and events in terms of similar attributes. The young child uses perceptual attributes, focusing on the surface sensory properties of events or objects. This is followed by a stage in which classification is based on what the child can arbitrarily do to or with objects ("egocentric functionalism"). Then there is progression to reliance on common appropriate uses. Finally, there is progression to the common linguistic classifiability. There is a shift from complexive rules, by which items are grouped according to several different attributes, none of which are common to all of the items, to rules based on superordination, in which classification is based on one or more attributes common to all the items included.

Studies by students of Bruner on grouping or classification have demonstrated the gradual freedom from the perceptual attributes of objects as children grow older. The youngest children studied (under 9 years of age) relied more heavily on perceptual attributes in their grouping than did the older children (9 to 12 years of age). The studies indicated that as perceptual (ikonic) ways of dealing with objects decreased, hierarchical structure with rules for hierarchical classification increased. Bruner ties this to language development: "As language becomes more internalized, more guiding as a set of rules for organizing events, there is a shift from the associative principles that operate in classical perceptual organization to the increasingly abstract rules for grouping events by the principles of inclusion, exclusion, and overlap, the most basic characteristics of any hierarchical system."[33]

Information seeking. One of the concurrent aspects of the development from enactive to symbolic representation—either an effect or one of the causes—is the "power for organizing acts of information processing into more integrated and long-range problem-solving efforts."[34] As children mature, they become more able to cumulate and utilize indirect information rather than sticking to the immediate situation. Such information is garnered by the kind of limiting and constraint-seeking questions that are most successful in the game of Twenty Questions; direct questions that attempt to get the answer immediately, usually fail. Older children are also able to cumulate information into a structure that can be manipulated by rules that go beyond simple association by similarly and contiguity. Both of these ways of operating enable the individual to "go beyond the information given," or that which is immediately present.

The mode of search changes in a rather regular way (at least in

Western culture). First, children deal with single features of a problem, one at a time, in a horizontal (rather than a hierarchical) order. They operate with images, attempting to match what they see with something in their heads. Later, they are able to deal with a number of alternatives simultaneously and hierarchically. "From then on, as information analysis rather than image-matching comes into play, the child grows in a regular fashion toward a lesser dependence upon redundance,"[35] becoming more efficient in information processing.

This system of processing information or environmental events involves the translation of experience into symbolic form, so that one can deal with the nonpresent both in space and time. Language provides a means for doing this.

Invariance. Invariance consists of the conservation of various forms of quantity across transformations in their appearances. The work of Bruner and his associates has shown that the achievement of the concept of conservation comes much earlier when a child engages in an activity, such as pouring water from one glass to another, rather than simply watching and then telling what will happen (Piaget's method). African children, who could not verbalize conservation as adolescents, nevertheless had no difficulty in actually handling conservation of liquids in their everyday life.

There is a fourth aspect of cognition which Bruner refers to as the *transcendence of momentariness.* This ability makes it possible for the individual to see coherence over longer and larger segments of experience beyond time- and space-binding representations. The child who first says that the larger of two half-filled glasses is fuller than the other, and then later says that it is also emptier, and still later, in response to questioning, says that it cannot be both fuller and emptier, is not evidencing transcendence of momentariness.

Intellectual or cognitive growth involves acquisition of ways to represent the recurrent regularities in the environment (equivalence), of the ability to seek out and analyze information, of the concept of conservation or equivalence, and of a means of transcending the momentary by ways of linking past to present to future. Growth in these areas can be conceived of as "the emergence of new technologies for the unlocking and amplification of human intellectual powers." The culture provides the child with "ways of responding, ways of looking and imaging, and, most important, ways of translating what one has encountered into language."[36]

With age, "language comes to play an increasingly powerful role as an implement of knowing. . . . Language shapes, augments, and even supercedes the child's earlier modes of processing information." Language as a medium for representation, translation, and transformation of experience frees the individual from immediacy, opening up "realms of intelleectual possibility that are orders of magnitude beyond the most powerful image-forming system."[37] Language provides the individual with the means of organizing and integrating his or her behavior; in organisms without language, integration is under the control of the stimulus situation.

The question of how language becomes internalized as a means of ordering experience is unanswered. Bruner speculates that the process of internalization depends on interaction with others and the need to develop corresponding categories and transformations as a basis for communal action.

Summary
Bruner does not claim to have constructed a "finished" theory of cognitive growth. He has instead constructed a "model" of intellectual and cognitive development.

In effect, this is a model of a model, since Bruner sees cognitive development as one's construction of a model of the world which allows one to deal with one's environment. Cognition is one's way of knowing one's world, through reducing and organizing complexity to a form in which one can deal with it or use it. The model allows one to go beyond the mode itself, to make predictions and to develop expectations about events, and to understand cause-effect relations.

Cognition (as well as perception) is thus selective; aspects of the world are selected for attention and action in terms of the intent or purpose of the action. Cognitive development is neither simply the result of the maturing or unfolding of inner structure nor entirely the result of shaping by the environment, but a product of both.

The individual's model involves representing the world. The child's earliest representation is through actions upon objects in the world (enactive representation). The child then develops the ability to go beyond immediate objects and to represent the world visually, in images (ikonic representation). Finally, with the development of language, he or she is able to deal with objects and events apart from their immediate presence or existence, in words (symbolic representation). Mature adults, while engaging in symbolic manipulation of their worlds, are also still able to deal with them ikonically and motorically.

The freedom from the immediately and visually present which symbolic representation provides, makes possible a higher order of thinking. Such thinking involves equivalence, invariance, and transcendence of momentariness.

Equivalence involves the recognition of the common characteristics of different objects and events, and is basic to classification. The ability to classify, especially in a hierarchical system, requires rules for inclusion, exclusion, and overlap. Its achievement allows individuals to free themselves from responding to and dealing with each individual object or instance as separate, distinct, and new. It thus simplifies reality and the problems of dealing with each event as distinct.

Invariance is similar to Piaget's concept of conservation; it involves the recognition of continuity in things or objects that are transformed in appearance, location, time, or the responses which they evoke. It is illustrated by the recognition that an amount of water remains the same when it is poured from a glass of one diameter to a glass of another diameter, even though the height (appearance) is different.

Transcendence of momentariness involves freedom from time and space and recognition of coherence among different time and space events or appearances.

All these forms of thinking are made possible by symbolization, or language. Language is thus at the center of intellectual development.

The modeling of reality is influenced by the characteristics and limitations of our human nature and neuromuscular system. But it is also influenced from the outside: Culture provides structured models which are impressed upon the individual. The modeling of reality is also influenced by its use, as when a cultural model is adapted by the individual for his or her own use. Bruner has suggested the term *instrumental conceptualism* to emphasize that models develop as a function of their uses.[38]

There are pressures in technical societies toward agreement or confirmation between the three modes of knowing—toward a correspondence between what we do, what we see, and what we say. A mismatching or confrontation may not always lead to the achievement of correspondence, however, or not for a period of time. For instance, recall the increase in contradictory errors with age, before the symbolic mode conquers. Bruner has called these "growth errors."[39] In a highly developed technical society there is a pressure to relate the three modes of representation or to translate them into each other. "We tend to reject those acts that do not lend themselves to a legitimate rendering or accountability, and perhaps to rule out of imagery those features of existence that have no enactive counterpart or words or sentences that render them communicable."[40]

Bruner closes with a caution about conceiving of conformity among modes as being desirable, especially the forcing of actions and images into conformity with language (lexicon and grammar). The enactive and ikonic operations may be the sources of valuable insights and intuitions, as in poetry.

THE PROCESS OF EDUCATION

Bruner became interested in the process of education very early in his studies of cognitive growth. He was convinced that "developmental psychology without a theory of pedagogy is as empty an enterprise as a theory of pedagogy that ignored the nature of growth."[41] Cognitive psychologists, after assuring themselves that a theory of intellectual growth meets certain theoretical criteria, must also ask themselves "whether we have contributed to our understanding of how to educate man to the point where he can use his intellectual heritage to the full. For if a theory of the growth of the mind cannot help in that enterprise, nor contribute to the understanding of education, it must surely be at fault."[42]

"Instruction," says Bruner, "is, after all, an effort to assist or shape growth. In devising instruction for the young, one would be ill advised to ignore what is known about growth. And a theory of instruction . . . is in effect a theory of how growth and development are assisted by diverse means. . . . The heart of the educational process consists of providing aids and dialogues for translating experience into more powerful systems of notation and ordering."[43]

Education as a Social Invention

Formal education is necessary for at least two reasons. First, in a complex society as distinguished from primitive (indigenous) societies, there is a sharp disjunction between the world of the child and the world of the adult. In primitive societies the child participates in the adult world from an early age, learning from modeling (imitating of adults in their daily activities), and by being shown how to act in the context of real activities. In complex societies children do not participate directly in the real world of adults. They learn from the adults by being told about real activities, out of context. (Teaching is thus often lacking in relevance. The school is removed from the immediate context of socially relevant action.) Schooling separates education from learning by experience and modeling. The school converts knowledge into a highly symbolic, abstract, verbal form.

A second reason for the existence of formal education inheres in the importance of language and symbolism in complex societies. The separation between the adult world and the child's world, with the child learning about the adult world through being told about it, makes language very important in the development of a model of the world. The acquisition of language is a long process. "The intellectual nuturing that makes it possible eventually to use language as a tool of thought requires long years and complex training."[44]

If society is to equip its young to deal with their world, there are five specifications that must be met: (1) Society must convert what is to be known—skills, beliefs, knowledge—into a form capable of being mastered by a beginner. (2) Emphasis must be placed on economy and transfer or generalization, or the learning of general rules or principles. (3) Emphasis must be placed on integrating knowledge and action, or moving from knowledge to action. (4) The interest of the young in learning must be maintained. (5) Society must assure that the necessary skills and knowledge which have been developed are passed on from generation to generation. (The school is not simply an agent of socialization, but a transmitter of basic skills. In our concern about what we should teach, however, we should not abandon the ideal that education should serve to produce well-balanced citizens for a democracy. The word *skills* is used in a broad sense; it includes skills in handling, in seeing and imaging, and in symbolic operations, as well as in cultivating or "disciplining" taste and deepening one's view of the world.)

Characteristics of a Theory of Instruction

The major task of a theory of instruction is to provide an understanding of how human beings can be assisted in their learning and development. A theory of instruction is concerned with the arrangement of the learning environment according to various criteria so as to optimize learning. A theory of instruction sets forth or *prescribes* rules for the most effective way to attain the desired results—the development of knowledge and skills in students. These rules also provide criteria for evaluating methods of teaching and learning. Thus, a theory of instruction is also *normative*, setting standards or criteria and specifying the conditions for meeting them. Such standards are general rather than specific, since specific conditions can be derived from the general.

A theory of instruction differs from a theary of learning in that it is prescriptive, while the latter is descriptive. Theories of learning tell what happens; a theory of instruction tells how to make it happen efficiently. A theory of instruction must be congruent with the theory or theories of learning and development to which it subscribes, since it is concerned with learning and development. That is, a theory of instruction must recognize that a curriculum must take into account not only the nature and structure of knowledge, but also those of the learner and the learning process.

There are four major characteristics of a theory of instruction:

1. It must specify those experiences or relationships with people and things in the school environment that will lead the child to be willing and able to learn. This includes the predispositions in the child which affect learning.
2. A theory of instruction should explicitly state how a subject or body

of knowledge should be structured so that it can be most easily mastered by the learner. Structure must then be related to the nature of the learner's status or cognitive level.
3. A theory of instruction must specify the sequences in which the materials are to be presented for effective learning.
4. A theory of instruction should describe the nature and pacing of rewards and punishments for the facilitation of learning. The relation of extrinsic and intrinsic rewards and their timing, as well as the place of immediate and deferred rewards, should be considered.

Aspects of these requirements as developed by Bruner will now be considered in more detail.

Predispositions. Under the rubric of predispositions to learning, Bruner includes personal factors in the learner—interest, readiness, motivation—as well as cultural factors and the teacher-student relationship. "The single most characteristic thing about human beings is that they learn. Learning is so deeply ingrained in man that it is almost involuntary. . . ."[45] There is an intrinsic motive to learn that does not depend upon extrinsic rewards.

Natural learning is self-rewarding. Learning which occurs as a result of curiosity, the urge toward mastery and competence, and through modeling the activity of another (older) human being is satisfying.

Curiosity characterizes an intrinsic motivation. It is aroused by something which is ambiguous, unclear, incomplete, or uncertain. The achievement of clarity, or even the search for it, is satisfying. Curiosity can be too great, however, in that attention is distractible, so that the individual is dominated by the changing environment and fails to attend adequately or long enough to its important elements. Sustained attention requires some constraints. The child does develop this sustained attention, apparently by becoming involved in the momentum of concrete activity. Little is known about how to help the young child achieve this attentiveness. The drama and uncertainty of a story plot or the uncertainty of play activities (building piles of blocks until they fall, for example) can sustain attention.

Competence is another intrinsic motive. Behavior is directed toward developing and perfecting one's capabilities. Play manifests this perfecting of ways of coping with the environment. Practicing and achieving are self-rewarding activities. What is done well is interesting. But the activity must have some meaning. The achievement of competence at one level encourages one to push ahead to a higher level. A sense of confidence in oneself develops.

Modeling, involving indentification with another, is a motive for learning. Identification can be with a group or a culture. It is a self-rewarding, and thus a self-sustaining, process, since the standards are interiorized.

Models may be "competence models." The teacher can be such a model, someone whose respect the student wants, whose standards he or she would like to adopt.

Reciprocity is the final intrinsic motive. It involves a basic need to respond to and cooperate with others. It seems to be its own reward. Joint action based upon reciprocity may be the basis of human society. The individual becomes a part of a group, and all learn together, though not always the same thing. Reciprocity is not a matter of conformity.

These motivational predispositions constitute the "will to learn." The will to learn is an intrinsic motive.

It is in the artificial setting of the school, where learning is verbal, often with lack of appropriate feedback, that problems arise. Learning in school—or education—is, as was noted above, learning out of context. Complex societies cannot depend upon casual learning of the culture. Education attempts to prepare children for the future—a future they do not know or understand, so that much of the content of education is irrelevant to them for the time being. The problem of interest, motivation, or the "will to learn" thus arises. Learning in school fails to engage the curiosity, desire for competence, aspiration to emulate a model, and commitment to social reciprocity which are the source of natural, spontaneous learning.

Interest in a subject is ideally the best stimulus to learning. It requires deep understanding and patient honesty to make subject matter interesting and still correct and comprehensible. However, making material interesting is not incompatible with presenting it soundly; in fact, accurate presentations are often the most interesting. "The best way to create interest in a subject is to render it worth knowing, which means to make the knowledge gained usable in one's thinking beyond the situation in which the learning has occurred."[46] This is the problem of relevance. It is also what Bruner refers to as the personalization of knowledge. This involves making the material meaningful in terms of the child's own feeling and attitudes.

Interest focuses attention and makes for continuing attention, so that periods (or episodes) in learning are longer in duration. Films, audio-visual aids, and other devices and fancy equipment or apparatus may arouse attention and interest in the short run; but they run the danger that the student may become passive and bored without them, and expect to be entertained. Learning is an active process, and the child should be encouraged to participate actively in the learning process. Interest is aroused and maintained by activity. The discovery method (to be discussed later) promotes interest. When children are faced with a real problem to be solved, they behave differently than when they are given facts to be memorized or when they feel there is no inherent rationality to the material—that it is simply random or arbitrary, and thus meaningless. When children are presented with problems, they naturally try to solve them, if they have not been discouraged by failure and poor teaching, leading them to fear failure or to fear being wrong. "With children in elementary schools, there is often a need to devise emotionally vivid special games, story-making episodes, or construction projects to reestablish in the child's mind his right not only to have his own private ideas but to express them in the public setting of the classroom."[47]

The intrinsic motives, particularly curiosity, with its accompanying uncertainty (or curiosity as a response to uncertainty), stimulate or activate the process of *exploration*. Routine, cut-and-dried tasks evoke little exploration; on the other hand, tasks that are two ambiguous and uncertain arouse anxiety and confusion and inhibit exploration. Learning and problem solving depend on the exploration of various alternatives.

Maintenance of exploration requires that its benefits be greater than its risks. Effective instruction reduces the risks, so that learning is less dangerous or painful than learning on one's own. Errors are less damaging.

Exploration, to be efficient, must be directed; that is, the end or the goal must be known, at least to some approximation, and the results of testing the alternatives must provide information with respect to the attainment of the goal. Instruction should be more helpful than "spontaneous" learning, in that it should provide better knowledge of results.

Relating knowledge to the learner. The pedagogical problem is how to represent knowledge, how to sequence it, and how to embody and present it in a form appropriate to the young learner. This is the function of the curriculum. "Let the curriculum consist of a series of prerequisites in knowledge and skill, to be mastered with a built-in reward in increased competence as the learner goes from one step to the next. Such a view assumes that for any knowledge or empowering skill that exists in the culture there is a corresponding form that is within the grasp of the young learner at the stage of development where we find him—that any subject can be taught to anybody at any age in some form that is both interesting and honest."[48]

This is Bruner's famous dictum, which he has restated a number of times in slightly different form, such as the following: "There is an appropriate version of any skill or knowledge that may be imparted at whatever age one wishes to begin teaching. . . . Any idea or problem or body of knowledge can be presented in a form simple enough so that any particular learner can understand it in recognizable form."[49]

The key to the dictum is the conversion of knowledge into a form which is understandable to the student and which provides her or him with valid knowledge. To do this conversion one must know the level of intellectual or cognitive development of the student. Any discipline, says Bruner, can be translated into a form appropriate for any level of intellectual development. A curriculum should tailor course material in a way that corresponds to the mode of representation at which the students are functioning.

Such tailoring involves the *structuring of subject matter.* Subject matter is voluminous and appears to be highly complex, especially in the sciences and mathematics. Yet, "the basic ideas that lie at the heart of all science and mathematics, and the basic themes that give form to life and literature are as simple as they are powerful."[50] The structure of a subject or discipline consists of fundamental ideas, issues, principles, and relationships. To recognize and develop these fundamentals into a curriculum requires the best minds in each discipline, together with experienced teachers and psychologists. This is what was attempted in the development of new curriculums in mathematics and science in the 1960s.

If such curriculums are to be appropriate for children at different levels of development, the content must be represented in a form which can be understood and assimilated by children at each level. Subject matter can be represented in three ways: by a set of actions designed to achieve a given result (enactive representation), by a set of images or graphics which summarize a concept without fully or completely defining it (ikonic representation), and by a set of symbolic or logical propositions which are elements in a system with rules for forming and transforming propositions (symbolic representation). Some subject matter areas are more difficult to represent in one or another of these areas than are other subject matters. But the basic principles in all presumably can be adequately represented in each mode, in an honest, or valid, form.

One of the advantages of a curriculum which is based on representation of the basic structure of subject matter in differing modes appropriate for learners at different levels of cognitive development is that any subject can be presented to beginning students. In addition, teachers can build on the subject matter not only by adding more detail and content, but by presenting it subsequently in the other modes, providing a continuity. The student is prepared for more advanced knowledge, and the gap between the elementary and the advanced is reduced. Material learned earlier is not absolute, out of date, or inaccurate by reason of being distorted through oversimplification. Later teaching builds on the earlier. "If earlier learning is to render later learning easier, it must do so by providing a general picture in terms of which the relations between things encountered earlier and later are made as clear as possible."[51] It might be argued that it is better to wait until the child is 13 or 14 before beginning the study of geometry, so that the process is continuous and condensed in time. But there is evidence that early training in the basic logical operations of mathematics and science makes later learning easier. The earliest work can be manipulative, followed by work involving images (diagrams and drawings), followed later by abstract notation. Thus, "if you wish to teach the calculus in the eighth grade, then begin it in the first grade by teaching the kinds of ideas and skills necessary for its mastery later."[52] This is what Bruner calls the "spiral curriculum." It involves revisiting basic ideas in different modes at successively higher levels.

The structuring of material and its presentation in a mode suited to the cognitive level of the child maintains the interest of the student. He is able to understand the fundamental ideas, and understanding makes the subject matter more interesting. Specific facts and isolated bits of information do not maintain interest. The timing of the steps in a progressive, spiraling process to match the unfolding capacities of the students is, however, a difficult question.

The structuring of knowledge in terms of fundamental ideas and principles makes for *economy* in teaching and learning. It reduces the amount of information which must be ingested, processed, and retained in order to achieve comprehension. The teaching of specifics outside the context of the fundamental structure of the subject is uneconomical; it is not as interesting, it is easily forgotten, and it doesn't lead to generalization or transfer. Principles and formulas are economical summaries of much detail. The mode of representation is related to economy: Some things are presented more economically in graphic form, others in symbolic, as in the case of formulas. Sequence, to be considered later, is also important.

The effective *power* of any specific way of structuring a body of knowledge relates to the state of the learner's ability to deal with it, including his or her set of learned propositions. Economy and power are theoretically independent, but a powerful structuring technique is unlikely to be uneconomical.

Sequence. There are certain orders of presenting materials and ideas which are more likely to lead students to basic ideas or principles. Instruction involves guiding learners through a series of statements and restatements in a subject or field of knowledge so that their ability to acquire, transform, and use what they are learning increases. Some routes are easier than others, though some are equal. The degree of ease or difficulty varies for different learners. An optimum sequence is likely one which progresses from enactive through ikonic to symbolic representation, although a learner well into the symbolic stage may be able to skip the first two stages. The question of the level of uncertainty and tension necessary to arouse and maintain interest in problem-solving activity is an empirical one.

Optimal sequences may vary depending upon the objective, whether speed of learning, resistance to forgetting, transferability, or economy and power, as these objectives are sometimes antithetical.

Transferability is of particular importance, since learning which cannot be transferred or generalized to similar situations is restricted and of little use in a complex environment. Effective learning is therefore learning which is transferable. The usual meaning of transfer of training is the specific application of learning to highly similar tasks which include identical elements. Such a concept of transfer is limited.

Bruner is concerned with nonspecific transfer, which is the transfer of principles and attitudes. It is this kind of transfer that is at the heart of the educational process, and to which instruction should be directed. This type of transfer is dependent upon mastery of the structure of the subject matter. "The teaching and learning of structure, rather than simply the mastery of facts and techniques, is at the center of the classic problem of transfer."[53]

Details and facts are not retained unless they become part of a structured pattern. The learning of general or fundamental principles reduces memory loss and makes possible the reconstruction of details when necessary. When specifics are seen as instances of a general case, a model is available for incorporating and understanding similar specific instances.

The form and pacing of reinforcement.　Bruner uses the word *reinforcement* to refer to knowledge of results, or feedback on the effects of one's actions. Such knowledge is "corrective knowledge" and is necessary for learning to occur. Its usefulness depends on timing, on when and where it is given and received.

Learning or problem solving consists of a cycle which includes a testing procedure, or a trial, and the comparison of results with some criterion, a cycle which is repeated again and again in an ascending or hierarchical order in the process of education. "Knowledge of results should come at that point in a problem-solving episode when the person is comparing the results of his try-out with some criterion of what he seeks to achieve."[54] Information given before that point is reached is not understood—it is not meaningful or relevant; information given later is too late to affect the next trial.

Since learning is usually piecemeal, with the eventual goal being distant and the learner not being clear about whether a particular cycle is leading toward this goal, instructors or tutors fill an important role. They provide information to learners about the longterm relevance of their efforts. Eventually, the learners must take over this function themselves, so they can learn without the presence of a tutor.

Information must be translated into the learner's method or approach to solving a problem if it is to be useful. Negative information—information about what something is not—is helpful. Corrective information must be given in the mode in which the learner is functioning in problem solving.

An important point, or caution, is that the object of instruction is to lead the learner to be self-sufficient. There is a danger that correction may encourage the learner to become dependent upon the tutor. Thus correction must be provided in a way that leads the learner to take over this function. Ideally, the learning situation should be set up to be self-correcting; for example, in experiments using apparatus such as balances, the effects of actions are immediately and clearly apparent. Learning occurs by feedback from the natural consequences of the actions. The instructor, of course, is involved in setting up the situation.

Learning is, or should be, its own reward. It provides satisfaction in achievement, in the sense of competence, and in the ability to move on to more difficult situations and problems. Thus, "to the degree that competence or mastery motives come to control behavior, the role of reinforcement or extrinsic pleasure wanes in shaping behavior."[55] Bruner suggests that the "satisfying state of affairs" emphasized by Thorndike's law of effect is not likely to be found consistently in "kind or harsh words from the teacher, in grades or gold stars, in the absurdly abstract assurance to the high school student that his lifetime earnings will be better by 80 percent if he graduates. External reinforcement may indeed get a particular act going and may even lead to repetition, but it does not nourish, reliably, the long course of learning."[56]

The domination of learning by strong extrinsic rewards and punishment can interfere with learning in several ways. First, it can create a pressure which leads to high anxiety, which inhibits learning—the child becomes unable to think. Also, where anxiety is too high, the learner is unable to use corrective information. Second, learning is narrowed to the specific aspects which are reinforced; learning is less generic and less transferable. Third, it masks the satisfaction of intrinsic rewards. Children who are led to expect a "payoff" from the teacher or instructor can be distracted from behavior which provides intrinsic rewards and become corrupted toward working for the extrinsic rewards. Their interest in the subject matter itself wanes, and attention and persistence decrease. They focus on trying to figure out what the teacher wants.

"Much of the problem in leading a child to effective cognitive activity is to free him from the immediate control of environmental rewards and punishments. That is to say, learning that starts in response to the rewards of parental or teacher approval or the avoidance of failure can too readily develop a pattern in which the child is seeking cues as to conform to what is expected of him."[57]

Discovery Learning

In 1961 Bruner published an article entitled "The Act of Discovery," which became the basis for a "school of pedagogy," emphasizing, says Bruner, discovery as a goal in itself without regard to what is discovered. Bruner intended to emphasize the importance of self-direction and intentionality in learning. In 1966 he published "Some Elements of Discovery," in an attempt to remedy the misuse of the concept of discovery learning.

Discovery learning does not refer to finding out something never before known; it refers to what one discovers for oneself. This is the most uniquely personal and all a person's knowledge. Discovery is "a matter of rearranging or transforming evidence in such a way that one is enabled to go beyond the evidence so reassembled to additional new insights."[58] New information is not necessary for discovery to occur.

Children engage in discovery learning naturally and continue to do so, to a greater or lesser extent, depending upon their learning environments. One important factor in its continuance is the expectation that there is something to discover, that there are regularities and relationships in the environment rather than that everything occurs at random. Discovery learning capitalizes upon and promotes the expectation of regularity and relatedness. It leads to the discovery of such characteristics in events and to efficient methods of doing so. "It is, if you will, a necessary condition for learning the variety of techniques of problem solving, of transforming information for better use, indeed for learning how to go about the very task of learning. Practice in discovery for oneself teaches one to acquire information in a way that makes that information more readily viable in problem solving. . . . To the degree that one is able to approach learning as a task of discovering something rather than learning about it, to that degree there will be a tendency for the child to carry out his learning activities with the autonomy of self-reward, or more properly by reward that is discovery itself."[59] The learner is thus freed from immediate stimulus control—external rewards and punishment—and is free to utilize success and failure as informative feedback. Behavior becomes more long-range in its orientation and operates more from the inside out. Bruner proposed these statements as hypotheses to be tested in the schools.

It is only through practice that one learns problem solving through discovery. Teaching can, however, facilitate the process. Bruner makes a distinction between teaching in the expository mode and teaching in the hypothetical mode. In the former, the teacher controls the process, and the student is a passive listener. In the latter, the student is involved as an active participant, and at times may be the principal actor. The student will be aware of alternatives and can evaluate the relevance of information as it comes. Bruner hypothesizes that this approach will facilitate discovery learning. In discovery learning the student incorporates information in a cognitive structure which he has developed, so that it is meaningful, and it is thus not only retained in memory but is more easily retrievable.

Discovery learning is, however, inefficient as a means of passing on the culture. Each individual cannot rediscover all that is known. Discovery cannot be the principal way that one learns about one's environment. And Bruner, in his later article, suggests that it is not the natural way. He points to the way language is learned as natural. In this process there are three elements. One is like discovery—the exploration of a situation. The child explores language usage. In the process he invents word combinations or patterns that have a certain innateness or develop out of basic characteristics of the nervous system. But these inventions become molded or shaped into adult grammar by the parents or other persons in the child's environment. Thus the process involves both active teaching and modeling as two elements in addition to discovery. The child is not permitted to discover haphazardly.

Bruner then discusses six problems in teaching by the discovery method so that children will use material appropriately in a variety of situations. First is the problem of arranging learning so that children recognize that there are connections or relationships between the things they have learned, so that they can go beyond the situation in which they have learned to other situations. This is an attitude; a belief in the learners that they have something in their own heads, implicit models, that are useful. "Discovery teaching generally involves not so much the process of leading students to discover what is 'out there,' but rather their discovering what is in their own heads."[60]

The second problem is the compatibility problem—how to get children to fit new material into their own systems of associations, categories, and frames of reference so that it becomes their own. Getting students to rephrase materials, using their own terms, is useful. Assisting them to form new and, to them, meaningful concepts and connections also helps.

The third problem is that of activating the children so that they can experience their capacity to solve problems and be successful enough that they are rewarded for thinking. Here Bruner reiterates the idea of competence as self-rewarding.

Fourth is seeing that children get practice in the use of information and problem solving. This can be fostered by teaching in the hypothetical mode, so that students get experience in hypothesis making as well as in hypothesis testing.

Fifth is what Bruner calls the "self-loop problem." Children can often do things but are not able to say to themselves what they have done and put it in a form which they can hold in mind. Discussions of how we say things and of how ways of saying things are the same or different, are helpful.

Finally, there is the problem of handling information flow so that it can be used in problem solving, or of engineering discovery so that it is more routine and less a matter of inspiration. Bruner emphasizes the importance of presenting material in contrastive form, as in showing aspects of life in different cultures. "We believe that by getting the child to explore contrasts, he is more likely to organize his knowledge in a fashion that helps discovery in particular situations where discovery is needed." The efficacy of the method of contrast "stems from the fact that a concept requires for its definition a choice of a negative case. Man is a different concept contrasted to standing bears, to angels, to devils. Readiness to explore contrasts provides a choice among the alternatives that might be relevant."[61]

Discovery learning is not, then, applied to all learning. The *method* of discovery learning is what appears to be emphasized by Bruner, and it is this which should be learned. This method involves the construction as well as the testing of hypotheses; its importance is in developing the ability to transcend the immediate or the familiar, and to take an as-if or if-then point of view which can lead in general to more creative thinking, as well as to specific discovery learning.

Disciplined Intuition

Intuition or *intuitive thinking* has at least two meanings, or connotations. On the one hand it refers to the antithesis of knowing by the scientific method, through experiment, empirical study, logical and statistical analysis, or mathematical proof. It is knowledge or understanding through art, poetry, myth, and the humanities. This is what Bruner refers to as knowledge from the left hand. In this sense the term *intuitive thinking* may be used pejoratively or deprecatingly.

But there is a use of the term in mathematics (as well as in the physical and biological sciences) which does not have this negative connotation. Intuitive thinking is valued in these disciplines—perhaps, Bruner suggests, because of the confidence in the power and rigor of these disciplines which its representatives possess.

The dictionary definition of intuition is "immediate apprehension or cognition." It is the achievement of a sudden solution to a problem on which one has worked a long time, the formal proof of which only comes later. It is also the recognition of a truth or solution without proof or the recognition of which of several approaches to a problem is likely to prove fruitful. Intuition "implies the act of grasping the meaning or significance or structure of a problem without explicit reliance on the analytic apparatus of one's craft. It is the intuitive mode that yields hypotheses quickly, that produces interesting combinations of ideas before their worth is known. It precedes proof; indeed, it is what the techniques of analysis and proof are designed to test and check."[62]

Intuitive thinking is in contrast to analytic thinking. Analytic thinking proceeds in a step-by-step fashion of which the thinker is aware. It may use deductive reasoning, or mathematics or logic, or a process of induction or experiment. Analytic thinking provides the proof of solutions or hypotheses achieved by intuitive thinking. Intuitive thinking may achieve solutions which might not be arrived at through analytic thinking, or perhaps only much more slowly. Intuitive thinking may even discover or invent problems which analytic thinking would not.

The importance of intuitive thinking is apparent. It is the source of many of the important problems and hypotheses which have led to advancement in the sciences. We need to utilize hunches, guesses, intuitions, which are forms of "knowledge by the left hand," by shifting them to the "right hand," so that they can be tested. It would appear to be desirable to encourage and improve intuitive thinking.

Bruner hypothesizes a number of things which might encourage intuitive thinking in students:

1. The development of intuitive thinking in children is more likely if their teachers think intuitively. The hypothetical mode in teaching would appear to be relevant here. The process of modeling through imitation or identification could be involved.
2. The providing of varied experience in a field should increase effectiveness of intuitive thinking in that field. Intuition is built upon a (thorough) knowledge of subject matter; the knowledge need not be formal, but something is necessary to work with.
3. Emphasis upon the structure or connectedness of knowledge increases facility in intuitive thinking. Structure emphasizes the important ideas, concepts, principles, and relationships which provide a basis for developing questions or hypotheses.
4. The teaching of heuristic procedures in problem solving should promote intuitive thinking. Such approaches are nonrigorous, as compared to an analytic or algorithmic procedure, and while heuristic procedures do not guarantee a solution (as does the algorithmic), they can be used when no algorithmic procedure for a problem is known. Such procedures include using methods appropriate for a simple problem similar to the one at hand; reasoning by analogy; appealing to symmetry; the examination of limiting conditions; and visualization of solutions. Such procedures free students to explore rather than restricting them to a single procedure.
5. The encouragement of guessing—not wild guessing but educated guessing founded upon some knowledge of a given subject—should increase intuitive thinking. Guessing is too often penalized. But often

in life it is necessary to act on incomplete knowledge, or in effect to make a guess. "What we should teach students to recognize, probably, is when the cost of not guessing is too high, as well as when guessing itself is too costly. We tend to do the latter much better than the former."[63] The use of guessing by teachers when faced with a question which they can't answer, followed by checking out the guess, could set an example.

6. Building self-confidence in students should foster effective intuitive thinking. Intuitive thinking often leads to correct solutions but may also lead to errors. There must be a willingness to risk being wrong, and such a risk is more likely to be taken by a student who is secure and self-confident.

7. Modifying the present system of rewards and punishments in schools which probably tends to inhibit intuitive thinking should increase intuitive thinking. Rewarding correct answers and the acquisition of facts with high grades, and punishing guessing and other manifestations of intuitive thinking with low grades, certainly discourages the latter.

These suggestions—intuitive though they are—are reasonable enough to merit consideration.

A compelling argument for attending to intuitive thinking in education is that it provides an entry to teaching the basic structure and fundamentals of a subject to young children, before they are able to understand analytic reasoning or formal thinking. The child at the concrete, or ikonic, stage of cognitive development is capable of grasping basic concepts of an intuitive level. In mathematics instruction particularly, it has been clearly shown that children are able to understand complex concepts when they are presented in a concrete form rather than by means of formal vocabulary. At higher levels, as in high-school plane geometry, teaching should begin with intuitive methods, including visual proofs. After an intuitive understanding has been achieved, the teacher can then move on to traditional and formal methods of proof.

The young child comes to school with an understanding, on an intuitive level, of a number of mathematical principles, which he may not be able to express verbally. The school, instead of beginning here, introduces "the premature use of the language of mathematics, its end-product formalism, which makes it seem that mathematics is something new rather than something the child already knows. . . . By interposing formalism, we prevent the child from realizing that he has been thinking mathematics all along. What we do, in essence, is to remove his confidence in his ability to perform the process of mathematics. At our worst, we offer formal proof (which is necessary for checking) in place of direct intuition. . . . It is important to allow the child to use his natural and intuitive ways of thinking, indeed to encourage him to do so, and honor him when he does well."[64]

Thus, rather than recognizing and encouraging the natural intuitive thinking of the child, the school inhibits it. The result is that the child is forced to go through the mechanical process of manipulating numbers without any intuitive sense of what it is all about. Bruner writes that observation of this process reminds him of the lines of Lewis Carroll: "Reeling and Writhing, of course, to begin with . . . and then the different branches of Arithmetic—Ambition, Distraction, Uglification, and Derision."

Acceleration

A word needs to be said about Bruner's view on acceleration, since he has been interpreted as disagreeing with Piaget on this matter. Actually, Bruner has very little to say about acceleration—the word does not appear in the indices of his books.

Bruner's position seems simply to be that the child needs, and will grow most rapidly in, situations which call for the exercise of those skills which are appropriate to its existing level of development. Or, as he has expressed it elsewhere, "instruction in scientific ideas, even at the elementary level, need not follow slavishly the natural course of cognitive development in the child. It can also lead intellectual development by providing challenging but usable opportunities for the child to forge ahead in his development."[65] If there is, as Bruner states, a way to teach basic ideas and concepts to children of any age, then, he suggests, one cannot or should not passively wait for readiness to develop. Readiness can be created by appropriate teaching.

Education of the Future

Education requires constant redefinition if it is to meet the requirements of succeeding generations. Bruner lists four changes in our own times that need to be considered in education:[66]

1. Increasing understanding of humans as a species. We are a tool-using species; our use of mind is dependent upon the ability to develop tools, instruments, or technologies that enable us to amplify our physiological and sensory powers. Language is a powerful technology. The educational system is the means of transmitting these technologies, which are necessary for the continuance of society. Emphasis must be placed on the teaching of skills related to technologies.
2. The increasing understanding of the nature of individual mental growth. Stages or steps in mental growth have been recognized. Although they are described differently by different investigators, there

appears to be general agreement. The implications of the fact that "unless certain basic skills are mastered [during early stages], . . . later, more elaborated ones become increasingly out of reach"[67] must be recognized.

3. A clearer understanding of the process of education. Education which is tailored to the mode of representation of the student makes it possible to begin early to teach difficult subjects. Success in high-level mastery at the symbolic level is best assured by beginning to teach the subject at lower levels, in the mode appropriate to the level of the students. The recognition that cognitive or intellectual mastery is rewarding provides the possibility of an approach to education which allows for greater progress in learning. The realization that evaluation should be continuous and built into the curriculum makes possible more effective curriculum change and development. The lack of a theory of instruction is a handicap which must be overcome.

4. The accelerating rate of change in society. The changing society forces a redefinition of education. The acceleration of technology has led to emphasis upon producing technicians, engineers, and scientists. But this does not provide what is needed to manage change. What is needed is men and women with skills in sensing continuity and opportunity for continuity.

Four general policies seem to follow from these considerations:

1. The first involves what is taught. Emphasis in education should be placed on skills, as noted above. A particular need is the education of perceptual-imaginal capacities, the training of subtle spatial imagery. Those who are trained in this mode appear to be able to view the environment with new discrimination and from new viewpoints.

2. Curriculums should involve the mastery of skills that lead, in self-rewarding sequences, to the mastery of higher-level, more powerful skills.

3. Adjustment to change requires the development of a metalanguage and "metaskills" for dealing with continuity in change. Mathematics is the most general metalanguage. "I find myself forced to the conclusion that our survival may one day depend upon achieving a requisite mathematical literacy for rendering the seeming shocks of change into something that is continuous and cumulative."[68] Poetry is also a discipline that seeks the likeness within change and diversity.

4. The accumulation of information requires that we move away from concern with history to a concern with the social or behavioral sciences. "It is the behavioral sciences and their generality with respect to variations in the human condition that must be central to our presentation of man, not the particularities of history."[69]

Adaptation to change requires that the educational system be more responsive. This means devoting far greater resources to designing our educational system. Among these resources is modern psychology. Educational psychology has fallen from its high status of a few decades ago. It has become preoccupied with learning and behavior in arranged environments where elements of behavior of theoretical interest can be observed. It has moved away from the psychology of learning in school to laboratory studies of short-term learning, such as the learning of nonsense syllables. This has not contributed to a theory of instruction, which must be concerned with arranging environments for optimum learning to meet various criteria.

Summary

Formal education is a necessity in a complex society, where the young cannot learn all that is required for functioning in the adult world simply by observing and imitating adults as they function in their daily activities. The young must learn by being told, rather than by being shown. Language thus becomes very important in the child's construction of its world by symbolic representation, and early schooling consists in large part of facilitating the acquisition of symbolic systems.

A theory of instruction must be concerned with the predispositions in the learner which influence learning; with the structuring of knowledge so it can be mastered by the learner; with the sequences in which materials should be presented; and with the nature and pacing of rewards and punishments to facilitate learning.

Natural learning is self-rewarding. The organism in nature is active, curious, seeking mastery and competence. There is a "will to learn"; motivation is not a problem. In the artificial setting of the school, where learning is separated from action and is highly verbal, with lack of natural or appropriate feedback, the content or subject matter may not seem to be relevant, and motivational problems arise. Interest in subject matter stimulates learning; it can be fostered by making the knowledge gained usable beyond the specific situation in the classroom where it is learned.

Knowledge can be related to the learner by structuring it so that basic concepts and principles are emphasized. These fundamental ideas and principles must and can be presented in a form which can be understood by the learner at his or her cognitive level (enactive, ikonic or symbolic) in an honest form. Any subject can thus be presented to beginning students, and should later be presented in different (as well as more detailed) form in the other modes of representation, building upon the earlier presentations in a "spiral curriculum."

Sequencing of materials involves presenting materials in an optimal order, usually beginning with the enactive (concrete) through the ikonic to the symbolic (abstract). Adequate structuring and sequenc-

ing makes for speed of learning, resistance to forgetting, and transferability, as well as economy and power in learning. Some of these
objectives may be inconsistent with others, however, so that there may
be no sequence which is optimal for all these objectives.

Reinforcement consists of feedback, or knowledge of the results
of one's actions. The teacher, in providing such "corrective knowledge"
or information relevant to the learner's progress toward a long-term
goal, plays an important role in learning. Learning which provides a
sense of achievement and competence is its own reward and leads to
efforts to cope with more difficult problems, since the earlier achievements provide a basis for continued success. Such learning is based on
intrinsic rewards. The use of strong extrinsic rewards or punishment
can inhibit learning, through the arousal of high anxiety, and can lead
to highly specific learning restricted to what is rewarded, thus lessen-
ing transfer.

Discovery learning is a useful method of learning in children, one
which is too often discouraged in education. It should be continued,
since it is a necessary condition for learning the techniques of problem solving. Discovery learning is self-rewarding and thus frees the
learner from stimulus control. It is fostered by teaching in the hypothetical mode as contrasted to teaching in the expository mode. Although discovery learning is inefficient as a means of passing on the
total knowledge of the culture, the method is important, since it is the
aproach to the discovery of new knowledge through the scientific
method.

The discovery of new knowledge involves intuitive thinking.
Intuitive thinking is the sudden solution of a problem or the recognition of a truth or solution without proof. These truths or solutions then
become hypotheses, which are tested or proved by analytic thinking.
Education tends to discourage intuitive thinking. It should rather encourage such thinking in several ways: by the example of teachers; by
providing a variety of ideas or approaches to a subject; by emphasis
upon fundamental ideas and concepts and their relationships; by pro-
moting heuristic procedures in problem-solving; by the encouragement
of educated guessing; by encouraging self-confidence in students so
they will risk a guess which may be wrong; and by abandoning the
system of rewarding "correct" answers and punishing guessing and
other manifestations of intuitive thinking.

Children are naturally intuitive in their thinking. Recognizing this
by presenting subject matter first in an intuitive mode makes it possible
for children to grasp basic subjects early. Feeling that they understand,
they then can be led to a more analytic or formal understanding without losing confidence in themselves and reverting to rote memorizing.

Education in the future must continually be redefined in terms of
increasing knowledge of humans as a species and increasing under-

standing of the nature of individual mental growth. A clearer under-standing of how to tailor the process of education to the mode of representation of the student will increase the efficiency and effective-ness of education. The accelerating rate of social change requires that we develop people who are capable of managing change, rather than simply turning out more technicians, engineers, and scientists.

The emphasis of education should be on the development of skills, in a broad sense, particularly the skill of spatial imagery, which seems to lead to innovative viewpoints with regard to the environment. The tremendous accumulation of information, which is highly specific with regard to time and place, cannot be dealt with in education. We must teach the principles and generalizations developed by the be-havioral sciences rather than items of historical fact. Education re-quires greater resources if it is to be responsive to change. Among these resources is an educational psychology which is relevant to learning in school environments and which can provide the basis for a theory of instruction.

EVALUATION

Bruner and Cognitive Psychology

The decade from the midsixties to the midseventies was dominated, in psychology, by behaviorism—or more accurately, by neo-neobehavior-ism. This influence of behaviorism began to be felt in psychology in the early fifties.

Bruner, as has been noted, has been critical of behaviorism. In 1969 he wrote: "It seems inconceivable that there stands between you and understanding a missing word of praise or a chocolate bar. Rather, what seems to be at work in a good problem-solving 'performance' is some underlying competence in using the operations of physics or whatever, and the performance that emerges from this competence may never be the same on two occasions. What is learned is compe-tence, not particular performance."[70]

Strike, referring to this statement in his review of Bruner's book, comments: "I suspect Bruner is correct here. Particularly, it is impor-tant to note that the degree to which a concept or a skill has this prop-erty of generativeness [that is, the capacity to generate or be applied to a variety of specific instances] will be the degree to which it will resist being stated as a behavioral repertoire. Anyone who takes the concept of generativeness as real and important should regard at-tempts to state educational goals in ways dictated by behaviorist as-sumptions as little more than the trivialization of education."[71]

Thus, Bruner has resisted the bandwagon trend toward behavior-ism. He was the forerunner, in the fifties, of the emphasis on cognition in psychology, an emphasis which has grown so strong that Millward notes that "today cognitive psychology dominates the Zeitgeist."[72] This dominance has penetrated behaviorism, which has become increasingly cognitively oriented. Indeed, the statement of current behavior theory by Bandura in his 1974 presidential address to the American Psychological Association is hardly recognizable as behaviorism, as the term has been generally defined.[73] Bandura's is a highly cognitive approach to behavior. To what extent Bruner has been responsible for this change is of course problematical; Bandura makes no reference to him.

Bruner and Piaget

In addition to comparing his position to that of Skinner, Bruner compares it to that of Piaget. He states that he is less of an environmentalist than Skinner, but more of an environmentalist than Piaget:

> Skinner attributes such order as there is to control of behavior by orderly stimuli in the world. Piaget sees more order than Skinner, so he attributes it to the inherent logical structures of mind, accommodating only slightly to the lessons of the environment. Skinner's solution has some of the monotony of nature. But it is much more fortuitous than nature could afford to be. The generativeness in behavior that makes it economical vanishes at Skinner's touch, even from language. With Piaget it is the opposite. The order and generativeness are all there from the start, like the shape of the mollusk, ready to eat so long as nutriment enters the system.
>
> We have no complaint against universality in human intellectual functioning, or against the shaping power of the environment. But we do have a complaint about theories that opt for internal universality in surfeit, or environmental shaping as the mold of such uniformity. Human beings are the most awkward species on earth, the most uneven in development, the most beset by obstacles that are not intrinsic to the task. We urge a new functional analysis of what it takes to grow up intelligent, a job description of growing up.[74]

Although it would appear that Bruner assigns Piaget a more extreme position than he deserves, it is clear that Bruner recognizes that intelligent behavior is a function of both the innate characteristics or nature of the individual and of the environment, or an interaction of the two.

Bruner has accepted much of the work and theory of Piaget. His enactive, ikonic, and symbolic modes, while not stages in the sense that Piaget conceives of stages, do closely parallel the stages of cognitive development described by Piaget (sensorimotor, concrete-operational, and formal operations). Bruner's description of cognitive development in broad outline is thus very similar to that of Piaget. Bruner writes that the "many points of disagreement are nevertheless minor by comparison with the points of fundamental agreement we share with Piaget."[75]

There are two major differences, however, between Bruner and Piaget; one is in the nature of the problem with which they are concerned, and the other concerns the place of language in cognitive development:

1. Piaget, as Bruner points out, is not mainly concerned with the psychology of cognition, but with epistemology. He is interested in the nature of knowledge and the development of knowing, or ways of knowing, in the child and adolescent. He describes the nature of knowledge at various stages in development in logical and mathematical form. Epistemology attempts to describe or explain how men *know*, how they think. "But in no sense does this formal description constitute an explanation or a psychological description of the processes of growth. The descriptive clarity, rather, poses the question for anybody who would deal with psychological explanation."[76]

   Bruner is mainly concerned with the psychological explanation of the process of cognitive growth—with how men *learn*. The difference in approach is illustrated in the interpretation of the behavior of children in the conservation problem involving the levels of water in glasses of different diameters. Piaget's interpretation is in terms of logical operations—compensation, reversibility, and, recently, quantitative identity. Bruner utilizes psychological (and intuitive) constructs, involving conflict in the ikonic and symbolic modes of representation. The achievement of symbolic representation, he believes, leading to the recognition of phenomenal identity, can resolve the conflict between the discrepant information provided by the ikonic representation and the symbolic representation.

2. This difference in interpretation is related to the difference in importance attributed to language by Piaget and Bruner. Bruner places great emphasis upon language as a mediator in the development of problem-solving skills in children of 6 to 7 years of age. Bruner and his colleagues found a correlation between the child's performance on tasks and the language he or she uses in describing the reasons for this performance (see above). Bruner then hypothesized that improvement in language should lead to improvement in task performance. This hypothesis was not studied, but the related supposition that activation of language habits already mastered by the child might also improve performance was studied. Bruner and his associates conducted a number of experiments which Bruner interprets as supporting his hypothesis. He concludes: "It is plain that if a child is to succeed in the conservation task, he must have some internalized verbal formula that shields him from the overpowering appearance of the visual displays."[77]

However, this conclusion is disputed by Inhelder and her colleagues on the basis of their experiments. They did find a parallel between a child's level of performance on conservation tests and its descriptive language. However, the "systematic teaching of the language of description appropriate" to the particular conservation concept being investigated did not necessarily lead to achievement of conservation, even though the children were able to use the language in their descriptions. They conclude: "Our evidence offers little, if any, support for the contention that language learning per se contributes to the *integration and coordination* of 'informational units' necessary for the achievement of the conservation concepts," though it does direct the child's focus to relevant dimensions and aids in the storage and retrieval of relevant information.[78] Language may be a correlate but not the instrument of performance, a symptom but not the source. Anglin suggests that although these results may indicate that language does not mediate conservation, they may also mean that the experimenters were not effective in teaching the language or that the language taught was not the appropriate language for the tasks.[79] Anglin's conclusion, however, is that the question is still open and unresolved.

The problem is a difficult one—whether the appropriate language or symbolic representation precedes appropriate performance, whether it is a concomitant of the performance, or whether it follows.

Burner seems to be inconsistent in his emphasis on the importance and priority of language symbolization and in his proposal that teaching should begin at the enactive level, proceed through the ikonic level, and then deal with the subject matter on the symbolic level—even with older children, when a new subject is introduced He cautions against too-early use of the formal language of logic and mathematics in education. Yet he writes: "Language is a major instrument of thought"; and, "The power of words is the power of thought"; and "The way of language in knowing is the most powerful means we have of performing transformations on the world, for transmuting its shape by recombination in the interest of possibility."[80]

There is no necessary contradiction between the emphasis upon the importance of language in human life and the recognition that action and visual representation precede symbolic representation in development, however. Language is the major instrument of thought and the most powerful way of knowing for the adult who has achieved a high semantic level of language. There would appear to be a danger, however, that Bruner's emphasis upon language could lead to overemphasis upon (premature) language training in children and neglect of attention to the development of enactive and ikonic modes of representation in the educative process. This appears to be the mistake of most compensatory programs of education for disadvantaged or deprived children. Bruner notes that class differences in language are not a matter of the amount of language or differences in language, but rather in the use of language. The upper classes use language in a more formal, impersonal, and analytic context, as compared to the more affective, personal, and situation-bound use by the lower class. Yet the lower-class child apparently can use language analytically under the appropriate conditions. Compensatory education should not, therefore, focus upon language per se, but upon the personal and situational variables that shape the use of language. In addition, Bruner notes that attempts to improve the intellectual performance of lower-class children by nonverbal means—discriminative and perceptual training—have been successful. Many programs focusing on language have not. The fact that, as Bruner has noted, the child's (syntactical) language is ahead of his capacity or ability to (semantically) benefit from it or to utilize it in conceptual thinking is perhaps relevant here. There appears to be some inconsistency in Bruner's emphasis upon the importance of language and his recognition that early development involves enactive and ikonic representation.

Bruner, Piaget, and Montessori

It seems to be appropriate here to note the parallels between Montessori, Piaget, and Bruner. Allowing for differences in time, language style, and the nature and context of their work, the three sound astonishingly alike in many of their concepts. It is remarkable how Montessori anticipated Piaget and Bruner. The support for many of her observations by the later studies and experiments of Piaget and Bruner strengthens the possible validity of her observations which have not yet been directly supported by research.

All three agree upon the concept of the child as an active learner, on behavior as intentional, and on the self-rewarding property of learning, that is, the importance of intrinsic rather than extrinsic reward. Their developmental stages closely parallel each other, with recognition of transition periods and plateaus, or periods of consolidation. Each recognizes, in some form, the existence of sensitive periods, or times when the organism learns optimally if opportunities are present. These opportunities represent the prepared environment of Montessori, and their necessity is the reason for formal education in Bruner's system.

Montessori appears to have some relevance for an approach to language development in young children. It will be recalled that retarded children began to write and read spontaneously at 4 to 5 years of age in Montessori's school. This they did without direct instruction; it occurred following the children's use of sandpaper letters and cutout letters, which were traced with the fingers and handled by feeling the outlines. In other words, language was approached through the enactive and ikonic modes, as Bruner recommends for other spheres of learning. The approach to language and reading by the enactive and ikonic modes is supported by recent work with brain-damaged patients with pure alexia (inability to read but ability to write). In these cases the use of three-dimensional letters leads to development of reading ability. Studies of Orientals with alexia have found that they may be able to read ideographic characters but not phonetic characters. These methods are being tried with children with learning disabilities involving reading.

Bruner's position regarding critical periods in development seems unclear. He recognizes the importance of the early environment: "It is plain that a stunted organism is produced by depriving an infant of the rich diet of impressions on which his curiosity normally feeds with such extravagance. Animals raised in homogenized environments show crippling deficits in their later ability to learn and to transfer what they have learned. Children 'kept in the attic' by misguided or psychotic parents show the same striking backwardness. Indeed, even the children who have suffered the dull, aseptic environment of backward foundling homes often show a decline in intelligence that can be compensated only by vigorous measures of enrichment."[81] Again, speaking of the importance of early experience, he refers to the "virtually irreversible deficits" produced in mammals by early deprivation, and to the "crippling effect of deprived human environments," which, however, can be compensated for, to some extent at least, up to adolescence.[82]

Again, referring to the effects of sensory deprivation and limitation of opportunity in animals, he writes: "There seems to be a critical period during which isolation from the world of rich stimulation has its maximum deleterious effect—during the first year principally. But there is evidence that there are effects, more or less irreversible, that are produced by prolonged exposure to dulled and homogenized environments during the formative years of any mammal." Then, referring to education, he says that "we should be asking whether there are critical periods for the introduction of training in mathematics and language and guiding myths. There probably are."[83] Yet he also writes: "There seems to be little evidence . . . for anything like critical periods in human growth—such that, for example, if a skill is not learned during a particular period in the life cycle, it cannot be learned later. The only exception may be in the sphere of language: we do not know whether language can be learned after a certain age, though we do know that if a certain language is *not* learned by ten or eleven, its phonology will never be fully mastered in the manner of a native speaker."[84]

The apparent inconsistency may be resolved perhaps by noting that although there may be no critical periods in the sense that once the period has passed the skill can never be learned (except possibly for language), there are apparently periods which are optimum for specific learnings, and such learnings may later be more difficult. And, as is noted above, Bruner states that unless certain basic skills are mastered, later more complex skills may not be achieved.

The matter of acceleration of learning is relevant here. Bruner appears to disagree with Piaget and Montessori on the possibility of acceleration. But it would appear that this difference can be reconciled if it is recognized that by acceleration Bruner is referring to introducing opportunities for the use and development of functions when the child is capable of exercising them; in other words, he is talking about providing a prepared environment. Bruner, characterizing his approach as context sensitive and Piaget's approach (and presumably that of Montessori) as context free, poses the Geneva (and Montessori) dilemma: If the child only takes in what he is "ready to assimilate," why bother to teach him before he is ready, and since he takes it in naturally once he is ready, why bother afterwards?[85] But it would seem that one may accept the first horn of the dilemma without accepting the second. The child who is ready to learn will not do so if the environment does not provide the opportunities for such learning, including a teacher to put the child in contact with the materials in an appropriate manner.

Bruner and Intuitive Thinking

Words have limits, Bruner notes, and he has emphasized the importance of the ikonic mode in getting a new or different view or perception of the problems with which we are faced, particularly, it might be suggested, the problems of relating to and efficiently utilizing our environment. Bruner links intuition, creativeness, and ikonic thinking, and relates all of them to a kind of knowledge which differs from "scientific" knowledge or knowledge which involves the symbolization of language and mathematics and the logical manipulation of these symbols. This knowledge, he has said, is derived from the left hand. Knowledge derived from the left hand has traditionally been considered as unscientific, subjective, and thus of little value. Yet, as Bruner points out, significant hunches and hypotheses emerge from such intuitive thinking. Both kinds of knowledge are necessary, and both should be encouraged and cultivated.

Bruner's intuitive recognition of these two kinds or two sources of knowing is supported by recent research on the human brain. This research indicates that the two hemispheres of the brain differ in their functions. It has long been known, of course that the right side of the brain controls and integrates the motor actions of the left side of the body, and that the left side of the brain controls the actions of the right side of the body. It has also long been known that the left side of the brain contains the language centers. But the other functions of the right side have not been clear. Now it appears that the right side contains centers for nonverbal, perceptual, mechanical, and spatial reasoning. Support for this conclusion comes from studies of artists who have suffered brain damage. If the damage is in the left hemisphere, language functions are disturbed or lost, but the artistic function continues, even improving, according to some reports. On the other hand, if the right hemisphere is damaged, artistic functioning is impaired. In cases of aphasia, resulting from damage to the left hemisphere, thinking involving spatial problems, differences in patterns and configurations, and the emotional or affective aspects of a situation may be preserved. "Knowing with the left hand," then, derives from the right side of the brain, as does also the motor activity of the left hand.

Thus it appears that a person has two brains, and each mediates a different way of knowing. One is dominant, however, so that each of us tends to be dominated by one way of thinking. However, we all have the potential for the other kind of thinking. It is of course the case that the two sides of the brain are connected, and communicate and interact with each other.

It would appear that since the ikonic mode of representation develops before the symbolic mode, the right side of the brain develops earlier than the left side. Education, as Bruner suggests, should recognize this earlier mode of thinking. Further, if some of us are right-brain dominant, it would also appear to be necessary to recognize this in our educational system, which now expects everyone to think in verbal, mathematical, or symbolic terms. Our present system favors the left-dominant individuals and discriminates against those whose "minor" hemisphere is dominant. Bruner's idea that we should encourage and develop intuitive, visual-spatial, or ikonic thinking throughout the educational process would appear to be a significant contribution. As a reviewer of *On Knowing* notes, "There are in this discussion the seeds of a theory of learning in a richer sense than psychology has thus far construed that term."[86]

SUMMARY

Bruner's orientation, in some contrast to that of Piaget, is psychological rather than biological and epistemological. Thus he is concerned not so much with the nature of knowledge and how people know, but with how people learn and the influences on the process of learning.

Bruner views the individual as an active being engaged in the construction of a world through seeking and selecting the stimuli to which he or she will respond, organizing and giving meaning to the environment, and guided by intention—the desire to achieve certain results. Cognitive growth is the process by which one increases one's mastery of the world by achieving and using knowledge. Cognition involves the means by which one represents one's experience of the world in the effort to reduce its complexity and to organize one's experiences and their effects for future use.

There are three modes by which the world is represented: the enactive mode, which consists of actions upon the world; the ikonic mode, which is representation through imagery; and the symbolic mode, which represents the world by symbols, particularly language. These modes develop in the order given, but as each new mode develops the preceding ones continue to function. Growth proceeds by stages, each of the major ones being characterized by one of these modes of representation.

Cognitive growth requires both internal factors (within the individual) and external factors (environmental stimuli) in interaction. Thus human evolutionary history, which has resulted in the manual use of tools, dependence on distance receptors, and the prolonged dependency of infancy, is involved in cognitive development. Culture is also an important factor in nurturing and shaping growth. Human behavior is more dependent on cultural techniques—tools, sensory amplifiers, language—than upon the characteristics of the human nervous system. Language exerts a particularly potent influence on thinking by providing the concepts in terms of which one organizes the world. While cultures vary and thus lead to cultural differences in cognitive development, there are also basic commonalities across cultures, including certain linguistic rules or principles. Both the human biological heritage and the specific culture place constraints on the limits of intellectual development.

Intellectual development involves acquisition of ways of representing the recurrent regularities in experience and events, development of the ability to seek out and analyze information, acquisition of the concept of equivalence (conservation across appearances), and acquisition of a means of transcending the momentary by linking past to present to future. Symbolic representation, especially language, provides the major tool for achieving this.

Conflicts among the modes of representation may arise. Problems are thus created, with social pressure to resolve them, or to create consistency between what we do, what we see, and what we say. Bruner cautions against forcing conformity among modes, especially forcing actions and imagery into conformity with language. Enactive and ikonic representations may be sources of valuable insights and intuitions.

Each individual thus constructs reality, or a world, through representation of his or her experiences with it. Education is concerned with assisting the individual in developing or constructing a world. Teaching is not the imparting of information or the transmission of the culture—there are more effective ways to transmit information.

Education is a social invention necessary in complex societies to prepare the child to participate in the adult world. Whereas in indigenous societies children learn by direct participation and modeling by adults (being shown what to do), in complex societies children learn out of context, in classrooms and through symbols (being told about real activities). Complex societies depend upon a high order of symbolic activity. This fact, in addition to the use of the symbolic in teaching, places a premium on high levels of symbolic activity, the attainment of which requires a long period of formal education. The separation of learning from experience reduces the relevance of what is learned and leads to so-called problems of motivation or interest in learning.

Instruction attempts to assist or shape cognitive growth. A theory of instruction specifies the arrangement of the learning environment to optimize learning in terms of various criteria—the acquisition and retention of information and knowledge, transfer or generalization utilizing principles and rules, and the acquisition of certain skills. A theory of instruction must take into account the nature of the learner. It must deal with the structuring of subject matter or knowledge for effective learning, and with the most effective sequencing of materials. Finally, it should specify the nature and pacing of rewards and reinforcements, including extrinsic and intrinsic rewards and immediate and delayed rewards.

The human organism is a natural learner. Natural learning is self-rewarding. Learning which occurs as a result of natural curiosity, the urge toward mastery and competence, and modeling after another human being (which are intrinsic motives) is satisfying. Motivation is not a problem in such learning.

Subject matter can be made interesting and still be presented accurately. The personalization of knowledge—making it meaningful and useful in relation to the child's thinking, attitudes, and feelings—creates interest. Learning is an active process, and the child should participate actively in the learning process. Activity promotes interest. The discovery method also engages the interest of the learner. The solving of real problems arouses interest. Curiosity, interest, and the urge toward competence and mastery lead to exploration, which is necessary for real learning and problem solving.

Bruner's dictum that any subject can be presented to a learner of any age in a form that is interesting and honest rests on the idea that any subject matter can be converted to a form appropriate for any level of cognitive development. This involves the structuring of subject matter in terms of basic themes, fundamental ideas, principles, issues, and relationships. These can be represented as a set of actions (enactive representation), by a set of images (ikonic representation), or by symbols (symbolic representation). Subjects can be presented sequentially in these modes, with the addition of detail and content, as students progress in school, thus constituting what Bruner calls the spiral curriculum. Later learning is easier when built upon earlier learning. Such structuring of subject matter or knowledge maintains the interest of the student. It also makes for economy in teaching and learning, and fosters retention and transfer, or generalization.

Reinforcement is feedback or the results of one's efforts or trials in problem solving. It is important that it come when it is most useful or relevant—not too early and not too late. In piecemeal learning, the teacher becomes important in providing knowledge of progress toward long-term goals, where the student is not clear about whether what she or he is doing is related to the achievement of this goal. Learning situations which are self-correcting are ideal; here the effects of actions become immediately apparent, as in experiments using apparatus such as balances. Extrinsic, external reinforcement does not foster continuation or persistence of learning. It may actually interfere with learning, by arousing too high a level of anxiety or by restricting attention and learning to the specific activities which are rewarded, thus discouraging transfer or generalization; and by weakening the satisfactions of intrinsic rewards through focusing the learner's attention on the "payoff" or on satisfying the teacher.

Bruner has emphasized the importance of intuitive thinking as well as analytic thinking. Intuitive knowledge derives from poetry, art, myth, and the humanities rather than from the application of the scientific method. It is the sudden apprehension of a truth or a solution to a problem. Proof or support comes later, through application of analytic thinking, or the scientific method.

Intuition provides fruitful hypotheses and creative ideas. As such it is important and should be fostered. Our educational system tends to discourage rather than to encourage such thinking. Bruner suggests a number of ways to encourage intuitive thinking in education. Emphasis on being right and giving correct answers restricts intuitive thinking, while encouragement of risking a guess should foster it. Children engage in intuitive thinking early, before they are capable of analytic thinking. Intuitive approaches to subject matter in the early years thus make it possible to present the fundamentals of a subject to young children.

Bruner suggests other changes in education that are necessary if it is to meet the needs of the future. It must emphasize the teaching of skills related to the technologies which we as a tool-using species have developed. Education must recognize and use the developing understandings of the nature of individual mental growth. It must incorporate this knowledge into a theory of instruction, along with what we know about the three modes of representation and the self-rewarding nature of learning based upon competence and mastery motives. It must support the development of persons who can manage the accelerating rate of change in society. The fostering of the imaginal and spatial-thinking capacities appears to be important if we are to relate to and control our environment for maximum human benefit. The development and use of a meta-language, especially mathematics is important. We must be less concerned about the particulars of history and more concerned about the generalizations for living which can be derived from the social and behavioral sciences. And psychology, or educational psychology, must move from laboratory studies of the learning of nonsense syllables to the development of a theory of instruction.

Bruner has been a significant figure representing cognitive psychology during a period when behaviorism has been ascendant. The tide has now turned, with cognitive elements perhaps being overemphasized in comparison to affective aspects of behavior. How much this dominance of cognitive psychology is due to Bruner's influence is difficult to say.

Bruner has many important things to say about education, as this summary should make clear. Not all of his contributions derive directly from his research or theory, since he has drawn broadly from the behavioral sciences. His influence might be greater if he had systematically drawn together all his work related to education. This presentation has attempted, however inadequately, to do this.

REFERENCES

1. For some illustration of the nature of the materials used and their effects, see R. M. Jones, *Fantasy and Feeling in Education* (New York: New York University Press, 1968). (Also published in paperback in Harper & Row Torchbook series.) Some excerpts are also presented in C. H. Patterson, *Humanistic Education* (Englewood Cliffs, N.J.: Prentice-Hall, 1973).
2. J. S. Bruner et al., *Studies in Cognitive Growth* (New York: Wiley, 1966), p. 8.
3. J. S. Bruner, *On Knowing: Essays for the Left Hand* (Cambridge, Mass.: Belknap Press of Harvard University, 1962), p. 129.
4. Bruner, *Beyond the Information Given,* ed. J. M. Anglin (New York: Norton, 1973), p. 298.
5. Bruner, et al., *Studies in Cognitive Growth,* op. cit., p. 1.
6. Ibid.
7. Ibid.
8. Ibid., p. 4.
9. Bruner, *On Knowing,* op. cit., p. 141.
10. Ibid., p. 142.
11. Ibid., pp. 134, 135.
12. Bruner et al., *Studies in Cognitive Growth,* op. cit., pp. 1–2.
13. Bruner, *On Knowing,* op. cit., p. 137.
14. Ibid., p. 138.
15. Bruner et al., *Studies in Cognitive Growth,* op. cit. p. 2.

16. Bruner, *On Knowing*, op. cit., p. 159.
17. Ibid.
18. Ibid., p. 2.
19. Bruner, *Beyond the Information Given*, op. cit., p. 247.
20. Ibid., p. 304.
21. Bruner et al., *Studies in Cognitive Growth*, op. cit., p. 16.
22. Ibid., p. 29.
23. Ibid., p. 26.
24. Ibid., p. 29.
25. Ibid., p. 37.
26. Ibid., p. 47.
27. Ibid., pp. 43, 48.
28. Bruner, *Beyond the Information Given*, op. cit., Chapter 19, "The Course of Cognitive Growth," pp. 325–351.
29. Ibid., p. 332.
30. Ibid., p. 333.
31. Ibid., p. 316.
32. Bruner, *Studeis in Cognitive Growth*, op. cit., p. 11.
33. Bruner, *Beyond the Information Given*, op. cit., p. 344.
34. Ibid., p. 345.
35. Bruner, *Studies in Cognitive Growth*, op. cit., p. 324.
36. Bruner, *Beyond the Information Given*, op. cit., p. 348.
37. Ibid., p. 349.
38. Bruner, *Studies in Cognitive Growth*, op. cit., p. 319.
39. Ibid., p. 322.
40. Ibid., p. 325.
41. Bruner, *The Relevance of Education* (New York: Norton, 1971), p. xiv.
42. Bruner, *Beyond the Information Given*, op. cit., p. 316.
43. Bruner, *Toward a Theory of Instruction* (Cambridge, Mass.: Harvard University Press, 1966; Norton, 1968, pp. 1, 21).
44. Bruner, *The Relevance of Education*, op. cit., p. 50.
45. Bruner, *Toward a Theory of Instruction*, op. cit., p. 113.
46. Bruner, *The Process of Education* (Cambridge, Mass.: Harvard University Press, 1963), p. 31.
47. Bruner, *The Relevance of Education*, op. cit., p. 62.
48. Ibid., p. 18.
49. Bruner, *Toward a Theory of Instruction*, op. cit., pp. 35, 44. See also *The Process of Education*, op. cit., pp. 12, 33; and *The Relevance of Education*, op. cit., p. 122.
50. Bruner, *The Process of Education*, op. cit., pp. 12–13.
51. Ibid., p. 12.
52. Bruner, *Toward a Theory of Instruction*, op. cit., p. 29.
53. Bruner, *The Process of Education*, op. cit., p. 12.
54. Bruner, *Toward a Theory of Instruction*, op. cit., p. 51.
55. Bruner, *Beyond the Information Given*, op. cit., p. 409.
56. Bruner, *Toward a Theory of Instruction*, op. cit., p. 128.
57. Bruner, *Beyond the Information Given*, op. cit., p. 406.
58. Ibid., p. 402.
59. Ibid., p. 406.
60. Bruner, *The Relevance of Education*, op. cit., p. 72.
61. Ibid., p. 81.
62. Bruner, *On Knowing*, op. cit., p. 102.
63. Bruner, *The Process of Education*, op. cit., pp. 64–65.
64. Bruner, *On Knowing*, op. cit., pp. 104, 105.

65. Bruner, *The Process of Education,* op. cit., p. 39.
66. Bruner, *Toward a Theory of Instruction,* op. cit., pp. 22ff.
67. Ibid., p. 29.
68. Ibid., p. 36.
69. Ibid.
70. Bruner, *The Relevance of Education,* op. cit., p. 111.
71. K. Strike, review of *The Relevance of Education, Contemporary Psychology* 18 (1973):466–468.
72. R. B. Millward, review of *Beyond the Information Given, Contemporary Psychology,* 20 (1975):492–494.
73. A. Bandura, "Behavior Theory and the Models of Man," *American Psychologist,* 29 (1974):859–869.
74. Bruner, *Beyond the Information Given,* op. cit., pp. 294–295.
75. Bruner, *Studies in Cognitive Growth,* op. cit., p. xv.
76. Bruner, *Toward a Theory of Instruction,* op. cit., p. 7.
77. Bruner, *Beyond the Information Given,* op. cit., p. 337.
78. B. Inhelder et al., "On Cognitive Development," *American Psychologist* 21 (1966):160–164.
79. J. Anglin, introduction to *Beyond the Information Given,* op. cit., p. xx.
80. Bruner, *Toward a Theory of Instruction,* op. cit., pp. 104, 105.
81. Ibid., p. 115.
82. Ibid., p. 28.
83. Bruner, *On Knowing,* op. cit., pp. 142, 143.
84. Bruner, *The Relevance of Education,* op. cit., p. 129.
85. Ibid., p. 153.
86. R. Jessor, review of *On Knowing, Contemporary Psychology* 8 (1963): 83–84.

Skinner and the technology of teaching

5

CHAPTER

5

INTRODUCTION

Burrhus Frederick Skinner (1904–   ) was born and grew up in Susquehanna, Pennsylvania. Keller writes that "the village atmosphere of Susquehanna, Pennsylvania, provided both variety and depth, together with sufficient time for dreaming. He grew up in a home where learning was esteemed, order prevailed, standards of conduct were high, affection was deep, and rewards were given when deserved. Here he learned to study, developed self-reliance, acquired the art of making gadgets, and came to love knowledge in a critical, questioning way."[1] He received his BA from Hamilton College, where he became interested in biology and literature. After graduation he decided to be a writer rather than following his father, who was a lawyer. He abandoned this goal, however, and decided to study psychology after reading a series of articles by Bertrand Russell on J. B. Watson's behaviorism in *Dial* magazine. In 1928 he entered Harvard University, where he studied psychology, receiving an MA in 1930 and the PhD in 1931. He remained at Harvard as a National Research Council fellow for two years and as a junior fellow in the Harvard Society of Fellows for three more years. It was during these years that he developed his approach to the study of voluntary behavior, now known as the experimental analysis of behavior.

In 1936 Skinner went to the University of Minnesota as instructor of psychology, becoming an Associate Professor in 1939. From 1942 to 1945 he conducted war research, first supported by and then sponsored by General Mills. During 1944–1945 he was a Guggenheim fellow. In 1945 he was appointed professor of psychology and chairman of the psychology department at Indiana University. While still holding this position he was William James Lecturer in Psychology at Harvard during 1947–1948. In 1948 he became professor of psychology at Harvard, where he has remained since. On January 1, 1958, he became

Edgar Pierce Professor of Psychology. Currently he is Emeritus Professor of Psychology.

His first major publication was *The Behavior of Organisms* (1938), in which he presented his experimental approach to behavior. In 1948 he published a utopian novel, *Walden Two,* depicting a community run on Skinnerian principles, in which everyone is happy and productive. It was his book *Science and Human Behavior* (1953), however, which stimulated the resurgence of behaviorism in American psychology.

Skinner's early work was with rats and pigeons. He extended his study, however, to the analysis of human verbal behavior (*Verbal Behavior,* 1957), to psychotic behavior, and to education, particularly the design of instructional devices or teaching machines (*The Technology of Teaching,* 1968).

Skinner has received honorary degrees from Hamilton College (1951), Ripon College (1961), North Carolina State College (1961), the University of Chicago (1967), the University of Missouri (1968), Alfred University (1968), the University of Exeter (England) (1969), Indiana University (1970), McGill University (1970), C. W. Post Center (1971), Rockford College (1971), Ohio Wesleyan University (1971), Dickenson College (1972), Farmington (Massachusetts) State College (1972) and Hobart and William Smith College (1972). Other honors include the Warren Medal of the Society of Experimental Psychologists in 1942, a Distinguished Scientific Contribution Award of the American Psychological Association in 1958, the National Medal of Science in 1968, the Gold Medal of the American Psychological Foundation in 1971, and the Joseph P. Kennedy, Jr., Foundation Award in 1971.

Among his professional memberships and honors are memberships in the National Academy of Sciences and the American Academy of Arts and Sciences and fellowship in the Royal Society of Arts. He is a member and fellow of the American Psychological Association, a member of the Swedish and British Psychological Societies, a member of the American Philosophical Association, and a member of the American Humanist Association.

Skinner is regarded by many as the greatest living psychologist, and his name repeatedly tops lists of psychologists most frequently referred to or most influential in psychology today or who will be remembered in history. Yet he is a highly controversial figure who has stimulated much criticism and even anger and enmity. His thesis, presented in *Beyond Freedom and Dignity* (1971), that behavior is under the control of environmental stimuli, and the proposal that therefore we should create an environment which will shape the kind of person we want, eliminating "freedom" (which in any case according to

Skinner does not exist), has resulted in attacks on him by psychologists and philosophers as well as laymen.

BACKGROUND

Behaviorism, or "the scientific study of behavior," as it is defined by behaviorists, originated in America in the work and writings of John Broadus Watson (1878–1958). Watson reacted against the then-current introspective or mentalistic psychology. He felt that psychology could only become a science if it gave up the study of conscious experience, which is not objectively observable, and limited itself to the study of behavior (muscular and glandular activities). His research was with animals, in which consciousness, if it existed, could not be studied but behavior could be. If the study of the behavior of animals could dispense with consciousness, then the study of human behavior could also. In 1913 Watson published an article entitled "Psychology as the Behaviorist Sees It." In 1914 his book entitled *Behavior: An Introduction to Comparative Psychology* was published, and in 1919 his book *Psychology from the Standpoint of a Behaviorist* appeared.

When the work of Ivan P. Pavlov (1849–1936), a Russian physiologist, became known in America, Watson accepted his principle of conditioning as the explanation for all learning. This principle is known as classical conditioning. In classical conditioning, a stimulus which does not naturally evoke a particular behavior, is led to do so by repeated presentations in association with the natural stimulus. The natural stimulus is the unconditioned stimulus, and the new stimulus is the conditioned stimulus (or conditional stimulus, as it was called by Pavlov). Pavlov's work was with dogs. In the process of studying gastric secretion, which involved the collection of saliva produced in response to placing food in the dog's mouth, he noticed that saliva was produced at the sight of the food, and even at the approach of the assistant with the food, which had become conditioned stimuli.

Pavlov then entered upon a long career of studying this conditional reflex behavior. He used a light and tones of varying frequencies as the conditioned stimuli. The presentation of a stimulus followed by food associated the stimulus with food, so that the light or tone alone came to produce salivation. It required a period of conditioning, or *reinforcement* of the neutral stimulus, to establish the association. If later the neutral stimulus alone was presented repeatedly without reinforcement, the association was dissolved, and the conditioned response would cease to occur, or would be *extinguished*. After an interval of time, however, the unconditioned stimulus would again elicit the conditioned response, showing *spontaneous recovery*. Pavlov was able to train dogs to discriminate between tones of different frequencies or between metronomes beating at different rates (stimulus differentiation). However, if the differences became small, the dog could not discriminate and became disturbed, a condition Pavlov called *experimental neurosis*.

While rejecting instinct as an explanation of human behavior, Watson believed that the emotional responses of fear, anger, and love are innate, and similar to reflexes; other emotional reactions are learned through association with them. He believed the natural stimulus for fear is a sudden loud noise. In a famous experiment with Albert, an 11-month-old boy, he and Rosalie Rayner showed that, although Albert was not afraid of white rats, when, in the presence of a white rat, a loud noise was sounded by a hammer striking a metal bar on seven occasions, Albert became afraid of the rat.[2] The fear extended (*generalized*) to a rabbit, and to a lesser extent to a dog, a fur coat, cotton wool, and a Santa Claus mask with whiskers. The fear persisted, though with lesser intensity, after a month. The loss of Albert as a subject prevented experiments to attempt to eliminate the fear. This is the first recorded example of an experimental conditioning of an emotional reaction in a human being.

In a second famous experiment (Peter and the rabbit), Mary Cover Jones attempted to eliminate an existing fear of a rabbit in Peter, a child of 2 years and 10 months of age. While he was hungry, Peter was fed while a rabbit was gradually introduced, at first in a cage and at a distance. Over a period of two months—with daily or twice-daily treatments—Peter lost his fear and finally held and petted the rabbit. In addition to direct conditioning (or reconditioning), Jones found social imitation (or modeling, as it would also now be called) to be effective in removing fear.[3]

Watson was a strong environmentalist who believed that human nature could be subjected to great change. This and his crusading spirit led him to take an extreme position at times. Such was his boast: "Give me a dozen healthy infants, well-formed, and my own specified world to bring them up in and I'll guarantee to take any one at random and train him to become any type of specialist I might select— Doctor, lawyer, artist, merchant-chief, and, yes, even beggar-man and thief, regardless of his talents, penchants, tendencies, abilities, vocations, and race of his ancestors."[4] He recognized that this was an exaggeration, that it went beyond the then-current facts, and that genetic or hereditary factors were important. But he was confident of the promise of the new approach to psychology and wanted to dramatize it.

Edward L. Thorndike (1874–1949), with his psychology of connectionism, is an important figure in the development of behavioristic psychology. Thorndike's early work was with animals, particularly cats. Since animal learning could be explained without recourse to the notion of reasoning, and since the fundamental laws of learning are the same for all species, then, reasoned Thorndike, the same principles involved in animal learning could explain human learning. Thorndike accepted the English associationistic tradition that learning is the formation of associative bonds, or connections, between physical and mental events. The process is passive, mechanical, trial-and-error; connections are "stamped in" or eliminated according as the responses lead to pleasurable or annoying consequences, or rewards and punishments. This is the law of effect.

Thorndike's theory, like Watson's, assumed that people are highly malleable; their behavior is not entirely or mainly genetically (or instinctively) determined, but is under the influence of the environment which controls its consequences (rewards and punishments). Learning is specific but can generalize, or transfer, to the extent that new situations or stimuli share identical elements with the old situation or stimulus.

Both the classical conditioning method of Pavlov and the connectionism of Thorndike include the idea of reinforcement. In the former, however, reinforcement refers to the association of the conditioned stimulus with the (natural) unconditioned stimulus which precedes it. For Thorndike, reinforcement consisted of the consequences of responses. Pavlov's classical conditioning applies to reflexive, or involuntary, behaviors. Thorndike dealt with voluntary behaviors. The term *instrumental conditioning* has been applied to this kind of learning, to indicate that the responses or behaviors are instrumental in achieving the consequences. (Skinner calls it *operant* conditioning—see below). It is being recognized that there is not a clear distinction between the two types of conditioning. It has been noted, for example, that if the classical conditioning experiment in which a conditioned stimulus is associated with a shock, leading to the dog's reflexively (involuntarily) lifting its paw when the conditioned stimulus is presented alone, is changed so that the animal can escape or avoid the shock by lifting its paw (voluntarily) *before* the unconditioned stimulus has occurred, then classical aversive conditioning becomes instrumental aversive conditioning.[5]

PHILOSOPHY, THEORY, AND PRINCIPLES

Philosophy

Skinner distinguishes between behaviorism as a philosophy and as a methodology. As an *ism*, behaviorism is a a philosophy of science, or more specifically a philosophy of psychology, or of the science of behavior. This philosophy does not reject consciousness, sensations, images, feelings, or thinking, that is, mental processes. A science of behavior must take into account such internal events. They are behaviors which happen to be inside the skin and are thus private rather than public events. As behaviors they can be studied, though it is more difficult to do so than to study overt behaviors.

Behaviorism as a philosophy of the science of human behavior poses such questions as: "Is such a science really possible? Can it account for every aspect of human behavior? What methods can it use? Are its laws as valid as those of physics and biology? Will it lead to a technology, and, if so what role will it play in human affairs?"[6] Skinner's answers to all of these questions appear to be in the affirmative.

Behaviorism as a philosophy of behavior does not, then, deny the existence of mental events. Methodological behaviorism, as a method or technique of studying behaviors, while accepting the existence of mental events, has ignored them because they cannot be studied by objective methods. What Skinner calls radical behaviorism takes a different view. It accepts both the existence of mental events and the possibility of studying them; it does not dismiss them because they are subjective, and it does not require agreement by others for acceptance of their truth. It does question the nature of such events, the extent to which they can be known by self-observation, and their importance. What is (introspectively) observed, or felt, is not a nonphysical consciousness, mind, or mental life, but the subject's own bodily processes and reactions. Mental events are not important, however, because they are not the causes of behavior. Behavior can be understood, predicted, and controlled without the consideration of mental events. As behaviors, mental events are effects or collateral products of the same causes as other, overt, behaviors. Further consideration will be given to mental events later.

Skinner begins with no presuppositions or assumptions about the nature of the human being. He takes humans (or rats or pigeons) as simply living organisms subject to study by his methods. They are, of course, products of the evolutionary process which has, through the process of selection (the shaping effects of environmental consequences) endowed each with particular anatomical and physiological characteristics and behaviors necessary for survival. Although genetic endowment is a factor in behavior, Skinner rejects the concept of instincts as causes of behavior. Such behaviors are the current effects of natural selection. Natural selection led to the development of certain behaviors which were necessary for survival. Survival is, then, contingent upon these behaviors.

There are two assumptions underlying Skinner's behaviorism. The first is that living organisms are constantly engaged in behaving. Such behavior does not have to be accounted for. It may originate from the inherent efforts of the organism to exist and survive in its environment, and it includes reflexive behaviors. As the organism interacts with its environment, new behaviors are learned. Skinner does not accept the concept of new behaviors developing in an autonomous manner, following a built-in design. New behaviors do not arise simply by a process of development. They arise either from the conditioning of reflexes or the conditioning of nonreflexive or *operant* behaviors.

Operant behavior is Skinner's term for the natural, ongoing behavior of the organism. It operates on the environment, producing consequences (in this way it is instrumental) which are reinforcing or aversive or which may be neutral. Operant behavior is, from the standpoint of the observer or experimenter, voluntary or "spontaneous" behavior, or, to use the technical term, *emitted* behavior, rather than *elicited* behavior, a term which refers to a reflexive response to a specific stimulus. Operant behavior is not uncaused; its causes are not necessarily immediate or clear, and in any event it is not necessary to know the causes. And although such behavior is often called voluntary behavior, it is not caused by an act of will or choice.

Operant behavior, then, exists and does not have to be accounted for. There is no need for a concept of motivation to explain the origin of behavior. "No one asks how to motivate a baby," says Skinner in his novel *Walden Two*. "A baby naturally explores everything he can get at, unless restraining forces have been at work, and this tendency doesn't die out."[7] (Since restraining forces do exist and operate in our society, motivation does become a problem, as in education.) The strength of a specific motivation, such as hunger, can be increased by limiting its satisfaction, such as with food, as is done in animal experiments in order to increase the reinforcement properties of food. As a matter of fact, Skinner defines motivation operationally not as the degree of hunger, but by the extent of deprivation (number of hours since feeding), which can be objectively measured.

Skinner's second assumption is that nature—including behavior—is orderly rather than capricious. Science, or the scientific method, is an attempt to discover this order. In the realm of behavior, the order consists of a set of systematic and functional relationships between the behaviors of the organism and the environment. When these are discovered, we will understand the causes of behavior, and will be able to predict and control behavior, that is, we will have a science of behavior.

Behavior, then, is assumed to be determined. Moreover, since we can discover its order and predict and control it without recourse to internal mental events, then it follows that the causes of behavior are entirely in the environment, either as currently present or as earlier experiences represented in the organism.

The results of Skinner's work and its implications raise problems of a philosophical as well as a theoretical nature. These come after, rather than prior, to his system of research. When we are dealing with animal behavior, few such issues arise; it is when we study the behavior of human beings and how it can be influenced or controlled that issues of a philosophical and ethical nature emerge. These issues will be considered later.

Theory

Skinner is avowedly atheoretical, even antitheoretical. He places description and empirical research above theory. In an early (1950) paper entitled "Are theories of learning necessary?" he says that theories may be used to give (universal) answers, and thus discourage research. Even the use of theory to generate research may result in much useless research: "Most theories are eventually overthrown, and the greater part of the associated research is discarded."[8] Research does not require a theory to guide it. Following the sequence of theoretical hypothesis, deduction, experimental test, and confirmation is not the way most scientists actually proceed. Theories are fun, Skinner says, but empirical research may produce more rapid progress in understanding than research designed to test theories. "When we have achieved a practical control over the organism, theories of behavior lose their point."[9] Yet Skinner admits that theory has a place as a critique of the methods, data, and concepts of science, as well as in integrating facts derived from scientific analysis into a systematic view of behavior. It is theory as an a priori framework from which hypotheses are deduced for testing by research that he rejects.

Skinner's research has been strictly empirical in nature. What is called the experimental analysis of behavior, or the functional analysis of behavior, attempts to identify, isolate, and demonstrate the environmental variables of which the behavior being investigated is a lawful function. For Skinner no theory is involved. Most of Skinner's work has been with pigeons and rats, where he has been able to exercise the strict controls which the scientist needs in order to make statements or conclusions which can be verified (or replicated) by others following the same procedures. He developed the "Skinner box," which contains only a lever, for rats (a disk is used for pigeons), connected to a recording system, and a food dispenser activated by the pressing of the lever (or the pecking of the disk). The experimenter can control the animals' behavior through reinforcement by food. Since organisms of different species share some basic similarities, the general principles of behavior, or of learning, are applicable to all species, including human beings. The behavior of rats, pigeons, monkeys, as well as cats, dogs, mice, and men, is indistinguishable when allowance "is made for differences in ways in which they make contact with the environment, and in the ways they act in the environment."[10]

Skinner's approach derives from Thorndike rather than from Pavlov or Watson. Instead of focusing upon classical, or respondent, conditioning, he has worked with instrumental or, as he has termed it, *operant conditioning.* Respondent conditioning is only of secondary importance; it enters his system in secondary reinforcement. *Reinforcement* is the reward in Thorndike's law of effect. The term *reinforcement* is preferred to *reward,* however, since the latter implies a mental event; that is, it implies that the effects or consequences of behavior are pleasant or satisfying. Reinforcement is empirically defined. A reinforcement is anything which increases the probability of the behavior which it follows. The reason that it increases the probability of the behavior is not that it feels good or is satisfying; it does so because it increases the chances of survival of the organism in the circumstances, or environment. Feelings are simply the bodily states generated by the reinforcer or accompanying the behaviors.

Skinner differs from other investigators of learning in that his experiments do not typically involve a number of subjects whose behaviors are averaged, with the results presented in tables of means and standard deviations or other data upon which other statistical analyses are performed. "Learning," he states, "is a process in the behavior of the individual."[11] He therefore studies the behavior of single subjects. Individual differences are not a problem, since their sources are controlled. Genetic differences and experience—the history of the organism—can be highly controlled in animal subjects. The controlled experimental situation eliminates the effects of many individual differences. Moreover, in experiments studying changes in behavior, the single subject can serve as its own control; the environment is then manipulated, and any changes in behavior are the result of changes in the environment, which remains constant except for the manipulation.

The behavior change which Skinner focuses upon as the most significant evidence of learning is the *rate of response,* which is studied under various conditions and types of reinforcement or lack of reinforcement. The rate of response and its changes under changing conditions of reinforcement can be plotted in the form of curves, which clearly depict the changes in behavior with no further statistical analysis. A single experiment with a single subject can demonstrate the effects of different conditions of reinforcement. There is no need to look for causes in theoretical concepts such as mental states or in physiological conditions, and no need for complex statistical analyses.

The prediction of behavior involves the prediction of the probability of a response under certain conditions. Learning is a change in the probability of response under specified conditions. These conditions involve changes in reinforcement, or the consequences of responding. Probabilities of responding correspond to the probabilities of reinforcement.

Skinner has developed his system entirely in terms of observable— and measurable—behaviors of organisms, the observable—and measurable—consequences of a behavior, and the observable—and measurable effects of changing the consequences, which are simply what follows behavior. The principles involved in this process of studying behaviors and their changes in this system are presented below. For completeness, several which have already been noted incidentally are repeated and elaborated.

Definitions and Principles

In its simplest form, Skinner's model, or theory of behavior, states that in the interaction of an organism with its environment there are three elements: (1) an occasion on which a response occurs (a discriminative stimulus); (2) the response; and (3) its reinforcing consequences, the interrelations of which constitute the contingencies of reinforcement. The reinforcing stimulus (the consequences) will occur only if the response is emitted in the presence of the discriminative stimulus. The term *discriminative operant* is applied to the total process. The discriminative operant is the basic unit in the analysis of behavior. The elements in the process, and other factors involved in a behavioristic analysis, will be considered here:

Operant behavior.   All living organisms engage in constant activity which brings them in contact with, and leads to interaction with, the environment. This behavior does not have to be accounted for, or its causes known. The ongoing behavior of the organism is *emitted* behavior, as distinguished from *elicited* behavior. Although the ongoing behavior may consist in part of behaviors elicited by stimuli from within and without, it is not elicited by the experimenter.

Contingency.   Operant behavior affects the environment; that is, it has consequences. A reinforcement can occur only if and when a response (behavior) occurs. In other words, reinforcement is contingent upon the behaviors of the organism. If a certain act is performed, certain consequences result. The act leads to the appearance of the reinforcer. It should be noted that in the case of classical conditioning, the reinforcer (unconditioned stimulus) precedes and causes the response; in operant conditioning the response precedes the reinforcer.

The term *response* may be misleading when used in operant conditioning. The response is not elicited by a stimulus, as in classical conditioning. Operant responses are emitted. They can be brought under stimulus control by reinforcement, in which case they would appear to be elicited by the environmental conditions which have become associated with (conditioned to) the reinforcer. Even here, however, it is usually stated that the environmental condition is the *occasion* for the emitting of the operant behavior, rather than that it elicits the behavior as a response, since the behavior is not an automatic, invariable response to a specified stimulus. Aspects of the environment which have been present when the operant response (behavior) has been reinforced are called *discriminative stimuli.* Again, however, they do not elicit the operant response but serve as cues that the reinforcement will occur if the operant response is emitted. The reinforcement is not a stimulus in the classical sense, since it does not elicit the operant response. It increases the probability that like responses will occur (be emitted) under similar conditions in the future.

The term *contingency* is used to indicate that there is no necessary or inherent reason why the consequence *should* follow the operant behavior. The pain following the touching of a hot object is not simply contingent upon the touching; it *must* follow the touching and is dependent upon the touching. Reinforcements, however, do not necessarily follow upon the behavior.

While the operant behavior results in the consequence, or reinforcement, it is not the cause of the reinforcement. Since the reinforcement controls the behavior, it is the cause of the behavior. While what follows a response cannot be the cause of that particular response, it is the cause of future responses.

Reinforcement. Consequences, or contingencies, may be positive, negative, or neutral. Positive consequences are reinforcers. As suggested earlier, a reinforcer is defined by its effect, not by any general characteristic it may possess. By *effect* is meant an increase in the probability of the behavior upon which it is contingent, not any presumed pleasant or satisfying feeling or state. Behaviors (responses) which are followed by a reinforcer tend to be repeated under the same or similar conditions. There are two classes of reinforcers:

1. *Positive reinforcers.* Stimuli (conditions) the presence of which, following an operant response, increase the probability of that response being repeated, are positive reinforcers. Food, water, sexual contact, praise, attention, and so forth, are positive reinforcers.
2. *Negative reinforcers.* Negative reinforcement is not, as might be supposed, punishment or an unpleasant consequence. Reinforcers *increase* the probability of a behavior occurring. Punishment or aversive stimuli decrease the probability of a response. Therefore, a negative reinforcer is a stimulus (condition) the removal of which (or escape from which) increases the probability of a response. An act which succeeds in removing (or accomplishing escape from) an aversive stimulus will tend to be repeated when the same, or a similar, stimulus is present.

Why reinforcers are reinforcing is not of particular concern to Skinner. It may be, he suggests, related to the preservation of the species on an evolutionary biological basis.

Schedules of reinforcement. Reinforcement may occur, or be provided, on many different timetables. Its occurence each and every time a response is made is *continuous reinforcement*. Continuous reinforcement is desirable in the early stages of learning, since it provides consistent reinforcement, leading to rapid and thus efficient learning. Once established, behavior can be economically maintained by occasional or *intermittent*, reinforcement.

Skinner reports his discovery of intermittent reinforcement as a humorous example of the hypotheticodeductive method. Running short of food pellets during an experiment and facing the time-consuming and laborious procedure of making more with his adapted pill machine, he asked himself why *every* lever press of the rat had to be reinforced. He decided to extend his supply by giving reinforcement once every minute.[12]

The differing timetables of noncontinuous or intermittent reinforcement are known as *schedules of reinforcement*. There are two main categories of intermittent reinforcement: *interval schedules* and *ratio schedules*.

1. *Interval schedules.* Interval schedules, based upon time, are of two kinds. In *fixed interval schedules*, reinforcements are given periodically, following a constant time lapse (30 seconds, 1 minute, 5 minutes, and so on). Responses on a fixed interval schedule are constant per reinforcement; that is, in a 30-second interval just as many responses will be emitted as in a 1-minute or 5-minute interval. But the responses are not distributed evenly over the interval. There are no responses immediately after a reinforcement, and then responses gradually accelerate, reaching a high level just before the next reinforcement, producing a scalloped curve. Although it would appear that the organism behaves as if it thinks, or is aware, that there will be no reinforcement immediately after one has occurred, and that, after a period of time, thinks or is aware that it is about time that it should obtain one, no such thinking or awareness is necessary for the behavior to occur. These behaviors are simply observed facts, explained or caused by the schedule.

   In *variable interval schedules*, reinforcements are given in a random, or variable order, each schedule having a mean time interval about which individual reinforcements vary. For example, reinforcements may be given at intervals of from 5 to 50 seconds, but averaging 25 seconds. Under a variable interval schedule the scallops or dips in the response curve (depicting the rate of response) disappear and it becomes essentially a straight line. The steepness of the curve depends on the average interval.

2. *Ratio schedules.* Ratio schedules are also of two kinds. In the *fixed ratio schedule*, reinforcements are given after a specified number of responses have been made (typically, with rats and pigeons, from 10 to 200). High rates of responding are usually built up by moving

from lower to higher ratios. The response curve is steep, with high rates of response, though with a brief pause after each reinforcement (except for small ratios). Skinner likens this schedule to piecework or piecerate payment in industry.

In *variable ratio schedules,* reinforcements are provided following differing numbers of responses, varying randomly around a given average. This is the reinforcement schedule of slot machines and other gambling devices. A high, uniform rate of response is generated, without the pauses after each reinforcement found in fixed ratio schedules. Gamblers playing a slot machine often do not pause to take up their winnings unless they need the coins to continue. As in gambling, the responding organism gets relatively little for its efforts.

There are numerous variations of these four schedules, including combinations of two or more schedules.

Conditioned reinforcers.   A stimulus or contingency that is not a reinforcer may become reinforcing by repeated association with (occurring just before or along with) a reinforcer. Such a reinforcer is a *conditioned, secondary,* or *derived reinforcer.* In operant conditioning experiments such reinforcers are useful in that they can be made to follow a response instantly, giving immediate reinforcement that prevents the intrusion of unwanted behaviors or responses, thus speeding up the process of conditioning.

All of the characteristics of the environment, and of the behavior of the organism just prior to the moment of reinforcement, through association with the reinforcer, become conditioned to the response and thus become secondary reinforcers.

Secondary reinforcers may become independent of the primary reinforcer and may in turn condition new reinforcers. Some secondary reinforcers tend to accompany (and become conditioned with) a wide variety of primary reinforcers, becoming *generalized reinforcers.* Money, attention, affection, and approval are such generalized reinforcers. They become independent of any single primary reinforcer, and persist indefinitely, probably because of intermittent reinforcement through occasional association with a primary reinforcer.

Extinction.   Extinction is the decline in rate of response and the eventual return of response rate to its operant or preconditioned level when reinforcement is discontinued. Skinner reports he discovered extinction in operant conditioning when the food magazine of his apparatus jammed and ceased dispensing reinforcements. He first considered this accident an interference in his experiment, but then he deliberately disconnected the apparatus to study the results. He writes: "I can easily recall the excitement of that first complete extinction curve. I had made contact with Pavlov at last! Here was a curve uncorrupted by the physiological process of ingestion. It was an orderly change due to nothing more than a special contingency of reinforcement. It was pure behavior!"[13]

The withdrawal of reinforcement may result in a temporary increase in the response rate—as if the organism were engaging in a frantic attempt to produce the reinforcement. The speed with which extinction occurs following the discontinuance of reinforcement depends upon a number of factors. The greater the number of reinforcements and the greater their magnitude, the slower is the rate of extinction. The greater the number of previous extinctions, the faster is the rate of extinction. The greater the deprivation (drive or motivation) of the organism, the slower is the rate of extinction.

An important factor in extinction is the schedule of reinforcement that established the response. Responses established by continuous reinforcement extinguish faster than those established by intermittent reinforcement. In fixed interval reinforcement, the first interval following the beginning of extinction is normal, ending with a high response rate, which continues for a time, then ceases when no response is forthcoming. Shortly, however, the responding resumes, and then stops again. The pauses increase in length, and the responding decreases, ultimately reaching the operant or preexperimental level. Variable interval conditioning is highly resistant to extinction; the longer the (average) intervals, the longer the responding persists. The rate of responding drops off slowly and gradually. Interval schedules in general lead to slower extinction rates than do ratio schedules.

Extinction following fixed ratio reinforcement consists first of the usual pause and then high response following the last reinforcement, followed by similar but increasingly longer pauses before responding is resumed, until the operant level is reached. Behavior on a variable ratio of reinforcement is more resistant to extinction. After the last reinforcement a high rate of response continues (as if the organism is adapting to a higher ratio), followed by a pause and then a resumption of a long period of responding. The pauses increase in length, and the responding decreases in duration, though maintaining a high rate, until the operant level is reached.

The resistance to extinction of behavior when it is no longer rewarded is in part a result of the similarity of the total environment during reinforcement and extinction. The entire environment during conditioning is associated with (conditioned to) responding, constituting numerous secondary reinforcers. The greater the extent to which conditions during extinction differ from the conditions during conditioning, the more rapidly does extinction occur. Where, as in most experiments, the conditions are almost exactly the same, responding will continue with little or no change for a long time. Skinner speculates that if it were possible to assure that the environment could be exactly the same (including the behaviors of the organism), no extinction curve would result. Responding would stop abruptly when exhaustion set in, but would resume again on recovery from the exhaustion. How long this would continue without any further reinforcements is, of course, unknown.

Spontaneous recovery. After a response has been extinguished, and a period of time has elapsed (outside of the experimental situation), responding at a high rate may occur when the organism is again placed in the experimental situation. This is known as spontaneous recovery. If no reinforcement is given, extinction again results, more rapidly than in the original extinction process. Skinner has suggested that this is the result of the same factors that may lead to resistance to extinction, that is, the association of responding with the entire experimental situation, with its secondary reinforcers, which recurs when it is presented again even after previous extinction.

These definitions and principles are those basic to operant conditioning. However, there are a number of other important principles that are necessary for an understanding of the conditioning of more complex behaviors.

Stimulus generalization. Responses that are reinforced under particular stimulus conditions occur under similar stimulus conditions. For example, a pigeon reinforced in the presence of a red circle will respond to a yellow circle of the same size, and also to a red square with the same area. It will also respond to a red circle that is slightly smaller or slightly larger than the original one. This spread of effect, or response, to similar stimuli is called generalization.

Stimulus discrimination. If there were no limit to generalization, then of course there would be no discrimination in responding, no association of responses with certain stimuli or situations, and hence no learning. However, a stimulus or stimulus situation that initially elicits a response because it is associated with reinforcement (that is, elicits a response because of generalization) will cease to elicit a response if it is not reinforced. The organism learns to discriminate. A simple example is the rat that is trained to press a lever to obtain food, and is then given food only when he presses while a light is on, food being withheld when the light is off. The rat discriminates between the two situations and presses the lever only when the light is on. Again, when a pigeon is not reinforced for responding to a yellow circle, or a red square, and is reinforced for responding to a red circle, it will cease the responding to the yellow circle and the red square that earlier occurred by generalization.

Discrimination results when behavior is reinforced in a particular stimulus situation (or closely similar situations) but not in another, less similar, situation. Generalization is thus limited or restricted; generalized responses are extinguished. It is possible to achieve discrimination without the usual process of extinguishing generalized responses by avoiding the development of generalization. Discrimination is thus achieved without error.[14]

Stimulus control. The influencing of the rate of response by the stimuli accompanying reinforcement is referred to by Skinner as *stimulus control.* Although operants are emitted rather than elicited, they are controlled by discriminative stimuli, as well as by reinforcers and conditioned reinforcers. Discriminative stimuli do not control responses in the automatic, invariable way in which an unconditioned stimulus controls a reflex; they are said to provide the cues or set the occasion for the response, or alert the organism to respond.

Response generalization. As responses generalize to similar stimuli, so do stimuli generalize to similar responses. When one operant is reinforced, similar, or related, or associated operants are also reinforced and will increase in their rates of response.

Response differentiation. Response differentiation is one of the most significant aspects of operant conditioning. If, as noted earlier, operant conditioning requires the existence of operant behavior that can be reinforced, how then can operant behaviors be changed or new behaviors developed? This is achieved through response differentiation, known as *shaping,* and by chaining. Shaping involves the combination of reinforcement and extinction in a process leading to successive approximations until the desired behavior is achieved. In response differentiation, reinforcement is made contingent upon differences in the properties of the response rather than, as in stimuli discrimination, differences in the properties of accompanying stimuli.

Shaping can involve the gradual increasing or decreasing of the duration of a response, or the forcefulness of the response, as in lever pressing. It can also be used to develop new behaviors. Pigeons do not usually hold their heads erect. But they can be trained to do so. On rare occasions a pigeon might hold its head erect long enough to be reinforced, but such behavior occurs so seldom that it could not be reinforced sufficiently to become conditioned—even if the experimenter had the time and patience to wait. But such behavior can be conditioned by successive approximations. When the pigeon raises its head to some degree, it is reinforced. This increases the frequency of raising its head slightly. Sometimes it raises its head a little higher than usual. Reinforcement is then given only for these higher elevations, and discontinued for lower elevations. As even higher elevations increase in frequency, these alone are reinforced. The pigeon then holds its head "abnormally" high for a pigeon—like a peacock. A rare response has become a highly frequent response.

It is important to realize that shaping requires close observation by the experimenter and providing reinforcements when he or she deems appropriate. An approximation response cannot be reinforced for too long, or it will persist and interfere with the emitting of better responses; but it must be reinforced enough so that it does not disappear and lead to regression rather than progression. Mechanical administration of shaping reinforcement is not possible, since no machine can (yet) select a series of approximate responses, reinforcing each just long enough but not too long—or going back to resume reinforcing at a lower level if progression is disrupted.

Response chains.   Complete acts, or complex behaviors, are, according to Skinner, sequences of movements (or discriminatory stimulus and response units) in which each response then becomes, or provides, a discriminative stimulus for the next response. Even the apparently simple behavior of a rat pressing a level is actually a response chain.

In establishing a response chain, one unit is developed at a time, beginning with the last in the chain. Shaping is often involved in the total process. Animal trainers achieve their apparently remarkable results by this method. Skinner reports training a rat to perform an elaborate series of responses: "The behavior consists of pulling a string to obtain a marble from a rack, picking the marble up with the forepaws, carrying it to a tube projecting two inches above the floor of the cage, and dropping it inside. Every step in the process had to be worked out through a series of approximations, since the component responses were not in the original repertoire of the rat."[15]

Skinner has trained pigeons to bowl with marbles, to play ping-pong, and to produce simple tunes (or sequences of notes) on a xylophone arrangement. The "experiment" on bowling was done in 1943 in the laboratory at General Mills, during time described by Skinner as waiting for decisions to be made in Washington on a request for a grant to train pigeons to guide missiles.[16] It was this experiment, in which Keller Breland and Norman Guttman were involved, that led to the discovery of shaping, when they grew tired of waiting for the pigeon to emit the operant behavior of striking the marble with its beak. They decided to reinforce any approach to the marble—even looking at it—and in a few minutes, "the ball was caroming off the walls of the box as if the pigeon had been a champion squash player."[17]

As a result of such experiments involving shaping and chaining, Skinner writes that "it is dangerous to assert that an organism of a given species or age *cannot* solve a given problem. As a result of careful scheduling, pigeons, rats, and monkeys have done things during the past few years which members of their species have never done before. It is not that their forbears were incapable of such behavior; nature had simply never arranged effective sequences of schedules."[18]

In a more literary vein, and reminiscent of Watson, he has the protagonist in "Walden Two" say: "What do you say to the design of personalities? . . . The control of temperament? Give me the specifications, and I'll give you the man!"[19]

Avoidance. Negative reinforcement, it was stated earlier, involves responding to aversive or noxious stimuli or conditions so as to escape from them or to stop them in some way. Many of our activities are directed toward avoiding aversive consequences rather than escaping from them or obtaining positive reinforcements. Conditioned stimuli serve as cues to avoid or postpone aversive stimulation, as in the case of the rat in a box whose floor is an electric grid that conveys shocks which the rat can avoid or postpone by pressing a lever. The aversive stimulus cannot be continuously or indefinitely avoided, however, since when it is avoided, extinction of the avoidance response occurs, because the response is not reinforced by the aversive stimulus. A single aversive stimulus reinstates the avoidance response for a considerable period of time, however.

Punishment. Punishment is the opposite of reinforcement: Positive reinforcers are removed, or negative reinforcers (aversive stimuli) are imposed. Withdrawing a positive reinforcer which is present is not the same as not providing a reinforcer, as in extinction. Response is reduced more rapidly by withdrawing an ongoing reinforcer than by withholding a reinforcer, as in extinction.

Skinner believes that punishment is relatively ineffective in controlling behavior because it suppresses responses only temporarily—unless it is very severe. If the punished behavior is strong (highly motivated) it will recur after a time, requiring further punishment. A further drawback of punishment is that the repetition of punishing behavior in the punisher is reinforced, since it leads to (temporary) cessation of the annoying or disturbing behavior. Punishment also arouses emotional responses in the recipient, increasing anxiety, which becomes attached to discriminated stimuli or cues conditioned to or associated with the punishment. Anxiety interferes with performance. For these reasons Skinner discourages the use of punishment, recommending that behavior be controlled by positive reinforcement. Undesirable behavior can be eliminated by extinction, by counter-conditioning (developing an incompatible response), or by satiation (negative practice).

Drive and emotion in operant conditioning. It was stated earlier that motivation in the sense of initiating behavior is not a problem for Skinner, since the organism is always engaged in operant behaviors which can be selectively reinforced and shaped. But it was also noted that the state of the organism is related to its responsiveness to reinforcement. A hungry animal will respond more rapidly to obtain food. What is reinforcing to one organism may not be reinforcing to another; what is reinforcing at one time is not at another. When a rat is well fed, its responses to food reinforcement will quickly decline as it becomes satiated. For this reason, animals in experiments where food is the reinforcement are kept below normal body weight to assure that food will be reinforcing. But where many would speak of the hunger drive or motivation, Skinner dispenses with any concept of a drive as a stimulus, or as a psychological state, or even as a physiological state. Drive, or level of motivation, is, in objective terms, the level of deprivation of the organism. It is defined as the number of hours since feeding, or the percentage of normal body weight. In human beings, what is a reinforcer and the strength or power of the reinforcer are empirically determined by trial and observation.

Emotions are not studied as separate responses by Skinner in his work with animals. (He does recognize them as responses worthy of study in human beings.) They are defined by changes in response under certain conditions. For example, rats trained to respond at a steady rate for food (by variable interval reinforcement) are given other trials in which a tone sounds for 3 minutes and is followed by an electric shock, resulting in classical conditioning of the tone to the shock. Then in regular trials, when the tone is sounded, the animal will study in human beings.) They are defined by changes in response This is an example of conditioned suppression, or conditioned emotional response. But the result of interest to Skinner is a reduction of the rats' responding by pressing the lever for food.

It was noted earlier that at the beginning of the extinction process, responding may actually increase. This may be indicative of emotion, according to Skinner—the first expression of frustration at failing to receive a reinforcement. Skinner writes: "When we fail to reinforce a response which has previously been reinforced, we not only initiate a process of extinction, we set up an emotional response—perhaps what is meant by frustration."[20] But the behavioral response which is relevant (in terms of Skinner's focus on frequency of responding) is the increase or decline of the previously reinforced response (of lever pressing in the rat, or disk pecking in the pigeon). Other, concurrent responses which Skinner notes—for example, the pigeon moves rapidly about its cage, flaps its wings rapidly in a squatting position—are not relevant to Skinner; they are simply accompaniments of the decline in responding under cessation of reinforcement. (Nevertheless, it was no doubt these responses which led Skinner to speak of "frustration" in relation to extinction.)

"Superstitious" behavior. There is an aspect of operant conditioning observed by Skinner which is interesting. "Superstitious" behavior is behavior which is accidentally related to reinforcement. Skinner reports the development of such behavior in a pigeon. A pigeon is fed at regular intervals without regard to its behavior. It happens to be behaving in a particular way the first time it is fed. This "accidental" behavior then tends to increase in frequency, being more likely to occur at the next reinforcement, and so on, until eventually it is performed regularly, as a conditioned response. The responses are of the form of fixed interval conditioning; they are subject to extinction and reconditioning. But the behavior is not instrumental in causing the reinforcer; it is a "ritual": "The bird behaves as if there were a causal relation between its behavior and the presentation of food, although such a relation is lacking."[21] Such conditioning can occur following a single reinforcement and can continue indefinitely. Conditioning of superstitious behavior can also occur to an adventitious stimulus whose presence (or absence) in the environment concurs with reinforcement.

Human Behavior

Skinner raises the question as to whether human behavior is an "exception where, unlike the order present in other species, spontaneity and caprice still reign."[22] While the great bulk of the research in operant conditioning has been done with animals, in recent years there have been numerous studies involving the operant conditioning or reinforcement of a wide variety of behaviors in normal and abnormal (psychotic and mentally retarded) human subjects. Curves of responding for normal humans and animals under the same reinforcement schedule are virtually indistinguishable.

There is no question that many human behaviors can be studied in terms of frequency of responding and that the frequencies can be influenced or controlled by methods of operant conditioning involving reinforcement.[23] The basic question is to what extent the complexities of human behaviors can be encompassed by the paradigm of operant conditioning. Are all human behaviors the result of genetic endowment and past and present environmental stimuli and contingencies? And, if so, is the only way the environment influences behavior through the conditioning process? Are internal states without effect on behavior? Are any differences that exist between the causes of behavior and behavior change in animals and the causes in humans, insignificant? The answers suggested by Skinner to all of these questions are in the affirmative.

Parallels have been suggested between animal behavior under

certain schedules of reinforcement and human behavior under piecework pay schedules and in gambling. Are these really more than
analogies? Certainly much human behavior can be reduced to, or described in, conditioning terms. Is there anything significant lost in this
translation? In his recent book devoted to a behaviorist analysis of
complex human behaviors, Skinner admits that "much of the argument
goes beyond established fact."[24] The argument is very persuasive,
however. Much of it is extrapolation from animal studies or, as Skinner
points out, interpretation, or even speculation. But it is an attempt by
radical behaviorism to deal with those events considered peculiarly
human, the mental (and emotional) events occurring in the private
world, or, to use Skinner's phrase, within the skin.

The world within the skin. The traditional mentalistic view is that
behavior is the result of internal states or characteristics whose list is
almost endless. They include, beyond instincts, such things as sensations, feelings, emotions, thoughts, needs, drives, wishes, wants, intentions, purposes, will, attitudes, beliefs, expectancies, and so on, and so
on. Behaviorism accepts the existence of mental states but denies that
they are causative factors in behavior. To assume mental events as
causes poses the problem of how mental events can cause physical
events. The causes of behavior are all in the environment and the
genetic endowment of the individual. But the existence of the mental
states must be explained. Mental states are results of external stimuli
or of the external consequences of behavior, or they are the corollaries
or accompaniments of overt behavior.

Mental states involve neurological or physiological processes, but
are not caused by these processes. Mental states pose an insoluble (and
false) problem for physiologists; behaviorism poses a realistic soluble
problem. But Skinner states that it is not necessary to understand the
neurological and physiological processes involved in behavior in order
to control behavior. Such understanding will eventually fill in a temporal gap between the time an organism is affected by contingencies of
reinforcement and later behaviors, explaining how the organism is
changed and why it behaves differently.

Mental activities cannot be modified directly; they are not accessible to direct contact or control. They can, Skinner notes, be changed
by surgery, drugs or electrical stimulation, but for practical purposes
they can be changed through the environment. Behavior modification
has demonstrated this. While feelings (as well as attitudes, opinions,
intelligence) may be helpful in predicting behavior, since they are
products of the same (past) contingencies which will also control
future behavior, behavior can be predicted more accurately on the
basis of direct knowledge of the history which also caused the feelings.

The fact that mental events are so inaccessible to observation and study has led to widespread speculations by philosophers and psychologists about their nature. Skinner says that "mental life and the world in which it is lived are inventions. They have been invented on the analogy of external behavior occurring under external contingencies, but in ignorance of the effects of environment on behavior."[25] The idea of the existence of mind in nonphysical space has dominated Western thinking for two thousand years. But, Skinner claims, "more and more of the behavior of organisms, including man, is being plausibly related to events in their genetic and environmental histories. If other sciences are any guide, human behavior may ultimately be accounted for entirely in such terms."[26] Thus, "the mentalist may insist that we act because we have stored memories of past actions and their consequences, which we now scan in order to reach certain expectations leading to an act of will which initiates behavior,"[27] but "the contingencies which affect an organism are not stored by it. They are never inside it; they simply change it. As a result the organism behaves in special ways under special kinds of stimulus control."[28]

Innate behavior. The human being is the product of an evolutionary process involving natural selection. As a living organism, it behaves, usually in interaction with its environment. Part of its behavior consists of reflexes. Other behaviors are commonly called instinctive, such as deeply ingrained behaviors of uncertain origins. But instincts, says Skinner, are not forces, and to label behavior as instinctive is not to explain it. Aggressive behavior, which may be a genetic response to injury or threat, is not caused by an aggressive instinct. Innate behaviors developed in the process of evolution because survival was contingent upon them. Reflexes developed because they promoted survival of the species. Conditioned reflexes, developed by the contingencies of reinforcement, promote the survival of the individual. Operant conditioning is also a product of natural selection and promotes the survival of the individual in a new or changing environment.

Consequences—or things—which are reinforcing are not reinforcing because they feel (or taste, smell, or look) good, but because they contribute to survival. "The feelings are merely collateral products of the conditions responsible for the behavior."[29] The feelings are immediate and more likely to be reported or verbalized than the effects. But such reports are considered as statements that their referents are reinforcing. Both contingencies of survival and contingencies of reinforcement place the cause of behavior in its consequences, that is, they eliminate the need for any prior purpose. The purpose is in the consequences.

Universality of behavior in a species does not mean that it is instinctive or innate. Contingencies of reinforcement may be universal and lead to species-wide behaviors. This, and not any innate endow-

ment, according to Skinner, may be the source of universal characteristics of language.

Behaviorists are often criticized for exaggerating the malleability
of behavior. Behaviorists emphasize contingencies of reinforcement
because they can be relatively easily manipulated, and because they
make possible the prediction and control of behavior. Skinner points out
that the relegation of behaviors to genetic endowment because they
cannot be controlled or modified does not explain the behaviors and
stops further attempts to analyze them. And *all* behavior is in a sense
inherited, since the organism is the result of natural selection.

Mind is not something which has developed in the process of
evolution. The organism has evolved certain behaviors which have
been explained by the invention of the concept of mind.

Verbal behavior. A major difference between animals and human
beings is the possession of verbal behavior by human beings. Skinner
has applied operant principles to verbal behavior. Since speech sounds
are emitted behaviors and are subject to reinforcement, the learning of
verbal behavior (or the "acquisition of language") can be accounted
for on the basis of operant conditioning, according to Skinner.[30] It
does not "develop" according to semantic rules which are innate or part
of a genetic code. Language is too recent a development to have a
genetic base. Semantic and grammatical rules are learned with the
learning of verbal behavior through reinforcement by other persons
who constitute the "verbal community." Word combinations never before heard or used can be verbalized under conditions of new combinations of stimuli in new settings, or as "mutations." Thus, although
verbal behavior differs from other kinds of behaviors, it is still subject
to the same conditions of control as nonverbal (including animal) behavior. No mentalistic explanation is necessary.

Verbal behavior is reinforced by its effects on other people, and
also on the speaker, who becomes a listener and can reinforce his or
her own behavior. The meaning of verbal behavior is in the consequences or effects it has, and has had in the past, on others. Meanings
are different for the speaker and the listener, since each has had different experiences with the same words. Thus communication can be
difficult. There are no standard meanings or contents as communications theory assumes or implies.

Much of our verbal behavior consists of metaphors or other figures
of speech, which can cause difficulties in relating the verbal behavior
to other behavioral processes. They arise through conditioning or
generalization. The statement that a person explodes with anger is the
result of the association of a behavior of an individual with the stimulus of the explosion of dynamite or a bomb. Our verbal behaviors also
are influenced by the fact that language developed at a time when

there was little understanding of the causes of behavior. Much of our verbalization about human behavior goes back to a time when inner causation by mental states was accepted. Such language must be translated into language which more accurately represents the actual causation of behavior. This is sometimes difficult because there may be no exact behavioral equivalents, "certainly none with the overtones and contexts of the original."[31] Skinner's attitude toward some of the inner states is apparent in his statement that "to spend much time on exact redefinitions of consciousness, will, wishes, sublimation, and so on would be as unwise as for physicists to do the same for ether, phlogiston, or *vis viva*."[32] Yet his discussion of human behavior consists essentially in translations and behavioral definitions of verbalizations about inner states.

Self-observation. No one can observe the conditions and processes which exist in another person. But if one is asked about these states and events, one can observe them in oneself and verbally describe them to others. Consciousness is simply observing one's behavior, internal and external, and being able to describe it verbally. The verbal descriptions are learned from the verbal community. Thus, when a child is hit or cut, an observer of the event says "That hurts" or "That's painful." The child associates the words with what it feels, and later uses them when it has the same or similar feelings. In addition, the community uses collateral or accompanying responses to the public stimuli of being hit or cut, such as crying, and uses the same words when such responses are present.

The descriptions of bodily states which are learned in this way are never completely accurate, however. Instruction is not systematic, and labels are sometimes based on inferences from the child's behavior. In addition, we do not have adequate means of contacting our own bodily states; the interoceptive, proprioceptive and exteroceptive nervous systems do not provide access to these states. *"But what is felt or introspectively observed is not an important part of the physiology which fills the temporal gap in historical analysis. . . .* We can never know through introspection what the physiologist will eventually discover with his special instruments."[33]

Self-statements involving characteristics or traits, such as "I am brave," refer to past behaviors in response to external stimuli. To say "I am brave" is to say that on a number of occasions in the past I have behaved in response to dangerous situations in a manner which is called brave, and it is likely that I will respond similarly in the future. What often happens, however, is that descriptive terms (adjectives) applied to behavior, such as *brave* or *courageous,* become entities (nouns), for instance, *bravery* or *courage;* then behavior is attributed to the entity. A state or quality inferred from the behavior becomes the cause of the behavior. A person learns to walk in a way described as cautious on ice; we say he walks with caution, or that he shows caution. But then we begin to say that he walks carefully *because* of his caution. Elaborate psychic entities and operations are built up, leading to seemingly profound statements.

Humans are the only animals that know that they behave. Self-knowledge has a social origin, resulting from the responses, including verbal labeling, of others. Questions by others about one's behavior lead to self-awareness, which makes it possible for the individuals to predict and control their own behavior.

Reports of the individual about his or her inner world are clues to that person's past and present behaviors and their causes, and therefore to his or her future behavior. But because of their inaccuracies they are not reliable predictors.

Thinking, reasoning, knowing, and the mind. Mentalistic formulations move behavior into the "mind." Behaviors related to thinking, such as attending, discriminating, seeking, and problem solving gave rise to the invention of the higher mental processes. But thinking is behaving; it is covert behavior, which may be either verbal or nonverbal. Reports of thinking may describe private conditions associated with public behaviors, though not necessarily caused by the public behaviors. Thoughts may be synonymous with talking to oneself, and "thinking out loud" makes the covert behavior overt.

Abstractions and concepts have no separate existence in the mind. They are simply terms used to refer to similar behaviors or responses to stimuli which consist of the common properties of different objects. They are learned as the result of reinforcement. Redness does not exist apart from its being a common property of a number of different objects. "A concept is simply a feature of a set of contingencies which exist in the real world, and it is discovered simply in the sense that the contingencies bring behavior under its control."[34]

In the mental parallel of physical search, no storehouse of memories of facts or images exists, which is scanned or searched. Recall is a matter of greater probability of occurrence as a result of previous experience and associations. Problem solving is emitting behaviors which will lead to a response which is lacking to produce a reinforcement. Steps are also taken to make the response more probable by altering the environment. Problem solving is originally acquired in overt form; when it becomes covert it is called thinking.

Choice is simply the solving of an aversive situation—the existence of two or more responses with nearly equal probabilities—by changing the setting so as to increase the probability of one response. To choose is to act; the choice is the act. Freedom of choice is the absence of external restraints so one can act on the basis of the probabilities which exist as a result of one's previous experience. Insightful problem solving is the result of many earlier learnings and discriminations. Creative thinking is the production of mutations which can be encouraged by certain settings and behaviors.

Thought processes are real as behaviors, but metaphorical when attributed to genetic endowment in the form of innate ideas, or to a mind. We have brains, but not minds. Thought is written or spoken behavior, and its contents derive from the environment.

The development of verbal behavior in humans made it possible to describe behaviors and their consequences, or cause-effect relationships. Commands, advice, warnings, directions, and instructions imply or embody such sequences. Folklore, maxims, and proverbs also describe cause-effect sequences. In complex societies, religious and secular laws are developed to codify contingencies of behaviors, which may be arranged or contrived in the form of punishments. Scientific laws formulate principles of cause and effect in the physical and biological realms.

Such descriptions of cause-effect sequences, or rules, make it possible for behavior to be learned or controlled without the actual experiencing of contingencies. Rules are useful in situations where learning by exposure to contingencies would be dangerous or require a long time, where the contingencies are long delayed, and where they are complex or unclear. Rules verbalize the contingencies which exist in the environment. It is not necessary, however, that the contingencies be verbalized or that the individual know the rules, in order for behavior to be controlled by the contingencies.

Reasons are the consequences of behavior implicit or explicit in advice, warnings, instructions, laws, and rules. We act reasonably without being aware of what we are doing, since behavior which takes contingencies, or reasons, into account is reasonable or rational behavior. Intuitive behavior is behavior which does not involve an analysis of the contingencies, or behavior for which no rule has been formulated. Faith is the result of strongly reinforced behaviors which have not been analyzed. Expectancy is similar in nature. Reasoning is the process of analyzing the reasons for behavior. Deliberate behavior follows an analysis of reasons; impulsive behavior is a direct effect of contingencies.

Inductive reasoning is the extraction of rules from individual instances of a class of events. It does not involve the drawing of inferences. The pigeon which learns to peck a disk when it is green, but not when it is red, does not draw inferences. Deduction is reasoning from generals to particulars and is involved in the application of rules, but it also may be the deriving of new rules from old rules. Induction and deduction are not objects of behavioral analysis, however.

Knowledge is not information stored somewhere; it is a repertoire of behaviors which the individual is capable of performing. We know something if we can repeat it, recite it, or do it. We know about something if we can work with it or do something with it. Such knowledge is based on experience. We may also know something on the basis of instructions, so that we can state directions, rules, and laws. We may also know in the sense of being able to report that we can or could do something under certain circumstances. All knowledge derives from the experiencing of contingencies. Behavior does not occur because we *know* the contingencies, but because they exist and occur.

Motivation: Needs, desires, wants, and wishes. The states associated with needing, wanting, wishing, desiring, hoping, yearning, and so on, are states of deprivation or of aversive stimulation. Want is a shortage of something; need is also. To be in need is to lack something, as is to be in want. These states are more likely to be felt if there is no relevant behavior immediately possible to achieve consequences which would reduce the lack. But an event, such as the presence of or eating of food, is not reinforcing *because* it reduces the need. States of wanting or needing exist when no reinforcement is available; but when reinforcement becomes available, the behavior is not caused by the want or need but by the deprivation or aversive stimulation which is responsible for both the state and the behavior. Feelings of want or need are the result of deprivation; feelings of satiation are the result of reinforcement. The relation between a state of deprivation and the strength of the appropriate behavior is presumably due to survival value. If behavior leading to ingestion were strong at all times, a person would grossly overeat and use his energies inefficiently."[35] Mentalistic terms applied to states of deprivation and effective reinforcers are often metaphors. Freud's dynamisms and defense mechanisms (repression, conversion, sublimation, and so on) are such metaphors. "They are not psychic processes taking place in the depths of the mind, conscious or unconscious; they are the effects of contingencies of reinforcement, almost always involving punishment."[36] People are portrayed as being driven by powerful drives, urges, and internal forces dwelling in the mind. Deprivation is not a driving force, and reinforcement does not create a motive or incentive, which are inferences from behavior. "We call a person highly motivated when all we know is that he behaves energetically."[37] "Motives" are feelings associated with consequences, not causes of actions.

Other feelings which are said to influence behavior are actually the results of consequences of previous behaviors. Expectations or anticipations are based on previous experience in the same or similar situations. Confidence, faith, belief, and feelings of certainty are results of frequent reinforcement in the past. Disappointment, lack of confidence, uncertainty, discouragement, and a sense of impotence are results of lack of reinforcement in the past. They do not account for behavior—they are not necessary to explain, predict, or control behavior. Statements about what one's expectations are or about what one is going to do, may be reports of covert behaviors likely to be emitted in certain circumstances, or predictions based on awareness of conditions with which the behaviors are associated.

Motivation: Will, purpose, and intention. In defining operant behavior, it was noted that it is behavior with no apparent immediate cause. This apparent lack has led to the invention of will as the initiating cause. Choosing is similar to willing, in the sense of choosing to act or not to act. But the act of willing or choosing must itself be explained. It was noted earlier that the causes of operant behavior are in the person's genetic makeup and past history. They are not immediately apparent and not of interest in operant conditioning, but they are there. "The critical condition for the apparent exercise of free will is positive reinforcement, as the result of which a person feels free and calls himself free and says he does as he *likes* or what he *wants* or is *pleased* to do."[38] Control by aversive consequences or punishment leads to the feeling of *having to do something* to avoid the consequences. But positively reinforcing consequences do not lead to avoidance or escape behavior; there is no feeling of being controlled, but instead a feeling of freedom and control. "Choice" is a matter of the relative effectiveness of reinforcers. "Will" simply means behaving or acting. Statements about what one will do are reports, though often in metaphorical form, of feelings, conditions, or stimuli which have preceded or accompanied the behavior in the past.

In stimulus-repsonse reflex conditioning, there is no question of intention, "but operant behavior is the very field of purpose and intention. By its nature it is directed toward the future: a person acts *in order that* something will happen, and the order is temporal."[39] But the purpose or intention is the effect of reinforcements. Reinforcements are often said to create motivation or give a person "a purpose." But the awareness of a purpose is the feeling or observing of a condition produced by reinforcement. Statements of inclinations, tendencies, intention, or purpose are statements of probabilities based on the existence of conditions in the individual (and also perhaps the environment) which have been associated with the intended or predicted behavior in the past.

The self or personality and self-management. "A self or personality is at best a repertoire of behavior imparted by an organized set of contingencies."[40] There may be several sets of contingencies, related to different situations in which the person lives. Conflicts may arise among them if the situations begin to overlap. All sets exists in one person and constitute the person.

Behavioral analysis thus does not deal with a self or a personality but with a person who behaves. The person is not an originating agent —the I who asserts and feels freedom is a product of a history which is not free and which determines what the I will do in the present.

Self-knowledge has focused on feelings, because that is what the verbal community has been interested in and asks questions about. Feelings have thus been identified with a sense of self or a self-image. If the focus of questioning is changed to the environment or external conditions, the individual is encouraged to look at the (real) reasons for his or her behavior—to know the contingencies which control the behavior. The observation of the behavior of others and the contingencies controlling it, helps us to understand ourselves.

Self-knowledge or self-understanding makes self-management possible. Self-management does not involve changing feelings or states of mind. It involves changing the environment in which one lives by analyzing contingencies to develop rules which can be applied to one's behavior. Rules developed by others can be helpful—maxims, proverbs, the Golden Rule. The Golden Rule deals with actions, not feelings—though feelings may accompany the actions. Self-management is concerned with consequences, which are often the result of actions by others.

Resolutions are rules for self-management, though they may not be particularly effective. Formulating a rule to avoid situations which lead to behaviors with undesirable consequences is a technique of self-management. Arranging an environment conducive to desired behaviors is another. Bringing one's personal history into the present helps one in self-control, or in transcendence of one's present environment, as in the case of an individual who refuses to be broken or demoralized or betray her or his principles.

When techniques of self-management have been learned, the individual may be able to move from the instructional contingencies provided by the verbal community to private effects or reinforcements. Self-management may become automatic, with the individual using stimuli unconsciously.

Managing others. Managing others is accomplished in the same way as one manages oneself—by changing the world in which they live. Arranging positive or negative contingencies is one way of changing the environment, and thus the behavior, of others. Describing contingencies—pointing them out, urging, exhorting, contracting, issuing warnings—is another, often with contrived aversive consequences added. Teaching, psychotherapy, governing, and entertaining are fields in which the behavior of others is managed.

The question of control. We start by recognizing that behavior is already controlled by genetic and environmental histories and the curernt environment. The individual is not a creating, initiating agent. Human behavior itself is a form of control, of both the physical environment and other persons, as well as of oneself. Education and government are controlling institutions. Existing controls, or methods of control, are in general haphazard and unplanned. If we are to create a world in which the potentialities of human beings will be realized, we must do so by applying the results of a scientific analysis of behavior.

It is of course possible to misuse the power to control behavior. Skinner writes, "The dangers inherent in the control of human behavior are very real."[41] And elsewhere, "The danger of the misuse of power is possibly greater than ever."[42] Control itself must be controlled. The first step is the exposure of controlling techniques. Awarness of control and its methods allows one to resist undesirable control. Aversive methods of control lead to countercontrol, by moving out of the orbit of the controller, protesting in some form, or, in the extreme case, by revolution. Control through positive reinforcement is control which is for the good of the controlled. Where aversive control results in the individual "having to" do something, under positive reinforcement the individual "wants to" do it. Wanting to do it leads to the feeling of freedom. "Feeling free is an important hallmark of a kind of control distinguished by the fact that it does not breed countercontrol."[43] Under positive reinforcement, the consequences of the controller's behavior are reinforcing to the controller, leading the controller to provide more positive reinforcement—and to be regarded as benevolent, compassionate, devoted, public spirited, and so on. Skinner is optimistic about the benefits of the application of his system to the entire field of human behavior. "For a long time men of good will have tried to improve the cultural patterns in which they live. It is possible that a scientific analysis of behavior will provide us at last with the techniques we need for this task—with the wisdom we need to build a better world, and, through it, better men."[44]

The objective or goal for a planned or designed culture is the survival of the culture, or of the human race. "The change does not require that we be able to describe some distant state of mankind toward which we are moving or 'deciding' to move. . . . We better ourselves and our world as we go. . . . We change our cultural practices because it is our nature as men to be reinforced in certain ways. This is not an infallible guide. It could, indeed, lead to fatal mistakes."[45] An example might be susceptibility to a virus as a result of advancements in sanitation which eliminate the development of immunity. Some objectives or values which could be developed on a transitional basis are that people be healthy, happy, productive, well behaved, skillful, wise. It is possible that something can go wrong in a culture—as it has in the past—and it will then need to be corrected by explicit design.

Control and the idea of control are resisted by most people. "People have suffered so long and so painfully from the controls imposed upon them that it is easy to understand why they so bitterly oppose any form of control."[46] Concern about aversive control has extended to all forms of control. In addition, the democratic philosophy is in conflict with the use of control, even to achieve the goals of the philosophy. Skinner is concerned that society may never profit from the science of behavior because of this. He suggests that while democracy served a purpose in freeing us from aversive control, it is an outmoded means to an end which now can be achieved by scientific means of control. "The hard fact is that the culture which most readily acknowledges the validity of a scientific analysis is most likely to be successful in that competition between cultures which, whether we like it or not, will decide all such issues with finality."[47]

> Who is to control? The question represents the age-old mistake of looking to the individual rather than to the world in which he lives. It will be a benevolent dictator, a compassionate therapist, a devoted teacher, or a public-spirited industrialist who will design a way of life in the interests of everyone. We must look at the conditions under which people govern, give help, teach, and arrange incentive systems in particular ways. In other words we must look to the culture as a social environment. Will a culture evolve in which no individual will be able to accumulate vast power and use it for his own aggrandizement in ways which are harmful to others? Will a culture evolve in which individuals are not so much concerned with their own actualization and fulfillment that they do not give serious attention to the future of the culture? These questions, and many others like them, are the questions to be asked rather than *who* will control and to what *end*. No one steps outside the causal stream. No one really intervenes. Mankind has slowly created environments in which people behave more effectively, and no doubt enjoy the feelings which accompany successful behavior. It is a continuing process.[48]

Summary

Behaviorism as a philosophy of a science of human behavior asserts that behavior can be studied scientifically, leading to the ability to account for every aspect of behavior and to prediction and control of such behavior. Laws of behavior can be developed similar to the laws of physics and biology. Methodological behaviorism provides the means for a science of human behavior. It is a method of observation which is objective. As such, it has rejected the study of internal events—feelings and thinking. The radical behaviorism of B. F. Skinner admits the study of internal events, by translating them into behaviors. Such internal events are not, however, involved in the causation of overt behaviors.

The organism is a behaving organism. Its ongoing behavior is called *operant* behavior and does not need to be accounted for. Learned behavior is a result of conditioning by the environment. A limited repertoire of behavior is acquired by *classical conditioning,* in which a *conditioned stimulus* which normally does not *elicit* a response, comes to elicit the response through association with (being immediately followed by) the natural or *unconditioned stimulus.* Most learned behaviors, however, are the result of *operant conditioning.* In operant conditioning, the rate of occurrence of *emitted responses* (operant behaviors) is controlled by the *consequences* of such responses. Responses which are followed by *reinforcement* (favorable consequences) increase. Reinforcement, which always increases the rate of response, may be *positive* (providing a favorable consequence) or *negative* (removing an aversive or noxious consequence).

Reinforcements occur on differing *schedules. Continuous reinforcement* is the occurrence of a reinforcement following each and every response. In *intermittent reinforcement* not every response is reinforced. There are four main schedules of intermittent reinforcement, divided into two types, *interval schedules* and *ratio schedules:* In *fixed interval schedules,* reinforcements occur periodically, each following a constant time lapse. In *variable interval schedules,* reinforcements occur randomly with respect to time, but varying about an average time interval. *Fixed ratio schedules* provide reinforcement regularly after a fixed number of responses have been emitted. *Variable ratio schedules* provide reinforcement irregularly with respect to the number of responses, but varying about an average number of responses.

Behavior which is not reinforced decreases in rate of response, eventually returning to the original or operant level. The decline in response following the withdrawal of reinforcement is called *extinction.* The rate of extinction is related to schedules of reinforcement. Behavior established under continuous reinforcement extinguishes more rapidly than does behavior established under intermittent reinforcement. (Continuous reinforcement is more effective and efficient in establishing the behavior, however.) After a lapse of time following extinction, responding at a high rate may occur again in the original, unreinforced, situation. This is known as *spontaneous recovery.*

A condition or event (or stimulus) which is not naturally reinforcing may become reinforcing through association with a natural reinforcer, and become a *secondary* or *conditioned reinforcer*. Characteristics of the environment and of the organism's behavior at the time of reinforcement, become conditioned to the response and act as secondary reinforcers.

Responses which occur under particular stimulus conditions occur under similar conditions; a pigeon trained to respond when a red circle is present will respond when a yellow circle is present, or when a red square is present. This is called *stimulus generalization.* The pigeon can be trained not to respond in a situation which, although similar in some respects, is significantly different, by not being reinforced. The pigeon will not continue responding in the presence of the yellow circle (or the red square) if it is not reinforced. *Stimulus discrimination* is then present.

Behavior is thus influenced by the conditions or stimuli which accompany reinforcement; that is, it is under *stimulus control.* This control is not the automatic control of a stimulus which elicits a response in reflexive behavior or classical conditioning.

An operant response similar to or associated with a response which is reinforced will also increase in rate, as a result of *response generalization.* Such generalization can be eliminated, however, if one fails to reinforce responses similar to the response desired. This is *response differentiation,* or *shaping.* By selectively reinforcing responses which increasingly approximate a desired ultimate response and ceasing to reinforce those which less closely approximate the desired response, behavior can be *shaped. Response chains*—a connected series of responses—can be developed by reinforcing the units of the chain in order. Shaping and chaining lead to new forms of behavior which were not a part of the operant repertoire of the organism.

Reinforcement increases the rate of behavior. *Punishment,* or the imposition of aversive or noxious conditions (or the removal of positive reinforcers), decreases the rate of response. Punishment is often used rather than extinction to eliminate an undesirable response because it works faster. Punishment has some undesirable consequences, however. To be really effective it must be severe, and its results are not long-lasting. It also arouses undesirable emotional responses in both the punished and the punisher.

Drive and emotion are concepts which are unnecessary in explaining behavior. As inferred states of the organism they are not objective or measurable. Objective measures of the state of the organism relevant to the effectiveness of certain reinforcers are provided by *deprivation* of the reinforcer. The reinforcing effect of food is directly related to the amount of time since the organism has been fed, or the ratio of its present body weight to normal weight. Emotions are internal states which are the result of environmental stimuli. They can be defined by changes in the rate of response. At the beginning of the extinction process, following the normal delay in reinforcement under the schedule being used, an organism may begin responding at an abnormally high rate. This may be interpreted as "frustration." But it is not an explanation of the behavior—it is an internal result of not receiving reinforcement, the objective or behavioral result of which is the change in responding.

The environmental control of behavior through the methods represented by reinforcement schedules has been amply demonstrated in laboratory experiments with animals. Experiments with human beings have demonstrated that human behavior is subject to the same methods of control. Verbal behavior, which is peculiarly human, is learned under the same contingencies of reinforcement as other kinds of behavior.

Human beings experience a variety of mental and emotional events or states which are not directly observable by others. Skinner recognizes their existence and the possibility of studying them through introspection and self-report. The inadequacies of verbal description and analysis make these reports inaccurate, however. And although these states are of interest, they are not important from the standpoint of predicting and controlling behavior. They are not causes of behavior, but the results of environmental stimuli or consequences, or accompaniments of the behavioral results of such external conditions. They are not entities, nor do they exist in a "mind"; they are actually behaviors occurring inside the body. The mind is simply an invention to explain mental events. Thinking is behavior of a covert nature, perhaps in part "talking to oneself."

Other concepts relating to mental life, such as needs, desires, wants, wishes, will, purpose, and intention, involve metaphors or figures of speech which, on analysis, can be translated into behavioral terms. The self or personality is simply a repertoire of behavior resulting from previous experiences with the environment. It does not exist as something apart from the person's behaviors.

A knowledge of oneself, based on observation of the effects of one's behavior on the environment, including other persons, makes self-management possible. Self-management involves altering or arranging the environment and its contingencies to control one's behavior.

In the same way one person can manage others—by changing or controlling their environments. We do this in education, psychotherapy, government, and entertaining. The control of others raises problems, including fears and resistance. This is because control has so often been achieved by aversive means for selfish purposes. There are dangers in the increasing ability to control behavior which the scientific analysis of behavior is making possible. But there is also the possibility of designing a culture which will improve the condition of humanity. The criterion for the design is the survival of the resulting culture. The use of positive reinforcement avoids the negative or undesirable aspects of control. In addition, the fact that human nature determines what is reinforcing provides some assurance that the results of control are desirable, though this is not an infallible guide.

Skinner believes that we must use the results of the scientific analysis of behavior if we are to accelerate progress toward a world which will achieve the ideals of democracy. Democracy, which has been useful in improving the state of humanity in a struggle against aversive control, is now an obstacle to the control which would lead to the achievement of its own goals.

EDUCATION: THE TECHNOLOGY
OF TEACHING

The educated person has been accounted for on the basis of three major processes, or *metaphors*, as Skinner calls them. Maturation, or *growth and development*, is the first. In this metaphor, change is mainly due to the natural development of innate characteristics and potentials, with minimal environmental influences. Education then consists in fostering natural development, or guiding growth. The result is the development of faculties, traits, cognitive powers, the intellect, or the mind. This metaphor does not account for behaviors which are obviously derived from the environment, such as speaking a particular language.

The second metaphor focuses on *acquisition* of knowledge, skill, and ideas from the environment. All of these are acquired with different degrees of receptivity—soaked up and digested by students, or inculcated, instilled, or drilled into them. The concern in this metaphor is with inner states or entities as outcomes of teaching—knowledge, meanings, concepts, ideas—not with behaviors. Behavior is not what is learned in this metaphor; behavior is simply performance based on what is learned.

The *construction* metaphor, the third metaphor, recognizes a genetic endowment which matures, but education or teaching is instruction, or construction, by which the student's behavior is given form or shape, or is built.

All three of these metaphors are commen in the language used to describe education. But metaphors are not particularly useful, since they do not specify just what is done in education, or by the teacher.

There are three other ways of describing learning and teaching which may be called *theories*. The first is *learning by doing*. Learning is an active process; "to know is to act effectively, both verbally and nonverbally."[49] Frequency, or repetition, and recency theories are proposed to account for learning by doing. But learning is more than going through the motions of behaviors. Learning by doing is inadequate as an explanation for learning.

The *experience theory* also is inadequate. Learning does not occur from experience alone. A two-factor theory in which experience is considered as stimulus or input and doing as response or output is also inadequate. It presumes that something is learned which connects the stimulus and the response so that the stimulus will produce the response. It neglects environmental variables.

The theory of *trial-and-error learning* explains learning as a result of the experience of the consequences of behavior—rewards and punishments. It assumes that learning is a slow process of eliminating errors, that errors are necessary. But "correct behavior is not simply what remains when erroneous behavior has been chipped away. . . . The term 'error' does not refer to the physical dimensions of the consequences, even those called punishment."[50]

These theories are incomplete rather than wrong. They include the three variables which compose the conditions of learning, or the contingencies of reinforcement: (1) an occasion upon which behavior occurs (learning by experience), (2) the behavior itself (the response, or learning by doing), and (3) the consequences of the behavior (learning by trial and error). It is not necessary to integrate these theories into a new theory. We simply need to analyze the changes which take place as a student learns, or to apply the experimental analysis of behavior.

The State of Teaching

An examination of what goes on in the usual classroom indicates clearly that education, which is the branch of technology most directly related to learning, has not benefited from advances in the science of learning. Efforts to improve education neglect method and are not based upon an analysis of teaching. Instead of attempting to improve teaching, we spend money for more and better school buildings, more teachers, audiovisual aids, new curriculums, and selection of better students. Teachers have not been trained in a technology of teaching. Even such training as has been attempted, in methods of teaching, has been disparaged, says Skinner, on the basis that knowledge of and interest in a subject matter is sufficient for good teaching.

From the standpoint of an experimental analysis of behavior, there are a number of things wrong with current teaching practices.

Aversive control. Corporal punishment in schools goes back to Rome and Greece. Its decline has been replaced with verbal punishment: ridicule, scolding, sarcasm, criticism. Other means of aversive control include incarceration after school hours, extra work, forced labor, ostracism, and fines. Clearly, schoolwork and school attendance are unpleasant experiences, something to be escaped from. To be excused from an assignment constitutes a reward. Students escape by being tardy and truant, dropping out, not paying attention, letting their minds wander and daydreaming, being restless, and forgetting. Or the student becomes inactive—sullen, stubborn, unresponsive, refusing to obey, and silently taking the punishment. Aversive control also breeds countercontrol—or counterattack. Students become unruly, rude, impertinent, impudent, even defiant. The situation may escalate until discipline becomes despotic or the teacher resigns.

Aversive control is easily learned by teachers. Its effects are immediate and clear. In mild form the undesirable by-products are not obvious. The system has produced well-disciplined, obedient, industrious, informed, and skilled students, who in later years may look back in appreciation at "tough" teachers. Aversive control may be justified by some because it toughens children to adversity, and because it prepares for adult life where government operates through aversive control.

Aversive control can get students to read, listen, talk, and do paperwork. But there are negative feelings—anxiety, fear, sullenness. Learning becomes unpleasant, painful—work, in other words. Getting the right answer is a minor event amid the mass of aversive consequences. Aversive methods also have undesirable effects on teachers. They become tense, unfriendly, aggressive—unable to relate with students in a way which is productive of learning. Aversive control corrupts both teachers and students.

Telling and showing. The child learns naturally in the real world; he seems to have a "natural curiosity" and "a love of knowledge." But only a small part of the natural world can be brought into the classroom. And when an attempt is made to bring some of it in by showing and telling the student something, an element necessary for learning is missing. That element is positive reinforcement, the natural consequences of the student's curiosity and wish to learn in real life. Reinforcements are given by the teacher. But these reinforcements are infrequent. In the learning of arithmetic in the first four years of school, Skinner estimates that some 25,000 contingencies are required by each student, but the total number which can be arranged by the teacher is only a few thousand. Moreover, in the typical classroom, the lapse of time between a correct response and reinforcement is too great for the reinforcement to be effective. The teacher, walking about the room observing the children doing problems, can catch only a few immediately after they have completed a problem. Intermittent reinforcement, it will be remembered, is effective for maintaining behavior; continuous reinforcement is more effective in establishing behavior.

Getting attention. To assist in focusing the child's attention, the classroom is isolated and freed of distractions, and silence is imposed. Earphones and TV screens are used. Audiovisual aids are resorted to. Colors, variety, sudden change, animation are introduced. The school and classroom may be made pleasant. But all these things come at the wrong time. They attract the child to school, to the material, to the book or content. But they do not assure that the child will read or listen.

The teacher as midwife. The concept of education as "educing" or drawing out what is there goes back to Plato and the Socratic or maieutic method. It is stated that the teacher cannot really teach, but can only help the student learn. But the famous scene in the *Meno,* in which Socrates takes the slave boy through Pythagoras's theorem on doubling the square is, says Skinner, "one of the great frauds in the history of education,"[51] and he contends that thousands of teachers have wasted years of their lives in application of the Socrates method.

The method of discovery is supposed to teach the seeking student to learn from the world of things. But "it is designed to absolve the teacher from a sense of failure by making instruction unnecessary. The teacher arranges the environment in which discovery is to take place, he suggests the lines of inquiry, he keeps the student within bounds. The important thing is that he should tell him nothing."[52] Learning without being taught, through discovery, does occur. But discovery learning is not the answer to the problem of education, since it is impossible for individuals to discover for themselves all they need to know. There are other problems with the discovery method. The teacher must pretend not to know, which can affect the teacher's relations with students. And in a classroom, all the discoveries will be made by a few good students, leading to problems.

The idols of the school. The Good Teacher Idol says that what a good teacher can do, any teacher can do. But these natural teachers are exceptions, and we do not yet know how to produce them. The Good Student Idol assumes that what a good student can learn, any student can learn. But these students are exceptions, who, because of superior endowments and environments, learn without being taught. We must abandon these idols and base teaching upon known methods of teaching and learning.

The Technology of Teaching

Skinner quotes William James who, in his book *Talks to Teachers on Psychology* (published in 1899), wrote: "You make a great, a very great mistake if you think that psychology, being the science the mind's laws, is something from which you can deduce definite programs and schemes and methods of instruction for immediate school-room use. Psychology is a science, but teaching is an art. . . ."[53]

But the scientific analysis of behavior provides principles which can be applied to the design of schools, equipment, texts, and class-room practices. These principles lead to methods which are alternatives to the aversive techniques which are so ineffective and harmful. Teaching consists of an arrangement of the contingencies of reinforcement so that students learn. The questions to be answered are: What behaviors are to be learned? What reinforcers are available? What operant behaviors or responses are available to begin a program of progressive approximation which will lead to the terminal behaviors? How can reinforcements be most efficiently scheduled to maintain the behaviors in strength? This is an applied science, not an art.

Three major applications of the principles derived from the scientific analysis of behavior are in classroom management, programmed learning, and teaching machines.

Contingency management in the classroom. Aversive methods of classroom management, or the attempt to achieve discipline through punishment, are ineffective. In fact, they lead to undesirable and disruptive behaviors rather than those which teachers desire. The alternative is not complete freedom. It is the application of contingencies of reinforcement.

If learning is to take place, children must come to class, and the general conditions in the classroom must allow learning to take place—irrelevant noise and activities must be at a minimum. The classroom must provide reinforcements for being present, and for behaving in ways that make learning possible. Social contingencies—the behaviors of other children and the teacher—are important. These are difficult to arrange, but the teacher does have some control, such as who sits near whom, what privileges are enjoyed by whom, when liked activities are engaged in, and so on. "Personal commendation is often a powerful reinforcer, but a merely synthetic approval or affection has its dangers."[54] The difficulty is to make reinforcers contingent on the desired behavior. A "generalized reinforcer" is needed. Credit points or *tokens* which can later be exchanged for privileges or other desirable reinforcers can be used. Students can be randomly selected and their behaviors observed for short periods of time, after which the student under observation is informed that he or she has or has not earned a token or credit. The desired behaviors begin to be reinforced in other ways, as learning increases in a conducive atmosphere.[55]

Such procedures have been called bribery, which is an implied contract ("If you do such-and-such, then I'll give you . . ."). "But a contract tends to destroy the effect of a reinforcer. Contingencies of reinforcement are most effective when there is no prior agreement as to terms."[56] It has been objected that the contingencies are artificial, or contrived. But punishment is artificial. "Artificiality is not the issue. We use contrived contingencies to set up behavior which will, we hope, be reinforced naturally under the contingencies of daily life. The *problem is to make sure that the behavior we set up will indeed be effective in the world at large.*"[57] Another objection is that reinforcers in real life are not immediate, and students must be taught to respond to remote consequences. But no one responds to remote consequences; it is mediating reinformers to which people respond. It is also objected that reinforcement in real life is intermittent, so that students should be accustomed to nonreinforcement. But this ignores the fact that continuous reinforcement is most effective in building up behaviors, and persistence is strengthened when reinforcements have been gradually extended.

Programmed instruction. Programming involves a series of progressive approximations to the *terminal performances* which are the goals of education. The first step is to define the terminal behaviors—what the student is to do as the result of the program. This is very difficult, because objectives are usually stated in vague terms rather than as behaviors—adapting; adjusting; surviving; acquiring knowledge, concepts, or meanings; or developing rational powers. The term *knowledge,* in the sense of being able to do something, is more useful in stating an objective. But objectives must involve behaviors—skillful behavior, not a skill; able or competent behaviors, not abilities or competency; that is, behaviors, not inner processes or states. Reading behavior, not an ability to read or knowledge of reading, is an acceptable objective.

When the behavior is defined, arrangements must be made to reinforce it when it appears. But one can't wait for it to appear all at once, and shaping by successive approximations is tedious. Other ways of achieving the behavior are more efficient. Behavior can be forced, as when the child's hand is manipulated so it can hold a pencil properly. But forcing can be aversive. Behavior can be elicited by appropriate stimuli. The most common method of evoking behavior to be reinforced is to use a stimulus called a *prime.* A common prime is modeling to induce imitation, which is then reinforced. Where the model can be seen, movement duplication is effective. Where the model cannot be seen, but the results are evident, product duplication (copying) can be used. Behavior may also be primed by nonduplicative repertoires—for example, verbal instructions. The teacher simply tells the students to do something and reinforces them when they do so. Shaping may, and sometimes must, be used. Behavior is learned not because of these procedures, however, but because it is reinforced, and one instance of the behavior is not sufficient for most learning. Reading once, aloud or silently, does not assure learning. The behavior must be under control of stimuli other than the prime if the prime is to be useful.

In facilitating other stimuli to take over in place of the prime, *prompts* are used. Prompts are part of the prime—just enough of the prime is given to prompt the behavior. Prompts are gradually reduced; to reduce the prompt is to *vanish* it. An example is gradually reducing the time of exposure of material which is being memorized. If, as some teachers believe should be done, maximal help is continually provided when the student has trouble responding, he or she will never become free of the prime. "To help a student learn, the teacher must so far as possible refrain from helping him respond."[58]

Programming complex behavior is difficult: It cannot be reinforced all at once, since it does not occur all at once but over a period of time, and it cannot simply be divided in parts which are reinforced part by part. It must be programmed in small steps in a sequence, constituting a segment; segments are then also sequenced. Narrative or time sequences are not always the best way to order materials; nor is an order from simple to complex, or an order in terms of difficulty, or an order based on the logical structure of the subject matter. The basic principle is to start with behavior which is available, as in shaping, and then move to behavior which even more closely approximates the terminal behavior, in steps which maximize success. The teacher working with an individual student uses primes and prompts and arranges sequences in relation to the student's level and ability, and enables the student to proceed at her or his own speed. "Arranging effective sequences is a good part of the art of teaching."[59]

By proceeding in small steps, programmed instruction minimizes trial-and-error learning, and thus mistakes. It thus minimizes or eliminates the need for aversive control—corrections or punishment. It capitalizes on positive reinforcement, both the extrinsic kind and the intrinsic reinforcement of success.

Programmed instruction is sometimes criticized because it focuses on specifics, ignoring the forest for the trees. But this is not a necessary outcome; the forest can be programmed. Similarly, to the criticism that students can't ask questions of a program it can be replied that neither can they ask questions of a book, and that important questions can be included in the program. Programming is a difficult process, but progress has been made and is still being made in moving toward a technology.

Teaching machines. The programming of instruction by the teacher allows for the development of individualized programs for students. But this is not a realistic possibility in the usual classroom of 30 students. Moreover, "the contingencies of reinforcement which are most efficient in controlling the organism cannot be arranged through the personal mediation of the experimenter. . . . Mechanical and electrical devices must be used. . . . Personal arrangement of the contingencies and personal observation of the results are quite unthinkable. . . . The simple fact is that, as a mere reinforcing mechanism, the teacher is out of date."[60]

Programs can be constructed in advance which apply to most students. They can be presented in the form of programmed textbooks, or of teaching machines. The first teaching machines, developed by S. L. Pressey in the 1920s, were essentially testing machines, not designed for programmed instruction. The teaching machines developed by or stimulated by Skinner incorporate the principles of programming and contingency management. Manipulation of the machine is interesting and thus reinforcing in itself. Reinforcement for the right answer is immediate, in the form of satisfaction with success and in the form of progression to the next step of a more difficult or challenging nature. Reinforcement is frequent, since the steps in the program are small. The operation of the machine requires activity on the part of the learner—responses are constructed, not selected; and emitted, not recognized. Students progress at their own rates. A student who has been absent can pick up where he or she left off, and can go back in the program to any point for review. If operation of the machine and the material itself is not sufficiently reinforcing, other supplemental reinforcers can be provided by the teacher. The teacher, free from the difficult task of programming for a number of children, can engage in supervision, observing individual children who may be having difficulty because a program is too hard, providing more difficult and advanced programs for those who are ready for them, suggesting collateral materials, and outlining further study. "The teacher may begin to function, not in lieu of a cheap machine, but through intellectual, cultural and emotional contacts of that distinctive sort which testify to her status as a human being."[61]

Skinner claims that material can be programmed to be taught by a machine in half the time that would be required if it were learned from a teacher, a text, or film, and with less effort. Materials designed for slow students will not unduly delay the fast student, who can proceed quickly through the material, or programs can be developed at different levels. The problem of gaps in learning or the missing of coverage of content caused by absences will no longer exist.

The Teaching of Thinking and Creativity

Programmed learning is not limited to simple facts and skills. Learning to explore new areas, to solve problems, to make decisions, to think, and to be creative can also be taught through programming. In fact, these things can be taught more efficiently when they are separated from the transmission of what is known, because they can be analyzed in terms of the terminal behaviors which actually indicate their presence or achievement. They are all behaviors; thinking, as noted earlier, is not an obscure cognitive activity of some faculty or power of the mind. This idea or belief results in the practice of developing thinking by presenting the student with tasks or problems to "exercise his mind" or "strengthen his rational powers," but this is not teaching. Application of the experimental analysis of behavior to thinking behavior provides a basis for teaching thinking.

Thinking is often identified with learning, discriminating, generalizing, and abstracting. These are not behaviors, however, but ways of indicating changes in behavior. The changes are a result of specific teaching and can be specified; it adds nothing to use the above terms in referring to the changes. There are no processes of discriminating, generalizing, and abstracting which are learned, but only changed behaviors. Thus, no special techniques for teaching these behaviors are necessary.

Thinking involves other kinds of behavior which can be analyzed and taught, however. "Some parts of our behavior alter and improve the effectiveness of other parts in what may be called self-management. Faced with a situation in which no effective behavior is available (in which we cannot emit a response which is likely to be reinforced), we behave in ways which make effective behavior possible (we improve our chances of reinforcement). In doing so, technically speaking, we execute a 'precurrent' response which changes either our environment or ourselves in such a way that 'consummatory' behavior occurs."[62]

Attending. Attention is a precurrent behavior which involves the selection of features of the environment to which to respond. Selection is in part or in some cases genetically determined or controlled. We respond naturally to loud noises and movement, and such stimuli are used to get attention. But *getting* attention is not the same thing as *paying* attention (which is why elaborate, colored illustrations in books and the use of films to arouse interest do not always improve learning). Paying attention can be taught by reinforcing attending behavior. But we cannot wait for attending behavior to be manifested; it is more efficient to use direct instruction and then reinforce the behavior.

Covert behavior. Much precurrent behavior involved in thinking is covert, and thus neglected in teaching. Talking to oneself is such covert behavior. It is necessary to make covert behavior overt if we are to use it in instruction. Instruction is thus conducted on the overt level; teaching reading is done through reciting aloud. The behavior of reading later reverts to the covert level, and reading (silently) is sustained by the automatic reinforcement of interesting content. In visualizing, or covert seeing, the seen object is so reinforcing that seeing it occurs in the absence of the object. Covert perception or seeing is not usually taught specifically, though it may be increased by reinforcement of successful outcomes, such as describing or copying maps, pictures, and so on. It may be directly taught by programming, however, moving from direct copying to reproduction after increasing intervals of time. But covert seeing may also be taught as overt seeing, by teaching and reinforcing effective ways of looking at or examining objects.

Learning how to learn. Studying is more than close attention or observation. Studying is usually taught indirectly; students are tested on material read, and those who do well, presumably because they have studied effectively, are reinforced. Much studying is done to avoid the aversive consequence of failing.

"To teach a student to study is to teach him techniques of self-management which will increase the likelihood that what is seen or heard will be remembered."[63] Repeated reading of material to learn it, as in learning to recite a poem, is not studying. Studying to learn a poem involves the gradual elimination of dependence on the material through the process of "vanishing" described earlier. Knowing how to study is knowing how much to focus upon for recall at each step and how long to wait before trying to recall. Learning or memorizing is maximized when the response is emitted just before it becomes too weak to be recalled. Learning to study is difficult because there are so many opposing contingencies for reinforcement for responding adequately at the moment, a situation which strengthens dependence on the material.

Learning material in a nonrote or nonmemorization manner is a different matter, and more difficult to teach or acquire. The method of prompts and vanishing is still appropriate, however. But the stimuli are not specific words; they are thematic stimuli. Underlining these and outlining or summarizing them lead to learning, or the ability to summarize or paraphrase without reference to the materials. Good programmed instruction builds thematic relations through introducing synonyms and other intraverbal responses.

Studying techniques must be taught at the overt level, though they eventually recede to the covert level, where they are maintained by their effectiveness in recall.

Problem solving. Paying attention and studying are parts of or preparation for problem solving. But problem solving includes "precurrent activities which facilitate behavior under a much greater variety of circumstances. We face a problem when we cannot emit a response which, because of some current state of deprivation or aversive stimulation, is strong. . . . We solve such problems either by changing the situation so that the response can occur . . . or by changing the deprivation or aversive stimulation. . . ."[64] Learning problem solving is much more complex than learning to pay attention or to study.

While a solution is not available in a problem situation, an effective response is, if the problem is soluble. The appropriate response to make the problem disappear must be found or selected. A problem which can be solved only by a sequence of steps requires the learning of responses appropriate for each step. Presenting students with problems to be solved by the standard sink-or-swim or trial-and-error technique is not teaching problem solving. Such an approach amounts to putting the student in the terminal situation with no preparation. Some of the responses evoked may prove effective, but problem solving is not learned.

Techniques of problem solving depend on the nature or type of problem to be solved. One way is direct instruction, which involves teaching a repertoire which leads to solution, as in a mathematical problem, where the verbal statement of the problem is translated into symbols, which are arranged and rearranged according to rules, leading to a solution. Simply showing students what to do and having them imitate the steps is not the same thing as teaching problem solving, even though they go through the behaviors. The behaviors must come under the control of stimuli which will lead the students to be able to solve similar problems without following the teacher or the printed instructions.

Productive thinking.   Attending, problem recognition, and problem solving may not appear to be thinking as a mental or cognitive process. Algorithmic problem solving (where known methods and techniques are applied) may not involve thinking, it may be claimed by nonbehaviorists, but certainly heuristic problem solving, involving discovery or invention of methods, must involve "productive" thinking. Such thinking is identified with solutions which have not been learned, but have been reached by "insight." But if heuristic problem solving is analyzed, it becomes simply a method of solving the problem of solving problems. Appropriate techniques can be analyzed and taught. These include the behavior of trying, understanding the problem, and relating it to similar problems, and the methods used to solve them. The solution may come surprisingly suddenly, as if it came from nowhere as an original idea. "But there is always an element of mystery in the emission of any operant response. A stimulus never exercises complete control. It is effective only as a part of a set of conditions, which build up to the point at which a response is emitted,"[65] often with a temporal lag. It is not possible to predict the moment of occurrence of a solution, and it may be difficult to explain what is happening during the temporal lag, but to call it insight does not explain it.

Having ideas. Although not always predictable, the occurrence of ideas can be encouraged by teaching certain kinds of precurrent thinking. Such thinking involves running through stimuli, such as going through the alphabet to aid in recalling a name, reviewing situations where the name has been used, and suppressing other thoughts. Since these are covert operations, they are hard to trace and are easily designated as mental activities. But they can be taught.

The role of the thinker. Although the possibility of productive thinking cannot be rejected, the fact that in our present state of knowledge we cannot now explain every instance of thinking does not prove its existence. Thinking consists of the manipulation of conditions which have some part of behavior as a function, and all thinkers proceed in the same way. The thinker engages in techniques of self-management which are the same techniques used by a teacher in getting the student to verbalize thoughts or engage in thinking behavior.

Thinking must be taught, and students who think well must give some credit to their teachers. Similarly, if a student does not think well, it is not only the student who has failed; the teacher is at least equally at fault. We tend to admire achievements which we can't explain as having been taught. As thinking is more successfully analyzed, so that it can be taught more effectively, more credit will go to the teacher and less to the thinker or learner. The experimental analysis of operant conditioning recognizes that "a student, like any organism, must act before he can be reinforced. In a sense he must take the initiative. All the behavior he eventually exhibits must have been his in some form before instruction began."[66] But it does not exist as some personal possession in full-blown form waiting to be drawn out. The teacher must induce the student to act, through primes and prompts. Such instructional contingencies are contrived, and temporary, and the behavior generated is taken over and maintained by contingencies in life outside the school.

The creative student. It would seem that the development of an effective technology of teaching would lead to regimentation (which we have now, in any case), and to the elimination of individuality in the form of originality, creativity, or "an inquiring spirit." "Since traits of this sort are distinguished by their introspective inscrutability, it is not too difficult to dismiss them from a serious analysis. We gain nothing in asserting that a student behaves creatively because he possesses something called creativity. Perhaps we can measure the trait,

compare people with respect to it, and test for the presence of associated traits, but we cannot change creativity itself. Those who take this
approach are reduced to selection rather than teaching—for example,
to talent searches intended to give creative students a chance to develop their special ability. If we are to design effective ways of furthering behavior said to show creativity, we must trace it to manipulable
variables."[67]

A deterministic science of human behavior, however, searches
for causes. It thus looks for the conditions under which creative behavior manifests itself, rather than attributing it to a capricious faculty
of creativity.

What are called freedom of the mind, originality, and creativity
can be developed. Such behaviors are important as "mutations" which
increase the chances of survival of a society. They thus should be encouraged so long as those that are obviously dangerous and harmful
can be avoided or dealt with.

Education furthers freedom by helping to develop a technology
which reduces aversive features of our physical and social environments and by teaching techniques of self-management which help in
dealing with remaining aversive elements. There are also positive
contingencies in which the long-run consequences are aversive. Education can help here in the same two ways.

Education can free students in the classroom by minimizing
aversive techniques and arranging positive contingencies which have
no objectionable by-products. The individuality of young artists can
be preserved by protecting them from conformity-inducing pressures.
Freedom also comes from self-reliance, which can be taught; one is
moved from control by others to control by environment stimuli—
clocks and calendars—which one can use by oneself. The technology
of instruction uncovers the dangers to freedom in older methods of
instruction and fosters freedom.

Although education attempts to provide the student with a behavior repertoire to meet the world, it can never prepare him completely. The student must also be taught to explore new environments
and to solve problems. Such behavior seems to be original, although
it is based upon earlier teaching of what is known about earlier solutions. Such knowledge, and the teaching of it, must not be too specific
or limited, but should be generalizable. Teaching unfortunately tends
to overemphasize literalness, accuracy, memorizing, and paraphrasing.

Paradoxically, by assigning students more than they can possibly
read effectively and by failing to program adequately, poor teaching
avoids rigidity and permits students (who can) to learn how to learn
on their own. A study of how such students learn could be used to
teach more efficiently.

The learning of facts in different forms, involving many translational repertoires, prepares the student to use knowledge more effectively in new situations. Programmed instruction has been criticized for redundancy, but its requirement that the student state a fact or proposition in different ways increases the student's repertoire. Independent and original thinking can be taught by these and other means. Teaching a student how to study, and to explore, leads to individuality and idiosyncracy in learning and behavior.

Behavior which is original, which cannot be traced to genetic endowment or environmental history, may be due to chance. "New responses are generated by accidental arrangements of variables as unforeseeable as the accidental arrangements of molecules or genes. Scientific discovery and literary and artistic invention can often be traced to a kind of fortuitous programming of the necessary contingencies."[68] Chance arrangements can be extended by deliberate design, as when scientists arrange for the occurrence of all possible combinations or permutations of chemicals, or more selectively rearrange genetic materials to produce mutations. By definition, original behavior cannot be taught, but the behaviors of rearranging environments in a way to increase the probability of original responses can be; accidents can be produced. The chances of a particular kind of desirable original behavior (such as art) being produced are greater when the quantity of behaviors of the particular kind is great. Contingencies of reinforcement influence the quantity produced. "Under contingencies which respect quantity, responses are emitted which would otherwise never be effective. The behavior is therefore likely to be original. . . . A powerful technology of teaching can strengthen these sources of originality—in any number of students. . . . The natural ultimate consequences of original behavior are deferred and often inconspicuous, and instruction is therefore all the more important."[69]

The Motivation of the Student

If all students were eager and diligent (as the Latin root of the word *student* implies), education would be greatly different, and more efficient. But underachievement, carelessness, inattentiveness, and doing just enough to get by characterize students at all levels. To attribute this to lack of motivation or lack of a desire to learn does not solve the problem. We have a belief that people have a natural curiosity or love of learning, that they naturally want to learn. "We do not say that about a pigeon; we say only that under the conditions we have arranged, a pigeon learns. We should say the same things about human students. Given the right conditions, men will learn—not because they want to, but because, as a result of the genetic endowment of the species, contingencies bring about changes in behavior."[70] Motivation is the result of schedules of reinforcement. Its manifestation is the increase in behaviors considered to be appropriate. In other words, a high rate of response is equated with interest, enthusiasm, or high motivation. It is necessary to examine the behavior involved to find the conditions which can be provided so that students will study more effectively. Reasons or purposes for studying are aspects of operant conditioning, so we must look at the consequences of studying.

The ultimate consequences or advantages of education—a better job, higher income, prestige, and so on—are too remote to be effective reinforcers. Grades, degrees, diplomas, and other evidences of progress toward the ultimate goal are used as conditioned reinforcers associated with the ultimate objective, but these are weak. Other, more immediate reinforcers are needed.

Contrived proximate reinforcers. Immediate consequences are necessary for arranging good instructional contingencies. Aversive consequences have been used because they are immediately available and are often effective. But although punishment suppresses unwanted behaviors it does not generate behavior, in addition to which it may have undesirable by-products. Positive reinforcers such as prizes, honors, and medals are infrequent and depend on deprivation. All students can't get prizes, or the top grades.

Personal reinforcers—attention, approval, friendship, affection, expressed verbally or physically—are powerful. But they raise problems of personal involvement (attachment and dependency) and of overuse. The contingencies are erratic and unstable. Attention is often given to undesirable behaviors. Approval may also go to fawners and flatterers, or be withheld when it is needed. There is also the problem of genuineness. "Simulated attention, approval, or affection will eventually cause more problems than it solves, and even the *deliberate* use of deserved attention cheapens the coinage."[71]

Natural reinforcers. The problems with contrived contingencies suggest that dependence should be on natural reinforcers. But little of the real world can be brought into the classroom. And it is not simply contact with the real world which leads to learning. Simple experience is no teacher, or at best it is a hard teacher. Learning in the real world depends upon deprivation and aversive stimuli. Much of what is learned in the real world is not very useful or relevant. Accidental contingencies breed superstitious behaviors. Contingencies are often too remote. The human race has learned very slowly from experience, often by accident. Education is designed to make learning more efficient. "The natural contingencies used in education must almost always be rigged."[72]

Improving contingencies. "The important distinction is not between nature and artificiality. The teacher is free to use any available reinforcer provided there are no harmful by-products and providing the resulting behavior can eventually be taken over by reinforcers the student will encounter in his daily life. . . . In improving teaching it is less important to find reinforcers than to design better contingencies using those already available."[73] Remote enforcers can be strengthened by using immediate reinforcers as evidence of progress. The satisfaction of knowing is reinforcing, but one must know that one knows, and it is difficult for the teacher in a large class to prvoide immediate reinforcement to let the students know that they know something. Programmed instruction does this. It may depend on external reinforcers at the beginning—aversive control, money, food, prestige, love. But its immediate and frequent reinforcement and the minimization of errors, maximize the effects of reinforcement inherent in being right and progressing in the material.

"Stretching the ratio."   Continuous reinforcement establishes behavior, but intermittent reinforcement strengthens the continuance of the behavior. "Stretching the ratio" involves increasing the number of responses per reinforcement (or reducing the proportion of responses reinforced) as rapidly as possible, without "losing" the student (or losing control of his behavior) by extinguishing the behavior through inadequate reinforcement. Pleasant experiences in school may be infrequent, but they often keep attendance regular. The precurrent behaviors involved in thinking and problem solving and in self-management are maintained by intermittent reinforcement. Once behavior is established by teacher comments of commendation, the comments can usually be reduced in frequency.

The hard-working student.   Diligence and industry are not traits or the results of a positive attitude toward learning, but the results of effective contingencies of reinforcement. Some of the consequences of working hard may be aversive, but hard work is not under aversive control. The positive reinforcements on an intermittent schedule outweigh the aversive consequences. (Behavior under aversive control is engaged in to avoid the aversive control and ceases when the control ceases to exist. Under aversive control no positive reinforcements are building up behaviors which will persist after the control is removed.)

The intermittent ratios which result in diligent and hard-working students are extremely difficult to design; such students are often the result of an accidental sequence of contingencies. Good books provide intermittent reinforcement, but the problem is programming a schedule which leads to the reading of good books. The dedicated person is the product of a gradually lengthening variable ratio schedule. "It is perhaps presumptuous to compare a Faraday, Mozart, Rembrandt, or Tolstoy with a pigeon pecking a key or with a pathological gambler, but variable ratio schedules are nevertheless conspicuous features of the biographies of scientists, composers, artists, and writers."[74]

An optimal program is perhaps to some extent accidental. But the principle of stretching reinforcements is valid. "Through a proper understanding of contingencies of reinforcement, we should be able to make students eager and diligent and be reasonably sure that they will continue to enjoy the things we teach them for the rest of their lives."[75] Motivation is not a matter of an inherent desire to learn but of the contingencies of reinforcement in the individual's history of learning and instruction.

The teacher as technologist. The failures of education are blamed on the teacher. People are always calling for better teachers. But little attention is given to how teachers can teach more successfully. The preparation of tecahers consists of subject matter courses and a brief period of practice teaching. The teacher is left to learn from the observation of other, presumably good, teachers, and from experience, a method which is inadequate for learning to teach. Pedagogy, or instruction in how to teach (methods courses), has fallen into disrepute. But there is nothing wrong with the idea of teaching teachers how to teach; they simply have not been taught adequately.

The technology of teaching offers an approach to teacher education. A scientific analysis of teaching clarifies the assignment. Instead of being told that the task is to "impart information," or "strengthen rational powers," which does not specify what the teacher does, the student-teacher is helped to specify terminal behaviors. A scientific analysis clarifies the process, and the variables which lead to the terminal behaviors. Programming contributes to an awareness of the requirements of learning: the need for short steps, preparation for the next step, avoidance of misleading, giving enough but not too much help—all things which do not characterize the usual teaching process.

A technology of teaching, rather than making the teacher a machine or automaton, frees the teacher as a human being. By providing technical equipment it creates time for those things for which the teacher is important—exposition, discussion, argumentation, exploration of new areas, concern with ethical behavior, and the common enjoyment of literature, art, and music.

A technology of teaching enables teachers to teach more than they know. Teaching machines (as well as taped or filmed lectures) relieve teachers of the necessity of being subject matter specialists, although it would still be desirable that teachers be well versed in the subject matter they teach.

Technology increases teachers' productivity, enabling them to teach more subject matter, more subjects, and more students. It thus contributes to the teachers' sense of accomplishment. "A technology of teaching by its very nature maximizes the teacher's achievement. The whole establishment gains. We cannot improve education simply by increasing its support, changing its policies, or reorganizing its administrative structure. We must improve teaching itself. Nothing short of an effective technology will solve that problem."[76]

The Function of Education

Education is part of the controlling environment. It is one of the methods used by society to control behavior. "A culture is no stronger than its capacity to transmit itself. It must impart an accumulation of skills, knowledge, and social and ethical practices to its new members. The institution of education is designed to serve this purpose."[77] The transmission of the culture is the first requirement for its survival.

Its survival depends on change, as well, however. "A culture must remain reasonably stable, but it must also change if it is to increase its chances for survival. The 'mutations,' which account for its evolution, are the novelties, the innovations, the idiosyncracies which arise in the behavior of individuals."[78] Society must therefore encourage novelty and diversity rather than conformity.

Our present educational system is highly standardized and regimented; such diversity as exists is accidental. But "an effective diversity must be planned. There is no virtue in accident as such, nor can we trust it. . . . Current differences among our students are for the most part accidents. A technology of teaching should permit us to diversify environmental histories and increase the range of mutations from which the cultures of the future will be selected."[79]

Education can increase diversity by its concern with the individual and his or her development as a creative person. "The goal of education should be nothing short of the fullest possible development of the human organism."[80] Few persons come even close to realizing their potential, even in the best of existing cultures. We do not know what the limits of human potential are. We have no model toward which to work. But the experimental analysis of behavior will enable us to go beyond the existing achievements of educated people and move toward the actualization of our potential.

There are, of course, dangers that a technology of teaching will be misused, or unwisely used, and like any powerful technology it will need to be contained and controlled:

> It could destroy initiative and creativity. It could make all men alike (and not necessarily in being equally excellent); it could suppress the beneficial effect of accidents on the development of the individual and on the evolution of a culture. On the other hand, it could maximize the genetic endowment of each student, it could make him as skillful, com-

petent and informed as possible; it could build the greatest diversity of interests; it could lead him to make the greatest possible contribution to the survival and development of his culture. Which of these futures lies before us will not be determined by the mere availability of effective instruction. The use to which a technology of teaching is put will depend on other matters. We cannot avoid the decisions which now face us by putting a stop to the scientific study of human behavior or by refusing to make use of the technology which inevitably flows from science.[81]

Summary

The scientific analysis of behavior, though a young science, has reached the point where it has practical applications in the field of human behavior. Its most effective technological step (with the possible exception of behavior therapy) has been in the development of a technology of teaching.

Teaching has not been particularly effective. It has used aversive control, which although having immediate effects in obtaining desired behaviors, is not effective in learning and has undesirable side effects and long-term effects. Positive reinforcement, which leads to effective learning without undesirable accompanying results is infrequent and irregular in the classroom. Attempts that are successful in gaining children's attention do not assure that they will continue to pay attention. The idea that the teacher can only draw out what is in the student (by the Socratic method) or allow the student to learn by discovery, is an abdication of teaching, transferring the responsibility for failure in learning to the student.

The technology of teaching has three major applications in education. The first is in classroom management. Positive reinforcement is more effective than aversive controls in developing and maintaining a classroom environment in which learning can take place.

Programmed instruction applies the principles of operant conditioning to the organization and presentation of subject matter for optimum learning. It focuses attention on objectives, in terms of desired terminal behaviors, and on the steps necessary to reach these behaviors. Programming involves small steps in sequence. Each step must be reinforced but, as in the shaping process with animals, then must lead to the next step, and so on. Assistance must be given when necessary but must be decreased (vanished), so that the student is not dependent on the teacher or the material.

The programming of instruction by the teacher is very difficult and requires individual instruction for each student, an unrealistic goal in most classroom situations. Programs can be developed which can apply to most students, or several programs at different levels can be developed, and presented in the form of programmed textbooks or by teaching machines operated by computers. Such programming is based upon the principles of operant conditioning. Programmed instruction by machines requires less time than instruction by the teacher or by means of standard textbooks or films.

Programmed learning is not limited to simple information, facts, and skills. It can be used to teach thinking, problem solving, and creativity. These are complex behaviors which can be analyzed into simple behaviors which can be programmed.

Motivation for learning is not a characteristic or trait possessed or not possessed by the individual. It is a result of schedules of reinforcement. Behavior which is reinforced occurs more frequently, and a high rate of response is called interest, enthusiasm, or high motivation. The ultimate advantages of education are too remote to be effective reinforcers—or motivators. More immediate, or proximate, reinforcers must be provided, which are often contrived reinforcers—prizes, honors, medals, grades, diplomas, degrees. The behaviors of the teacher —attention, approval, friendship, affection—are powerful reinforcers but raise problems. They must be genuine, not simulated, to be effective. It is not always possible to use natural reinforcers in the classroom, and these reinforcers are not always the most effective, especially when they are remote.

Teaching is a matter of using all available reinforcers and arranging effective contingencies of reinforcement. The principle of "stretching the ratio" of reinforcement, that is, moving from the continuous reinforcement which is more efficient in establishing behavior to intermittent reinforcement, which is more efficient in maintaining behavior, is important, though very difficult to put into practice.

Teacher education is ineffective because it does not provide the teacher with the necessary technology of teaching. A technology of teaching does not eliminate the need for teachers or reduce the teacher to a machine. It provides the teacher with time to engage in those activities which only a teacher, and not a machine, can do—exposition, discussion, argumentation, exploration of new areas, concern with values and ethical behavior, and provision of opportunities to enjoy art, literature and music.

The function of education is to transmit the culture and to provide for the changes necessary to assure the survival of the culture. These changes are dependent upon "mutations," the development of novelties and innovations. These can be encouraged by the fostering of diversity. Our present educational system is regimented, leading to conformity. A technology of teaching can enable us to increase diversity. In doing so, it is concerned with the development of individual potential. The extent of human potential is unknown. The scientific analysis of human behavior can contribute to the development of this potential and thus increase the chances of the survival of the culture and of the human race.

EVALUATION

Skinner's position is, as noted earlier, highly persuasive. Its adherents are strongly committed to it and can produce apparently iron-clad arguments for it. It is perhaps because many of its opponents—or doubters and questioners—although convinced that the position is inadequate and has flaws, are unable to make any impression on its adherents or penetrate their arguments (or dogmatism) that they react with frustration and emotion. Behaviorists stimulate negative reactions because of their attitude of having *the* answer; their claim that behaviorism is *the* science of behavior, or even of psychology; their claims of success and effectiveness in prediction and control in all areas of behavior; their brushing aside or rejection of all other theories, methods, or approaches to the study of human behavior; their optimism about the ability of the method of behaviorism to lead to the understanding of all human behavior or experience; and their rejection of the importance of central processes and lack of concern for what many consider the most human aspects of behavior.

Skinner challenges—and rejects—many strongly held beliefs and attitudes about human behavior. This has led many to reject behaviorism out of hand, without adequate examination of its nature. In other cases, criticisms have been based upon inadequate understanding of the approach, or misunderstanding deriving in part no doubt from strong emotional reactions against it.

We shall first consider a number of common criticisms, enumerated by Skinner. Many of these criticisms are based upon inadequate understanding or misunderstanding of Skinner. Skinner responds to these criticisms, adequately in some cases, but (in the writer's opinion at least) inadequately in others. In the discussion of these criticisms we shall comment on Skinner's responses when they are considered to be inadequate. Some of these criticisms involve important questions or issues. The specific criticisms with which Skinner deals will be followed by consideration of some of these basic issues regarding human behavior raised by behaviorism.

Common Criticisms of Behaviorism

1. *It ignores consciousness, feelings, and states of mind.* Skinner admits that this criticism does apply to methodological behaviorism (and it must be pointed out that many behaviorists, particularly applied behaviorists are methodological behaviorists). But Skinner's radical behaviorism, as noted earlier, does not "behead the organism,"

or "sweep the problem of subjectivity under the rug." Internal stimulation affects behavior, and a person can be conscious of this stimulation, while under its control. Introspective knowledge, however, is not accurate, though within limits self-knowledge is useful. But they are useful as indicators or products of environmental causes. Furthermore, consciousness of internal stimuli and self-knowledge do not require a "mind."

Thus, though Skinner acknowledges the existence of consciousness, feelings, and states of mind, they are of little importance and unnecessary for the understanding of behavior, since they have no causal influence on behavior. "A completely independent science of subjective experience would have no more bearing on a science of behavior than a science of what people feel about fire would have on the science of combustion. Nor could experience be divorced from the physical world in the way needed to make such a science possible."[82] Thus, it is not simply that it is difficult to study consciousness, feelings or so-called states of mind; they are irrelevant, and attention to them interferes with the study of more important things.

This view of internal states is a result of the definition of science which Skinner has adopted, a restricted definition which will be considered later in another context. It takes the position that if behavior can be predicted and controlled without the assumption of consciousness or the knowledge of inner states, then these are not important. But there may be other bases for ascribing importance to inner states. Our concern about human beings (and animals as well) goes beyond a concern for their behavior only; feelings, emotions, attitudes, beliefs, and so on are of concern. To be sure, behaviorism insists that since these are the products of environmental conditions or are associated with environmentally determined behavior we are creating "good" inner states when we create good behaviors. But the question can be raised as to whether a person as an identity, or a personal identity, is nothing more than an assortment of behaviors. Why did inner states, and awareness of them, arise in evolution? Have they no purpose, no meaning, no value—even survival value? And beyond this, there is the possibility that certain complex human behaviors may not be predictable and controllable entirely by environmental conditions. This possibility will be returned to later.

2. *It neglects innate endowment and argues that all behavior is acquired during the lifetime of the individual.* While some behaviorists may act as if the individual is almost completely malleable, few would deny the importance of genetic endowment. Behaviorism is a counterbalance to an extreme hereditarian viewpoint. Particularly in education it is important to recognize the importance of environmental influences.

3. *It formulates behavior simply as a set of responses to stimuli,*

thus representing the person as an automaton, robot, puppet, or machine. Operant behaviorism is not stimulus-response psychology. As noted earlier, stimuli do not *elicit* responses; they change the probabilities that repsonses will be emitted. It is the contingencies of reinforcement, notes Skinner, that control behavior.

But there is a dilemma posed by the concept that, on the one hand, emitted behavior is voluntary, or initiated, behavior, operating on the environment, but on the other hand such behavior can be brought under the control of the environment. One who can control the environment of another can, theoretically, make the other a puppet or robot. The problem of control will be considered in more detail later.

4. *It does not attempt to account for cognitive processes.* A behavioral analysis, says Skinner, does not reject "higher mental processes." But such processes (which include searching, generalization, discrimination, problem solving, and so forth) are behaviors, though often covert rather than overt. A behavioral analysis investigates the contingencies under which they occur.

The translation (or, as some would contend, the reduction) of cognitive processes to behaviors does not satisfy many critics, however, who feel that not all mental processes have been, or can be, reduced to behaviors; that in some cases those which are lose something in the process; and that sometimes the results are less than convincing—that the behaviors as explained do not represent or substitute for what is denoted or connoted by the cognitive concept. Skinner admits that human thinking is complex and has not been accounted for or explained even by a behavioral analysis, but he insists that mentalistic explanations explain nothing. Further reference to this will be made later.

5. *It has no place for intention or purpose.* Operant theory treats purpose not as an antecedent intention or plan, but as a result of subsequent selection by contingencies of reinforcement. "A person disposed to act because he has been reinforced for acting may feel the condition of his body at such a time and call it 'felt purpose,' but what behaviorism rejects is the causal efficacy of that feeling."[83]

This treatment of purpose and intention would be considered inadequate by many critics, and we shall return to this problem again.

6. *It cannot explain creative achievements*—in art, for example, or in music, literature, science, or mathematics. Skinner's view on this has already been presented: Special contingencies of reinforcement may explain such achievements without recourse to "creative mind" or a trait of creativity, and such achievements can be increased by discovering appropriate contingencies, as well as by arranging conditions which foster the unexplained "mutations" which are original and sometimes creative. Thus, for Skinner, creativity can be explained.

7. *It assigns no role to a self or sense of self.* According to Skinner,

the self or person develops as a human organism acquires a repertoire of behaviors. More than one self can exist if different and more or less incompatible repertoires of behavior develop. Self-knowledge and self-management are of social origin, products of the contingencies of survival and of reinforcement. Identity consists in the uniqueness of each person. But "there is no place in the scientific position for a self as a true originator or initiator of action."[84]

The question was raised earlier as to whether a repertoire of behaviors constitutes an identity. The paradox of the person engaging in self-management (as well as controlling the environment), yet not originating action, also appears. It is a basic paradox of behaviorism to which we shall return.

8. *It is necessarily superficial and cannot deal with the depths of the mind or personality.* Skinner admits that there is "a grain of truth" to this contention. But behavioristic analysis questions the causal role of what is inside the skin—in the mind or personality. Here again it is apparent that behaviorism gives importance only to cause-effect elements, and rejects or is unconcerned about anything which is not important in this frame of reference.

9. *It limits itself to the prediction and control of behavior and misses the essential nature of human beings.* Behaviorism replies in essence that behavior—action—and its prediction and control, which involve the relation between behavior and its genetic and environmental antecedents, *is* the nature or essence of the species.

10. *It works with animals, particularly white rats, but not with people, and its picture of human behavior is therefore confined to those features which human beings share with animals.* The experimental analysis of behavior has been applied to human beings, however, with the result that the same basic processes occur in both animals and people. Human behavior is of course far more complex, and the long and complex history of human subjects before the experimental studies creates special problems. Skinner, as noted earlier, admits that much of his discussion of human behavior goes beyond the facts, but he is confident that the experimental analysis of behavior will eventually yield all the facts necessary for the understanding of human behavior. This is a faith not shared by his critics, some of whom would argue that behaviorism is limited by its theory and method and can provide only partial understanding of the human being. Further consideration will be given to this later.

11. *Its achievements under laboratory control cannot be duplicated in daily life, and what is said about human behavior in the world at large is therefore unsupported metascience.* It is recognized that extrapolation from the laboratory to everyday behavior involves interpretation. But this is the case in all the natural sciences. Laboratory research makes it possible to identify the relevant variables. The proof

of the usefulness of laboratory investigations is the practical effectiveness of technologies derived from such studies. One would expect that there would be some loss of effectiveness or efficiency between the controlled laboratory and the outside world. In physicis, the law of falling bodies applies in the atmosphere as well as in a vacuum, but the resistance of the air must be taken into consideration. Thus, Skinner, with some basis, rejects this criticism.

12. *It is oversimplified and naive, and its facts are either trivial or already well known.* To this Skinner replies that it is the critics who are naive about their knowledge of the scientific analysis of behavior. It is rather the mentalistic explanations that are oversimplified. Nevertheless, simple principles are characteristic of all the sciences, though the data from which they are derived are complex. And though it is true that many before the behaviorists recognized the existence of reinforcement, it was the behaviorists who demonstrated its universality and importance. The development of a behavioristic technology is new. And the violence of the attack on behaviorism belies its triviality.

13. *It is scientistic rather than scientific. It merely emulates the sciences.* This criticism has been directed at many of the behavioral and social sciences; it is not applicable, says Skinner, to the experimental analysis of behavior, whose assumptions, methods, procedures, and data are straightforward and simple.

14. *Its technological achievements could have come about through the use of common sense.* While in retrospect this may appear to be so, it should be asked why the practices were not used before the advent of an experimental analysis of behavior. Moreover, "the disastrous results of common sense in the management of human behavior are evident in every walk of life, from international affairs to the care of a baby,"[85] in contrast to the results of the application of a technology of behavior. This criticism, therefore, is unwarranted.

15. *If its contentions are valid, they must apply to behavioral scientists also, and what they say is therefore only what they have been conditioned to say and cannot be true.* Skinner recognizes that the behaviorist is in the causal stream and cannot observe behavior from a special vantage point. The behavior of the logician, mathematician, and the scientist, is very complex, but it is not necessarily different in kind from other behavior, nor does it require a different kind of analysis. Scientific *knowledge* consists of verbal rules, and they are "true" in the sense that they result in effective action. Skinner acknowledges that there may be limits to the behavior of the scientist and the nature of scientific knowledge, and beyond such limits indeterminacy may exist, but we have not reached these limits if they do exist.

It may be objected that rule-governed behavior, which Skinner agrees comes under different operants than contingency-shaped behavior, is enough different from contingency-shaped behavior to be a different kind of behavior, beyond the complete control of the environment and involving internal determinants. Skinner does, as noted above, admit the possibility of indeterminacy in human behavior; but there is not only the question of possible indeterminacy, but, within the context of determinism, the possibility of the existence of other determiners besides genetic endowment and environmental stimuli and consequences.

16. *It dehumanizes people; it is reductionistic and destroys the human being* qua *human being.* This criticism usually implies that the picture of the human being provided by behavior analysis is incomplete, that it omits consideration of certain complex human qualities. Skinner replies that this criticism does not specify what has been left out. While behaviorism claims that human behavior is lawful, it does not deny its complexity. If what is meant by this criticism is that behaviorism has no place for choice, purpose, intentions, and creativity, then the answer is that the behavior from which these are inferred can be subjected to behavioral analysis. "I know of no essentially human feature that has been shown to be beyound the reach of scientific analysis. . . . The point [that behavioral analysis dehumanizes man] is often made by arguing that a scientific analysis changes man from victor to victim. But man remains what he always has been, and his most conspicuous achievement has been the design and construction of a world which has freed him from constraints and vastly extended his range."[86]

Behaviorism, says Skinner, is not reductionistic. "It simply provides an alternative account of the same facts. It does not *reduce* feelings to bodily states; it simply argues that bodily states are and always have been what is felt. It does not *reduce* thought processes to behavior, it simply analyzes the behavior previously explained by the invention of thought processes. It does not *reduce* morality to certain features of the social environment; it simply insists that those features have always been responsible for moral behavior."[87]

Here again critics would argue that something is lost in translation and that actually behaviorism *is* reductionistic. The translation is simply a verbal restatement into behaviorist language, which may be less meaningful than natural language, and thus less useful. The behaviorist language does not necessarily result in greater understanding, or a solution to the complex problem of mental processes or feelings. A behaviorist explanation is not really an explanation. It may be no less a metaphor than the natural language. If not reductionistic, it is simplistic. It is a forcing of all experience into the procrustean bed of behavior, a refusal to recognize that man is anything but behavior. Rather than encouraging, or engaging in, the attempt to analyze and understand internal events, which Skinner admits exist, it avoids their study unless they can be converted to behaviors, because that is the only thing which behaviorism can study or is interested in studying. What has been left out is suggested later in this evaluation.

17. *It is concerned only with general principles and therefore neglects the uniqueness of the individual.* Skinner emphasizes that individuals are unique, since they have different genetic endowments and different reinforcement histories. But he admits that science cannot provide the whole story about an individual case, if only because of the cost and the fact that greater benefits will result from the development of general principles. It is possible to develop an understanding of another person through intensive psychotherapy, but this is beyond the reach of science, with its emphasis upon generalities.

18. *It is necessarily antidemocratic, because the relation between experimenter and subject is manipulative, and its results can therefore be used by dictators but not by people of good will.* Skinner admits that operant conditioning *can* be used to control others. But those who use aversive methods or methods which are exploitative (with deferred aversive consequences) are subject to countercontrol. "Democracy is a version of countercontrol designed to solve the problem of manipulation."[88] Control is not always manipulative or bad—it exists in education, psychotherapy, and government in nonexploitative form. It is unreasonable to end behavioral research because the results can be used by despots and tyrants; these results can also be used in countercontrol.

The power of behavioral control in everyday situations has perhaps been overrated. However, some critics who minimize and reject behaviorism's claims, at the same time raise the specter of tyrannical control. Skinner notes that you can't have it both ways.

The methods *are* potentially powerful, particularly in situations where total environmental control is possible, as in institutions such as prisons, mental hospitals, schools for the retarded, and even the ordinary classroom. MacMillan writes enthusiastically of the "endless possibilities of shaping school behaviors."[89] And there is evidence that it has been misused in institutions of the kind listed, and considerable public and legal reaction has occurred. Its misuse in the school classroom has as yet created little negative public reaction, perhaps because the public, as well as teachers and educational administrators, approve of the results. In a review of studies of behavior modification in the classroom, Winett and Winkler[90] found that it has been used in maintaining order and control in the classroom. Their survey of studies found that behavior considered to be inappropriate, and thus to be controlled (eliminated), included being out of one's seat, talking, singing, whistling, standing up, running, hopping, skipping, jumping, crying, tapping feet, rattling papers—that is, any behavior which interferes with order, quiet, and stillness. Desirable behaviors were those indicated in the title of their paper: stillness, quietness, and docility.

Skinner has recognized the dangers of the misuse of methods of con-

trol, and has been concerned that the methods be used for the benefit of humanity. Neither he nor the methods can be criticized because
of the misuse of behavior modification. Unfortunately, a great many
of those who are now using these methods appear to have little concern about the nature of their goals or objectives. The ethics of behavior modification are receiving increasing attention.[91]

The problem of means-ends relates to this issue. While Skinner
appears to be ready to dispense with democracy, most people would
not agree with him on this. Thus, even if one were to accept the goals
of Skinner for humanity—happiness, productivity, the feeling of freedom—one could question the undemocratic methods of control by
which Skinner would achieve them, including the deception that would
be involved in creating a sense of freedom where it in fact did not exist.

19. *It regards abstract ideas such as morality and justice as fic-
tions.* According to Skinner, "the behavior we call moral or just is a
product of special kinds of social contingencies arranged by govern-
ments, religions, economic systems, and ethical groups. We need to
analyze those contingencies if we are to build a world in which people
behave morally and justly, and a first step in that direction is to dismiss morality and justice as personal possessions."[92]

The denial of morality and justice, as well as compassion and responsibility, as personal possessions or attributes would seem to
pose problems. If persons are moral, just, compassionate, or responsible only because of the consequences, that is, because that is the way
they have been shaped by their environments, then there is, as Skinner
notes, no virtue in such behaviors. If as Skinner agrees, benevolent,
devoted, compassionate, or public-spirited behavior are lacking when
countercontrol is lacking, that is, if they are ways of avoiding aversive
consequences of aversive control, then they are self-serving and not altruistic behaviors. But this is not an undesirable situation, according to
Skinner, since the consequences, for others upon whom these behaviors
fall, are the same as if the behaviors were altruistic; that is, the consequences are good. Similarly, if responsible behavior is the result of
contingencies of reinforcement, individuals can take no credit for
being responsible. But neither can they be blamed for being irrespon-
sible—in fact, the concept of responsibility is inappropriate, and Skinner suggests that the term *controllability* should be substituted. Nothing would be lost or changed, since the behaviors we now designate
as responsible would continue. And presumably, if a person were
uncontrollable, he would be imprisoned. But Skinner's analysis would
appear to leave many social problems unresolved.

20. *It is indifferent to the warmth and richness of human life, and
it is incompatible with the creation and enjoyment of art, music, and
literature and with love for one's fellow human beings.* But, says
Skinner, "there is nothing in a science of behavior or its philosophy

which need alter feelings or introspective observations. The bodily states which are felt or observed are acknowledged, but there is an emphasis on the environmental conditions with which they are associated and on insistence that it is the conditions rather than the feelings which enable us to explain behavior."[93] Knowing the conditions or causes need not affect the enjoyment experienced in art, music, and literature. Nor should love and affection be endangered by understanding their nature and origin in terms of reinforcement. They are effects, not causes, of behavior and thus not of concern in behavioral analysis.

Skinner has identified most of the common criticisms of behaviorism. A number of them, as we have just seen, are based on misunderstanding of the nature of behaviorism, and Skinner's answers are adequate. Some of them, however, represent basic issues and problems, and Skinner's responses are less than adequate. We shall consider these criticisms in more detail.

Freedom and Choice Versus
Determinism and Control

The problem of freedom versus determinism is one which scientists and philosophers have never resolved; it is perhaps not possible of resolution. The principle of indeterminacy in physics (Heisenberg's principle) is accepted by some as evidence against complete determinism; others see it only as representing a present inability to verify determinism. In any event, it is not possible either to accept or reject determinism. It is an assumption.

It is likely that the problem is not an either/or problem. That the terms *freedom* and *determinism* both exist, and have continued to exist, indicates that they both refer to something important. Neither would be a meaningful concept with the other. If there were no idea of determinism, freedom would be incomprehensible. Both freedom and determinism may operate in human behavior. Determinism is necessary for freedom to be possible as an alternative, and vice versa. Complete freedom, with no cause-effect relationships, would mean chaos; complete determinism would leave no room for innovation nor even the mutation Skinner accepts. It does not seem to be possible to demonstrate or prove determinism in creative thinking or problem solving. Thus it may be maintained that both freedom and determinism exist, and neither is absolute.

Skinner recognizes that determinism is an assumption, not a demonstrated or verified fact: "We cannot prove, of course, that human behavior is fully determined, but the proposition becomes more plausible as facts accumulate, and I believe a point has been reached at which its implications must be seriously considered."[94] Skinner appears to believe that if everything were known, the causes of behavior could be identified. But the problem is that Skinner not only considers this belief as a hypothesis; it is a basic assumption of behaviorism. Its consequences are incorporated in his system; thus his entire system rests upon it. If it is false, then his entire system collapses. But even if it is in fact false, accepting it as an assumption does make an undesirable difference in one's behavior, in the way one treats other people.

A problem of definition appears to be involved in Skinner's rejection of freedom as choice and autonomy in decision making. For Skinner, freedom is manifested in the avoidance of and escape from aversive conditions. The behaviors which lead to this kind of freedom are based on the biological tendency to avoid noxious conditions, and are learned through the contingencies of reinforcement. Thus, they are determined, and are not free. Clearly, this definition is a peculiar use of the term *freedom*.

Freedom is also used by the behaviorists in another way, to mean the accumulation of knowledge and skills which widen or increase alternatives. The limits are still determined. Personal autonomy is also still ruled out; there is really no freedom of choice among the alternatives, since the alternative "chosen" must be chosen given the conditions and circumstances of the individual's history and the situation. Again, this is not what is usually meant by freedom.

Skinner rejects the usual definitions of freedom. Freedom as the possibility of doing what one wants to do is rejected, because wants are not expressions of free will but of environmental determinism—what one wants is actually determined. The idea that freedom is good because all control is bad, is rejected since all control is not exploitation. Controls are inevitable, as part of the natural environment, and are necessary and beneficial for individual development. Planned control reduces control by chance and caprice. It protects the individual from aversive control. Control through positive reinforcement benefits the individual who is reinforced. There is general agreement, Skinner says, on what is good and desirable for human beings and what is bad and wrong. Those who cry for freedom often themselves use aversive (punishing) control. Finally freedom as a feeling is not freedom—it is simply the result of absence of aversive control or coercion. Freedom cannot be something one possesses, then, since it is simply the feeling resulting from an environment in which restraint and coercion are absent.

For Skinner, the environment does the selecting. Yet the environment can be ambiguous—more than one kind of behavior may be reinforced, and what the individual will do may not be clear from his or her past history. And it can also be contended that the organism does the selecting, from among a number of possible actions or responses, either randomly emitted or consciously produced, of that response which results in or produces the reinforcement. Emitted, or operant, behavior is admittedly not clearly caused or determined—it is not clearly related to a stimulus or previous consequences, and it changes the environment. It thus would appear to allow for self-initiated behavior. It is puzzling that Skinner appears unconcerned about bringing such behavior within the realm of determined behavior. It is also puzzling that he accepts mutations as accidents, without concern for their causation.

Skinner's concept of freedom is thus limited and is not what the ordinary person means by the term. Skinner (1) denies the existence of a will to be free, and (2) declares that what appears to be a person's struggle for freedom is due to certain behavioral processes, characteristic of the human organism, which avoid or lead to escape from aversive aspects of the environment. Skinner's effort to make a will to be free and avoidance of aversive consequences appear to be incompatible is, according to Scriven, "simply a con job. There is absolutely no good reason to take the first alternative to be incompatible with the second; Skinner is simply wrong to think that there is. Certainly he gives no plausible reason to suppose it incompatible."[95] The second alternative could well be a [partial] definition of what is meant by the will to be free. This, like many other of Skinner's translations, is simply an awkward way of saying what is better said in the more traditional way. "In fact," says Chomsky, "Skinnerian translation, which is easily employed by anyone, leads to a significant loss in precision, for the simple reason that the full range of terms for the description and evaluation of behavior, attitude, opinion, and so on must be 'translated' into the impoverished system of terminology borrowed from the laboratory (and deprived of its meaning in transition). It is hardly surprising then, that Skinner's translations generally miss the point, even with the metaphorical use of such terms as 'reinforce'."[96]

Skinner acknowledges that there are no exact behavioral equivalents for some of the traditional terms, since there is no popular vocabulary for expressing the role of the environment in the control of behavior. Thus, the technical word or phrase will often seem forced or roundabout. Mentalistic terms have become embedded in our language and will thus seem more natural and meaningful.

A form of freedom (in addition to emitted operant behavior) which goes beyond freedom from aversive control is the cognitive activity of thinking, involving analysis, evaluation, hypothesis making, and invention. None of these is adequately or convincingly explained by Skinner. Such activities make it possible to, or free one to, engage in many new behaviors. These behaviors are not defensive behaviors—against aversive stimuli—nor simply reactive behaviors. They involve initiating activities, not avoidance or escape behaviors. Skinner's analysis of creative thinking in behavioristic terms is not adequate to account for its nature—its innovative, inventive results. Such results, in turn, make possibile new freedoms of a positive nature.

Skinner on the one hand makes translations of mentalistic concepts and statements in behaviorist terms, yet on the other hand continually makes statements which involve these terms in their ordinary meanings. These statements cannot be taken simply (as he claims) as the use of traditional terms in casual discourse. Skinner presents humans as decision-making beings—yet humans do not and cannot make choices, according to him. The individual affects, influences, or controls the environment, yet is completely controlled by the environment. ("A person does not act upon the world, the world acts upon him."[97])

To further illustrate inconsistencies in Skinner, operant behavior is said to operate on the environment—in human interaction the controller is controlled by those he or she controls. That is, the behavior of those controlled influences the controller. Aversive control breeds countercontrol; positive reinforcement supposedly avoids this and produces satisfied subjects. A cartoon reproduced in one of Skinner's papers presents the paradox of who controls whom. A rat in a Skinner box, in the act of pressing a lever, remarks to another rat: "Boy, have I got this guy conditioned. Every time I press the bar down he drops in a piece of food."[98] Yet Skinner clearly states that the rat is controlled by the schedule of reinforcement.

Skinner writes: "Once we have arranged the particular type of consequence called a reinforcer, our techniques permit us to shape the behavior of an organism almost at will."[99] But will, says Skinner, does not exist. How does it happen that Skinner or anyone else can, by choice and with intent, control the behavior of others?

If we are completely controlled by our environments, how can we control the environment? If the environment controls us, how can we engage in self-management? Skinner says we do so by arranging our environment. But if we cannot initiate behavior, how can we do this? There is no will to control ourselves in our minds, says Skinner. Self-control is thus not a case of freedom, but simply a function of environmental consequences of behavior—the avoidance of aversive consequences. This argument is hardly convincing.

Skinner argues for control on the basis that control exists anyway, and it is desirable that we plan and use it consistently for good rather than evil, and that we use positive reinforcement rather than aversive controls. Control is necessary if we are to assure the survival of the culture. Survival takes precedence over freedom and dignity. Control which has no aversive consequences is not bad, even though it restricts, or eliminates, freedom. But in his curious way, Skinner argues that freedom exists when control is not by aversive means, since the individual is not aware that he is being controlled; the means of control are invisible. Chomsky, one of the strongest critics of Skinner, in his critique of Skinner's book *Beyond Freedom and Dignity*, points out that there is nothing in Skinner's approach that is incompatible with a police state, in which the threat of dire punishment pervades the system. In such a system behavior which would be punished might never occur. Skinner would of course argue that this would not be his idea of a desirable culture. But one could question why it is not. It would not be legitimate to argue that it is because people would be living in fear, because fear is an inner state which does not influence behavior. The behavior is "good"; fear is simply an accompaniment of the desirable behavior.

It could also be argued that such control is aversive, and would breed countercontrol. But note that if no one is ever punished, there are no aversive consequences. Skinner could perhaps argue that a *threat* of dire punishment could not continue to be effective if dire consequences never occurred.

One can object that this is not control by positive reinforcement. Consider, then, the situation in which people are controlled by positive reinforcement. Skinner describes such a society in *Walden Two*. Skinner writes: "We can achieve a sort of control under which the controlled, though they are following a code much more scrupulously than was ever the case under the old system, nevertheless *feel free*. They are doing what they want to do. . . . There's no restraint and no revolt. By a careful design, we control not the final behavior, but the *inclination* to behave—the motives, the desires, the wishes."[100] (This is an example of his use of terms referring to mental states, which are not supposed to exist.)

Is this a better society? Everyone is well behaved, happy, productive, and feels free. (Parenthetically, it can be questioned whether the feeling of freedom could exist without any awareness of control, or in the absence of any idea of the lack of freedom.) Are the results of positive reinforcement always desirable and good for the person being controlled? Skinner uses the cartoon of the rat referred to earlier to suggest that the only successful means of control is unselfish; that is, positive reinforcement benefits the controlled. Skinner suggests that the organism responds to reinforcing consequences because of a built-in tendency to respond to what is good for it, in terms of survival. It is questionable that this is always the case. It is not necessarily the case that positive reinforcement is always and necessarily for the basic and ultimate good of the individual. One can be exploited through positive reinforcement, with no aversive consequences to lead to revolt or countercontrol. Skinner seems to believe that the exploited person will become aware of the fact and act to protect himself. This is questionable, however; and in any event, awareness of exploitation might not occur before a long period of continuous exploitation had taken place.

It does not seem to be true that we can always depend on the controlled to govern the behavior of controllers by their reactions to control, any more than it is true that the experimenter is actually controlled by the reactions of the rat to his or her behavior. In addition to the fact that aversive reactions to control—rebellion, revolution, and so on—may be eliminated because of overwhelming power in the hands of tyrants and fear of the consequences of an abortive revolt, and in addition to the danger that exploitation will be implemented through positive reinforcement, there is the possibility that control will involve deception, so that the controlled are prevented from attributing aversive consequences of control to the controller.

That contrived positive reinforcement is not always good for the individual is indicated by at least two kinds of possible undesirable effects. In schools and other institutions or situations, candy or cigarettes are often used as reinforcers. Clearly, there are negative consequences of such reinforcers—"spoiling" of appetite for regular meals, with resultant poor nutrition; and possible lung cancer. In addition, a second undesirable effect is dependence on a contrived reinforcer for the continuance of the desired behavior. Skinner emphasizes the desirability of moving from contrived reinforcers to natural or intrinsic reinforcers. He admits, however, that "natural reinforcers may not automatically replace the contrived positive reinforcers of the classroom."[101] But he neglects to tell just how one can move from contrived to natural reinforcers. The maintenance of behavior without contrived reinforcers has not been a concern in behavior modification. Researchers and demonstrators have entered the classroom to show that control of behavior can be achieved by behaviorist methods, using contrived reinforcers. They compare the results with a base period, showing the change in behavior. They withdraw the reinforcers, showing the reversion of behavior to the base rate again, and then resume dispensing reinforcers to show their effect. Then, having achieved their demonstration or collected their data for a publication, they withdraw, leaving the teacher with a dilemma: If she or he ceases to administer the reinforcers, the class will be back where it started. But how is the teacher to maintain the behaviors without continuing the reinforcers?

The harmful effects, as well as the lack of long-term effects, of extrinsic positive reinforcers are pointed out by Levine and Fasnacht. They refer to studies which show that an intrinsically interesting or rewarding activity was worked at for less time when an extrinsic reward was given than when none was given; that an extrinisic reward for an intrinsically interesting activity led to a decrease of the response when the reward was withdrawn; and that external rewards led to less reported interest in game activities than when no reward was given. Tokens given for interesting classroom activities thus will lead to a decrease of interest. "Reinforcement may shift attention from the activity to the reinforcer." Tokens do not seem to lead to long-term learning, or to generalization. The children have learned how to obtain tokens, not to value the activities involved. When tokens cease, extinction occurs. The authors write: "Therefore, once token-type programs are instituted, it may never be possible to fully withdraw tokens without behavior going at least back to baseline. Furthermore, since tokens tend to decrease the intrinsic value of an activity, they may actually do more harm than good."[102]

In a school situation, behavior control may be achieved by one teacher, but the results do not transfer or generalize to other teachers and other classrooms. The failure of behaviorists to be concerned about this problem, say Scriven, is due to rejection of the concept of autonomy, a characteristic of the inner man. "If one is mostly interested in behavior and its external conditions, one runs the risk of not focusing on the inner man. But only the inner man goes up to the next grade, the reinforcers do not. . . . [Skinner] cannot quite bring himself to the task of modifying the *interior* of the organism in such a way that it will continue to follow a certain behavior pattern in the *absence* of the contingencies that are presently reinforcing for it. To do so is to recognize a further dimension of autonomy in man—his capacity to develop new valences, new sets, new values."[103]

It is true, as Skinner notes, that there is a strong antipathy to the idea of control, whether it is by aversive means or not. This is simply behavioristic terminology for what is called a "will to freedom." Control exists, to be sure, as Skinner emphasizes. But to say that control exists does not justify extending control until it is complete. There are degrees of control and of freedom, and people appear to desire to retain a certain amount of, if not to maximize, personal freedom. In setting up a utopia or designing a culture, it may be necessary to recognize this desire and to include in the goals, possibly at the expense of order and efficiency, the preservation of an acceptable degree of freedom.

It is, of course, possible that human behavior is not completely determined and that therefore human behavior *cannot* be completely controlled. The acceptance of the assumption of determinism in human behavior is an extrapolation from relatively simple and highly controlled experiments with animals, whose histories have been controlled and whose behavior has been limited or restricted. The extrapolation of determinism into all of human behavior is based on belief, faith, and expectation, not upon fact or experiment. Those experiments which have found people to respond in the same ways as do rats and pigeons have been concerned with limited behaviors. Human beings have been subjected to the restrictions of a controlled environment in these experiments—they have been treated as animals. It is possible that human behavior is subject to control only when the individual is placed in a completely controlled situation and treated as an animal. Freedom or choice will not be exhibited where the situation prevents it.

The rejection of absolute determinism does not require the acceptance of nondeterminism. As Scriven notes, it simply raises the question of whether all the complex actions of human beings "are wholly determined by external factors which *override* any variation in mental state—in which case we are not free—or whether one of the intervening determiners is a mental state or event such as preferring or choosing."[104]

There is no satisfying answer to the problem of freedom versus determinism. But Skinner's treatment of the problem is inadequate. It involves the assumption of determinism, and it avoids the basic issues in behavior control by a questionable translation—or reduction—of the concepts representing those issues into a behaviorist terminology.

Intention and Purpose

Skinner's treatment of purpose and intention in human behavior is as unsatisfying as his treatment of freedom and control. Again, it consists essentially of a translation (or reduction) of these concepts into behaviorist terminology. As inadequate as this translation is, there is the added ambiguity of the behaviorist terminology. In operant behavior, a person acts *in order that something will occur,* or in order to receive reinforcement. That is, behavior is instrumental; it tries to achieve something, a reinforcement. It is said to operate upon the environment. Yet behavior engaged in to produce a reinforcement is not, Skinner says, intentional. It does not involve any expectation of the consequences. Though the behavior (cause) leads to the reinforcement (effect), there is no intention involved. Doing something to achieve certain consequences is not intentional. Purpose, says Skinner, is simply a fanciful inner process: "A person disposed to act because he has been reinforced for acting may feel the condition of his body at such a time and call it 'felt purpose,' but what behaviorism rejects is the causal efficacy of that feeling."[105] Motives and purposes are the effects of past reinforcements. Awareness of the feeling of purpose or intention is not necessary for behavior to occur; the awareness is simply observing a condition produced by reinforcing.

Skinner recognizes that operant behavior is directed (by outside forces) toward the future. Yet the future can have no effect on the behavior itself; it is not the future reinforcement that controls the behavior, but the effects of past experiences. What are called expectancy and anticipation are the results of past reinforcement schedules. These effects, however, are not stored in the mind where they can operate as determiners of behavior, directing the person to act in order to achieve future reinforcement. Skinner is thus unclear about how past experience affects behavior. Behavior is influenced by, but not caused by, earlier reinforcement. It requires something else, at least a cue, to trigger it off, as Skinner recognizes. The effects of previous reinforcement change the organism in some way not clearly explained by Skinner. He simply says that the organism is different as a result of experience, and the different organism responds differently than it did before the experience. If there is to be any explanation of the difference, he says, it will be given by neurology and physiology.

Behavior, according to Skinner, can be explained without recourse to purpose, intention, or expectation. Yet he himself is unable to avoid the use of these concepts. His entire proposal for designing cultures would seem to depend on people planning and designing, as well as initiating, a course of action intended to achieve certain expected future consequences. It is difficult to reconcile such a proposal with the behaviorist definitions of the terms involved in it. If the behaviorist definitions are accepted, it is difficult to see how people can create the kind of future environment envisioned by Skinner. If the changes in the environment resulting from operant behavior are not planned, with foresight and purpose, how can people design a culture? It may well be that the history of the human race to date has not involved any design, plan, or purpose, but to achieve the culture proposed by Skinner would appear to require planning and purpose.

Again we have a paradox: A person who is shaped and controlled by the environment engaging in planning and intelligently choosing future goals and designing a culture to achieve them. No one intervenes, no one can initiate behavior, no one can choose, will, or intend an effect, no one can have a purpose. Nor does evolution, biological or social, have a purpose. Species and cultures *evolve* under the contingencies of environmental reinforcements. Yet people can manage themselves, change and create environments, plan and design cultures. But how can they, if the former statements are true? Is not the concept of planning, like the feelings of freedom, choice, intention, and purpose, nothing but an illusion, a figure of speech? Yet, according to Skinner, people can control their environment or let it control them. If this is so, then they have a choice, they are free.

Although Skinner states that operant conditioning is future-oriented, he does not recognize the importance of the future for the individual. He notes that no one responds to remote consequences; yet people are or can be influenced by such consequences. Skinner himself recognizes that people must be influenced by such consequences if they are to survive. But how? It is not clear how this is possible in the behaviorist system.

It is perhaps here that the most significant difference between animals and the human race exists—a difference greater than, though possibly related to, speech. The human being is the only creature who has an awareness of a past and a future as well as a present. We exist in a dimension of time, with a memory of the past and an awareness of the future. Doob maintains that the point at which an organism becomes human is when it becomes aware of existence in a temporal medium.[106] This is a difference not recognized by Skinner. It must make a difference in the behavior of people and of animals.

An awareness of a future involves—indeed, requires—the existence of intention, purpose, expectation, anticipation, and hope, as well as anxiety or fear. These are characteristics of Skinner's own behavior, even though he denies them. The awareness of time makes the field of human behavior different from that of animal behavior. It is true that some, even much, of human behavior is similar to that of animals, in that awareness of future consequences of behavior may not always be present. But when this awareness does exist, human behavior differs radically from that of animals. It may not be justified to say that a pigeon pecks a disk in expectation of reinforcement, but it is justifiable, and important, to say that a human being does something *because* of the expectation of certain results or consequences. Certainly such behavior is influenced by past experiences, but the awareness of the past makes possible a conscious prediction for the future, resulting in an expectation.

Behavior can be radically changed, however, if the expectation is changed by verbal means or instruction. A man may have been led to expect certain consequences on the basis of past experiences, so that he should (be expected to) respond in a certain way on the basis of this experience; but if he then is told (or is informed in some way) that the consequences experienced in the past will no longer be forthcoming, he will not respond on the basis of his past experience. Behavior which would have a high probability of occurring because of its previous reinforcement will have little or no probability of occurring. In other words, unlike the gradual curve of extinction found when reinforcement is discontinued with the pigeon, behavior will extinguish immediately. Thus it is not adequate to say, for human beings, that the probability of response or of a particular behavior, is a result (or function) of the frequency or schedule of reinforcement. It is more adequate to say that the reinforcement schedule creates a state in the organism designated by the term *expectancy,* of a certain degree of strength, which leads to behavior with a certain degree of probability. But there are other methods of creating, and changing, expectancies of varying degrees of strength in human beings.

A human characteristic related to time and expectation is belief. Scriven notes that although thinking that something is true cannot make it true in the natural sciences, in psychology this is not the case. People can be led to believe that they can do something, and then can succeed in doing it, when otherwise they could not have done so. Thus they demonstrate a new capability, not dependent on previous reinforcement, as well as demonstrating the possession of autonomy and freedom. People achieve many things on the basis of faith in their ability to do so. This is in contradiction to Skinner's statement that such claims regarding the power of belief are philosophically unsound. As Scriven points out, "Skinner himself is an excellent example of someone who got things done by transcending the apparently reasonable. (And what drove him was a vision of how things should be, an inner state if there ever was one.) . . . Some of man's internal states which are involved in his information-processing and information-acquiring activities and of which he is aware by his own perceptions of his own brain states (i.e., introspection) often dominate his overt behavior, explain it, and even control the truth of predictions about his later behavior."[107] The best prediction about what a person will do is often that person's statement of intention.

Skinner's claim that no theory changes what it is a theory about—or that no beliefs about people change human nature—is, says Scriven, false and unscientific, and incompatible with the evidence about the effects of self-fulfilling beliefs, as well as with Skinner's own discussion about self-management and the control of cultural evolution. In this respect, it makes no difference whether a doctrine or belief is true or false; it is the consequences of belief which are important. The implications for belief in determinism or in freedom should be clear.

Attitudes and opinions are related to beliefs and expectations. Skinner rejects these as influences on behavior. They are reduced in behaviorist terminology to verbal behavior. It is then verbal behavior, not attitudes or opinions, which is changed or influenced through contingencies or reinforcement (or to some extent through persuasion, which Skinner accepts as a weak behaviorist method of control). But Chomsky notes the inadequacy of this translation: "Taken literally, this means that if, under a credible threat of torture, I force someone to say, repeatedly, that the earth stands still, then I have changed his opinion."[108]

In this connection, also, Skinner is not consistent with his rejection of inner states as influencing behavior. He attributes resistance to the acceptance of scientific control to an *attitude* toward control, an attitude that must be changed so that we can proceed to design a controlled culture. "The productivity of any set of conditions can be evaluated only when we have freed ourselves of the attitudes which have been generated in us as members of ethical groups."[109] And in speaking of the need to change our educational system from one in which learning is not hard work done under compulsion but engaged in because learning is pleasant, he notes: "But an adjustment in attitudes is needed."[110] Presumably, changes in attitudes are causative of changes in behavior.

Skinner cannot avoid recognizing, inadvertently, the influence of inner states on behavior, hard as he may try to do so. He recognizes persuasion as a weak form of control, yet it is his major method, in his own writing, for attempting to change behavior. He attempts to reduce persuasion to the manipulation of environmental contingencies. Chomsky analyses this reduction, pointing out that to use the concept of reinforcement to account for any behaviors favorable to behaviorism resulting from reading Skinner goes beyond any technical meaning of reinforcement. The mere verbal attachment of a favorable (or unfavorable) consequence to a description of desired (or undesired) behavior is not sufficient for persuasion. Persuasion is effective or not depending on the nature and content of the argument, not upon verbal reinforcements. Persuasion, then, is not a behaviorist method, yet it can lead to changes in behavior. Therefore, all behavior change is not the result of behaviorist methods or of environmental consequences. "Since persuasion cannot be coherently described as a result of the arrangement of reinforcers, it follows that behavior is not entirely determined by the specific contingencies to which Skinner arbitrarily restricts his attention."[111]

The rejection of intention and purpose in human behavior appears to be the result of an unwarranted extrapolation from animal behavior which fails to recognize a fundamental difference between animals and human beings. This difference involves the dimension of time, or the awareness of time in human beings. This awareness of a future involves, or at least makes possible, the existence of expectations, purpose, and intention in human behavior. Awareness of the consequences of behavior allows for behavior to be influenced not only by the past but by the future. It is people's present awareness of a future that leads them to be concerned about the future, and to plan and design a culture for purposes which they can choose.

The Limits of Behaviorism

Behaviorism began with Watson as the study of overt, observable muscular and glandular behavior. Skinner has extended behaviorism to the study of verbal behavior. Its method of measurement, essentially frequency of response, is appropriate for the study of such behavior. Behaviorism has always proclaimed itself as the science of behavior. As such it has been limited to only a part of what has been considered to be the field of psychology. However, it has become extended, and, particularly with Skinner's acceptance of mental states as existing and worthy of at least some interest and study, it appears to want to be considered as constituting all of psychology. Skinner's approach is to attempt to reduce mental states to behaviors, or failing that, to treat them as unimportant variables to be studied in a limited and restricted way through introspection. It can be maintained that this is an unwarranted extension of the term *behaviorism;* by calling everything that psychology is interested in *behavior,* then behaviorism becomes all of psychology. But behaviorism has simply described mental events in behavioral terms—so far it is nothing more than a translation, to use Skinner's term—or even a reduction. The method of behaviorism cannot study mental events, as Skinner appears to be aware. The reason that it can't is that they are not behaviors in the behaviorist (objective) sense of the term. They are experiences and are not subject to study by counting frequencies of responding.

The Skinnerian experimental paradigm or model, in which behavior is controlled and shaped by its consequences, clearly is effective in modifying simple operant motor behaviors in rats, pigeons, and people. That it operates in or accounts for all learning or behavior change, even of motor events, is questionable. All of us acquire and retain many ideas, items of information, and facts of varying degrees of importance, on the basis of single, isolated, unimportant, nonreinforced happenings, or through casual reading.

If covert behavior, such as trains of thought, is beyond the realm of observation by others and thus not subject to environmental consequences, it is difficult to see how it can be included in the operant model. Skinner's discussion of complex human behaviors and experiences goes beyond the facts, as he admits, and is simply speculative. While *he* is confident (on the basis of experience or belief?) that the method of behaviorism will eventually explain these experiences, it is difficult to see how it can do so.

Here again we see the inadequacy of translation of concepts into behaviorist terminology. While Skinner disclaims that his translations and interpretations are reductionist, it would appear that in many cases they are. In fact, Skinner himself has spoken of reduction: "Statements which use such words as 'incentive' or 'purpose' are usually reducible to statements about operant conditioning."[112] Behaviorism's reductionist statements are no more (or are even less) helpful than the terms which they purport to explain. The behaviorist explanations are long, awkward, contrived, and not particularly convincing. The so-called mentalistic statements are not necessarily misleading and confusing, as Skinner suggests. They are useful at least as generalizations of experience, and further as representations of the effects of experience, referring to the changes made in a person by experiences, or the person who is changed. As noted above, Skinner does not provide any satisfactory explanation as to how the organism is changed by experience—he simply says that since the organism behaves differently, it is a different organism than it was prior to the experience. There is no doubt a neurological or physiological difference. But there is also the difference that the individual has different beliefs, attitudes, concepts, expectancies, and so forth about him- or herself and the world which cannot be reduced to or equated with physiological or neurological changes.

Chomsky, from the field of psycholinguistics, has made some

telling criticisms of the behaviorist treatment of verbal behavior and language analysis, stating that it is a surface analysis and fails to recognize or handle the "deep structure" which may give the same word different—even opposite—meanings when used in different syntactical structures.[113] Psycholinguistics, Chomsky notes, has not moved in the direction of behavioral analysis, which is considered to be limiting, but toward a cognitive psychology.

To a great extent, the extension of behaviorism to concern with inner experience, and Skinner's treatment of this area with his translations of ordinary language into behaviorist terms, appears to be a play upon words. That Skinner is not really concerned about inner experience seems evident; he recognizes that there is a gap between the terminal events in behavioral analysis (environmental conditions at one end and behavior at the other), which he says may be filled by mentalistic events, conceptual inner events, or physiological events as explanations, but he clearly prefers to believe that the explanation will be in terms of biological or physiological events. He does not seem to be concerned or embarrassed about this gap, as he was in his consideration of covert verbal behavior, where he wrote: "In a sense verbal behavior which cannot be observed by others is not properly part of our field. It is tempting to avoid the problems it raises by confining ourselves to observable events, letting anyone extend the analysis to his own covert behavior who wishes to do so. But there would then be certain embarrassing gaps in our account."[114] Chomsky argues that knowledge of the terminal events (input-output, S-R) does not provide an explanation of behavior; it is the internal structure, states, and organization of the organism that produce the relation between these events which is of interest to science.[115]

Thus, while Skinner does not deny the existence of inner states, (1) he contends that, although the method of introspection is acceptable it is not scientifically adequate, and that if these states are to be understood, it must be by means of behavioral analysis. (However, he also appears to believe that there is no adequate method for their study.) (2) He appears to deny that they are important. They are not important because they are not causal and not necessary in the prediction and control of behavior. Although this position is progress from the earlier logical positivism of methodological behaviorism, it actually represents no change in terms of method—it simply attempts to extend the method to the study of internal variables or, where this is not possible, to ignore them except for speculative translations into behaviorist terminology.

A question may be raised about the relegation of inner states to an unimportant position—as useless epiphenomena of behavior. What then is their significance in human evolution? Why did they develop? Are they accidents of evolution? Or are they vestigial remains from a time when feelings had significance as precursors of environmental stimuli? Their existence must be accounted for in some way, in terms of meaning or significance. Behaviorism avoids this question.

Ignoring inner states as irrelevant (in a causal sense) is only possible as long as there is a one-to-one correspondence between environmental conditions and behavior. In simple animals and in simple behaviors, or where there is complete control of the organism and the environment (with the organism in a controlled situation where only limited responses are possible), this assumption of a one-to-one correspondence seems to hold up. The question is whether it holds for more complex human behaviors in the real world. Experience suggests that it does not.

Skinner constantly refers to acts or behaviors which cause changes in the behaver and in his or her environment. Such behaviors appear to be voluntary or emitted acts without specific, accountable, or obvious causes deriving from the individual's endowment or environment. It would appear that states of mind have results on the individual: Feelings change the individual in some way; they do not simply exist. The fact that we do not know how this occurs does not eliminate the possibility or justify rejecting the possibility that they affect behavior by denying that mind can act on matter (as Skinner does). Skinner opens the door a little when he talks about the effects of private stimuli on behavior, but he never really considers what these private stimuli are or how they influence behavior. To accept the influence of inner states does not reject determinism. It simply adds a third causative influence to endowment and environment. Inner states exist, and their existence must make a difference in the individual and his behavior.

The difficulty is that behaviorism is still wedded to a single method which it insists is *the* scientific method, and the only way to achieve knowledge. While Skinner talks about another kind of knowledge, that is, the understanding that can come through intensive psychotherapy, he does not accept this as scientific knowledge. Such understanding or knowledge cannot be observed and measured in terms of rate of response. It cannot be manipulated in terms of the terminal variables—the environment as an independent variable and the behavior as the dependent variable—which manipulation is the method of science. Anything in between these variables, or what psychologists call intervening variables, or what philosophers and other more cognitively oriented psychologists call psychological concepts, are "explanatory factors" which do not explain, because they are not necessary for the prediction and control of behavior. All such variables are, as indicated earlier, reducible to operant conditioning terms. They represent nothing new, different, or useful—not even as generalizations. They are simply metaphors. To attempt to find observable variables which would serve as indexes of the internal variables is not useful, since the internal variables themselves are not important.

Behaviorism as a philosophy of science is, Malcolm points out, based on the philosophical doctrine of physicalism, which states that all statements and laws must be in terms of physical concepts, conditions, and occurrences, which can be tested and verified objectively in terms of observable phenomena.[116] While the philosophical doctrine accepts physiological conditions as physical variables, Skinner accepts only external behaviors. Mental concepts, if they are to be studied, must be reduced to physical (behavioral) variables.

The behaviorist assumption is, then, that the descriptions of internal states, what Malcolm calls first-person sentences, such as "I am excited," are based on observations of the state and behaviors of one's own body. This is rarely, if at all, the case, says Malcolm. Behaviorists assume that first-person psychological sentences have the same basis or content, and the same verification, as corresponding third-person sentences. But while we verify what others are feeling by observing their behavior, that is not the way we verify what we ourselves are feeling: In fact we do not normally verify it at all—we simply feel. The notion of verification does not apply—first-person reports are not based on observations, either of inner states (introspection) or outer events or behaviors (behaviorism). If a person says he or she feels a certain way, we often (usually) accept this testimony even though we may not be able to verify the feeling in the person's behavior. First-person statements are not always, nor perfectly, correlated with behavior. But "the testimony that people give us about their intentions, plans, hopes, worries, thoughts, and feelings is by far the most important source of information we have about them. This self-testimony has, one could say, an autonomous status."[117] Self-statements are important because the behavior of the human being, as a linguistic animal, includes many such statements, which are significant in human relations and in people's understanding of each other. They cannot be studied by, or reduced to, observable behaviors. They are not based on the individual's observation of her- or himself as an object, nor can they be replaced by observations by another person. Behaviorism regards the individual solely as an object, and thus cannot deal with such statements and their implications.

The issue is the nature of knowledge and how it is obtained. Behaviorism limits science to its methodology, and knowledge to what can be learned from that methodology, which is external observation of external behaviors. In effect it rules out of consideration the whole of human experience (as contrasted with behavior) and, further, discourages the study of such experience by other methods by insisting that if it is important or relevant it can be reduced to behaviors which can eventually be studied and understood by behaviorist methodology, which is the only method of science. Hilgard and Bower pose the following question: "Is psychology to be the science of the mind, or the science of behavior? Is physics the science of things or the science of meter readings? Do behaviorists confuse the subject matter of the field with the evidence available about drawing inferences about this subject matter?"[118]

Skinner rejects much of what is considered to be psychology: study and research in perception, cognition, learning, motivation, personality, social psychology (attitudes and opinions). He has remained closely consistent with his basic position, attributing all causation to endowment or the environment, and rejecting the possibility of the contribution of central processes—inner states—to the causation of behavior. He has persisted in his insistence that a science of behavior is concerned only with observable behaviors in response to contingencies of reinforcement, leaving to the anatomist and physiologist the explanation of how and why the organism changes and behaves in a particular way in a given situation.

In an article entitled "The Steep and Thorny Way to a Science of Behavior,"[119] he lists what he calls diversions which have impeded progress toward a science of human behavior. One of these is the preoccupation with feelings and their relation to, or presumed influence upon, behavior. Another is concern with other inner correlates or collateral products of behavior—wishes, intention, ideas, will, as well as memory and the so-called higher mental processes of cognitive psychology. A third is concern for the individual as an agent, initiator, and creator, which produces the attack on and rejection of the control of human behavior.

Skinner recognizes that he does not speak for all behaviorists. As a matter of fact, it appears that he is beginning to stand almost alone, along with a group of laboratory researchers in clinging to the extreme environmentalist and anti-mentalist position. Many behaviorists are moving beyond this and are incorporating other aspects of human experience, particularly the cognitive, into their thinking. One of these is Bandura, who still is considered, and considers himself, a behaviorist.

Bandura does not believe that the empirical facts of human behavior support the theory that behavior is completely and automatically controlled by conditioning, either classical or operant (or both), to the exclusion of inner affective and cognitive factors. "It is well documented," he says, "that behavior is influenced by its consequences much of the time. . . . But external consequences, influential as they often are, are not the sole determiners of human behavior, nor do they operate automatically."[120] The consequences of behavior provide information which, through thought, serves to guide action. Consequences also motivate behavior by enabling the individual to represent possible outcomes symbolically. We act, or fail to act, to gain anticipated benefits or to avert possible aversive consequences. "The widely accepted dictum that man is ruled by response consequences thus fares better for anticipated than for actual consequences."[121] When a fixed-ratio schedule is used, for example, with every fiftieth response reinforced, 96 percent of the responses are not reinforced; behavior is maintained in spite of its lack of reinforcement. "As people are exposed to variations in frequency and predictability of reinforcement, they behave on the basis of the outcomes they expect to prevail on future occasions. When belief differs from actuality, which is not uncommon, behavior is weakly controlled by its consequences until repeated experience instills realistic expectations. Had humans been ruled solely by instant consequences, they would have long become museum pieces among the extinct species."[122]

This view of reinforcement, recognizing the influence of expectations, resolves two problems faced by Skinner's theory. First is the question of how remote consequences influence behavior, especially when remote consequences are aversive while immediate consequences are not. Skinner says that we are not influenced by remote consequences—we cannot be, until they have occurred. Yet we must be, if we are to design a culture, an undertaking which must take into consideration long-term future consequences. Second is the fact that Skinner talks about probability of response as the basic dependent variable in behavior. Actually, however, the only thing he measures is the rate of response. A probability exists before the response is made, but where does it exist, if inner events do not influence behavior? The recognition that behavior is influenced by expectancies resolves this problem. Awareness, or consciousness, thus does influence behavior. Awareness of what is being reinforced affects the influence of consequences on behavior.

Social factors also influence the effects of consequences on behavior. Behavior can be influenced by observed consequences (vicarious reinforcement) as well as by direct experience. Human beings also develop personal standards of conduct that lead to actions having self-reinforcing properties. These may be in conflict with external outcomes: If the consequences for the self-concept are negative, external influences are relatively ineffective. Behavior in a social context is influenced by personal as well as social factors. "Personal control is clearly more complex and flexible than the theorizing implies."[123]

Self-management or self-regulation of behavior involves self-control and even though external influences are involved, self-influence (through internal or inner variables) is also involved. "The recognition of self-directing capacities represents a substantial departure from exclusive reliance upon environmental control."[124]

Bandura claims that empirical evidence, rather than supporting the behaviorist contention that cognitions are unnecessary in causal analysis, has shown the opposite. "A large body of research now exists in which cognition is activated instructionally with impressive results. People learn and retain more by using cognitive aids that they generate than by repetitive reinforcement. With growing evidence that cognition has causal influence in behavior, the arguments against cognitive determinants are losing their force."[125] Learning occurs by observation of others (modeling), by reading about something, or by listening, in situations where, in any strict definition of the terms, there is no stimulus, no contingency, no response or overt behavior.

Thus, the individual is a source of influence.

It is true that behavior is regulated by its contingencies, but the contingencies are partly of a person's own making. By their actions, people play an active role in producing the reinforcing contingencies that impinge upon them. Thus, behavior partly creates the environment, and the environment influences the behavior in a reciprocal fashion. To the oft-repeated dictum, change contingencies and you change behavior, should be added the reciprocal side, change behavior and you change the contingencies. . . . To contend, as environmental determinists often do, that people are controlled by external forces, and then to advocate that they redesign their society by applying behavioral technology undermines the basic premise of the argument. If humans were in fact incapable of influencing their own actions, they could describe and predict environmental events but hardly exercise any intentional control over them. When it comes to advocacy of social change, however, thoroughgoing environmental determinists become ardent exponents of man's power to transform environments in pursuit of a better life.[126]

Summary

Skinner's behaviorist or reinforcement model of behavior fails to deal adequately with or resolve some basic problems in human behavior. These include the issues revolving around freedom versus determinism, control by the environment versus control of the environment, and the existence and place of intention and purpose in human behavior. The extension of the results of animal experiments to human behavior does not provide the basis for an adequate model or theory of human behavior. If one observes the ordinary behavior of individuals outside the laboratory or not under controlled experimental conditions, one will find it difficult to accept the assumption that all their complex behaviors are controlled by environmental stimuli or conditions. That they are, is an assumption that has not been supported by research.

Although Skinner insists on the importance of empirical analyses of behavior as a basis for knowledge, his description or theory of human behavior is not based upon such empirical analyses. This is not to say that there has been no behaviorist research involving human beings. There has been a great deal, and it has supported, in general, the assumption that behavior is a function of its consequences, or of reinforcement. The principle is not invalid or erroneous; it simply does not appear to be sufficient to explain all of the complex aspects of human behavior. The human being is an animal, but a different, much more complex animal than any other. Language is one major differentiating factor. Skinner has attempted to apply the behaviorist model to verbal behavior, but the results have not been satisfying or acceptable to psycholinguists. Moreover, the implications of the fact that man exists in a temporal dimension have not been adequately recognized or dealt with by Skinner.

The promised control of behavior through the application of reinforcement contingencies has not materialized in real life—with retarded children, autistic children, psychotic adults, or even programmed instruction. Where results have been obtained, they cannot be attributed to the simple application of behaviorist techniques. Persistent and consistent concern, caring, and other personal relationship variables have been important. And even when results have been obtained, they often do not continue; the problem of the maintenance of changes in behavior has not been resolved. The repeated claim of practitioners that their techniques have been shown to be effective on the basis of research is not justified in the case of complex human behavior.

Thus, operant conditioning does not work in real life as well as in the laboratory. It is not possible to shape the behavior of human beings as effectively as one can train pigeons to bowl or play ping-poing, or chickens to play the piano. The model is incomplete. The principles of reinforcement are valid. But, as Kendler notes, "the reason that the reinforcement model is not more effective in controlling human behavior is that significant processes tend to be ignored, such as those related to the transformation of external stimuli into symbolic reactions that guide behavior."[127] Many behaviorists have recognized the limitations of a behaviorism which rejects cognition and other inner states as being important in behavior. In particular, Bandura, a recognized behaviorist, has extended behaviorism by incorporating cognitive psychology in his social learning theory. His approach fills many of the gaps and resolves some of the inconsistencies in Skinner's approach.

The critique of Skinner's behaviorism has been rather detailed (though by no means including all the criticisms that have been or could be made) because of the wide and optimistic claims made for its effectiveness in changing behavior, claims which tend to present it as a panacea; and because of a resulting wide acceptance on an uncritical basis. The evidence appears to indicate that Skinner's extreme, monolithic form of behaviorism is on the decline and is not generally accepted as a sufficient approach to human behavior by psychologists.

SUMMARY

The behaviorism of B. F. Skinner is a development from the work of Thorndike rather than from that of Pavlov and Watson. The conditioning model is not the so-called classical model, but what has been called instrumental conditioning, more commonly known now by Skinner's term of *operant conditioning*. In classical conditioning, a conditioned stimulus becomes the stimulus for a response which it does not normally elicit by being repeatedly associated with the normal or unconditioned stimulus for that response. In operant conditioning, the probability of a response occurring in a particular situation is increased by reinforcing the response when it appears (is *emitted*) in that situation.

The science of behavior—or the experimental analysis of behavior, to use Skinner's term—consists of analysis of the systematic and functional relationships between the environment and the behaviors of the organism. The process in which the organism interacts with its environment is called the discriminative operant and forms the basic unit in the analysis of behavior. There are three elements in the process: (1) an occasion upon which a response occurs (a discriminative stimulus); (2) the response; and (3) its reinforcing consequences. The interrelations of these elements constitute the contingencies of reinforcement. The reinforcing stimulus, or reinforcement, will occur only if the response is emitted in the presence of the discriminative stimulus.

The organism is constantly behaving, or emitting operant behaviors. These behaviors have consequences, which affect the future probabilities of their emission in situations where discriminative stimuli are present. The consequences of behavior are positive or negative. Positive consequences are reinforcers—they increase the probability of the behaviors which they follow. Negative reinforcers are noxious consequences whose *removal* (or the escape from which) reinforces the behavior which succeeds in their removal. Why reinforcers are reinforcing is not of concern to Skinner; it is sufficient to know what consequences are reinforcing for a given organism or individual.

Reinforcement may follow every instance of the behavior being conditioned, in which case it is known as *continuous reinforcement*, or it may occur *intermittently*, on various schedules. The most common *schedules of reinforcement* are *interval schedules*, involving reinforcement at specified time intervals, and *ratio schedules*, in which reinforcements are delivered following a given number of responses. Both interval and ratio schedules may be fixed or variable (varying around an average interval or ratio).

Continuous reinforcement is most efficient in establishing a response. Intermittent reinforcement is most efficient in maintaining the response and in delaying extinction when reinforcement is removed.

A stimulus which is not reinforcing may become a *conditioned reinforcer* by being associated with a reinforcer. Some conditioned reinforcers (for example, money) may become associated with a large number of primary reinforcers, becoming *generalized reinforcers.* Responses may occur in situations which are similar to a particular stimulus situation, indicating *stimulus generalization.* On the other hand, such generalization can be prevented if one withholds reinforcement in similar situations, producing *stimulus discrimination.* Responses which are similar to a reinforced response tend to increase, indicating *response generalization.* Again, such generalization can be avoided if one reinforces only specific responses and does not reinforce similar responses, thus producing *response differentiation.*

Response differentiation makes possible the *shaping* of behavior. In shaping, a desired specific response is achieved by reinforcing any approximation to the desired response, and then successively reinforcing closer approximations while ceasing to reward the lesser approximations. New behaviors can be developed in this way and can be chained together, as in the training of pigeons to bowl or play ping-pong, or chickens to peck a series of tuneful notes on the piano.

Punishment is the opposite of reinforcement. Here positive reinforcers are removed, or negative reinforcers or aversive stimuli are imposed. Skinner believes that punishment is relatively ineffective in controlling behavior, because it is short-lived and has undesirable effects on both the punisher and the one being punished.

Skinner's method and the principles of reinforcement were developed in empirical research with animals. The methods have been extended to work with human beings in laboratory experiments, in institutions for the emotionally disturbed and retarded, and in school classrooms. Research has demonstrated that the response frequencies of many overt behaviors in humans can be influenced or controlled in laboratory or experimental situations by the methods of operant conditioning. The basic question is the extent to which complex and nonovert behaviors of humans can be influenced or controlled in natural environments. Is the paradigm or model of operant conditioning, which places all the causes of behavior in the environment (except for genetic factors, or limitations), sufficient? Are inner states—feeling, thinking, intending, willing, and the like—never involved in the causation of behavior? Skinner answers yes to the first question, and no to the second (that is, he rejects inner states as causes).

Admitting that much of his argument goes beyond the known facts, Skinner extends the principles of operant conditioning to complex human behavior, including the covert behaviors of thinking, problem solving, and creative activities. He translates these activities, as well as feelings, needs, drives, intentions, purpose, and so on into behaviorist terminology. In his view, mental states are caused by environmental conditions, or are corollaries of behaviors caused by external stimuli or the consequences of the behaviors. They are not causes of behavior, and behavior can be predicted and controlled without consideration of them. Mental events and processes are inventions and are essentially metaphors. To the extent that they exist they are (covert) behaviors which can be dealt with in behaviorist terms. Skinner believes that ultimately all human behavior, including mental behaviors, can be accounted for entirely in terms of genetic and environmental conditions.

Motivational terms, such as needs, desires, wants, wishes, and so on, are mentalistic terms referring to states of deprivation. The organism is always active, and reinforcers which eliminate a deprivation increase the behavior which leads to the reinforcement. Motivational terms apply to feelings which are associated with the consequences of actions, and are not causes. Choosing, willing, and intention also refer to feelings resulting from the effects of behavior. Positive reinforcement leads to a feeling of freedom, while aversive control leads to the feeling of being forced to do something, or of not being free.

Behavioral analysis is concerned with a person who behaves, not with a self or personality. *Self* is simply a term applied to a repertoire of behavior developed from experiences of reinforcement. The person is a product, not an originator of behavior. Self-knowledge involves an understanding of the environmental causes of one's behavior. It makes possible self-management through control of environmental contingencies. Management or control of others is achieved in the same way —by controlling their environment through positive and negative contingencies.

All behavior is controlled. The problem of control is to replace unplanned control with planned control and to prevent abuse of the power to control which develops as the science of behavior advances. Aversive methods of control lead to counter-control. Control through positive reinforcement leads to a feeling of freedom and does not breed countercontrol; the consequences are presumably desirable and good for those who are controlled. It is our nature to be reinforced in certain ways. Yet Skinner recognizes that natural susceptibility to certain types of reinforcement is not an infallible guide to the ideal culture or the survival of a culture, which is the objective of his designed society. Control is resisted, because in the past it has been aversive in nature. But control is not in itself bad. Democracy is in conflict with control, and while in the past it served the purpose of freeing man from aversive control, it may have to give way to scientifically based control.

An examination of education reveals that teaching has not benefitted from the results of the experimental analysis of behavior. Control in the classroom depends on aversive methods, or punishment, which breeds the negative behaviors characteristic of countercontrol.

The content of the curriculum is to a great extent and by necessity artificial and irrelevant to the lives of the students and is not naturally reinforcing. The teacher becomes the source of reinforcement. But reinforcement is infrequent, delayed, and unsystematic. Students who do learn, do so on their own, without being taught.

The scientific analysis of behavior provides principles which can be applied to the educational environment and to classroom practices, resulting in a technology of teaching. There are three major applications of these principles in education:

1. In classroom management, the principles of behaviorism can be used to assure that children attend class, engage in those behaviors necessary for learning to take place, and do not manifest behaviors which are disruptive to learning. Discipline is achieved through the application of contingencies of reinforcement, emphasizing positive reinforcement. Systems involving the use of tokens which earn certain privileges can be used. Though contrived, such reinforcement may lead to natural or intrinsic reinforcers taking over as learning becomes pleasant and self-rewarding.

2. Programmed instruction utilizes the principles of behavioral analysis in selecting and defining objective terminal behaviors which are desired as the outcome of learning, and then constructing a graded sequence of steps toward the objective, each of which is reinforced until it is established, at which time the next step is presented. Behaviors are elicited by the teacher through the use of *primes*—modeling, use of copying, direct instruction. The behaviors must be reinforced when they occur. As the behaviors are repeated, primes are replaced by *prompts* (which are abbreviations of the prime—just enough to prompt the behavior), until the prompt is no longer necessary, or is *vanished*. Programming classroom learning is difficult, since it requires breaking down complex behavior into steps of just the right size. The size may vary with the student; individual instruction is almost necessary.

3. Teaching machines are an efficient method of presenting programmed instruction. Programs can be constructed in advance which are appropriate for most students. Short steps which are necessary for some learners can be gone through rapidly by the better students. Programs can be constructed at different levels. Delivery of reinforcements can be more systematic and immediate than when it is dependent on the teacher. Students are active in the learning process, constructing rather than selecting answers, and can progress at their own rate, and review if they wish. The teacher is freed for those activities which cannot be done by a machine—for instance, individual attention, discussion, exploration of new areas, and providing cultural activities in art, music, and so on. Teaching machines can be used not only to teach simple facts and skills, but to teach thinking, problem solving, and creativity.

Motivation to learn is not the result of a natural curiosity or love of learning, but the result of schedules of reinforcement. Remote consequences do not influence behavior, and natural consequences in the real world are often aversive. Education must depend on immediate or more proximate and contrived reinforcers. Reinforcers are often already available but are not used systematically. Personal reinforcers (attention, approval, friendship) are powerful but raise problems of personal involvement and of overuse. Also, they cannot be simulated and be effective. Even when deserved or merited by the student, deliberate use is not advocated by Skinner.

For establishing behaviors, continuous reinforcement is more effective than intermittent reinforcement, but more difficult to provide. Once behavior is established, "stretching the ratio" of reinforced to nonreinforced responses is effective. But the most effective programs of reinforcement are difficult to carry out and are often achieved accidentally, as in the case of highly motivated and productive individuals working against odds with relatively few reinforcements.

The scientific analysis of teaching provides a basis for a more effective aproach to teacher education. It focuses on the specification of desired terminal behaviors and the process of achieving them through the application of the principles of programming. Technology increases the teacher's productivity and thus leads to a sense of accomplishment.

Education is an important part of the controlling environment, transmitting the knowledge, skills, and social and ethical practices which are necessary for the survival of a culture. It is also important in encouraging the "mutations" and innovations which are necessary for the changes which also contribute to survival. Education at present promotes conformity rather than diversity, however. Education must concern itself with fostering creativity through emphasis on the development of the potentials of each individual. The experimental analysis of behavior can enable education to produce individuals who can more nearly actualize their potentialities. Whether we achieve this, rather than producing the conformity which can also be achieved by a technology of teaching, depends on our decision.

Behaviorism, with its threat of control and manipulation and loss of individual freedom, has aroused extensive criticism. Much of this criticism is a result of misunderstanding or is based on emotional reactions. Behaviorists have often stimulated such reactions by their confidence and dogmatism, their rejection of other points of view, and their insistence that theirs is the only scientific approach to the study of behavior. There is also the real threat of abuse or misuse of the techniques of behavior modification, which Skinner recognizes: The controllers must be controlled.

Skinner lists a number of criticisms of behaviorism which he believes represent misunderstanding or misconceptions, and he answers them. However, his answers are not entirely satisfying or acceptable, and he fails to recognize still other objections or criticisms. It is interesting that, while rejecting the influence of attitudes and beliefs on behavior, behaviorism, in challenging or rejecting many strongly held beliefs and attitudes about human behavior, has felt the effects of the resulting negative attitudes.

Skinner's presentation of behaviorism is simple (probably oversimple or simplistic) and logical, and convincing and persuasive. Thus behaviorism has been widely—and often uncritically—accepted, though its influence is apparently waning and many of its adherents are modifying or extending their position. It is important, therefore, that the criticisms of behaviorism be carefully examined.

The first major basis for criticism is the failure of behaviorism to deal adequately with some of the basic aspects of human behavior and experience. While Skinner does not reject the existence of inner or mental states, he does not feel that we are able, or ever will be able, to study them scientifically; in any event, and more important, he does not consider them necessary for predicting and controlling behavior, since they have no causal influence on behavior. To many people, including many psychologists, these states are important aspects of human existence, which could and may influence complex behaviors. They are thus worthy of attention and study.

Cognitive psychology has become an increasingly important area of the field of psychology, yet it is completely rejected by Skinner. Skinner's treatment of inner states, including feelings, attitudes, opinions, beliefs, intentions, and the higher mental processes, consists simply of translating them into behaviorist terminology. He admits that his treatment of these aspects of human existence is not based upon fact, but upon translation (some would say reduction) and interpretation, and extrapolation from animal studies. His translations are often peculiar and awkward ways of talking about complex mental events or processes in order to avoid using terminology which implies that they influence behavior. There are inconsistencies in his discussions; even Skinner cannot seem completely to avoid recognizing the importance and influence of these events in human life. The major difference between humans and other animals, for Skinner, is language, or verbal behavior, which Skinner treats as just another kind of behavior, subject to the principles of behaviorism.

This treatment of inner and mental states seems to be little more than a verbal device to avoid basic problems and issues which behaviorism is not able to handle. These issues center around freedom versus control or determinism, and the existence of will, intention, and purpose in human behavior. These are complex problems, to which there are no clear solutions at present, but behaviorism does not resolve them and thus cannot reject them.

A second major source of criticism, deriving from the first, concerns the limitations of behaviorism. By limiting itself to observable behavior—or more specifically to the frequencies of motor responses—and refusing to recognize other aspects of human existence as accessible to or relevant for scientific study, it limits the field of psychology. The tremendous amount of study and research in perception, cognition, personality, and social psychology is ignored or rejected by Skinner. If Skinner is right, vast amounts of time and money have been wasted in these studies.

Many, if not most, psychologists who are identified as behaviorists, have moved from Skinner's extreme position of rejection of cognition and have incorporated cognitive elements in the behaviorist framework. For these psychologists, of whom Bandura is an outstanding example, behavior is not completely or automatically determined by its actual consequences. Consequences provide information which guides action. Consequences motivate behavior by representing possible outcomes which can be dealt with cognitively, so that the individual can decide to act or not in order to obtain or avert certain outcomes. Anticipated rather than actual consequences thus influence behavior. Behavior can also be influenced without direct experiencing of consequences by vicarious experience (observation of others), by reading about something, and by listening, activities which involve no objective stimulus, no overt response, and no contingencies or actual reinforcement.

Behavior is also influenced by social experiences. But in a social context, personal elements or standards also are involved: A person may eschew an external reinforcement because it is inconsistent with consequences for the self-concept.

Thus, it is being increasingly recognized that, while the principle of reinforcement is valid, it does not operate simply, automatically, or without the influence of internal affective and cognitive factors in much of human behavior. Behaviorism is not wrong; however, in its simple form based on experiments with animals in the laboratory it is not adequate to account for complex human behaviors. In many situations, nonetheless, an understanding and application of the principles of reinforcement can lead to an understanding and influencing of much human behavior. Environmental conditions, or contingencies, are real and important, and recognition of this in education can lead to many improvements in classroom management and in teaching and learning. But behaviorism is not a panacea, and as a technology will not be sufficient to create a utopian culture. People of good will, with deep feelings of respect and concern for others and a purpose directed toward a goal which includes freedom and mutual respect, are needed to design that culture. Such people will not be produced by an educational system modeled on a narrow technology derived from a limited behaviorism. Skinner's vision of human perfectibility and his humanistic concern for people go beyond his scientific analysis of behavior, which must be recognized as a part but not the whole of an approach to the understanding of the human race and the improvement of the human condition.

REFERENCES

1. F. S. Keller, in his citation of Skinner for the Gold Medal Award of the American Psychological Foundation, published in *American Psychologist* 27 (1972):71.
2. J. B. Watson and R. Rayner, "Conditioned Emotional Reactions," *Journal of Experimental Psychology* 3 (1920):1–14.
3. M. C. Jones, "A Laboratory Study of Fear: The Case of Peter," *Pedagogical Seminary (Journal of Genetic Psychology)* 31 (1924):308–315. See also M. C. Jones, "The Elimination of Children's Fears," *Journal of Experimental Psychology* 7 (1924):382–390.
4. J. B. Watson, *Behaviorism*, rev. ed. (New York: Norton, 1930), p. 104. (First edition, 1924).
5. A. J. Yates, *Behavior Therapy* (New York: Wiley, 1970), p. 34. See also E. R. Hilgard and G. H. Bower, *Theories of Learning*, 4th ed. (Englewood Cliffs, N.J.: Prentice-Hall, 1975), pp. 209–212.
6. B. F. Skinner, *About Behaviorism* (New York: Knopf, 1974), p. 1.
7. Skinner, *Walden Two* (New York: Macmillan, 1948), p. 101.
8. Skinner, "Are Theories of Learning Necessary?" *Psychological Review* 57 (1950):193–216. Reprinted in Skinner, *Cumulative Record: A Selection of Papers*, 3rd ed. (Englewood Cliffs, N.J.: Prentice-Hall, 1972), pp. 69–100.
9. Skinner, "A Case History in Scientific Method," *American Psychologist* 11 (1956):221–233. Reprinted in Skinner, *Cumulative Record*, op. cit., p. 120.
10. Ibid., *Cumulative Record*, p. 129.
11. Skinner, "Are Theories of Learning Necessary?," op. cit., p. 72.
12. Skinner, "A Case History in Scientific Method," op. cit., pp. 110–111.
13. Ibid., p. 110.
14. See Hilgard and Bower, *Theories of Learning*, op. cit., pp. 226–228; Skinner, *Cumulative Record*, op. cit., p. 187; and Skinner, *The Technology of Teaching* (Englewood Cliffs, N.J.: Prentice-Hall, 1968), pp. 71–72, 82–83.
15. Skinner, *The Behavior of Organisms: An Experimental Analysis* (Englewood Cliffs, N.J.: Prentice-Hall, 1938), pp. 339–340.
16. Skinner, "Pigeons in a Pelican," *American Psychologist* 15 (1960):28–37. Reprinted in Skinner, *Cumulative Record*, op. cit., pp. 574–591.
17. Skinner, "Reinforcement Today," *American Psychologist* 13 (1958):94–99. Reprinted in Skinner, *Cumulative Record*, op. cit., p. 159. The ping-pong-playing pigeons are described in "Two 'Synthetic' Social Relations," *Journal of the Experimental Analysis of Behavior* 5 (1962): 531–533. Reprinted in Skinner, *Cumulative Record*, op. cit., pp. 533–537.
18. Skinner, "Reinforcement Today," op. cit., p. 163.
19. Skinner, *Walden Two*, op. cit., p. 243.
20. Skinner, "Are Theories of Learning Necessary?," op. cit., p. 83.
21. Skinner, " 'Superstition' in the Pigeon," *Journal of Experimental Psy-*

chology 38 (1948):168–172. Reprinted in Skinner, *Cumulative Record,* op. cit., pp. 524–532.

22. From Skinner, "The Experimental Analysis of Behavior," *American Scientist* 45 (1957): 343–371. Reprinted in Skinner, *Cumulative Record,* op. cit., p. 150.
23. The literature is now so large that no single reference is adequate. Many brief reviews and summaries, often of special areas, are available in text-books in educational psychology. A more extensive review will be found in F. H. Kanfer and J. S. Phillips, *Learning Foundations of Behavior Therapy* (New York: Wiley, 1970).
24. Skinner, *About Behaviorism,* op. cit., p. 17.
25. Ibid., p. 107.
26. Skinner, "Man," *Proceedings of the American Philosophical Society* 108 (1964):482–485. Reprinted in Skinner, *Cumulative Record,* op. cit., p. 51.
27. Ibid.
28. Skinner, *About Behaviorism,* op. cit., p. 112.
29. Ibid., p. 48.
30. Skinner, *Verbal Behavior* (Englewood Cliffs, N.J.: Prentice-Hall, 1957).
31. Skinner, *About Behaviorism,* op. cit., p. 17.
32. Ibid., p. 18.
33. Ibid., pp. 222, 223.
34. Ibid., p. 98.
35. Ibid., p. 51.
36. Ibid., p. 161.
37. Ibid., p. 52.
38. Ibid., p. 55.
39. Ibid., p. 56.
40. Ibid., p. 153.
41. Skinner, "Some Issues Concerning the Control of Human Behavior," *Science* 124 (1956):1057–1066. Reprinted in Skinner, *Cumulative Record,* op. cit., p. 33.
42. Skinner, "Freedom and the Control of Men," *American Scholar,* Winter 1955–1956. Reprinted in Skinner, *Cumulative Record,* op. cit., p. 11.
43. Skinner, *About Behaviorism,* op. cit., p. 202.
44. Skinner, "The Experimental Analysis of Behavior," op. cit., p. 157.
45. From Skinner, "The Design of Cultures," *Daedalus,* Summer 1961. Reprinted in Skinner, *Cumulative Record,* op. cit., p. 49.
46. Skinner, *About Behaviorism,* op. cit., p. 206.
47. Skinner, "Man," op. cit.
48. Skinner, *About Behaviorism,* op. cit., pp. 211–212.
49. Skinner, *The Technology of Teaching,* op. cit., p. 5.
50. Ibid., pp. 7, 8.
51. Ibid., p. 61.
52. Ibid., p. 109.
53. Ibid., p. 59.
54. Skinner, "Contingency Management in the Classroom," *Education,* 90 (1969):93–100. Reprinted in Skinner, *Cumulative Record,* op. cit., p. 231.
55. In the last few years there has been a proliferation of brief books (usually in paperback) on classroom management. The following list is representative: Ackerman, J. M. *Operant Conditioning Techniques for the Classroom Teacher.* Glenview, Ill.: Scott, Foresman, 1972; Buckley,

N. K., and Walker, H. M. *Modifying Classroom Behavior: A Manual of Procedures for Classroom Teachers.* Champaign, Ill.: Research Press, 1973; Dollar, B. *Humanizing Classroom Behavior: A Behavioral Approach.* New York: Harper & Row, 1972; Fargo, G. A., Behrens, C., and Nolan, P. *Behavioral Modifications in the Classroom.* Belmont, Calif.: Wadsworth, 1970; Glover, J. B. *Behavioral Strategies for Classroom Management: A Programmed Text.* New York: New Century, 1970; MacMillan, D. L. *Behavior Modification in Education.* New York: Macmillan, 1973; Meacham, M. L., and Wiesen, A. E. *Changing Classroom Behavior,* 2nd ed. New York: Intext, 1974; Morreau, L. E., and Daley, M. F. *Behavioral Management in the Classroom.* Englewood Cliffs, N.J.: Prentice-Hall, 1972; O'Leary, K. D., and O'Leary, S. G. *Classroom Management,* 2nd ed. New York: Pergamon, 1977; Poteet, J. A. *Behavioral Modification: A Practical Guide for Teachers.* Minneapolis: Burgess, 1973; Sarason, I. G., Glaser, E. M., and Fargo, G. A. *Reinforcing Productive Classroom Behavior.* New York: Behavioral Publications, 1972; Stephens, T. M. *Implementing Behavioral Approaches in Elementary and Secondary Schools.* Columbus, Ohio: Merrill, 1975; Sulzer, B., and Mayer, G. R. *Behavior Modification Procedures for School Personnel.* Hinsdale, Ill.: Dryden, 1972.
56. Skinner, "Contingency Management in the Classroom," op. cit., p. 232. Skinner here appears to be in disagreement with those who have developed contingency contracting programs for the classroom, such as L. Homme et al., in *How to Use Contingency Contracting in the Classroom,* rev. ed. (Champaign, Ill.: Research Press, 1973).
57. Ibid. Emphasis added.
58. Skinner, *The Technology of Teaching,* op. cit., p. 216.
59. Ibid., p. 223.
60. Ibid., pp. 21–22.
61. Ibid., p. 27.
62. Ibid., pp. 120–121.
63. Ibid., p. 129.
64. Ibid., p. 132.
65. Ibid., p. 137.
66. Ibid., p. 143.
67. Ibid., p. 170.
68. Ibid., p. 180.
69. Ibid., pp. 183–184.
70. Skinner, "Contingency Management in the Classroom," op. cit., p. 229.
71. Skinner, *About Behaviorism,* op. cit., p. 190.
72. Skinner, *The Technology of Teaching,* op. cit., p. 155.
73. Ibid.
74. Ibid., p. 165.
75. Ibid., p. 168.
76. Ibid., p. 258.
77. Ibid., p. 110.
78. Ibid., p. 171.
79. Ibid., p. 236.
80. Skinner, "Why We Need Teaching Machines," *Harvard Educational Review* 31 (1961):377–398. Reprinted in Skinner, *Cumulative Record,* op. cit., p. 193.
81. Skinner, *The Technology of Teaching,* op. cit., p. 91.
82. Skinner, *About Behaviorism,* op. cit., pp. 226–227.
83. Ibid., p. 230.

84. Ibid., p. 231.
85. Ibid., p. 240.
86. Ibid., p. 246.
87. Ibid., pp. 247–248.
88. Ibid., p. 250.
89. MacMillan, *Behavior Modification in Education,* op. cit., p. 29.
90. R. A. Winett and R. C. Winkler, "Current Behavior Modification in the Classroom: Be Still, Be Quiet, Be Docile," *Journal of Applied Behavioral Analysis* 5 (1972):499–504.
91. C. H. Patterson, "Humanistic Concerns and Behavior Modification," a paper presented at a conference on "Moral and Ethical Implications of Behavior Modification," University of Wisconsin, Madison, March 20–21, 1975.
92. Skinner, *About Behaviorism,* op. cit., p. 251.
93. Ibid., p. 252.
94. Ibid., p. 194.
95. M. Scriven, "The Philosophy of Behavior Modification," in C. E. Thoresen, ed., *Behavior Modification in Education.* (*The Seventy-second Yearbook of the National Society for the Study of Education,* Part I) (Chicago: National Society for the Study of Education, 1972), p. 431.
96. N. Chomsky, "The Case Against B. F. Skinner," *New York Review of Books,* December 30, 1971, 18–24. Also in N. Chomsky, *For Reasons of State* (New York: Pantheon Books, 1971).
97. Skinner, *Beyond Freedom and Dignity* (New York: Knopf, 1971), p. 211.
98. Skinner, "A Case History in Scientific Method," op. cit., pp. 122–123.
99. Skinner, *The Technology of Education,* op. cit., p. 10.
100. Skinner, *Walden Two,* op. cit., p. 218.
101. Ibid., p. 162.
102. M. Levine and G. Fasnacht, "Token Rewards May Lead to Token Learning," *American Psychologist* 29 (1974): 816–820.
103. Scriven, "The Philosophy of Behavior Modification." op. cit., pp. 438, 439.
104. Ibid., p. 435.
105. Skinner, *About Behaviorism,* op. cit., p. 230.
106. L. W. Doob, *The Patterning of Time* (New Haven: Yale University Press, 1971).
107. Scriven, "The Philosophy of Behavior Modification," op. cit., p. 426.
108. Chomsky, "The Case Against B. F. Skinner," op. cit.
109. Skinner, "Some Issues Concerning the Control of Human Behavior," op. cit., p. 28.
110. Skinner, "Freedom and the Control of Men," op. cit., p. 15.
111. Chomsky, "The Case Against B. F. Skinner," op. cit.
112. Skinner, *Science and Human Behavior* (New York: Macmillan, 1953), p. 87.
113. Chomsky, review of Skinner's *Verbal Behavior,* in *Language* 35 (1959):26–58. Also in L. A. Jakobovits and M. S. Miron, eds., *Readings in the Philosophy of Language* (Englewood Cliffs, N.J.: Prentice-Hall, 1967).
114. Skinner, *Verbal Behavior,* op. cit., p. 434.
115. Chomsky, "The Case Against B. F. Skinner," op. cit.
116. N. Malcolm, "Behaviorism as a Philosophy of Psychology," in T. W. Wann, ed., *Behaviorism and Phenomenology: Contrasting Bases for*

Modern Psychology (Chicago: University of Chicago Press, 1964), pp. 141–155.
117. Ibid., p. 153.
118. Hilgard and Bower, *Theories of Learning,* op. cit., p. 250.
119. Skinner, "The Steep and Thorny Way to a Science of Behavior," *American Psychologist* 30 (1975):42–49.
120. A. Bandura, "Behavior Theory and the Models of Man," *American Psychologist* 29 (1974):860–869.
121. Ibid., p. 860.
122. Ibid., p. 280.
123. Ibid., p. 861.
124. Ibid., p. 863.
125. Ibid., p. 865.
126. Ibid., pp. 866, 867.
127. H. H. Kendler, review of Skinner's "Contingencies of Reinforcement: A Theoretical Analysis," in *Contemporary Psychology* 15 (1970): 529–531.

Carl Rogers and humanistic education

6

CHAPTER

6

INTRODUCTION

Carl Ransom Rogers (1902–   ) was born in Oak Park, Illinois, the fourth of six children in a home which he describes as marked by close family ties, a very strict and uncompromising religious and ethical atmosphere, and what amounted to the virtue of hard work." He writes that he was "a pretty solitary boy."[1] When he was 12, his family bought a farm, as a hobby for his well-to-do father, but also, Rogers speculates, to keep the growing children from the "temptations" of suburban life. On the farm Carl became interested in and studied the great night-flying moths and became a student of scientific agriculture, a background which later led him to recognize the importance of research in evaluating the effectiveness of counseling or psychotherapy.

Rogers entered the University of Wisconsin to study agriculture, but, influenced by a religious conference, decided he would enter the ministry. He then changed his major to history, which he felt would be better undergraduate preparation. In his junior year (1922) he was selected as one of a dozen American student delegates to the World Christian Federation Conference in China. This experience, lasting six months in all, led to his recognizing that there were great differences in religious doctrines, and he broke with the doctrines of his parents.

After graduation from college in 1924 (Phi Beta Kappa), Rogers married a childhood sweetheart and, with her, went to Union Theological Seminary, where he spent two years. Here, he and some other students, dissatisfied with teaching in which they felt that ideas were being fed to them, asked for, and were allowed to set up, their own seminar (with an instructor sitting in). The result was that Rogers and some of the others "thought themselves right out of religious work." He had been interested in lectures and courses in psychology at Teachers College, Columbia University, and moved gradually into clinical psychology, working in child guidance. He obtained an internship at the just-established Institute for Child Guidance, where he came under the influence of Freudian psychology.

After receiving the MA degree from Columbia University in 1928, he was employed as a psychologist in the Child Study Department of the Society for the Prevention of Cruelty to Children in Rochester, New York. In 1930 he became director of the department. He received the PhD from Columbia University in 1931, while continuing to work in Rochester. In 1938 he helped organize, and became director of, the Rochester Guidance Center. In 1939 his first book, *The Clinical Treatment of the Problem Child,* was published, based on his experience with children.

It was during the years at Rochester that Rogers began to question the effectiveness of the traditional directive, or "the-therapist-knows-best," approach to counseling or psychotherapy. It was also during this period that he became aware of and influenced by the work of Otto Rank, through a social worker trained at the Pennsylvania School of Social Work.

In 1940 he accepted a position as professor of psychology at Ohio State University, and in 1942 published his second book, *Counseling and Psychotherapy: Newer Concepts in Practice.* This was a statement of an approach which came to be called nondirective counseling or psychotherapy, and later, client-centered counseling or psychotherapy. In 1945 he went to the University of Chicago as professor of psychology and executive secretary of the university counseling center, where he remained until 1957, and wrote *Client-Centered Therapy: Its Current Practice, Implications and Theory* (1951), In 1957 he was appointed professor of psychology and of psychiatry at the University of Wisconsin, where he directed a study of psychotherapy with hospitalized patients in a mental hospital, the results of which were published in *The Therapeutic Relationship and Its Impact: A Study of Psychotherapy with Schizophrenics* (with E. T. Gendlin, D. Kiesler, and C. B. Truax). In 1962–1963 he was a fellow at the Center for Advanced Study in the Behavioral Sciences at Stanford University.

Rogers then went to the newly established Western Behavioral Sciences Institute in La Jolla, California, as a resident fellow. In 1968 the Center for Studies of the Person was formed by Rogers and others from the institute, and he has continued there as a resident fellow. During this period he became involved in the group movement and has extended his theory to the basic encounter group: In 1970 he published *Carl Rogers on Encounter Groups.* He also became interested in the application of his theory to education, and in 1969 published *Freedom to Learn.* More recently he has become interested in the marriage relationship, and in 1972 published *Becoming Partners: Marriage and Its Alternatives.*

Rogers has been visiting professor or has taught part-time at Columbia University, the University of California at Los Angeles, Harvard University, Occidental College, California Western University, and the University of California. He was awarded the Nicholas Murray Butler Medal (Silver) by Columbia University in 1955, and the Doctor of Humane Letters by Lawrence College in 1956. In 1956 he was among three psychologists who received the first Distinguished Scientific Awards of the American Psychological Association. In 1972 he received the first Distinguished Professional Contribution Award of the association. Rogers was a charter member and later a fellow and president (1944–1945) of the American Association for Applied Psychology. He is a fellow of the American Psychological Association, of which he was president in 1946–1947, and was president of its Division of Clinical and Abnormal Psychology in 1949–1950. He is a fellow of The American Orthopsychiatric Association, of which he was vice president in 1941–1942. He was a charter member, and president in 1956, of the American Academy of Psychotherapists.

Although Rogers began his clinical work with children, most of his experience has been with adults. His client-centered therapy has been widely taught and practiced, and has been the subject of more research than any other method of counseling or psychotherapy. This is no doubt because Rogers himself has been an unusual combination of therapist and researcher. He has also been interested in theory regarding the nature of the individual and human personality and development as revealed in the process of therapy. In his 1951 book he presented a theory of personality and its change, which he developed further, and more systematically, in a 1959 publication, which is the source from which the following summary is drawn.[2]

CONCEPTS AND THEORY

Certain basic convictions and attitudes underlie the theoretical formulation:[3] (1) Research and theory are directed toward the satisfaction of the need to order significant experience. (2) Science is acute observation and careful and creative thinking on the basis of such observation, not simply laboratory research involving instruments and computing machines. (3) Science begins with gross observations, crude measurements, and speculative hypotheses, and progresses toward more refined hypotheses and measurements. (4) The language of independent, intervening, and dependent variables, while applicable to advanced stages of scientific endeavor, is not adapted to the beginning and developing stages. (5) In the early stages of investigation and theory construction, inductive rather than hypotheticodeductive methods are more appropriate. (6) Every theory has a greater or lesser degree of error; a theory only approaches the truth, and it requires constant change and modification. (7) Truth is unitary, so that "any theory, derived from almost any segment of experience, if it were complete and completely accurate, could be extended indefinitely to provide meaning for other very remote areas of experience."[4] However, even a slight error in a theory may lead to completely false inferences when the theory is projected to a remote area. (8) Although there may be such a thing as objective truth, individuals live in their own personal and subjective worlds. "Thus there is no such thing as Scientific Knowledge, there are only individual perceptions of what appears to each person to be such knowledge."[5]

These attitudes, convictions, or assumptions may be taken as representing the approach of humanistic (and phenomenological) psychology. They underlie the theoretical statements which follow. Humanistic psychology focuses upon the experiencing person and his distinctively human qualities—choice, creativity, valuation, dignity and worth, and the development of his potentials. Phenomenological psychology studies behavior from the point of view or frame of reference of the behaving person. Both thus emphasize the individual person, rather than group averages or characteristics. Both derive from an existential-phenomenological philosophy of human beings and their worlds.

Human Nature and the Individual

The common concept of human beings is that they are by nature irrational, unsocialized, and destructive of themselves and others. The client-centered point of view sees people, on the contrary, as basically rational, socialized, forward-moving, and realistic.[6] This is a point of view developing out of experience in therapy rather than preceding it. Antisocial emotions exist—jealousy, hostility, and the rest—and are evident in therapy. But these are not spontaneous impulses which must be controlled. Rather they are reactions to the frustration of more basic impulses for love, belonging, and security. People are basically cooperative, constructive, and trustworthy, and when they are free from defensiveness their reactions are positive, forward-moving, and constructive. There is then no need to be concerned about controlling people's aggressive, antisocial impulses; given the possibility of fulfilling their basic impulses, they will become self-regulatory, balancing their needs against each other. A person's need for affection and companionship, for example, will balance any aggressive reaction or extreme need for sex, or other needs that would interfere with the satisfactions of other persons. Human beings are thus basically good, though with potential for aggressive or antisocial behavior, which is provoked by threat to or frustration of basic needs.

Individuals possess the capacity to experience in awareness the factors in their psychological maladjustment and have the capacity and the tendency to move away from a state of maladjustment toward a state of psychological adjustment. These capacities and this tendency will be released in a relationship which has the characteristics of a therapeutic relationship. The tendency toward adjustment is the tendency toward self-actualization. Psychotherapy is thus the releasing of an already existing capacity in the individual. Philosophically, the individual "has the capacity to guide, regulate, and control himself, providing only that certain definable conditions exist. Only in the absence of these conditions, and not in any basic sense, is it necessary to provide external control and regulation of the individual."[7] When the individual is provided with reasonable conditions for growth, his or her potentials will develop constructively, as a seed grows and becomes its potential.

Definitions of Constructs

The theory of therapy and personality makes use of a number of concepts or constructs. These are briefly defined prior to their use in the theory:[8]

> *Actualizing Tendency:* "The inherent tendency of the organism to develop all its capacities in ways which serve to maintain or enhance the organism."
>
> *Tendency Toward Self-Actualization:* The expression of the general tendency toward actualization in "that portion of experience of the organism which is symbolized in the self."
>
> *Experience* (noun): All that is going on in the organism at a given time, whether in awareness or potentially available to awareness, of a psychological nature; the "experiential field," or the "phenomenal field" of Combs and Snygg.[9]
>
> *Experience* (verb): To receive in the organism the impact of sensory or physiological events which are happening at the moment.
>
> *Feeling, Experience of a Feeling:* "An emotionally tinged experience, together with its personal meaning."
>
> *Awareness, Symbolization, Consciousness:* The representation of some portion of experience.
>
> *Availability to Awareness:* Capability of being symbolized freely, without denial or distortion.
>
> *Accurate Symbolization:* The potential correspondence of symbolization in awareness with the results of testing the transitional hypothesis which it represents.
>
> *Perceiving, Perception:* "A hypothesis or prognosis for action which comes into awareness when stimuli impinge on the organism." *Perception* and *awareness* are synonymous, the former emphasizing the stimulus in the process. Perceiving is becoming aware of stimuli.
>
> *Subceive, Subception:* "Discrimination without awareness."
>
> *Self-Experience:* "Any event or entity in the phenomenal field dis-

criminated by the individual as 'self,' 'me,' 'I,' or related thereto."

Self, Concept of Self, Self-Structure: "The organized consistent conceptual gestalt composed of perceptions of the characteristics of the 'I' or 'me' and the perceptions of the relationships of the 'I' or 'me' to others and the various aspects of life, together with the values attached to these perceptions."

Ideal Self: "The self-concept which the individual would most like to possess."

Incongruence Between Self and Experience: A discrepancy between the perceived self and actual experience, accompanied by tension and internal confusion and discordant or incomprehensible (for example, neurotic) behavior. The discrepancy arises from conflict between the actualizing and self-actualizing tendencies.

Vulnerability: "The state of incongruence between self and experience," with emphasis on "the potentialities of this state for creating psychological disorganization."

Anxiety: "Phenomenologically, a state of uneasiness or tension whose cause is unknown. From an external frame of reference, anxiety is a state in which the incongruence between the concept of the self and the total experience of the individual is approaching symbolization in awareness."

Threat: "The state which exists when an experience is perceived or anticipated (subceived) as incongruent with the structure of the self"; an external view of what is, phenomenologically, anxiety.

Psychological Adjustment: Complete congruence, complete openness to experience.

Psychological Maladjustment: The state which exists when the organism denies or distorts awareness of significant experience, resulting in incongruence between self and experience; incongruence viewed from a social standpoint.

Defense, Defensiveness: "The behavioral response of the organism to threat, the goal of which is the maintenance of the current structure of the self."

Distortion in Awareness, Denial to Awareness: Denial or distortion of experience which is inconsistent with the self-concept, by which the goal of defense is achieved; the mechanisms of defense.

Intensionality: The characteristics of the behavior of the individual who is in a defensive state—rigidity, overgeneralization, abstraction from reality, absolute and unconditional evaluation of experience, and so on.

Extensionality: Perception which is differentiated, dominated by facts rather than concepts, with awareness of the space-time anchorage of facts and of different levels of abstraction.

Congruence, Congruence of Self and Experience: The state in which self-experiences are accurately symbolized in the self-concept: integrated, whole, genuine.

Openness to Experience: Absence of threat; the opposite of defensiveness.

Mature, Maturity: An individual is *mature* "when he perceives realistically and in an extensional manner, is not defensive, accepts the responsibility of being different from others, accepts the responsibility for his own behavior, evaluates experience in terms of the evidence coming from his own senses, changes his evaluation of experience only on the basis of new experience, accepts others as unique individuals different from himeslf, prizes himself, and prizes others." *Maturity* is the behavior exhibited by an individual who is congruent.

Contact: The minimal essential of a relationship, in which each of two individuals "makes a perceived or subceived difference in the experiential field of the other."

Positive Regard: One's perception of some self-experience of another which makes a positive difference in one's experiential field, resulting in a feeling of warmth, liking, respect, sympathy, acceptance toward the other.

Need for Positive Regard: A secondary or learned need for love, affection, and so on.

Unconditional Positive Regard: Perception of the self-experiences of another with discrimination as to greater or lesser worthiness; prizing, acceptance.

Regard Complex: "All those self-experiences, together with their interrelationships, which the individual discriminates as being related to the positive regard of a particular social other."

Positive Self-Regard: "A positive attitude toward the self which is no longer directly dependent on the attitude of others."

Need for Self-Regard: A secondary or learned need for positive self-regard.

Unconditional Self-Regard: Perception of the self "in such a way that no self-experience can be discriminated as more or less worthy of positive regard than any other."

Conditions of Worth: The valuing of an experience by an individual positively or negatively "solely because of . . . conditions of worth which he has taken over from others, not because the experience enhances or fails to enhance his organism."

Locus of Evaluation: The source of evidence as to values, either internal or external.

Organismic Valuing Process: "An ongoing process in which values are never fixed or rigid, but experiences are being accurately symbolized and continually and freshly valued in terms of the satisfactions organismically experienced." The actualizing tendency is the criterion.

Internal Frame of Reference: "All of the realm of experience which is available to the awareness of the individual at a given moment"; the subjective world of the individual.

Empathy: The state of perceiving "the internal frame of reference of another with accuracy, and with the emotional components and meanings which pertain thereto, as if one were the other person, but without ever losing the 'as if' condition."

External Frame of Reference: Perceiving "solely from one's own subjective frame of reference without empathizing with the observed person or object."

A Theory of Personality[10]

Characteristics of the human infant. Infants perceive their own experience as reality; for them, their own experience is reality. They are endowed with an inherent tendency toward actualizing their organisms. Their behavior is goal directed, directed toward satisfying the need for actualization through interaction with their perceived reality. In such an interaction an infant behaves as an organized whole. Experiences are valued positively or negatively, in an organismic valuing process, in terms of their maintaining or not maintaining the infant's actualizing tendency. The infant is adient toward (approaches) positively valued experiences, and abient toward (avoids) those which are negatively valued.

The development of the self. As a result of the tendency toward differentiation (which is an aspect of the actualizing tendency), part of the individual's experience becomes symbolized in awareness as self-experience. Through interaction with significant others in the environment, this self-experience leads to a concept of self, a perceptual object in the experiential field.

The need for positive regard. With awareness of the self, the need for positive regard from others develops. The satisfaction of this need is dependent on inferences regarding the experiential fields of others. Satisfaction of this need is reciprocal in human beings, in that one's positive regard is satisfied when one perceives oneself as satisfying another's need. The positive regard of a significant social other can be more powerful than the individual's organismic valuing process.

The development of the need for self-regard. A need for self-regard develops from the association of satisfaction or frustration of the need for positive regard with self-experiences. The experience of or loss of positive regard thus becomes independent of transactions with any social other.

Development of conditions of worth. Self-regard becomes selective as significant others discriminate the self-experiences of the individual as more or less worthy of positive regard. The evaluation of a self-experience as more or less worthy of self-regard constitutes a condition of worth. The experiencing of only unconditional positive regard would avoid the development of conditions of worth and lead to unconditional self-regard, to congruence of the needs for positive regard and self-regard with organismic evaluation, and to the maintenance of psychological adjustment.

The development of incongruence between self and experience. The need for self-regard leads to selective perception of experiences in terms of conditions of worth, so that experiences in accord with one's conditions of worth are perceived and symbolized accurately in awareness, but experiences contrary to the conditions of worth are perceived selectively or distortedly, or denied to awareness. This presence of self-experiences which are not organized into the self-structure in accurately symbolized form results in the existence of some degree of incongruence between self and experience, in vulnerability, and in psychological maladjustment.

The development of discrepancies in behavior. Incongruence between self and experience leads to incongruence in behavior, so that some behaviors are consistent with the self-concept and are accurately symbolized in awareness, while other behaviors actualize those experiences of the organism which are not assimilated into the self-structure and have thus not been recognized, or have been distorted to make them congruent with the self.

The experience of threat and process of defense. An experience which is incongruent with the self-concept is subceived as threatening. If this experience were accurately symbolized in awareness it would introduce inconsistency in the self-structure and a state of anxiety would exist. The process of defense prevents this, keeping the total perception of the experience consistent with the self-structure and the conditions of worth. The consequences of defense are rigidity in perception, an inaccurate perception of reality, and intensionality.

The process of breakdown and disorganization. In a situation where a significant experience demonstrates the presence of a large or significant incongruence between self and experience, the process of defense is unable to operate successfully. Anxiety is then experienced, to a degree depending on the extent of the self-structure which is threatened. The experience becomes accurately symbolized in awareness, and a state of disorganization results. The organism behaves at times in ways consistent with the experiences which have been distorted or denied and at times in ways consistent with the concept of the self, with its distorted or denied experiences.

The process of reintegration. For an increase in congruence to occur, there must be a decrease in conditions of worth, and an increase in unconditional self-regard. The communicated unconditional positive regard of a significant other is one way of meeting these conditions. In order to be communicated, unconditional positive regard must exist in a context of empathic understanding. When this is perceived by the individual, it leads to the weakening or dissolving of existing conditions of worth. The individual's own unconditional positive regard is then increased, while threat is reduced and congruence develops. The individual is then less susceptible to perceiving threat, less defensive, more congruent, has increased self-regard and positive regard for others, and is more psychologically adjusted. The organismic valuing process becomes increasingly the basis of regulating behavior, and the individual becomes more nearly fully functioning. The occurrence of these conditions and their results constitute psychotherapy.

A Theory of Interpersonal Relationships[11]

The conditions of a deteriorating relationship. "A person Y is willing to be in contact with person X, and to receive communications from him. Person X desires (at least to a minimal degree) to communicate to and be in contact with Y. Marked incongruence exists in X among the following three elements: his experience of the subject of communication with Y; the symbolization of this experience in his awareness, in its relation to his self-concept; [and] his conscious communicated expression (verbal and/or motor) of this experience."

The process of a deteriorating relationship. Under the above conditions, the following process occurs: "The communication of X to Y is contradictory and/or ambiguous, containing expressive behaviors which are consistent with X's awareness of the experience to be communicated [and] expressive behaviors which are consistent with those aspects of the experience not accurately symbolized in X's awareness. Y experiences these contradictions and ambiguities. He tends to be aware only of X's conscious communication. Hence this experience of X's communication tends to be incongruent with his awareness of same [and] . . . his response tends also to be contradictory and/or ambiguous. . . . Since X is vulnerable, he tends to perceive Y's responses as potentially threatening." Thus he tends to perceive Y's response in a distorted way, congruent to his own self-structure. He also perceives Y's internal frame of reference inaccurately and thus is not empathic. As a result, he cannot and does not experience unconditional positive regard for Y. Y thus experiences the receipt of at most a selective positive regard, and a lack of understanding and empathy. He is thus less free to express his feelings, to be extensional, to express incongruencies between self and experience, and to reorganize his self-concept. As a result, X is, in turn, even less likely to empathize, and more likely to make defensive reactions. "Those aspects of experience which are not accurately symbolized by X in his awareness tend, by

defensive distortion of perception, to be perceived in Y." Y then tends
to be threatened, and to show defensive behaviors.

The outcome of a deteriorating relationship.   The process of deteriora-
tion leads to increased defensiveness on the parts of X and Y. Communication becomes increasingly superficial. Perceptions of self and
others become organized more tightly. Thus, the incongruence of self
and experience remains in status quo, or is increased. Psychological
maladjustment is to some degree facilitated in both X and Y.

The conditions of an improving relationship.   "A person, Y', is willing
to be in contact with person X', and to receive communication from
him. Person X' desires to communicate to and be in contact with Y'. A
high degree of congruence exists in X' between the three following
elements: (a) his experience of the subject of communication with Y';
(b) the symbolization of this experience in awareness in its relation
to his self-concept; [and] (c) his communicative expression of this experience."

The process of an improving relationship.   "The communication of X'
to Y' is characterized by congruence of experience, awareness, and
communication. Y' experiences this congruence as a clear communication. Hence his response is more likely to express a congruence of his
own experience and awareness." Y', being congruent and not vulnerable, is able to perceive the response of Y' accurately and extensionally,
with empathy. Y' feels understood and experiences satisfaction of his
need for positive regard. "X' experiences himself as having made a
positive difference in the experiential field of Y'." X' reciprocally tends
to increase in feeling of positive regard for Y', and this positive regard
for Y' tends to be unconditional. The relationship Y' experiences has
the characteristics of the process of therapy. "Hence communication in
both directions becomes increasingly congruent, is increasingly accurately perceived, and contains more reciprocal positive regard."

Outcomes of an improving relationship.   As a result of an improving
relationship, all the outcomes of therapy may occur, within the limitations of the area of the relationship.

A tentative law of interpersonal relationship.   "Assuming a minimum
mutual willingness to be in contact and to receive communication, we
may say that the greater the communicated congruence of experience,
awareness, and behavior on the part of the individual, the more the
ensuing relationship will involve a tendency toward reciprocal communication with the same qualities, mutually accurate understanding

of the communications, improved psychological adjustment and functioning in both parties, and mutual satisfaction in the relationship."[12]

The concept of congruence is important. Congruence is the accurate matching of physiological experiencing with awareness, and the matching of these with what is communicated. When congruence is lacking, there is ambiguity in communication—words don't match nonverbal communication. When there is incongruence between experiencing and awareness, the incongruent individual does not recognize this. For example, a man may be unaware that his bodily actions and tone of voice communicate anger, while in words he is claiming to be cool, rational, and logical in an argument. An incongruence between awareness and communication may also be deliberate, however, when a person is deceitful and insincere. When a person is congruent, we know where he or she stands; but we don't know what an incongruent person really means or feels, and we have difficulty relating to or interacting with him or her. When two persons who are congruent interact, they are able to listen to each other without defensiveness, to understand each other empathically, to develop respect for each other, in short, to be therapeutic for each other. Each will benefit in improved psychological adjustment, becoming more unified and integrated, less in conflict, more mature, and more satisfied in the relationship. In the case of each person, the receiver of the communication must perceive the communication of the other as it is, or is intended, without distortion or misunderstanding. To the extent that each is congruent and to the extent that each does not feel threatened, this is more likely to occur.

A Theory of the Fully Functioning Person
The endpoint of optimal psychotherapy or of facilitative interpersonal relationships, the state of maximal psychological growth, is the fully functioning person. There are three characteristics, or aspects, of such a person, though they integrate in a unitary organization or whole:

1. *Openness to Experience*. Having positive regard from others, and positive self-regard, the fully functioning person is free from threat, and thus free from defensiveness. The person is open to all his or her experiences, and stimuli are received and processed through the nervous system without selectivity or distortion. Though there is not necessarily a self-conscious awareness of organismic experiences, there is availability to awareness, there are no barriers or inhibitions to prevent the full experiencing of whatever is organismically present.
2. *An Existential Mode of Living*. Openness to experience means that there is a newness to each moment of living, since the same situation of inner and outer stimuli has never existed before. There is a fluidity of experiencing in which the self and personality emerge

from experience; since each experience is new, the person cannot predict specifically what he or she will do in advance. There is a participation in experience without complete control of it. Living is characterized by flexibility and adaptability, rather than rigidity. The personality and the self are in flux; openness to experience is the most stable personality characteristic.

3. *The Organism as a Trustworthy Guide to Satisfying Behavior*. The fully functioning person does what "feels right" and finds this to result in adequate or satisfying behavior. This is so since, being open to all experience, she or he has all relevant data available, without denial or distortion of any elements. These data include social demands as well as the person's own complex system of needs. The total organism, including the person's consciousness, processes these data like a complex computer. The total organism is often wiser than consciousness alone. The organism is not infallible, since data may be missing or unavailable. But the resulting unsatisfying behavior provides corrective feedback.

The fully functioning person is characterized by optimal psychological adjustment, optimal psychological maturity, complete congruence, complete openness to experience, and complete extensionality. To help a person become fully functioning is the goal of optimal psychotherapy.

These characteristics of the fully functioning person have relevance to values and the valuing process. The locus of evaluation in the organismic valuing process is internal, within the individual. This is characteristic of the infant's approach to valuing, but in the process of socialization the locus of evaluation usually becomes externalized as the individual seeks love, acceptance, and social approval from significant others in his or her environment. Value patterns are thus introjected, rather than being the result of the person's own organismic valuing processes or experiencing. They are rigid, and though they often include contradictory values, they are rarely examined. They are often at variance with experiences, and this discrepancy, Rogers believes, is the basis of insecurity and alienation within the individual. In a therapeutic climate, in life or in therapy, some individuals achieve the openness to their experiences and the maturity which return the locus of evaluation to themselves. Although their valuing process is like that in the infant, it is more complex, involving all the individual's past experiences, including the effects or consequences of resulting behaviors on the self and others. The criterion of the valuing process, as in the infant, is the degree to which behaviors lead to self-enhancement or self-actualization.

The value directions which develop in persons as they become more fully functioning are not idiosyncratic or unique but have a commonality which extends through different cultures, suggesting that they are related to the human species, enhancing the development of the individual and others, and contributing to the survival and evolution of the species. These directions include, according to Rogers, being real rather than presenting a facade, valuing one's self and self-direction, valuing being a process rather than having fixed goals, valuing sensitivity to and acceptance of others, valuing deep relationships with others, and finally, and perhaps most important, valuing an openness to all one's inner and outer experiences, including the reactions and feelings of others. In other words, the older values of sincerity, independence, and self-direction, self-knowledge, social responsivity, social responsibility, and loving interpersonal relationships appear to have a universality arising out of the nature of human beings as they become, under conditions which have been found to be effective in psychotherapy, fully functioning persons. The characteristics of the fully functioning or self-actualizing person include the conditions for the development of such persons.

There are several implications of this concept which are of interest:

1. *The fully functioning person is a creative person.* Such a person could be, notes Rogers, one of Maslow's "self-actualizing people," one of whose characteristics is creativeness.[13] His or her sensitive openness and existential living would foster creativeness through allowing awareness of relationships not observed by others. He or she is not a conformist, and perhaps not always "adjusted" to the culture, but is able to live constructively and satisfy basic needs. "Such a person would, I believe, be recognized by the student of evolution as the type most likely to adapt and survive under changing environmental conditions. He would be able creatively to make sound adjustments to new as well as old conditions. He would be a fit vanguard of human evolution."[14]

2. *The fully functioning person is constructive and trustworthy.* The basic nature of individuals is good, individually and socially, when they are functioning freely. When we are able to free individuals from defensiveness, so that they are open to the wide range of their own needs, as well as the range of environmental and social demands, their reactions may be trusted to be positive, forward-moving, constructive. We do not need to ask who will socialize them, for one of each person's deepest needs is affiliation with and communication with others. When people are fully themselves, they cannot help but be realistically socialized. We do not need to ask who will control the individual's aggressive impulses, for when one is open to all of one's impulses, the need to be liked by others and the tendency to give affection are as strong as impulses to strike out and seize for oneself. The individual will be aggressive in situations in which aggression is realistically appropriate, but there will be no runaway need for aggression. When a person is open to all his or her experience, his or

her total behavior, in these and other areas, is balanced and realistic behavior appropriate to the survival and enhancement of a highly social animal.[15]

3. *His or her behavior is dependable but not predictable.* Since the particular pattern of inner and outer stimuli at each moment is unique, fully functioning people are not able to predict their behavior in a new situation, but they appear dependable to themselves, and are confident that their behavior is appropriate. Upon later analysis by another person, a scientist, for example, the fully functioning person's behavior will appear lawful; the scientist can postdict but not predict it. Science cannot collect and analyze all the necessary data, even with a computer, before the behavior has occurred. This suggests that the science of psychology, when it deals with the fully functioning person, will be characterized by understanding (of the lawfulness of behavior which has occurred) rather than by prediction and control.

4. *The fully functioning person is free, not determined.* Science has shown that we live in a world where cause and effect operate. Behavior can be controlled by external or environmental conditions and events. Yet the individual can be free to choose how to act. Rogers reports his experiences with clients in therapy who in the process have made decisions and choices which have changed their behaviors and their lives. He says: "I would be at a loss to explain the positive change which can occur in psychotherapy if I had to omit the importance of the sense of free and responsible choice on the part of my clients. I believe that this experience of freedom to choose is one of the deepest elements underlying change."[16]

This freedom is an inner freedom, an attitude or realization of one's ability to think one's own thoughts, live one's own life, choosing what one wants to be and being responsible for one's self. It is something that is phenomenological rather than external. It is not a contradiction to the cause and effect apparent in the psychological universe, but a complement to such a universe. "Freedom rightly understood is a fulfillment by the person of the ordered sequence of his life. The free man moves out voluntarily, freely, responsibly, to play his significant part in a world whose determined events move through him and through his spontaneous choice and will."[17] It exists in a different dimension than external cause and effect.

Individuals differ in the extent to which they are free from influence and control by others and external events. Rogers cites the findings of several studies in which subjects who yielded or conformed or were susceptible to control in psychological experiments differed from those who did not conform. They panicked under stress, showed feelings of inadequacy and personal inferiority, were lacking in openness and freedom in emotional processes and in spontaneity, and were emotionally restricted and inhibited. The nonconformists, on the other hand, were able to cope effectively with stress, were more self-contained and autonomous in their thinking, had a sense of competence and personal adequacy, and were more open, free, and spontaneous. Thus the sense of personal freedom and responsibility make a difference in behavior.

Rogers points out the parallel between the characteristics of these subjects and of those individuals who experience freedom and responsibility as they progress in therapy, and the fully functioning person:

> He wills or chooses to follow the course of action which is the most economical vector in relation to all the internal and external stimuli, because it is that behavior which will be most deeply satisfying. But this is the same course of action which from another vantage point may be said to be determined by all the factors in the existential situation. Let us contrast this with the picture of the person who is defensively organized. He wills or chooses to follow a given course of action, but finds that he *cannot* behave in the fashion that he chooses. He is determined by the factors in the existential situation, but these factors include his defensiveness, his denial or distortion of some of the relevant data. Hence it is certain that his behavior will be less than fully satisfying. His behavior is determined, but he is not free to make an effective choice. The fully functioning person, on the other hand, not only experiences, but utilizes, the most absolute freedom when he spontaneously, freely, and voluntarily chooses and wills that which is absolutely determined.[18]

The ideal fully functioning person does not exist. There are persons who can be observed moving toward this goal in therapy, and in the best family and group relationships, and in good educational experiences.

Summary
Scientific research and theory are attempts of man to order his experiences. Science begins as empirical observations, leading to inductive speculations and hypotheses and theory construction. Theory approaches truth, but we can never know objective truth; we live in our own personal worlds, the worlds that we subjectively perceive. One's experience of one's world is one's reality.

The infant thus creates its own reality, its own world, on the basis of its experiences with the physical and personal elements with which it interacts. Its behavior is directed by one basic motive: to actualize the capacities or potentials of the organism. Certain experiences are recognized as self-experiences and are organized into a self-concept.

With awareness of the self the need for positive evaluation or regard of the self from others, and of positive self-regard develop. But the regard of others is not unconditional and thus creates conditions of worth—the individual is more or less worthy of positive regard from others, and thus of positive self-regard. The need for positive self-regard, however, leads to selective perception of experiences, with those experiences which are inconsistent with positive self-regard being denied to awareness or distorted. There is then incongruity between self and experience, or psychological maladjustment.

Experiences which are inconsistent with the self-structure are threatening and lead to defensiveness to avoid anxiety. Rigidity develops. Where the inconsistent experience is strong, defense is unsuccessful, anxiety develops, and disorganized or inconsistent behavior occurs.

Reorganization or reintegration occurs when there is a decrease in conditions of worth, with an increase in unconditional positive regard from others in an empathic atmosphere. Positive self-regard increases, with congruence between the self and experience. The individual is more congruent, less defensive, and more open to his experiences, showing more positive regard for others. He is psychologically better adujsted, a more fully functioning person.

It is apparent that one's adjustment is a function of the nature of one's interpersonal relationships. In poor interpersonal relationships there is inconsistent or incongruent communication; lack of understanding—a failure to perceive another's internal frame of reference accurately; the feeling of threat, and lack of unconditional positive regard. In good interpersonal relationships, on the other hand, there is clear or congruent communication, lack of threat, empathy, and unconditional positive regard. These become reciprocal in each participant.

Human beings are characterized by a tendency to move from a state of maladjustment toward psychological adjustment. This is a manifestation of the tendency toward self-actualization. Good interpersonal relationships facilitate this tendency. The person who is free from external threat grows and develops. Although the capacity for negative, irrational, aggressive behavior exists in people, such behavior is manifested under conditions of threat and frustration. When people are free from threat and experience congruence, unconditional positive regard, and empathic understanding from others, they are basically rational, constructive, and social. Such people are fully functioning, open to all their experiences, living existentially, and trusting their organism as a guide to satisfactory behavior. They are creative, constructive and trustworthy, dependable though not predictable in advance, and free rather than determined in their behavior. Their locus of evaluation is internal; their values are those which enhance the actualizations of the organism and the self. These values are not self-centered or antagonistic to others; they are related to the needs of the human species and its survival, and are common or universal among cultures. They include the traditional values of sincerity or honesty, autonomy, responsibility, and love.

FREEDOM TO LEARN

In *Freedom to Learn,* Rogers brought his thinking and experience about education and teaching together in a book directed toward educators and teachers. This book, like a number of earlier papers, is based on his experience and research in psychotherapy. As his work in psychotherapy has focused upon the person and attitudes of the therapist rather than upon techniques, so does his writing on education and teaching focus upon the person and attitudes of the teacher rather than upon methods or techniques of instruction. He expresses this focus in his statement of the aim of education as the facilitation of learning:

> We know that the facilitation of such learning rests not upon the teaching skills of the leader, not upon his curricular planning, not upon his use of audiovisual aids, not upon the programmed learning he utilizes, not upon his lectures and presentations, not upon an abundance of books, though each of these might at one time or another be utilized as an important resource. No, the facilitation of significant learning rests upon certain attitudinal qualities which exist in the personal relationship between the facilitator and the learner.[19]

The Crisis in Education

Education, says Rogers, is facing challenges the response to which "will be one of the major factors in determining whether mankind moves forward, or whether man destroys himself on this planet, leaving this earth to those few living things which can withstand atomic destruction and radioactivity."[20] The crisis is represented by a number of questions which he poses:

1. Can education free itself from the past and past goals and prepare individuals and groups to live in a world of accelerating change, if it is possible for human beings to do so?
2. Can education deal effectively with increasing racial tensions and prevent civil war among the world's races?
3. Can education prepare us to deal responsibly and communicatively with increasing irrational nationalism and international tension, and help us prevent nuclear destruction?
4. Can educators and educational institutions satisfy the revolt and objections of youth against the imposed curriculums and impersonality of secondary and higher education, or will learning move out of our institutions of learning, leaving them to indoctrinate conformity?
5. Can the conservative, traditional, bureaucratic, rigid educational

system break out of the shackles of pressures for social conformity and deal with the real problems of modern life?

6. Will education be taken over by business, with more innovation and responsiveness, but with the motive of profit-making and emphasis upon producing profitable "hardware"?

These are not issues of technology; they are philosophical, social, and psychological issues. And they clearly relate not to the traditional subject matter of education, that is, information and knowledge, or even cognitive or intellectual development, but to the area of personal development and interpersonal relationships.

The Goal of Education

To resolve these crisis questions and to assure human survival, the goal of education must be the facilitation of change and learning. "The only man who is educated is the man who has learned how to learn; the man who has learned how to adapt and change; the man who has realized that no knowledge is secure, that only the process of *seeking* knowledge gives a basis for security. Changingness, a reliance on *process* rather than upon static knowledge, is the only thing that makes any sense as a goal for education in the modern world."[21]

This goal includes, but goes beyond, cognitive or intellectual education, to include the education of the whole person. It involves personal growth and the development of creativity and self-directed learning. The goal of education is the same as the goal of psychotherapy: the fully functioning person. Openness to experience; an existential way of living in which life is not static but an ongoing, flexible, adaptive process; and trust in the organism as the basis for behavior are characteristics of the person who is capable of continuing to learn and to adapt to change, to meet the issues involved in the crisis in education. The traditional concept of the "educated person" is no longer relevant to our modern society.

The educator of the future "must know, at the deepest personal level, the stance he takes in regard to life. Unless he has true convictions as to how his values are arrived at, what sort of individual he hopes will emerge from his educational organization, whether he is manipulating human robots, or dealing with free individual persons, and what kind of a relationship he is striving to build with these persons, he will have failed not only his profession, but his culture."[22] This is a far cry from, but more fundamental and important than, concern with curriculums, methods, administration, and teaching techniques.

Two Kinds of Learning

Learning may be conceived of as falling along a continuum of meaning. At one end is meaningless learning—rote learning, exemplified by the

learning, or memorization, of nonsense syllables. Such learning is difficult and does not last. Much of what is taught in schools involves such
learning. The material has no personal meaning for the student, does
not involve feelings or the whole person; it is learning occurring "from
the neck up."

The learning which takes place in everyday life, experiential
learning, has meaning and personal relevance. Such learning is quick
and is retained. Learning a language in a native environment, as
compared to learning it in a classroom, illustrates the difference.
Even though the stimulus for learning in the first case may come from
outside, from the necessity to adapt to the society, it is in a real sense
self-initiated. It also represents a personal involvement. It is pervasive,
influencing the total person, including attitudes and behavior. It is
evaluated by the learner in terms of his or her needs—the locus of
evaluation is internal. And its essence is meaning.

Education traditionally has involved the first, meaningless kind of
learning, though many teachers and educators recognize the value of
the second. To implement the second approach would amount to a
revolution in education. The difficulties of implementing it in a practical way have stood in the way of those who accept it theoretically.
Rogers proposes ways in which it can be implemented.

This second kind of learning is not noncognitive in nature. It involves cognitive elements or aspects; but it combines these with the
affective elements involved in personal meaning. It recognizes that
meaningful learning, even of a cognitive nature, involves the total
person.

The Nature of Significant Learning

Significant—personal, experiential—learning is learning which makes a
difference to the person, in behavior, attitudes, and personality. It is
learning which leads to the individual becoming a more fully functioning person. Such learning involves certain principles (or hypotheses)
which relate to the theory of human nature and of human behavior
presented earlier.

1. Human beings have a natural propensity for learning. They are by
   nature curious; exploratory; desirous of discovering, knowing, and
   experiencing. Yet there is an ambivalence toward learning; significant learning involves some pain, either connected with the learning itself or with having to relinquish earlier learnings. Learning to
   walk involves bumps and bruises. Learning that some others are
   better than oneself in some respects is painful. But the gains and
   satisfactions of learning, of developing one's potentials, are usually
   greater than the pain, and learning continues.
2. Significant learning takes place when the subject matter is perceived by the student as having relevance for her or his own pur-

poses. A person learns significantly only those things which are perceived as involving the maintenance and enhancement of the self. Two students of equal ability learn quite different things, or amounts, depending on how they perceive the material as relating to their needs and purposes. The speed of learning also varies. The time for learning may be reduced by as much as two-thirds to four-fifths when material is perceived as relevant to the learner's purposes.

3. Learning which involves a change in self-organization, or the perception of the self, is threatening, and tends to be resisted. The self includes one's values, beliefs, and basic attitudes, and when these are questioned they are defended. To recognize that something new and different may be better, that one is behind in things or inferior in some way, or inadequate, is defended against.

4. Those learnings which are threatening to the self are more easily perceived and assimilated when external threats are at a minimum. Pressure, ridicule, shaming, and so on, increase resistance. But an accepting, understanding, supportive environment removes or decreases threat and fear and allows the learner to take a few steps or to try something and experience some success. Teaching machines incorporate this idea.

5. When threat to the self or self-concept is low, experience can be perceived in a differentiated fashion, and learning can proceed. This is why learning is inhibited by threat and assisted by its lack. Threat disorganizes thinking: It leads to distortion of perception, restriction of the perceptual field (a kind of tunnel vision), even, in strong threat, to paralysis of thinking and action. Freedom from threat to one's security, or ego, frees one to see the total situation and to examine it—to "take it apart," manipulate it, put it together —and to learn. Threats to the *organism*—even life-or-death threats— can be handled or responded to with all one's powers; but threats to the *self* or the self-concept interfere with learning. Another way to view it is that threat to the self leads to all-out efforts to *maintain* the self as it exists, but not to change or growth in the self.

6. Much significant learning is acquired through doing. Experiential involvement with practical or real problems promotes learning. Meaningfulness and relevance are inherent in such situations.

7. Learning is facilitated when the student participates responsibly in the learning process. When students choose their own objectives and directions, formulate their own problems, discover their own resources, decide on and follow their own courses of action, and experience and live with the consequences, significant learning is maximized. Self-directed learning is meaningful and relevant.

8. Self-initiated learning which involves the whole person of the learner—feelings as well as intellect—is the most lasting and pervasive. The learning is the learner's own, and becomes incorporated in her or him; it is not something external or accepted on authority, and thus vulnerable to questioning or another authority.

9. Independence, creativity, and self-reliance are all facilitated when self-criticism and self-evaluation are basic and evaluation by others is of secondary importance. Creativity needs freedom, freedom to try something unusual, to take a chance, to make mistakes without being evaluated or judged a failure.

10. The most socially useful learning in the modern world is the learning of the process of learning, a continuing openness to experience and incorporation into oneself of the process of change. Change is a central fact of current life, and learning must be continuous.

Significant learning requires that we focus upon something other than the usual concerns of teaching or education. It makes the question of what should be taught, the curriculum, minor. Teaching as the imparting of knowledge is useful in an unchanging environment. But in this modern world, are we justified "in the presumption that we are wise about the future and the young are foolish? Are we *really* sure as to what they should know? Then there is the ridiculous question of coverage . . . based on the assumption that what is taught is learned. . . . I know of no assumption so obviously untrue."[23] In a continually changing world, information and knowledge quickly become out of date or obsolete.

Significant learning involves the whole person; it combines cognitive and affective-experiential elements. It is a unified learning, yet with awareness of the different aspects. It does not separate the mind from the heart, from feelings, as most education attempts to do. Rogers quotes Archibald McLeish in this regard: "We do not feel our knowledge. Nothing could better illustrate the flaw at the heart of our civilization. . . . Knowledge without feeling is not knowledge and can lead only to public irresponsibility and indifference, and conceivably to ruin."[24] Personal meaning, relevance, significance involve feelings, attitudes, and beliefs.

Teaching and Learning

If the only learning which can significantly influence behavior is self-discovered, self-appropriated personal learning, can learning be taught? Rogers, on the basis of his experience both in psychotherapy and in teaching, has raised some serious questions. He states them personally as follows (not all are listed here):

> *It seems to me that anything that can be taught to another is relatively inconsequential and has little or no significant influence on behavior. . . .*
>
> *Self-discovered learning, truth that has been personally appropriated and assimilated in experience, cannot be directly communicated to another. . . .*
>
> When I try to teach, as I do sometimes, I am appalled by the results, which seem a little more than inconsequential, because sometimes the

teaching appears to succeed. When this happens I find that the results are damaging. It seems to cause the individual to distrust his own experience, and to stifle significant learning. *Hence I have come to feel that the outcomes of teaching are either unimportant or hurtful.* . . .

As a consequence, *I realize that I am only interested in being a learner, preferably learning things that matter, that have some significant influence on my own behavior.* . . .

I find that one of the best, but most difficult, ways for me to learn is to drop my own defensiveness, at least temporarily, and to try to understand the way in which his experience seems and feels to the other person.

I find that another way for me to learn is to state my own uncertainties, to try to clarify my own puzzlements, and thus get closer to the meaning that my experience actually seems to have.[25]

Such experience, he concludes, would imply that we do away with teaching. Learning would take place in groups of people who wanted to learn. But can this be done with children? What is the place of the teacher in the learning of children?

The Teacher as the Facilitator
of Learning

Teaching, as usually defined and practiced, involves instruction, imparting information, knowledge, or skill; it is "to make to know," "to show, guide, direct." These are activities of the teacher. But are they necessary for learning, or even related to learning as defined earlier? "Teaching," says Rogers, "is a vastly over-rated function."[26]

The function of the teacher is to facilitate learning in the student by providing the conditions which lead to meaningful or significant self-directed learning. The objective is to develop a group, including the teacher, into a community of learners. In such a community, curiosity is freed, the sense of inquiry is opened up, everything is open to questioning and exploration. "Out of such a context arise true students, real learners, creative scientists and scholars and practitioners, the kind of individuals who can live in a delicate but everchanging balance between what is presently known and the flowing, moving, altering, problems and facts of the future."[27] Such a community facilitates learning, or learning how to learn.

How can we achieve such a community of learners? We now have considerable knowledge about how to do so, about how to stimulate self-initiated, significant learning by the whole person. There are three major conditions, or qualities or attitudes, which, when present in an interpersonal relationship, facilitate such learning. These conditions were first identified and demonstrated to be effective in counseling or psychotherapy; there is now evidence that they apply to classroom learning as well as learning in psychotherapy.

Realness is the facilitator of learning. Learning is facilitated when the teacher is not playing a role prescribed by the educational system but rather is himself or herself, genuine, authentic, honest. Relationships with students are direct personal encounters; the teacher is a real person, with no professional facade. He doesn't feel one thing and say something else; he doesn't conceal his feelings, either positive or negative. But in expressing his feelings he accepts them as his own, without projecting blame for his negative feelings onto the students. If he is irritated, he says "I feel irritated," not "You irritate me." He can be bored as well as enthusiastic. "He can like or dislike a student product without implying that it is objectively good or bad or that the student is good or bad. He is simply expressing a feeling for the product, a feeling which exists within himself. Thus he is a person to his students, not a faceless embodiment of a curricular requirement nor a sterile tube through which knowledge is passed from one generation to the next."[28]

A sixth-grade teacher who changed from the traditional teacher-dominated method to one which gave her students considerable responsible freedom found that she couldn't live with the mess which they made during the art period, though it didn't bother the students. She expressed her feelings: "One day I told the children . . . that I am a neat and orderly person by nature and that the mess was driving me to distraction. Did they have a solution? It was suggested there were some volunteers who could clean up. . . . I said it didn't seem fair to have the same people clean up all the time for others—but it would solve it for me. 'Well, some people like to clean,' they replied. So that's the way it is."[29]

It is not easy to be real in this sense, without evaluating, judging, or blaming others. Note that the teacher above did not say: "You are the messiest children I have ever seen. . . . You are just terrible." They may not have been excessively messy; they may have been excited and absorbed in their art work. It was the teacher who felt they were messy. Being real is not a license to judge and condemn others, to project one's feelings on others, to take out one's own anger and frustrations on one's students. Nor is using the "right" words or verbal formula being genuine if there is a judgmental attitude behind them. "Only slowly can we learn to be truly real. For first of all, one must be close to one's feelings, capable of being aware of them. Then one must be willing to take the risk of sharing them as they are, inside, not disguising them as judgments, or attributing them to other people."[30]

Prizing, acceptance, trust.   If one is not to express judgments and evaluations, one must not be judgmental in one's attitudes. This is related to the second attitude which facilitates learning. The learner is accepted as a person of worth, a unique individual, and is respected; his or her feelings, opinions, and person are prized. The learner is seen as trustworthy. There is a caring for him or her. And all this is unconditional; there is no demand that the learner be different or conform in some way to be accepted and respected. Fears as well as satisfactions, apathy as well as enthusiasm, anger and resistance as well as pleasantness and cooperation, are all accepted as aspects of an imperfect human being.

Underlying this attitude is a trust in the human organism, its capacity for developing its potential, choosing its own directions, given the opportunity. It is a confidence that the direction of change and learning will be toward the fulfillment or actualization of the person's potentialities, toward growth and development.

Empathic understanding.   Empathic understanding is not the usual evaluative understanding based on a diagnostic analysis from an external point of view. It is understanding which comes from putting oneself in the place of the student to understand his or her reactions from the inside, to experience the student's perceptions and feelings about what is happening.

> This attitude of standing in the other's shoes, of viewing the world through the student's eyes, is almost unheard of in the classroom. One could listen to thousands of ordinary classroom interactions without coming across one instance of clearly communicated, sensitively accurate, empathic understanding. But it has tremendous releasing effects when it occurs.[31]

Rogers goes on to suggest that if a teacher were able to make even one nonjudgmental empathic response to a student's expressed feeling each day, he or she would discover the power of such understanding.

The Student's Contribution to Learning

If the teaching-learning process is a relationship or an encounter between a facilitator and a learner, then the learner must be a participant in the process. There are three conditions involving the learner which are necessary for learning to occur.

Perception of the facilitative conditions.   If realness, prizing, and acceptance and empathic understanding are to be effective in facilitating learning, they must be perceived or felt by the student. Students, because of their previous experience, may at first think that the genuineness or realness of the teacher is a new kind of phoniness whose purpose is to manipulate them. But students overcome this disbelief when the teacher is in fact not pretending or trying a new role, and recognize the realness and humanness of the teacher.

Awareness of a problem. Real learning occurs in response to a situation perceived by the student as a problem. Otherwise there is little if any stimulation to learn or to change. This is essentially the problem of relevance. It requires that if real learning is to be facilitated, education must present students with situations they perceive as real, as relevant, meaningful problems and issues regarding their existence which they must resolve.

Motivation. Conceivably, problems can be ignored, avoided, or resisted. But there is a natural motivation for learning in all normal individuals. This motivation is the tendency to fulfillment or toward self-actualization. When faced with a problem, or an obstacle to self-actualization, the natural tendency of the individual is to face it, work on it, and attempt to solve it. Unfortunately, this natural motivation to learn is often suppressed rather than supported in our current educational system.[32] The school and the classroom are highly threatening to many students, and this threat inhibits the natural motivation to learn. The presence of facilitative conditions in the teacher minimizes threat and thus allows the motivation to learn to manifest itself.

> When a facilitator creates, even to a modest degree, a classroom climate characterized by all that he can achieve of realness, prizing, and empathy; when he trusts the constructive tendency of the individual and the group; then he discovers that he has inaugurated an educational revolution. Learning of a different quality, proceeding at a different pace, with a greater degree of pervasiveness, occurs. Feelings—positive, negative, confused—become a part of the classroom experience. Learning becomes life, and a very vital life at that. The student is on his way, sometimes excitedly, sometimes reluctantly, to becoming a learning, changing, being.[33]

Implementing the Conditions[34]

The conditions for facilitating learning are attitudes, not techniques. Teachers may ask, however, just how they are to be real, to manifest their prizing and respect, and to express their empathic understanding. Some suggestions follow:

Being real. Being real does not mean simply venting all one's negative feelings on students nor does it mean uninhibited expression of feelings or behaviors such as directing, bossing, controlling, punishing, and disciplining. There is no place for the impatient, easily irritated, emotionally disturbed teacher in the classroom; nor is an authoritarian personality a facilitative teacher. The attitudes being expressed in being real must be attitudes of respect, warmth, caring, liking, and understanding.

The expression or explosion of pent-up irritations or accumulated negative feelings can be harmful to children. The teacher must be aware of such feelings and deal with them before they reach this stage. A student of the author reports an experience in student teaching in which she learned this:

> Last semester I went through a traumatic and distressing time, in connection with my student teaching. I had been given advice by teachers on how to conduct a good classroom. I was told not to smile too much, to establish my authority at the outset, and never to show my emotions, because the students would then know they could "get my goat." For six weeks I labored to follow this advice, because it came from supposed experts. One day I became so angry at the noise in the classroom that I burst out in an emotional attack on the students, screaming at them for their terrible behavior. The students were startled; they felt that I had been unfair. If I had been more real in this situation I would have been able to tell the students that I got annoyed at the noise much earlier, and we could have worked out some sort of compromise on the noise level. This realness could have avoided my personal attack on them as bad persons. It could also have helped me avoid my tremendous feelings of guilt; for even though my cooperating teacher felt that the students got what they deserved, I knew that I had been most unfair. In the future, when in the teaching situation, I will try my personal best to be real, to express my feelings as they occur in my awareness.

Being real means that teachers do not pretend that they know everything or have all the answers, or are perfect. Again, a student of the writer expresses this nicely:

> If I am real, my students will be able to relate to me as I am—a human being with feelings and ideas, not an authority figure who issues mandates from above. They will realize that I am being my whole "self," and that I can and do make mistakes; furthermore, when I make mistakes, I will be able to admit them. It is only human to make mistakes, but very few teachers are accustomed to letting their students know that they are less than infallible. In my opinion, students would feel more at ease with a teacher who is able to admit errors, and who relinquishes his role of all-knowing authority. The teacher would also become a learner in the eyes of the student if he were able to admit that his ideas are not always absolutely correct.

Genuineness or realness is not a method or technique, something outside oneself, but a manifestation or expression of oneself as a person. A teacher who is real is thus not preoccupied with following a method or technique.

Manifesting prizing, trust, and respect.   Prizing or respecting another is a positive thing; it is not simply a grudging acceptance. It is more than the gushing "I love all children." It is probably not possible for a teacher to like all children, or like them equally well. Prizing or respect does not require that the teacher like or accept all a student's characteristics or behaviors; the teacher prizes the student as a person worthy of respect. And it is also true that when one is really able to understand another, one almost always finds some basis for liking and respecting the other as a person. But if a teacher cannot feel some respect and liking for a student as a human being, then it is better that the child be placed with a teacher who can.

Prizing or respect is manifested in certain behaviors in a teacher:

1. *Listening.* Studies of teaching have found that teachers in the classroom talk on the average about 75 percent of the time. Even when they are not talking, and students are talking, teachers often are not really listening, in the sense that they are really trying to understand and are interested in what the students are saying and why. Usually they are evaluating a student's answer to a question: Is it right or wrong?

   Real listening to another is not evaluative, nor is it selective in terms of whether the other is sticking to the point, being relevant to the question, or logical. It involves attending to everything the other person says, and being interested in the other's thoughts, ideas, and feelings, recognizing them as worthy of being expressed and heard rather than rejecting or putting them down as inadequate, wrong, or poorly thought out or expressed. To facilitate real learning, the student must feel free to express ideas and feelings without being negatively evaluated, criticized, or condemned for having them, even if they are negative. Such listening shows respect and prizing of the student.

2. *Responding.* In responding to a student the teacher communicates that she or he has been attending to what the student has been saying, that the student has been heard and hopefully, to some extent at least, understood. Such responses may be simply "yes," "I see," "I understand," "uh-uh." A simple restatement of what was said also indicates that the teacher has heard accurately. If the teacher does not understand, the response indicates this: "I don't understand," "I'm not sure I follow you," "Can you say that again," "I'm not sure I know what you mean," "Are you saying . . . ?" This can lead to clarification by the student. The student's feelings or thinking may

be confused, and such responses help the student to try to communicate what is being expressed clearly. Ignoring a student who does not give the right answer or who is not clear or not understood happens all too frequently and does not convey respect. The teacher should not pretend to understand when he or she does not.

Understanding empathically. In addition to the manifestation of respect for the student, listening and responding to the student are the basis for empathic understanding and the communication of that understanding. Empathic listening involves putting oneself in the place of the other and trying to see things as the other sees them. If the teacher does this in regard to the student giving a wrong answer to a question, the teacher can often see and understand what leads the student to give such an answer, and is thus able to help the student understand the question. Empathic understanding goes beyond the cognitive aspects of what the student is saying. It also includes the affective or feeling aspects, which must be recognized and responded to if significant learning is to occur.

Facilitative teaching involves a personal relationship which includes mutual genuineness, respect and trust, and understanding. It is at its best a spontaneous personal encounter. It may involve disagreement, conflicts, or controversies which are resolved in a confrontation. Differences may not be resolved, but they are recognized, faced, and accepted. When the facilitative conditions are present the relationship is one which is free from the threat which inhibits exploration and learning.

Methods of Building Freedom

In addition to being concerned about implementing or manifesting the facilitative conditions, teachers will be interested in ways in which they can provide opportunities for self-reliant learning in the classroom. As in the case of implementing the attitudes, these methods of building freedom will be related to the style of the teacher, and many will be personal and in a sense unique. There are a number of approaches or methods, however, which Rogers indicates have been used successfully by teachers:

Building upon problems perceived as real. In education, as in our culture, we seem to attempt to insulate students from real problems in life. But "it appears that if we desire to have students learn to be free and responsible individuals, then we must be willing for them to confront life, to face real problems. . . . Some real confrontation by a problem seems a necessary condition for this type of learning."[35]

Real problems derive from students, and the teacher must be sen-

sitive to and willing to respond to and nourish those problems or issues which relate to the course or subject being taught. Because of the
insulation of students from problems, it may be necessary for the
teacher to confront them with situations which will pose real problems.
Some of the following approaches are designed to do this.

Providing resources. In counseling or psychotherapy the resources
are within the person; the therapist does not supply them. In education
there are many resources which the teacher can provide for students
without forcing them upon the students. The facilitative teacher, instead of spending most of the time organizing lesson plans and lectures, devotes it to discovering, obtaining, and making easily available
the kinds of resources relevant to the needs of students. Resources include not only books, articles, laboratory equipment, tools, maps, films,
recordings, and so on, but also human resources—persons who can contribute knowledge. The teacher, of course, is perhaps the most important resource, but his or her knowledge and experience is not forced
upon students in lectures, but is offered and made available when
students need and want it. "If we spent the same amount of time that
is now spent on planning for prescribed curricula, lectures, and examinations on the imaginative provision of resources for learning, we
would come up with all kinds of new ways of surrounding the student
with a learning environment from which he could choose those elements which best met his needs."[36] Lectures or expositions of subject
matter by the teacher are not, then, a necessary part of education, imposed upon all students, but may be a part of education when desired
by students.

Use of contracts. Student contracts can give security to students as
well as placing responsibility upon them. They provide a transitional
experience between the requirements of a program or educational institution and complete freedom of the student. A student who for whatever reason (lack of interest in a required course, for example) wants
only a passing grade in a course may make a contractual agreement
with the teacher about just what he or she will do—perhaps reading
certain material and taking an examination on it. A student who wants
a higher grade may also propose a course of study, and when this is
agreed upon with the instructor it also becomes a contract. Students
know that if they perform their part they will receive the agreed-upon
grades. Class discussions can become freer—students aren't worried
about the effects on their grades of disagreeing with the instructor.

Division of the class. Freedom should not be imposed on those who
do not want it. Thus, provision should be made for those who desire

the alternative of conventional instruction; students should be free to learn passively as well as to initiate their own learning. Programmed learning provides another alternative.

Self-initiated learning also is perhaps more productive in small groups. Large classes can be divided in various ways, and the smaller groups can function in different ways, with the members assuming various kinds of responsibility.

The conduct of inquiry. The inquiry method of learning is a participative, experiential process. The subject (usually it has been science) is not considered as a set of absolute, already discovered facts. The teacher in inquiry learning poses problems and serves as a resource to the students in their solution of the problems. Students thus function as scientists. Whereas traditional educational methods make children less autonomous, less open, and less empirical as they progress in their education, inquiry methods lead to independent thinking and openness, as well as to new, deeper, and more lasting understandings. The inquiry method can, however, become a technique or routine in a teacher-imposed curriculum.

Simulation as a type of experiential learning. A simulation is a miniature or model representing a real situation—a family, a school, a corporation, a legislature, a nation, a world. A simulation experience requires knowledge of the system and some preparatory training before engaging in it. The experience has built into it certain situations, events, or problems, but the process and outcomes are partly determined by the responses and decisions of the participants. Consequences of responses and decisions are provided, based upon calculations following formulas developed for the simulation.

Simulation can provide students with experience with complex real-life processes involving decisions affected by incomplete or inadequate information, by difficulties in communication, by misunderstandings, and by interpersonal relations. The importance of these factors in decision making becomes impressed upon the student. Students become involved and feel that they learn about real-life situations. Responsibility for the conduct of the simulation is in the hands of the students once the teacher introduces it.

Programmed instruction as experiential learning. Programmed instruction may be used to facilitate self-initiated learning. A student who becomes aware of a gap in information or knowledge necessary for a problem or project in which he or she is engaged, can turn to an appropriate unit of programmed instruction to fill the gap. The need for the information or knowledge is real, and the motivation to acquire it is present. Students can obtain the material on their own, when they need it, at their own rate, efficiently and with a positive experience in learning. Programmed learning cannot be substituted for broader approaches to learning meanings and patterns of thinking, however.

The basic encounter group. An important new approach to experiential learning is the basic encounter group, or "sensitivity training." Although widely used in business and government, the encounter group has not been used extensively in education. There are many kinds of group experiences being advocated and practiced, but the basic encounter group is an unstructured experience in which facilitation helps the group express itself and the members to interact in such a way as to achieve a meaningful, mutually helpful experience. The facilitator does this by providing the conditions for facilitating learning which have been described earlier. Such an experience leads to the members of the group becoming more accepting, respecting, understanding, and genuine.[37]

Evaluation in Meaningful Learning

Significant learning, or personal learning, is difficult if not impossible to measure and evaluate in terms of external criteria. Rogers writes:

> I believe that the testing of the student's achievements in order to see if he meets some criterion held by the teacher, is directly contrary to the implications of therapy for significant learning. In therapy, the examinations are set by *life*. The client meets them, sometimes passing, sometimes failing. He finds that he can use the resources of the therapeutic relationship and his experience in it to organize himself so that he can meet life's tests more satisfyingly next time. I see this as a paradigm for education also.[38]

Means of fulfilling the requirements for many life situations would be among the resources provided by the teacher or counselor in the school. These requirements include prerequisites for courses and requirements for graduation, for college entrance, for certain college curriculums, and for employment in various occupations. Certain scores on objective tests of achievement are required for some of these and other life situations. These requirements are set as tickets of entrance. The students would be free to choose whether they wanted to obtain a given ticket.

Self-initiated learning becomes responsible learning when one evaluates one's own learning. Goals and criteria are established by the individual, who decides to what extent he or she has achieved them. Self-evaluation must thus be a part of experiential learning.

There are various ways to incorporate self-evaluation into learning: mutual discussion between teacher and student, written evaluations and self-grading, demonstration of fulfillment of a contract; self-analysis in comparison with standards or norms or in discussion with other students.

Criteria may vary among students, so equivalent evaluations or grades do not always mean the same thing, which can constitute a problem in a conventional educational program or institution. There are other problems also in such situations, including the influence of competition for grades in a system and society where grades are so important in indicating educational progress.

Implications for Teacher Education

A combination of the cognitive and the affective in education and a focus upon the interpersonal conditions for facilitating significant learning, require changes in the preparation of teachers. Teacher education currently emphasizes subject matter and methods of cognitive learning. A basic question is "Is it possible to develop interpersonal qualities in teacher-education students?" It has been possible to do this in counselor education, so it should be possible in teacher education.

Such a program of preparation would require many capable facilitators of small-group processes. Task-oriented groups of staff members and students should be formed to consider the question "How can this school help the whole person learn?" These groups would not be limited to cognitive discussion, but would focus upon the whole person. The groups would consist of volunteers who were willing to become involved experientially as well as cognitively. They would meet together for three weeks of intensive group experiences, followed by weekly meetings, and a weekend session three months later.

Turbulence would be created among staff members, with innovators and traditionalists opposing each other. But no one would be discharged or punished for dissent. A probable outcome would be a "free university" type of teacher-training institution, "in which the students would form their own curricula, participate in the facilitation of learning, and find other means of evaluation than grades. And what would this student do as a new teacher in his own classroom? Most importantly he would simply *be* the attitudes I have already described, and because of this fact new participatory methods would emerge."[39]

Implications for Administration

The approach to education described above has implications for the administration of a school or educational system. Administration would follow what D. M. McGregor calls Theory Y, rather than what he calls Theory X, or the traditional or conventional view of administration.[40]

In the conventional management pattern, a school administrator . . .
sees his task as that of harnessing the energy of faculty and students so
that the goals and requirements of the educational system will be met.
In the first place he sees himself as responsible for organizing the available money, equipment, and people in such a way as to achieve the
educational goal which he has in view. This means that he must motivate and direct his faculty, and through them the students. It means
that one of his main functions is to control the actions and to modify
the behavior of all members of the school in such a way that the educational goal will be achieved. Central to his policies is the view that both
faculty and students would be, if left to their own devices, apathetic to,
or resistant to, the educational goal. Consequently, they must be rewarded, punished, persuaded—through use of both the carrot and the
stick—so that they work toward the goal which the administrator, or his
board of trutsees, or the state, has defined as "being educated."[41]

The administrator may be "hard" or "soft" (using aversive control or positive reinforcement), but in either case directs, controls,
manages, and manipulates his or her subordinates, who are considered
as apathetic, not willing or able to take responsibility, and needing to
be guided and led.

This approach to administration has been questioned by research
and experience in the behavioral sciences and industry. McGregor's
theory Y exemplifies the newer approach. This approach rests upon the
view of human nature which underlies the approach to education
described above.

In terms of this theory the educational administration is responsible for
organizing the resources of the institution—the teachers, the students,
the funds, the equipment and materials in such a way that all of the
persons involved can work together toward defining and achieving *their
own* educational goals. The mainspring of the organization is the motivation for development and learning which is inherent in each person.
The task of the administrator is to so arrange the organizational conditions and methods of operation that people can best achieve their own
goals by also furthering the jointly defined goals of the institution.[42]

The administration attempts to facilitate the ability of teachers
and students to develop and use their potentials, though removing obstacles (such as red tape) and creating a climate of valuing, prizing,
and trusting. Everyone participates in the organizational process, sharing initiative, responsibility, and authority. In-service training would
be used to develop facilitative leaders—persons who could listen, accept, understand, clarify, and communicate—who could help individuals and groups grow and develop.

A PLAN FOR SELF-DIRECTED
CHANGES IN AN EDUCATIONAL
SYSTEM

The goal of and approach to classroom education developed by Rogers would require not only changes in teachers, administrators, and their preparation, but in the entire educational system, including parents. "A way must be found to develop a climate in the *system* in which the focus is not upon *teaching,* but on the facilitation of self-directed *learning*."[43]

The intensive group experience is such a way. As it can be used to change teacher education, so it can be used to change the educational system. The intensive group or "workshop" provides an unstructured situation in which participants have freedom for expression and exploration of personal feelings and for interpersonal exploration in a safe, nonthreatening atmosphere, promoted by the facilitator. The group experience is conducted intensively for periods of three days to two or three weeks. The objective is to bring about change in the organizational climate and structure in which the members work. Such groups have been successfully used since 1947 with industry and government executives and administrators, with professional groups, and more recently educational groups, including administrators, teachers, and student-teacher groups, student groups, dropouts, predelinquents and delinquents, and others. But few attempts have been made to use the intensive group experience to change a total educational system. Educators who have participated in the group experiences away from the school have returned to the same system, where their new attitudes and open behaviors have not been welcomed.

The first step in implementing a plan for change through the group experience in an educational system would of course be a commitment by the chief administrator and one or two of his or her associates or school board members. Then a group experience could be offered on a voluntary basis to board members and administrators, away from the locality, when school was not in session. Experienced facilitators from outside would be employed. Costs might be subsidized by an outside agency or foundation, though participants would pay part of the cost as evidence of their commitment. Small group experiences would be supplemented by presentations to the total group in general meetings.

Interpersonal feelings and relationships would be explored; the participants would get to know each other as they had never done in years of working together. Concealed negative feelings and antagonisms which had prevented real cooperation and progress would come to the surface and be resolved with increased understanding and acceptance. With trust and openness, ideas, ideals, and proposals would be expressed. The way would be open to plan organizational and system change. The chief administrator would be more open to innovative ideas; more person-oriented and acceptant of others; more democratic and able to utilize the potentials of staff members; more able to communicate clearly and realistically with superiors, peers, subordinates, and the board.

It is likely that the decision would be made to go ahead with planning for change, and to involve others in the system. This could include an intensive group experience for the teachers who wished it. Those who participated would be more open and able to listen to students, more sensitive to and accepting of students' feelings and creative ideas, and able to develop better relationships with them. They would become more humanistic teachers. Innovations developed from the group experience are more likely to be implemented than those coming from outside—they are self-chosen and are likely to be supported by their superiors who have had the group experience.

Students could be involved in a group experience with their teachers—not away from the school, probably, but with trained facilitators. Not all students in a large system could be involved, but those who were would be freer to express their feelings in class, would work with other students and teachers in cooperative ways, would take responsibility for their own learning, and would learn more because they would have greater motivation and more energy to devote to learning.

A school system which goes this far will arouse attention and interest in the community. Parents will want to be involved, and should be. A group experience might be offered to PTA officers and chairmen, or to parents of children involved in a group experience, in the form of a weekend session, 24-hour marathon, or weekly 3-hour evening sessions.

Finally, in addition to the group experiences for peers or near-peers, vertical groups could be attempted. On invitation, two each of school board members, administrators, parents, teachers, highly achieving students, failing students, and dropouts could form a group. Such a diverse group might have some difficulty getting started, and a theme such as "What I like and don't like about our schools and what I would like them to be" might be suggested. Such groups can develop greater understanding among the various members and be the source of great change in individuals. In Rogers' words, "It scarcely has to be added that even a very few such vertical groups would drastically change the climate and flavor of any educational system."[44]

The holding of workshops before the academic year and each month during that year, each involving from one to ten small groups, would involve hundreds of people in the system and assure lasting effects. But a plan for continuing change should be built into the system. Opportunity for members of the system, selected on the basis of attitudes (nondefensiveness, realness, and genuineness in interpersonal relationships, awareness of and ability to express feelings, empathy with others, caring and concern for others) manifested in the group experience, should be given the opportunity for summer training as group facilitators. During the following year these people would serve as cofacilitators of groups with outside facilitators, and when ready, would themselves become facilitators, with outside facilitators serving as consultants. The system then would have its own facilitators for continuing the process, involving more members of the system.

The nature of these groups must be emphasized, since there is a negative reaction to encounter groups, by many who fear they will be forced to reveal themselves and will be attacked and criticized by others. It is true that there are some groups where this does happen, and group leaders who force or encourage such behaviors. But the groups discussed here are not of that type; they are built upon the facilitative conditions for learning which have been discussed earlier.[45] All participation would be voluntary.

The resulting process of change might not be smooth; constructive turbulence occurs in the process of significant or rapid change. Elements of the community might be threatened and resist any change of the traditional method of education; such persons would not be likely to become involved in the intensive group experience, and thus could not be reached or changed. Yet if change is to occur, it must be attempted, even though it is difficult and will be opposed by some. The process would be subjected to evaluation and assessment by those in the system and by outside professional observers and evaluators. More rigorous research programs could also be developed.

Self-Directed Educational Change
in Action

The plan summarized above was tried in two school systems, one private and one public.

A private school system. The private system consisted of Immaculate Heart College (which included teacher education), 8 high schools, and 50 elementary schools in Los Angeles. Financial support was provided by private foundations and individuals.

The top administrators and many other leaders were enthusiastic about the plan. Forty-five administrators and College faculty members and thirty-six administrators and faculty from three high schools met for two weekends in encounter sessions in small groups. One-hundred-and-eighty teachers and administrators from twenty-two elementary schools met in small groups for two weekends over a period of time. Forty student leaders from a high school met in three groups for one weekend, and for a second weekend a month later with faculty, who at first were reluctant to meet in small groups with students. Groups were facilitated by members of the staff of the Center for the Study of the Person; staff members also met with faculty on innovation in education and later on the encounter group program, discussing questions and criticisms. Staff members also participated in an assembly with the college students, which was also attended by a number of faculty members. Later, the administrative council of the college was helped to plan task-oriented groups. Workshops for teachers and principals of the elementary schools were held, some of which were disappointing and some highly successful.

Although there was some criticism of some of the facilitators and groups (too "pushy," too personal), the reactions of the faculty were generally positive, with faculty who were not involved in the first groups attending later groups. Interest in encounter groups for faculty and students within departments developed. Communication and relationships among faculty improved, and faculty meetings improved. After the first series of groups, others were conducted at the request of groups in the system. Faculty members instituted changes in their classroom teaching and relationships with students. The atmosphere of the schools changed.

Over the three-year period of the program other changes occurred. The administrative structure was changed to involve more participation, more student participation in both class and out-of-class functions was encouraged, with more faculty-student interaction and cooperation. After the experimental period ended, changes continued. Teacher-education methods were changed to include more contact of the students with schools and classrooms. Several people from the system obtained training as facilitators so encounter groups could continue.

Project transition. In 1970 a similar program was initiated in the Louisville, Kentucky school system, with support from the U.S. Office of Education (which had declined to support the earlier program). Almost 60 percent of the more than 60,000 children in the district were black; over one-third were below poverty level or receiving welfare. Most of the poor and the black were in inner-city schools. The district had the highest number of underachievers, the highest dropout rate, the most delinquency, the highest student and teacher turnover, the highest unemployment, and the highest segregation in housing of any district in Kentucky. The project was supported by the three white and two black members of the school board and by the new superintendent (who had had encounter group experience).

There were three components of the project. One was an organizational development program throughout the system involving a series of weekend encounter groups (on paid time) for administrators, teachers, trustees, and some parents. The encounter groups for administrators were followed by communication laboratories and human potential seminars, and training sessions for administrators in group dynamics, conflict management, team building and interpersonal skills. Over 1,600 school personnel were involved over a six-month period. The objective was to improve communication and participation in policy and program decisions in the system. The second component involved the teaching staff in proposing and developing programs directed at reaching the student population through more humanistic teaching, through more relevant curriculums, through differentiated staffing patterns, and through more flexible educational structuring. Team teaching, teacher corp interns, and parent volunteers were involved. The third component consisted of the decentralization of administration, with the development of neighborhood school boards which became involved in the development of school philosophy, curriculum selection, teacher selection, and teacher evaluation.

The project led to much ferment and turmoil, at the upper administration level and in individual schools. But positive results occurred, including greater interest of parents and students, with resulting lowering of dropouts and gains in student academic achievement. The continuing or long-term effects of the project have been lost or obscured by the turmoil following a court order for desegregation in the Louisville schools, which includes merging of the Louisville city schools with suburban schools in Jefferson County.

Summary

The necessity of adapting to a world characterized by rapid change and by tensions between groups and nations poses a crisis in education. The goal of education must be the development of persons who can adapt and change, who know how to learn. Such a person is the fully functioning person described earlier. Education must go beyond concern with knowledge and cognitive development; it must include the whole person and must promote affective development, personal growth, and creativity. The focus must be upon significant learning, which is personally meaningful learning rather than meaningless learning like the enforced acquisition and memorization of information and facts. Traditional learning has involved the latter, which has been the focus of research in learning and instruction. To promote the second kind of learning is the focus of what is designated by many as humanistic education and requires a revolution in education. It does not reject cognitive learning, but combines it with the affective, recognizing that they cannot be separated.

Learning—significant learning—is a natural characteristic of the organism in its inherent tendency to maintain and enhance itself, to develop and utilize its potentialities. Such learning occurs when the subject matter is perceived as being relevant to this basic motivating tendency. But change, particularly change in the self-organization, is threatening, and tends to be resisted. However, such learning is more likely to occur when external pressures or threat are at a minimum—when the environment is accepting, understanding, and supportive. When threat to the self or self-concept is minimized, learning is promoted, since experiences can be accurately perceived in a differentiated manner and can be explored, analyzed, taken apart, and reintegrated in a meaningful manner.

Learning is facilitated by the student's experiential involvement with practical and real (relevant) problems, with the student participating actively and responsibly in the learning process. This is self-initiated learning, involving the whole person of the learner. Self-initiated learning, together with self-evaluation and self-criticism, leads to independence, self-reliance, and creativity, and to learning how to learn.

If significant learning is self-initiated, self-discovered, self-appropriated, and personally meaningful, questions arise about the nature and usefulness of teaching. Teaching, says Rogers, is vastly overrated; little if anything of a consequential nature can be taught. Rather than being an instructor, the teacher's function is to facilitate learning. The teacher does this by providing the conditions under which significant learning occurs. There are three major conditions which do this: realness, congruence, or genuineness in the teacher; a prizing, acceptance, and trust of the student; and an empathic understanding of the student.

If these conditions are to be effective, they must be communicated to and perceived by the student. The student must also be in a state of readiness to learn, which involves motivation. Unless something has happened to inhibit or destroy the student's natural drive toward the maintenance and enhancement of the self, motivation is present and is aroused in response to a situation presenting a real problem, something that is perceived by the student as relevant to his or her development. The presence of the facilitative conditions minimizes the threat which may exist in any new problem situation, allowing the motivation to learn to function.

These facilitative conditions are attitudes of the teacher rather than techniques or methods as such, divorced from the person of the teacher. They are, however, manifested in and communicated to the student in behaviors. Behaviors which implement the conditions include openness and honesty and admission of lack of knowledge and of mistakes. They include showing respect for students by listening to them to understand how they feel and how they see things, and by responding to communicate this understanding. Teaching becomes a personal relationship, a spontaneous personal encounter which frees the student to learn.

The teacher contributes to the student's freedom to learn by recognizing and centering education upon problems that are real to students. The teacher also provides as many resources as possible, including his or her own knowledge. Programmed instruction, small group methods, inquiry learning, and simulation may be used. The teacher allows students to select their own objectives and set their own levels of achievement, which may involve the use of contracts.

Evaluation of significant learning poses a problem in our present educational settings. Personal learning is difficult if not impossible to evaluate by external criteria of the kind usually available. If the individual sets her or his own goals and criteria, self-evaluation is the most appropriate form of evaluation. Beyond this there is evaluation in terms of the requirements of life situations, some of which can be provided by educators as part of the resources made available to students.

In addition to the facilitation of cognitive learning, there are other outcomes of this approach to teaching and learning. Students enjoy learning, and motivation is not a problem. Students take responsibility for their learning. They work harder and longer at their self-imposed tasks. They work together; there is cooperation rather than competition, sharing rather than hoarding of information. Students develop positive self-regard and positive self-concepts; they have confidence in their ability to learn. They develop positive regard and respect for others and the contributions of others. Creativity is manifested in the learning process. Students grow as persons. In short, they become more fully functioning persons.

This approach to education has implications for teacher education and for administration. Teachers must be prepared to function as facilitators of learning, and administrators must accept this approach to teaching and support it. Further, the educational system (and with it the community) must undergo changes, so that a climate for self-directed learning exists. The intensive small-group experience is a method for system change which has now been used in enough situations to warrant its introduction into any system where there is a desire to change on the part of top administrators and school boards.

EVALUATION

Origin and Development

The approach to education presented by Rogers is derived from his experience and research in counseling or psychotherapy, mainly with young adult and older clients. This experience and research has led to the recognition, definition, and measurement of the basic or essential conditions for positive personality or behavior changes. These conditions are certain characteristics of personal or interpersonal relationships.

If these conditions lead to changes in personality and behavior in psychologically or emotionally disturbed persons in counseling or psychotherapy, then the question presents itself, would they not also lead to changes in so-called "normal" persons, including children in educational settings? The relevance of this question is increased by the evidence of research that the kinds of clients, problems, and personality characteristics and behaviors which are affected by the conditions have been shown to be very extensive in kind or variety. Not only do the conditions lead to emotional or affective changes, but to cognitive or intellectual changes. Truax and Carkhuff summarize this as follows:

> The person (whether a counselor, therapist or teacher) who is better able to communicate warmth, genuineness and accurate empathy is more effective in interpersonal relationships no matter what the goal of the interaction (better grades for college students, better interpersonal relations for the counseling center out-patients, adequate personality functioning and integration for the seriously disturbed mental patient, socially acceptable behavior for the juvenile delinquent, or greater reading ability for the third grade reading instruction student).[46]

The evidence for cognitive changes in children following classes taught by teachers who are empathic, respecting, and real in their relationships with students will be presented later. Here it can be stated that the concern of those who fear that such an approach to education will neglect cognitive development is unfounded. Attention to and concern with the student as a person, a feeling person, fosters intellectual development as well as affective development.

The recognition of the importance of the personal relationship in learning is, of course, not a discovery unique with Rogers. Not only have the great and good teachers of all times manifested this in their teaching; it has been recognized by educators beginning at least with the early Greeks and continuing through Erasmus, Comenius, Locke, Rousseau, Pestalozzi, Froebel, and Montessori.[47] As Rogers notes, his experience was a rediscovery of effective principles which have been discovered over and over by competent teachers, and of principles which have been stated by others, including Dewey and Kilpatrick.[48] That experience in a different area, that is, counseling or psychotherapy, has led to the discovery of the same principles and is corroboration of their significance, makes it irrelevant and unjustified to criticize Rogers because he "has not thought it necessary to be a student of education before advocating a revolution"[49] and to belittle his contribution because Rousseau and Dewey wrote about meaningful learning.

Rogers and Humanistic Education

Rogers identifies himself with the movement known as humanistic psychology, being one of the founders of the American Association for Humanistic Psychology. Yet he does not use the term *humanistic* to designate his approach to education. In fact, he has no specific designation for it. Perhaps he is reluctant to use a label, remembering the difficulties and even misunderstandings associated with the terms *non-directive counseling* and *client-centered therapy* which he used successively (1942 and 1951) to designate his approach to counseling or psychotherapy.

Yet the term *humanistic education* is being widely used to refer to a concept or philosophy of education which is essentially that developed by Rogers. Unfortunately, however, many if not most of those who have written about humanistic education are unfamiliar with his work. Their writings lack an explicitly developed philosophical and psychological foundation and are thus unsystematic and fragmentary. Most of the attention and concern is devoted to techniques, rather than to principles and attitudes. Rogers' work provides the systematic foundation upon which humanistic education must be based.[50]

There are, however, some aspects of humanistic education which Rogers does not develop. Humanistic education may be conceived of as including two major aspects: (1) the general psychological conditions for all learning, and (2) affective education, or concern with the affective development of the student as well as the student's cognitive development. Rogers has focused upon the first. The general psychological conditions do apply to affective development as well as cognitive development; there are, however, additional aspects of affective development or affective education.

In providing the conditions of empathic understanding, acceptance, prizing or respect, and realness or genuineness, the teacher is fostering affective learning, or changes in personality, attitudes, and values. The teacher is doing this by example, or, to use the technical term, by modeling. Students who are exposed to a teacher who manifests these characteristics develop them in themselves or in their relations with others. Modeling is a highly effective method for teaching complex behaviors. Children learn from what the teacher does more than from what the teacher says. If the teacher is not the kind of person he or she is trying to teach students to be, he or she cannot successfully teach this, even though students may be told, "Do as I say, not as I do." This is a very important principle, since no matter how much the schools may claim that they do not teach attitudes and values, they cannot avoid doing so. It therefore is necessary that we be aware of what attitudes and values are actually being taught and decide if they are those that we want to teach or think should be taught.

Although indirect teaching through modeling is a powerful

method and usually supersedes what is taught directly if there is inconsistency, direct or didactic teaching contributes to the efficiency of instruction. It helps to be able to put into words, in the form of principles, what is being modeled. The affective aspects of development, or humanization or human relations, can be taught in part through instruction. This can be done through the standard curriculum.[51] The course of study referred to earlier in the section on Bruner, called "Man: A Course of Study," is a deliberate attempt to do this.

Recently there have been many attempts to develop specific methods or curriculums in affective education. These approaches can be subject to a number of criticisms. One is that they are often forced into a standard curriculum format, complete with lesson plans and teacher manuals. They thus become subject-matter-oriented rather than person-oriented. Related to this is another difficulty: The structuring of affective experiences may become a matter of techniques, with neglect of the attitudes, which are basic. Simulations, games, exercises, and such can be useful, but they can also lead to unnatural, controlled, contrived experiences, rather than natural, spontaneous, real experiences. The development of commercial materials and expensive kits can foster this unnatural, technique-oriented approach. The emphasis upon structured, teacher-controlled techniques with predetermined specific objectives is inconsistent with the goals of affective education, which include spontaneity, student-initiated activity, open, free discussion and interaction in a natural setting, and self-directed exploration and learning. Even the current emphasis on social or interpersonal skills can result in neglect of the attitudes of respect, acceptance, and a desire to understand others, which are basic to good interpersonal relationships.

In addition to modeling and didactic instruction, there is a third approach to affective education. This is the experiential approach. Experiential learning is particularly relevant in affective education, which involves human or interpersonal relations. We learn to live with others most effectively by living with others. It is here that the basic encounter-group approach developed by Rogers is relevant. Not only is it useful educating teachers and changing educational systems; it is perhaps the most important and effective approach to educating children in interpersonal relations. Small-group experiences should be a continuing part of the educational experience. Actual experience in groups seems so clearly superior to any other method of learning in human relations that it is difficult to understand why it has not been widely used in human relations education in the school. It has been widely used outside the school with adults.

A student sitting in a classroom with 30 other students, being psychologically alone, not really knowing the other students, not interacting with or relating to them, while listening to a teacher talk about "mental hygiene" or "human relations," is not undergoing a real learning experience. Nor is being in a classroom and going through a structured series of games or exercises the most effective way of learning to relate to others. In a small encounter group of six to ten students with a trained facilitator, without assigned subject matter or an agenda other than to talk about themselves or whatever is of concern to them, students can learn through experience to:

> listen to others
> accept and respect others
> understand others
> identify and become aware of their feelings
> express their feelings
> explore their feelings
> become aware of the feelings of others
> experience being accepted and understood by others
> develop greater awareness of themselves
> recognize basic commonalities in human experience
> change themselves in the direction of being more the selves they want to be
> help others accept themselves
> help others understand themselves and each other.

In such groups, learning occurs without the input of external content, in a natural setting, through experience. The teacher, while an expert in interpersonal relations, is a facilitator, teaching through modeling rather than didactically through providing content or subject matter. A cognitive understanding of the group experiences can be developed through analysis in discussion of the experience and through didactic teaching of the principles of human relations, as suggested earlier.

Research Support

There is now extensive research support for the effectiveness of the three conditions for facilitating positive personality change in individual and group counseling or psychotherapy. Support for the effectiveness of the conditions in classroom teaching is accumulating.

An early study of Emmerling[52] indicates that teachers who differ in their orientation toward teaching and students are perceived differently by students. One group of high school teachers saw the problems of teaching as helping children think for themselves and be independent, getting students to participate, learning new ways of helping students develop their maximum potential, and helping students express individual needs and interests. A second group, on the other hand, saw the urgent problems as trying to teach children who don't even have the ability to follow directions, teaching children who lack a desire to learn or who are not able to do the work required for their grade, and getting children to listen. Students saw teachers in the first groups as more real, more acceptant, more empathic than they saw teachers in the second group.

In a study by Bills,[53] four teachers rated adequate and effective by their superiors and four rated inadequate were compared. The more adequate teachers were rated by their students as more real, more empathic, and as having a higher level of regard for their students than the teachers rated as inadequate.

These two studies used the Barrett-Lennard Relationship Inventory, first developed to measure clients' perception of empathy, level of positive regard, unconditional positive regard, and genuineness in their counselors or therapists, and then adapted to measure students' perceptions of these attitudes or conditions in teachers. In a study by Lewis, Lovell, and Jesse[54] an adaptation of another instrument which had been developed for use with clients was used (Teacher-Pupil Relationship Inventory). Sixth-grade students of teachers who were rated high (by students) showed significantly greater gains over the school year on the Iowa Tests of Educational Development than did the students of teachers rated low. For a group of ninth-grade students the difference in gains was greater for the students of high-rated teachers, but not significantly so, but the teachers (English teachers) had the students in only one class, while the sixth-grade teachers had the same students for the entire day.

A study by Macdonald and Zaret[55] analyzed recorded interactions of nine teachers and their students. The behaviors of teachers which were classified as "open"—clarifying, stimulating, accepting, facilitating —were followed by student responses which were classified as "productive"—discovering, exploring, experimenting, synthesizing. But when teacher behaviors were "closed"—judging, directing, reproving, ignoring, probing—student behaviors were "reproductive"—parroting, guessing, acquiescing, reproducing facts, remembering.

A number of studies have involved the use of rating scales of the teachers' empathic understanding, respect or positive regard, and genuineness or congruence. Aspy[56] used the Carkhuff scales of these attitudes or conditions to rate tape recordings of teachers' interactions with third-grade students in reading instruction groups. Ratings were obtained for two one-week periods, two months apart. The students of teachers of three classes who were rated high on these scales showed a significantly greater gain on the Stanford Reading Achievement Test than the students of teachers of three classes who rated low on these conditions. In a further study, Aspy and Hadlock[57] found that third- to fifth-grade students taught by teachers rated high in genuineness, respect, and empathy showed a reading gain of 2.5 years during a five month period, compared to a gain of 0.7 years by students of teachers rated low on the conditions.

Carkhuff and Berenson, reviewing these and other studies state:

> When we look at the data, we find that high-level functioning teachers elicit as much as two-and-one-half years of intellectual or achievement growth in the course of a school year, while teachers at low levels of facilitative conditions may allow only six months of intellectual growth over the course of a year: students may be facilitated or they may be retarded in their intellectual as well as emotional growth, and these changes can be accounted for by the level of the teacher's functioning on the facilitative dimensions and independent of his knowledge-ability.[58]

Summary

Rogers has extrapolated from his experience and research in counseling or psychotherapy and proposed an approach to education which focuses on teaching as a facilitative interpersonal relationship, in which the facilitator is characterized by three basic attitudes or conditions: empathic understanding; respect, positive regard, prizing, or trust; and realness, genuineness, or congruence. In doing so he has provided a systematic psychological foundation for what is becoming known as humanistic education.

Humanistic education does not neglect or minimize cognitive or intellectual development. The facilitative conditions promote such development, as well as fostering affective or emotional growth, which is considered an important aspect of education. Affective development centers upon interpersonal relationships. Such development can be fostered through aspects of the regular curriculum, through didactic teaching of human relations, and especially through experiential learning in basic encounter groups.

Research studies have supported the effectiveness of the facilitative conditions in counseling or psychotherapy. Similar research is now accumulating to support their effectiveness in classroom teaching.

Education of the future is described by Rogers as follows:

> Education will not be a *preparation* for living. It will be, in itself, an experience in living. Feelings of inadequacy, hatred, a desire for power, feelings of love and awe and respect, feelings of fear, dread, unhappiness with parents or with other children—all these will be an open part of [the student's] curriculum, as worthy of exploration as history or mathematics. In fact this openness to feelings will enable him to learn content materials more readily. His will be an education in becoming a whole being, and the learning will involve him deeply, openly, exploringly, in an awareness of his relationships to the world of others, as well as an awareness of the world of abstract knowledge.[59]

SUMMARY

Carl R. Rogers, who has devoted his lifetime to practice and research in counseling or psychotherapy, has developed an approach to education derived from this experience and research. This approach is based upon a positive conception of the nature of man. Human beings, as they are experienced in Rogers' client-centered therapy, are basically rational, socialized, forward-moving, and realistic. They are active and proactive, in addition to being reactive to stimuli in their environments. They are basically cooperative, constructive, and trustworthy. Anti-social emotions—jealousy, hostility, competitiveness—do exist but they are defensive reactions to threat and the frustration of more basic impulses for love, belonging, and security.

These positive capacities and tendencies are aspects of the single basic motivation toward the actualization of the individual's potentials, or toward self-actualization. The drive toward self-actualization is not simply an unfolding from the inside, automatic and without regard to the environment. Rather it requires certain conditions if it is to manifest itself and lead to the development of a self-actualizing or fully functioning person. These conditions are certain basic attitudes manifested by other human beings in their relationships with the individual. Three major attitudes or conditions have been identified and defined, and scales for their measurement have been developed on the basis of experience and research in counseling or psychotherapy. They are empathic understanding; respect, trust, or positive regard; and genuineness, congruence, or realness.

Self-actualizing or fully functioning people have a number of characteristics which can be described, although they integrate in a unitary organization with the person: (1) These people are open to all their experiences, since they are free from defensiveness. (2) They live in an existential mode, experiencing each moment of life anew. They are flexible and adaptable, changing with new experiences over time. (3) Their organisms are trustworthy guides to satisfying behavior, since, being open to all their experiences, these people incorporate all relevant data in their behavior. If any data are missing, openness to corrective feedback leads to modification of behavior and toward greater satisfaction of the need for self-actualization.

If one is fully functioning, one's locus of evaluation is internal, rather than external, though one will of course be influenced by external factors. One's values are one's own, but are not necessarily idiosyncratic or unique, since one shares the basic motivation and need of the species. Among the common values (which contribute to the survival of the species as well as of the individual) are realness, sensitivity to and understanding of others, and acceptance of and respect for others—that is, the conditions for the development of self-actualizing persons.

There are a number of implications of the concept of the fully functioning person: (1) One who is fully functioning is a creative person, since creativeness is fostered by sensitive openness to experience. (2) Since one is free from defensiveness, one's basically good nature will manifest itself; one is constructive and trustworthy. (3) One is dependable, but not necessarily predictable, since one will respond to the unique pattern of internal and external stimuli at each moment. (4) One is free, and not determined. Though the freedom-determinism issue is complex, there is a sense in which fully functioning individuals choose and experience freedom even though their behavior is determined, since being open to all elements in the situation, they will behave in a way that will be satisfying and self-actualizing.

The goal of education is or should be the development of fully functioning or self-actualizing persons. Only such persons can survive—and thus make possible the survival of the human race—in a rapidly changing world characterized by tensions among races, nations, and other groups. The fully functioning person is adaptable and has learned how to learn.

To educate toward a fully functioning person requires that education cease focusing on imparting facts, information, and knowledge, that it go beyond the objectives of development of the intellect or of thinking persons, to concern for the development of the affective, emotional, and interpersonal relationship qualities of individuals. The whole person must be educated.

Learning related to the development of the whole person is significant learning, learning which is personal and experiential and which makes a difference in the person. The individual doesn't have to be motivated toward significant learning—the motivation is inherent in the drive toward self-actualization. Significant learning occurs when the learner perceives the subject matter as relevant for his or her own purposes. Significant learning for those whose self-concepts are formed may require a change in the self-organization, and this may be threatening, but in such cases learning is facilitated when external threats to the self are at a minimum. Freedom from threat enables the learner to explore, to differentiate, to try out new ideas, to change. Significant learning is facilitated by experiential involvement with real problems. Initiation of the process and participation in it by the learner fosters significant learning. Self-evaluation rather than external criticism and evaluation fosters independence, creativity, and self-reliance. Significant learning, involving all these elements, is learning how to learn.

Significant learning involves the whole person and requires that we change our focus in education from cognition to a combination of the cognitive and the affective, and from teaching and the teacher to learning and the learner. The teacher becomes the facilitator of learning by providing the conditions for self-initiated, self-directed learning.

There are three major conditions for such learning. They are, of course, the three conditions which lead to positive personality change in counseling or therapy, and to the development of fully functioning persons—realness in the facilitator; prizing and acceptance of or trust in the learner, and empathic understanding. The contribution of Rogers is significant in that it goes beyond traditional psychological and educational theories of learning, which consider learning almost solely in terms of individual or intrapersonal determinants and impersonal environmental stimuli, to recognition of the social or interpersonal relationship of students with the teacher and with each other and the atmosphere or psychological climate of the school.

Learning also depends, of course, upon the learner. Motivation is a normal, natural characteristic of human beings if it has not been suppressed or destroyed by mistreatment. Stimulation by problem situations also occurs naturally in normal persons. Finally, the learner must perceive the facilitative conditions in the teacher, and here, also, individuals who have not been mistreated, deceived, conned, or turned off will be open to and recognize these conditions.

The teacher may need some help in implementing the facilitative conditions, and some suggestions are made. The real teacher does not know everything and does not pretend to. He or she can admit mistakes. The teacher manifests prizing, acceptance, and trust by really listening to the student, without evaluating her or him, and by responding to what the student says—to the attitudes and feelings expressed as well as to the content. Listening also evidences the attempt to understand, and responding attempts to communicate understanding. Teaching becomes a real, spontaneous, personal encounter with students.

The teacher also facilitates learning by building upon real problems in the lives and culture of students, by providing many easily accessible resources (including his or her own knowledge), by developing contracts with students through which they can develop their own learning programs, by providing programmed instruction units, by small group sessions and discussions or projects, by inquiry learning, by simulation learning, and by encounter-group sessions.

Evaluation of learning in self-initiated, self-directed learning should be done by the learner. Criteria are necessary, however. These should be realistic, that is, they should reflect the requirements of life, as set by society and its institutions, and made available to students by teachers, counselors, or others in the school. Students can then evaluate themselves in terms of these criteria.

It should be obvious that this approach to education and learning has important implications for teacher education and for school administrators. To use this approach teachers would need preparation which focused upon the teaching relationship and the facilitation of encounter groups. Administrators adhering to what McGregor designates as theory Y than what he labels theory X would fit into such a system.

Educational systems as they now exist would have to change considerably if they were to incorporate this approach to education. A plan for self-directed change in a school system is outlined. With the initiative and support of a few top administrators and school board members, a program of intensive small-group experiences could lead to such change.

This approach to education could well provide the basis for an integrated system, bringing together the cognitive contributions of Piaget and Bruner, the conditioning methods of Skinner, and the humanistic ideas of Montessori and of others currently developing humanistic education. It recognizes the involvement of the whole person in education—that cognitive learning involves affective elements, and that emotional and affective development must be a concern of education.

Our educational system is obsolete. It is obsolete not only in curriculum but in methods. Methods of instruction ignore much of what we know about the conditions of learning. The application of conditioning methods through the use of programmed instruction is not a sufficient answer. Our curriculum focuses on cognitive learning and ignores affective learning, which is nevertheless occurring in an unplanned, haphazard manner. In the world in which we live and will be living, we need persons who are not only mature intellectually but affectively, who can not only think but who can feel and relate to others.

A humanistic approach to education addresses these problems. It provides an understanding of the psychological conditions of learning, of cognitive and affective development leading to self-actualizing or fully functioning persons. The conditions are the attitudes of respecting, prizing, and trusting others; of realness, genuineness, or honesty in dealing with others; and of empathic understanding of others.

To change our educational system in this direction will require a real revolution in education, since not only the methods but the goals of education must be changed. It will not be easy; there is and will be opposition, from those who see the change as displacing or detracting from cognitive education and from those who believe that affective education is the province of other social institutions, of the family and the church. But these institutions are not performing this task, a task which must be performed if society is to survive. If the school does not perform it, some other institution must be developed to do so. It would be inefficient and ineffective to attempt to split the individual into cognitive and affective elements, each to be educated in a different institution. The individual is a whole, and his or her cognitive and affective development intermesh and must be developed together. The same psychological conditions are essential for cognitive and affective development.

REFERENCES

1. This, and the following unfootnoted quotations and material, are from C. R. Rogers, "This Is Me," Chapter 1 in *On Becoming a Person* (Boston: Houghton Mifflin, 1961).
2. C. R. Rogers, "A Theory of Therapy, Personality, and Interpersonal Relationships, as Developed in the Client-centered Framework," in S. Koch, ed., *Psychology: A Study of Science* (New York: McGraw-Hill, 1959), study I, *Conceptual and Systematic*, vol. 3, *Formulations of the Person and the Social Context*, pp. 184–256.
3. Ibid., pp. 188–192.
4. Ibid., p. 191.
5. Ibid., p. 192.
6. Rogers, *On Becoming a Person,* op. cit., pp. 90–92, 194–195.
7. Rogers, "A Theory of Therapy, Personality, and Interpersonal Relationships," op. cit., p. 221.
8. Ibid., pp. 194–212.
9. A. W. Combs and D. Snygg, *Individual Behavior: A Perceptual Approach to Behavior,* rev. ed. (New York: Harper & Row, 1959).
10. Rogers, "A Theory of Therapy, Personality and Interpersonal Relationships," op. cit., pp. 222–233.
11. Ibid., pp. 236–240.
12. Ibid., p. 216.
13. A. H. Maslow, "Self-actualizing People: A Study of Psychological Health," in C. E. Moustakas, ed., *The Self: Explorations in Personal Growth* (New York: Harper & Row, 1956), p. 16.
14. Rogers, *Freedom to Learn* (Columbus, Ohio: Merrill, 1969), p. 290.
15. Ibid., pp. 290–291.
16. Ibid., p. 268.
17. Ibid., p. 269.
18. Ibid., pp. 294–295.
19. Ibid., pp. 105–106.
20. Ibid., p. vi.
21. Ibid., p. 104.
22. Ibid., p. 218.
23. Ibid., pp. 103–104.
24. Quoted from James Reston, "The Forgotten Factor," *New York Times,* November 29, 1970, p. 11, by Rogers, in "Bringing Together Ideas and Feelings in Learning." In D. A. Read and S. B. Simon, eds., *Humanistic Education Sourcebook* (Englewood Cliffs, N.J.: Prentice-Hall, 1975), pp. 39–49.
25. Rogers, *Freedom to Learn,* op. cit., pp. 152–154.
26. Ibid., p. 103.
27. Ibid., p. 105.
28. Ibid., p. 106.
29. Ibid., p. 108.
30. Ibid., p. 114.
31. Ibid., p. 112.
32. See, for example, J. Holt, *How Children Fail* (New York: Pitman,

1964); J. Kozol, *Death at an Early Age* (Boston: Houghton Mifflin, 1967); C. E. Silberman, *Crisis in the Classroom* (New York: Random House, 1970); and C. H. Patterson, *Humanistic Education* (Englewood Cliffs, N.J.: Prentice-Hall, 1973).

33. Rogers, *Freedom to Learn,* op. cit., p. 115.
34. The ideas in this section are adapted from Patterson, *Humanistic Education,* op. cit.
35. Rogers, *Freedom to Learn,* op. cit., p. 130.
36. Ibid., pp. 132–133.
37. See Rogers, *Carl Rogers on Encounter Groups* (New York: Harper & Row, 1970); Pattreson, *Humanistic Education,* op. cit., Chapter 11, "Groups in Humanistic Education."
38. Rogers, *On Becoming a Person,* op. cit., p. 290.
39. Rogers, "Bringing Together Ideas and Feelings in Learning," op. cit., p. 47. See also "The Preparation of Humanistic Teachers," Chapter 12 in Patterson, *Humanistic Education,* op. cit.
40. D. M. McGregor, "The Human Side of Enterprise," in W. G. Bennis, K. D. Benne, and R. Chin, eds., *The Planning of Change* (New York: Holt, Rinehart and Winston, 1961), pp. 431–442. [First published in *Adventures in Thought and Action: Proceedings of the Fifth Anniversary Convocation of the Schools of Management* (Cambridge, Mass.: M.I.T. Press, 1957.)] See also D. M. McGregor, *The Human Side of Enterprise* (New York: McGraw-Hill, 1960).
41. Rogers, *Freedom to Learn,* op. cit., p. 206.
42. Ibid., pp. 207–208.
43. Ibid., p. 304.
44. Ibid., p. 315.
45. See Rogers, "The Process of the Basic Encounter Group," in J. F. T. Bugental, ed., *The Challenges of Humanistic Psychology* (New York: McGraw-Hill, 1967), pp. 261–276; Rogers, *Carl Rogers on Encounter Groups,* op. cit.
46. C. B. Truax and R. R. Carkhuff, *Toward Effective Psychotherapy.* (Chicago: Aldine, 1966), pp. 116–117.
47. Patterson, *Humanistic Education,* op. cit., chapter 3.
48. Rogers, *Client-centered Therapy* (Boston: Houghton Mifflin, 1951), p. 386.
49. M. A. White, review of Carl Rogers' *Freedom to Learn, Contemporary Psychology* 15 (1970): 175–176.
50. The writer's *Humanistic Education,* op. cit., is an attempt to build on this systematic foundation.
51. F. T. Wilhelms, "Humanization via the Curriculum," in R. R. Leeper, ed., *Humanizing Education: The Person in the Process* (Washington, D.C.: Association for Supervision and Curriculum Development, 1967).
52. F. C. Emmerling, "A Study of the Relationships Between Personality Characteristics of Classroom Teachers and Pupil Perceptions" (doctoral diss., Auburn University, 1961).
53. R. E. Bills, unpublished study, cited by Rogers in *Freedom to Learn,* op. cit., pp. 117–118.
54. W. A. Lewis, J. T. Lovell, and B. E. Jesse, "Interpersonal Relationships and Pupil Progress," *Personal and Guidance Journal,* 44 (1964):396–401.
55. J. B. Macdonald and E. Zaret, "A Study of Openness in Classroom Interactions" (unpublished manuscript, Marquette University, 1966), cited in Rogers, *Freedom to Learn,* op. cit., p. 118.

56. D. N. Aspy, "A Study of Three Facilitative Conditions and Their Relationships to the Achievement of Third-Grade Students" (unpublished doctoral diss., University of Kentucky, 1965); D. N. Aspy, "The Effect of Teacher-offered Conditions of Empathy, Positive Regard, and Congruence upon Student Achievement," *Florida Journal of Educational Research* 11 (1) (1969):39–48. This study and a number of other studies are summarized in D. N. Aspy, *Toward a Technology for Humanizing Education* (Champaign, Ill.: Research Press, 1972).

57. D. N. Aspy and W. Hadlock, "The Effects of High and Low Functioning Teachers upon Students' Academic Performance and Truancy" (unpublished study), cited in R. R. Carkhuff, *Helping and Human Relations,* vol. II (New York: Holt, Rinehart and Winston, 1969), p. 258.

58. R. R. Carkhuff and B. G. Berenson, *Beyond Counseling and Therapy* (New York: Holt, Rinehart and Winston, 1967), p. 14.

59. Rogers, "Interpersonal Relationships: U.S.A. 2000," *Journal of Applied Behavioral Science* 4 (1968):265–280.

INDEX OF NAMES

INDEX OF SUBJECTS

77 78 79 80 9 8 7 6 5 4 3 2 1